Expert Podcasting Practices

Practices

FOR

DUMMIES®

Expert Podcasting Practices

FOR DUMMIES®

by Tee Morris, Evo Terra, and Ryan Williams

BICENTENNIAL
1807
WILEY
2007
BICENTENNIAL

Wiley Publishing, Inc.

Expert Podcasting Practices For Dummies®

Published by
Wiley Publishing, Inc.
111 River Street
Hoboken, NJ 07030-5774
www.wiley.com

WILEY

About the Authors

Tee Morris: Tee entered 2005 with an idea: podcasting a novel in order to promote its sequel. His podcast of *MOREVI: The Chronicles of Rafe & Askana* went on to become the first book podcast in its entirety and was nominated for a 2006 Parsec for Best Podcast Fiction. Podcasting *MOREVI* also led to writing with Evo Terra the #1 book in podcasting, *Podcasting For Dummies*. Tee's other podcasts include the Parsec-nominated *Survival Guide to Writing Fantasy, Podcasting For Dummies, Give Us a Minute, Speaking of Beer's MicroBrewed* with Phil Rossi, and "Behind the Mic" for *Blogger and Podcaster Magazine*. He continues to podcast fiction as well with "Dear John" (from BenBella Books's *Farscape Forever: Sex, Drugs, and Killer Muppets*) for *The ScapeCast;* and "Asleep at the Wheel" for the podcast anthology *VOICES: New Media Fiction*, edited by Mur Lafferty. Following 2007's *Billibub Baddings and The Case of The Singing Sword* podcast, Tee will podcast *Legacy of MOREVI* in preparation for the 2009 print release of *Exodus from Morevi*. Find out more about Tee Morris and his podcasts at www.teemorris.com.

Evo Terra: Evo Terra has a penchant for infecting others with the New Media bug. His credits in the field include launching the premier destination for serialized audiobooks, Podiobooks.com. A pioneer in the world of podcasting, he's the co-author of *Podcasting For Dummies* and *Expert Podcasting Practices For Dummies* (both published by Wiley).

His personal and professional blog, FunAnymore.com, serves as Evo's soapbox and testing ground, where he pontificates and proselytizes the bleeding edge of Web 2.0 applications that are reshaping how we define "the conversation."

Ryan Williams: Ryan Williams is a multimedia designer, author, and bassist based in Indianapolis, Indiana. He's shared the stage and studio with everybody and everything from Grammy Award–winning hip-hop artists to a full band of bagpipes and drums. He's the author of *Windows XP Digital Music For Dummies* and *Teach Yourself Visually Bass Guitar* (both published by Wiley). He has also written several articles and tutorials on music and music technology for several publications and Web sites. He is the technical editor for *Second Life For Dummies* and *Composing Digital Music For Dummies*. He is a frequent panelist on digital music and home studios at music conferences around the nation. He received his master's degree in music technology from the Indiana University School of Music in 2003.

Dedication

This book is dedicated to the life, memory, and laughter of Joe Murphy. May he live on forever in the hearts and minds of podcasters and listeners the world over. We miss you, Joe. (http://joemurphymemorialfund.org)

Authors' Acknowledgments

Tee Morris: *Expert Podcasting Practices For Dummies* has truly been a challenge, raising the bar for myself as a writer and a podcaster. I cannot thank Evo Terra and Ryan Williams, my co-authors, enough for their incredible work on this title. You are only as good as the company you keep, and I am in incredible company. This also extends beyond the writing. Steve, Kim, Barry, and Linda (a/k/a Team Wiley) have gone to the wall to make this title even better than its predecessor; and along with our Technical Editor, *Escape Pod*'s Steve Eley, I believe we have done so. Thank you all for keeping me honest and for keeping the book timely and concise. A huge heart-felt thank you to Samson Technologies, Abode Systems, Audio-Technica, The Kennedy Center, The International Spy Museum, Dancing Cat Studios, and podcasters everywhere who have contributed their time, resources, and passion for the podosphere in helping me put all this together. Finally, to my family and friends for weathering storms, tolerating my long hours and deadlines, and for believing in me.

Evo Terra: I would like to thank many people for their help and support along the way for my sophomore effort, which I found infinitely more challenging than my first book.

First, quite obviously, goes to my lovely wife Sheila and superb son NJ, for their support, understanding, and unwavering encouragement through the entire writing process. Second, the podcast community at large, for their enthusiasm and unending inspiration. You have all helped to create a landscape and community that is worthy of helping to move forward.

Finally, I would like to thank Kim and Steve from Wiley for their exceeding coolness. They serve as shining examples of all that is right and good in the publishing world. This book — and my involvement — certainly would not have been possible without them.

Ryan Williams: My contribution to this book would be impossible without the tireless efforts and patience of my fellow authors, Steve Hayes, Kim Darosett, and Barry Childs-Helton. Thanks are also due to the staff and users of Indianapolismusic.net, and the creator of WFMU's Downtown Soulville, maybe the finest podcast I've ever heard.

This book is dedicated to my wife, Jennifer. Thanks for letting me stay up late.

Publisher's Acknowledgments

We're proud of this book; please send us your comments through our online registration form located at www.dummies.com/register/.

Some of the people who helped bring this book to market include the following:

Acquisitions, Editorial, and Media Development

Project Editor: Kim Darosett

Executive Editor: Steven Hayes

Senior Copy Editor: Barry Childs-Helton

Technical Editor: Stephen Eley

Editorial Manager: Leah Cameron

Media Development Project Manager: Laura Atkinson

Media Development Assistant Producer: Kit Malone

Editorial Assistant: Amanda Foxworth

Sr. Editorial Assistant: Cherie Case

Cartoons: Rich Tennant (www.the5thwave.com)

Composition Services

Project Coordinator: Erin Smith

Layout and Graphics: Stacie Brooks, Jonelle Burns, Carrie A. Cesavice, Shane Johnson, Stephanie D. Jumper, Barbara Moore, Brent Savage, Julie Trippetti, Christine Williams

Proofreaders: Melissa Buddendeck, Cynthia Fields

Indexer: Potomac Indexing, LLC

Anniversary Logo Design: Richard J. Pacifico

Publishing and Editorial for Technology Dummies

Richard Swadley, Vice President and Executive Group Publisher

Andy Cummings, Vice President and Publisher

Mary Bednarek, Executive Acquisitions Director

Mary C. Corder, Editorial Director

Publishing for Consumer Dummies

Diane Graves Steele, Vice President and Publisher

Joyce Pepple, Acquisitions Director

Composition Services

Gerry Fahey, Vice President of Production Services

Debbie Stailey, Director of Composition Services

Contents at a Glance

Table Of Contents

Introduction

To put it bluntly, all of us — from authors to editors — are a bit uncomfortable with the "Expert" part of this title. Not because of any lack of experience on the part of your authors, but because of the do-it-yourself — and (perhaps more importantly) do-it-your-*way* — nature of podcasting. To quote Daniel Quinn, "there is no one right way" to make a podcast. In fact, many of the most popular podcasts (and you can measure popularity in a variety of ways) ignore or break the rules of just about every practice we discuss in this book. But while there may be no one right way to make a podcast, we've tried to fill this book with a series of *best* practices — which are certainly among the right ways to do specific podcasting-related tasks.

At the time of this publication, *Podcasting For Dummies* has been on the shelves for just over two years. While that book helped many people get started in podcasting, a need has arisen to go beyond what the first book covers. For many, starting a podcast is the easy part. It's the *Now what?* question that plagues many who seek to take their existing podcasts to the next level.

We hope this book can answer that question, providing a few paths — some well-trodden and some relatively uncharted — toward success. Having said that, your authors are staunch supporters of the Law of Multiple Success Variables, which we just made up. It states, both basically and in its entirety, that every podcaster will have his or her own metrics of success, and that the merits of one cannot and should not be judged by those of another. Podcasting isn't broadcasting. It's not radio, TV, or any other form of mainstream media that came before. It is a difficult form of media to describe to your grandmother and likely to be misunderstood by your peers. Its very amorphous nature is what keeps its fans and creators coming back for more.

With a little luck, some judicious planning, and the wise decision to implement some of these practices in your podcasting, we hope to move the needle higher on your own metrics of success. Enjoy.

About This Book

This book is written for — and by — podcasters. It's filled with a series of practices, tips, tools, and techniques designed to take your podcast "to the next level" — whatever the heck that means to you. By its very nature, a podcast can be many things to many different people. We understand that and have tried very hard to assemble practices that are helpful to the widest possible audience of podcasters.

We cover a lot of technical territory in this book, from choosing better headphones to switching to a video-podcasting format. We also help define the softer side of podcasting — helping you understand your options for scripting and providing suggestions for generating more audience interaction. Yet we're not afraid to take on the heavier issues, and we offer some definite opinions on advertising, networks, and the ever-present issue of *podfading* (disappearing from the podosphere — yes, it does happen).

While we don't promise to answer all possible questions in this book, we do provide a lot of perspective for the podcaster looking to break new ground, try new things, or even breathe new life into a floundering project. Some advice is very specific, some much more general. But all of it — we hope — will be of use to someone wishing to make a podcast even better.

What You're Not to Read

While most *For Dummies* books aren't necessarily designed to be read from front to back, that goes doubly well for this book. So in case it wasn't clear before, you have our permission to skip entire practices — or even parts — if they don't apply to you. We've tucked lots of cross-references into the book, so you shouldn't miss anything important.

You may notice a few sidebars in gray text throughout the book. These are more like anecdotes and asides than independent content. They're for adding clarity, dimension, and the occasional example to topics discussed in the text. While we're positive the writing is as brilliant as we are modest, you can skip them without fear of offending us — or missing anything terribly important.

Foolish Assumptions

As stated earlier, we're working under the impression that you are familiar with the basics of podcasting. In a perfect world, you're already a podcaster and don't need us to define terms like RSS or guide you through your first time FTPing a file to a server. We figure you won't be puzzled if you're looking at a wave form for the first time. If that gives you pause, then allow us to highly recommend picking up a copy of our first book, *Podcasting For Dummies,* where all of that lovely stuff — and much more — gets covered at an appropriate level of detail.

Beyond that, we assume you are a generally curious person who's familiar with the basics of getting new programs installed on your computer, signing up for online services, and adapting broad instructions to your specific environment. As with any *For Dummies* book, you get step-by-step instructions where they're called for, without having to endure somebody talking down to you. Of course, in keeping with the "Expert" part of our book title, we sometimes start the hand-holding a bit further along in the process. We figure you've already got a handle on the simple, up-front stuff.

How This Book Is Organized

As stated earlier, this book offers a series of distinct practices, provided in a loosely linear fashion. Each practice is designed to be read by itself, with any necessary and relevant cross-references added. Similar practices are clustered together in parts that move (generally speaking) from relatively basic to relatively advanced.

Okay, this book isn't set up like a novel; it's not designed to be read from cover to cover, though you may find that individual parts are easiest to understand and implement if you read 'em in more or less the sequence in which we present the practices. Often a consistent theme of an entire part is easier to understand if you read all the practices in it, in order. Or not. Your mileage may vary. Do what works for you.

Part I: Planning Out a Podcast

Even though this book is designed for those who are already podcasting, we recognize that some of you will ignore that advice and jump into that world right here. (You probably skip the prologues in your novels as well, don't you? Well . . . so do we.)

Assuming you already have experience in recording, editing, producing, or even creating your own podcast, you may have that unmistakable itch that can only be scratched by creating another podcast. This part takes you through the process of getting ready to podcast. It covers a range of topics — figuring out what to talk about, finding who else is talking about it, getting a handle on how you should talk about it, and what to do to make sure that others *care* that you are talking about it.

Part II: Going for a Professional Sound

The second part in this book is all about the recording process. We help you pick out quality microphones and headphones — and help you put them to good use. We offer some perspective on various types of recording environments so you can increase your flexibility in deciding where to capture the perfect sound. Additionally, we get into some more advanced recording topics, covering professional software and techniques to step up your game and make your show sound fantastic.

Part III: Post-Production Approaches

The audio engineers in the crowd will tell you — the magic happens in post-production. Unless you are of the "record and release" school of podcasters, you'll probably find that an efficient post-production session dramatically increases your show's sound quality. This part covers topics in that vein — ways to fix problem audio files, adding in just the right effects, navigating the nuances of mp3 files, and weighing the pros and cons of doing *enhanced* podcasts.

Part IV: The Final Steps Before Episode #0

This may be the smallest part of the book, but the practices inside can mean the difference between a fun show that's enjoyed by a few and a fun show that's easily discovered and enjoyed by *many more*. In this part, we leave the engineering tricks behind and discuss often-overlooked aspects of podcasting — including proper ID3 tagging, creating valid RSS feeds, and making the most of your corresponding Web site.

Part V: Building Your Audience

With all the work that went into building your show and podcast episodes, you'd probably be a lot happier if a few more (or a *lot* more) people were listening to your show. That's why this part provides plenty of ways you can get the word out about your show. Social media, networking with other podcasters, and mobilizing your fan base are all great ways to increase your podcast's visibility. We discuss those opportunities and a whole lot more.

Part VI: Creating a Video Podcast

Some podcasters are naturally drawn to the wonders of moving pictures and feel compelled to create video versions of their podcasts. This part provides an overview of adding video to your podcast, with enough information to get you started down the path. Truth be told, there aren't enough pages in this book to fully cover making a professional video podcast. That's a topic for another day. And another book. But we give you a solid place to start.

Part VII: Podcasting as a Business

Although many podcasters do it for fun, some do it as a job. In this part, we cover the business side of podcasting. Whether you do business-based podcasting on your own or are paid to do it for an organization or corporation, this part will help you navigate the waters between hobby and vocation.

Practice VIII: Reengineering Your Podcast

The final part of this book takes an honest and straightforward look at the reality of podcasting — sometimes it's just not fun anymore. Although (quite often) that can mean throwing in the towel (we talk about that), in many cases a spark still exists that can be nurtured back to a roaring blaze. It's all about changing your perspective — and sometimes topics or personnel.

Bonus Content on the DVD

We know we cover a lot of ground in this book, so we brought along a goodie bag for you to enjoy on your journey. On the DVD, you'll find samples of podcasts, *podsafe* music (music that's okay to use in your podcast without fear of violating prohibitive copyright or licensing agreements), and a few screencast tutorials that illustrate some basic podcast techniques. You'll also find sample files you can use to follow along with some of the step lists in the book to help develop your podcasting skills. For your convenience, the DVD also provides live links to sites for the podcasts, software, and equipment mentioned in the book.

Conventions Used in This Book

This book uses some consistent design features to help you get around the topics and spot the important stuff at a glance. For instance . . .

- ✔ **Computer typeface:** We use `text that looks like this` to denote commands, paths to files, or the URLs of Web sites, much like what you'd see in your browser window.

- ✔ **Command arrows:** When writing about drop-down navigation of menus on your computer, we use a ⇨ to denote a shift from one menu to the other. For example, File⇨New indicates that you should select the New option from the File menu.

Icons Used in This Book

We've pared down the icons in this book to only four. They are:

These are shortcuts or helpful hints along the way. They may not work for you in every case, but often they get you to a useful destination in the shortest amount of time.

Some things bear repeating and reinforcing to drive the point home. When you see this Remember icon, expect to take a moment to reflect on the content.

Be very careful about taking specific steps when you see this Warning icon. Yes, there are some things you can do that can cause significant damage to your media files, Web site status, and relationship with your dedicated listener base. Proceed with caution — and don't take the steps unless you are absolutely sure of the outcome.

Remember our comment about "no one right way" earlier? It's still true, but we use this Insider Secrets icon to tell you at least one common way to get something done. These pearls of practical wisdom may not always work for every situation, but each one is certainly a known entity for at least one of your authors.

Where to Go from Here

You already know you can skip around to your heart's content in the book. If you're relatively new to podcasting, we suggest starting with Practice 1. Those who want answers to the *How do I make money with this?* question can jump right into Part VII. Wherever you feel like starting, we hope you find it enjoyable.

To help with that enjoyment, we'd like to let you know that we have companion podcasts available for both books — *Podcasting For Dummies* and *Expert Podcasting Practices For Dummies*. Co-author Tee Morris has produced several episodes — and will be producing several *more* episodes — of free content that showcases many of the topics discussed in the two books. You can subscribe to the podcast (free of charge, naturally) at

```
http://etips.dummies.com/rss/
    podcastingfd.xml
```

Part I

Planning Out a
Podcast

The 5th Wave   By Rich Tennant

Practice 1

Selecting the Right Topic for Your Podcast

A s Kermit the Frog said, "It's not easy being green." While the veracity of this statement is subject to debate, we, the authors of this book, posit to you that selecting the right topic for your podcast is not easy either. The key word in that statement is "right." We heartily agree that all too many podcasts are chosen without sufficient foresight and planning — the collective decision of one or more parties after too much alcohol, too little sleep, and the auspicious statement, "You know, this would make a great podcast!"

Well, no, we're not talking about that at all. The title of this book has the words *expert practices* in it, and we're certainly not about to start off breaking from the code on the very first practice of the book (even though the authors of this book have been guilty of the aforementioned, on more than one occasion). Heck, by some accounts, the story of how we decided to write our first book together, *Podcasting For Dummies*, is eerily similar.

In this practice, we advocate the use of rational and logical thought to help guide you toward one of the many "right" topics you may choose for your podcast. The truth is, there are probably many topics you are qualified to speak about, that are of interest to a potential audience, and that allow you (as well as any co-hosts or support staff you might employ) to grow and expand. Podcasting is fun. But podcasting with a purpose is sublime.

Taking Inventory of Your Interests

Let's start this off with the most important person in the equation: you. No, it's not your audience. It's not the community you aim to serve. It's not even the person who might have paid you to pick up the mic and start cranking out episodes. We'll even tell you that it isn't your spouse, though as we say this we cast a wary eye over our shoulders, burning through even more SPUs (which we explain later).

The host of the show is the lifeblood of the show. We're not trying to put undue pressure on you, but your show won't get very far if the topic isn't something that you (a) want to talk about and (b) can talk about while (c) demonstrating that you know what you're talking about. So what can you talk about? What do you want to talk about?

To be fair, you may have had the idea of doing a podcast thrust upon you as part of your job. That's fine. Unless your boss has arranged for someone to hand you a completed script to read in front of the microphone (in which case, you probably aren't reading this anyhow), you'll still benefit from the suggestions in this section.

List what aspects of your job interest you

Like it or not, we spend a lot of time at our jobs, developing skills and competencies we use in our personal lives as well. While there is no question that some of your daily tasks at a job might fall into the *mind-numbing* category, examine those parts of your job that you do find interesting.

Notice we didn't say *day job*. The reality is that for many people with the drive and ambition to even consider becoming podcasters, the wearing of two hats is commonplace. It's not uncommon to take off the Accountant hat at 5:30 and assume the mantle of Community Organizer, Sports Memorabilia Collector, or Classic Car Restorer. These are every bit as much of a profession as that which provides the majority of your household income. The pay just stinks.

We recommend making a list of the things you do in your profession that most interest you, keeping the following points in mind:

- ✔ You can get very specific or very broad — you can always refine or group tasks together later.

- ✔ Be sure to include the aspects of professional affiliations, groups, or associations to which you may belong. Within all of these are hidden gems that may very well lead you to the right topic.

Jot down what you like to do for fun

What else turns your crank that you enjoy doing in your leisure time? All work and no play makes Jack a very boring podcaster whom no one much wants to listen to or talk with. And let's face it, the possibilities for entertainment-focused podcasts are endless.

Look — you don't *have* to be in this for the money. Some of the best-produced and most rewarding shows are created by people for the sheer fun of it. Perhaps you are an avid bowler and would like to share your passion with others. Maybe you know a ridiculous amount about beer. Perhaps your friends all turn to you for information when it comes to obscure knots and stitches, and everyone knows it takes you half as long to knit a sweater than anyone else on the block.

The idea is to find out what you are passionate about. Jot down a few ideas and see if you can come up with five or six subtopics worthy of further discussion. And remember that you don't have to be the most knowledgeable person on the planet on a given topic. If you have the passion, it might be fun to take your listeners on the journey as you learn more.

Filling a Niche by Focusing on a Specific Area of Interest

Deciding what topics you can talk about is an important step, but it's time for the application of what we like to call *Jurassic Park* logic. JP logic requires you to ask yourself this question: You've spent a lot of time thinking about whether you *could,* but have you figured out whether you *should?*

While we're not trying to put you into tidy boxes or for an instant suggest that adding your voice to a busy conversation is a waste of time, we *are* suggesting that you strive to introduce a new topic to the podosphere, or find an underserved audience. Yes, you could create yet another music podcast featuring an eclectic mix of podsafe music artists. But realize that you will be competing with the dozens — perhaps hundreds — of shows out there doing basically the same thing.

The suggestions in the previous section should have given you more than one idea. If one of those ideas is adequately (and only you can decide this) covered by a host of other shows, consider moving on to the next topic. Practice 2 covers a few podcast-discovery ideas.

You'll best serve the current and future audience of podcast listeners by selecting a niche topic. This stands in stark contrast to traditional broadcast media, where the idea is to select broad-reaching topics to maximize the coverage area. That's fine in a world where only so many stations fit on a radio dial, but that's not where we live. Go for the small and focused. It's where you'll find the most loyal audience just waiting for you to start talking.

Determining whether you'll have enough to talk about

One of the perils of *going niche* is making sure you have enough material with which you can create new episodes. A show centered around the intricacies of reattaching lost buttons to ladies' blouses might limit your options in the future. However, that might make an excellent episode of a podcast about tailoring or seamstressing (is that a word?).

Our advice is to write down the topics and subtopics that come to mind. Don't worry — you're not planning out your show production schedule for the next six months. If you can list ten items of interest with only a few minutes of thought, you'll probably be fine.

 You never know when show topics will hit you, so figure out a system for jotting down the inspirations when they strike. One of your authors uses a portable Moleskine notebook (overpriced notebook, claims the second); the other keeps an outliner application at the ready (though the first wonders why inspiration only strikes at the keyboard). Figure out what system works best for you. Heck, sticky notes are a great way to start. Anything that allows you to collect ideas as they come is good to have.

Considering whether anyone will listen

Once you know you have enough to get started on your first five to ten episodes, you'll want to do a final sanity check: Is there anybody out there waiting to listen? We hesitated before putting this section out there and remain torn as of this writing. But in the end, practicality won out. You can have exceptional diction, excellent production values, and extraordinary content — but someone other than you and your mom needs to care.

Luckily, this shouldn't be a problem for you; more (sometimes way more) than one person always seems to be interested in the most obscure things out there. Keep in mind, however, that audience size and podcast topic are intimately related. If a large audience is your goal (and we're not saying it should be), then select a topic that appeals to many.

Narrowing Your Focus to Make Your Show Unique

Let's revisit that music podcast we spoke of earlier in this practice. You've got the DJ bug bad, and no amount of rationale or arguing will sway you from your goal. Fine. Far be it from us to get in the way of your passion. A surefire way to differentiate yourself from other shows is to dig into the minutiae of your chosen topic.

Hyperspecialization

So maybe that crazy idea we had about sewing buttons on ladies' blouses isn't so crazy after all? Let's face it — there are lots of types of buttons out there and lots of places on which you can sew them. Different configurations, styles, backings . . . and don't get us started on the various types of button-holes and the related stitching!

This might seem an extreme example, but it's easily ported into nearly any topic. Instead of covering something as broad as sports marketing, how about focusing on the extreme sports market or promoting and financing Ultimate Fighting Championship matches?

When you narrow your focus to specific elements within a specific topic, sometimes you can actually uncover more content. Now, that may sound counterintuitive, but consider the extreme-sports marketing angle. A show on general sports marketing might turn off an audience if the host delves into the venue-selection process for rock climbing to maximize sponsorship branding. And if you can make a compelling podcast about that topic. . . .

Hyperlocalization

Even though podcasts can and do reach a global audience, going *hyperlocal* is another great way to set your show apart from the rest. Forget covering sports marketing for the entire U.S. market — cover the challenges and rewards of doing the job in Peoria, Illinois. How many community, school, or enthusiast teams are there in an area — each giving you a number of potential listeners?

And don't think that hyperlocal means that only local people will listen. While the content may be local and relevant to those in a local area, the concept may appeal to a wider audience. It's no big leap of faith to assume that someone working to market a disc-golf tournament in Flagstaff, Arizona, could get some great advice from the sports marketer in Peoria — even if the producers never specifically talk about disc-golf tournaments.

Broadening Your Focus to Appeal to New Listeners

Strange as it may sound, taking the opposite road — broadening your focus — can also lead to a great podcast topic. Often, in fact, this advice can offer the most benefit to established podcasters looking to step up their game or appeal to a wider audience.

And while we love the idea of getting down to brass tacks with your topic, it's not always the right path for every show.

Becoming multifaceted

Just because you neatly fill a niche with your show doesn't mean that's the only niche you *can* fill. (Specialization may be the most commonly offered evidence of natural selection, but it's the ability to survive when the nature of the game changes that keeps the species going.)

 If you're going for multiple niches, make sure they are related in some way. Combining your passion for extreme-sports marketing and your fascination with button application might be taking things a bit too far, and you're almost guaranteed to alienate half of your audience — unless (say) there's some new extreme sports with some equally extreme fastening mechanisms. But no, probably not even then. . . .

Becoming multifaceted often happens after a show has been underway for a while, as the host discovers "niches within the niche" — and perhaps even tangential affinities — while exploring the main topic at hand. While these can certainly digress from the show's original intent, they can also indicate an untapped interest — for the podcaster and the listening audience.

Go ahead and explore these side projects. Let your audience know that you're taking a brief off-topic stroll if you feel it necessary. Change is a natural part of life, and as long as you're not going completely off the deep end, your audience will allow you some latitude.

Tapping into the community

Speaking of your audience — ask your listeners what they think and where you should take the show.

A little of this technique goes a long way. Don't use it as a crutch when you're out of things to talk about. And certainly don't use it in your first 20 episodes. There are few things more annoying than a show host begging the audience to come up with ideas. Audiences see that as laziness on the part of the host, and they quickly find someone else willing to put forth the necessary effort to keep producing the content they want to hear.

Instead of asking your listeners outright what you should do, pay attention to the feedback they provide you about the shows you produce. We go into great detail about feedback and how to get it in Practice 34.

One thing you'll learn is that podcast listeners aren't afraid of letting you know what they think of your show. When something out of the ordinary that you do strikes a chord with them — either positively or negatively — they'll speak up. Pay attention to this feedback and look for ways to keep doing more of the things they like.

You can also consider learning more about your audience and tailoring the show to their needs. If your show on women's hat fashion from the 1960s is frequented by a high percentage of listeners from the Eastern seaboard (you can find this in your server log files), consider adding a recurring segment dedicated to the life and times of Jackie Kennedy-Onassis.

The idea is to play to the audience. Find out about them with surveys and server logs, or engage them in an ongoing dialogue. Yes, the show is about you, by you, and should be of primary importance *to* you. But surely there is some common ground between you and your audience, or they wouldn't be listening to you in the first place.

Practice 2

Keeping Up with the Joneses

In This Practice

- Finding other podcasts on podcast directories
- Knowing where — and how — to search
- Staying abreast of new content while staying afloat
- Remembering the world outside your computer

There is an old adage worthy of modification to make it relevant to the podosphere: People listen to other podcasts more than they listen to yours. That's because a lot of podcasts are out there clamoring for attention, and it's highly likely that your listeners are listening to many of them. It's a prudent podcaster who understands the playing field and has at the least a passing knowledge of the other podcasts in the game.

But in a world of over 100,000 video and audio podcasts, it's simply not practical to try and listen to all of them, though many poor souls make a valiant effort. In this practice, we not only give you some practical tips on searching and finding podcasts relevant to your needs, but also show you some simple ways to keep your head above water when the flood of shows starts coming in.

Watching Podcast Directories

Podcast directories are probably the easiest place to get started in your search to find other shows with content similar to yours. Directories serve not only to aggregate content but also to categorize the shows listed — making it easy to sample many related shows in one sitting. True, there may be many more shows of a similar nature out there that have not been collected by a directory, but we'll get to that in a minute. For now, Table 2-1 lists some popular all-purpose directories to start your search.

Of course, Table 2-1 isn't a full listing of podcast directories. In fact, well over 150 podcast directories exist as of this writing. Rob Walch, one of the most respected podcasters and host of the *podCast411* podcast, maintains a comprehensive list on his site at `http://podcast411.com/page2.html`.

There are two ways to find information on directories — and they lead to very different results. If you're looking for many podcasts of a certain style, try browsing these directories. iTunes and Podcast Pickle provide the most meaningful results here; they incorporate a healthy subcategorization schema. Alternatively, you can utilize the search box on the directory; keep in mind, however, that this may not show you all the similar podcasts of the type you're looking for.

TABLE 2-1: POPULAR PODCAST DIRECTORIES

Directory	URL
iTunes	`http://itunes.com` (requires desktop installation)
Podcast Alley	`http://podcastalley.com`
Podcast Pickle	`http://podcastpickle.com`

Browsing within subcategories

On "the Pickle," follow these steps to search within categories:

1. Navigate to `http://podcastpickle.com`, shown in Figure 2-1.

• **Figure 2-1: The Podcast Pickle is a community site and directory site for audio and video podcasts.**

2. **Pull down and choose from the Genres tab in the middle of the screen.**

3. **Choose from the list of shows displayed on the page.**

For results beyond the first 30, use the page selector at the bottom of the screen.

On iTunes, your trip starts in the iTunes Store. Follow these steps:

1. **Launch the iTunes application and click the iTunes Store link on the left-hand side.**

2. **Click the Podcasts link.**

iTunes likes to move that link around with new versions of the application, but it's always under the iTunes Store.

From there, you see a list of categories, as shown in Figure 2-2.

• **Figure 2-2: The iTunes Music Store podcasting section, with various categories on the left side.**

3. **Select the category you're interested in searching.**

Depending on the category selected, you may see a list labeled `More [category name]` for further refinement.

iTunes does a great job of showing you Featured, Top Rated, and other New and Notable podcasts relevant to your selections along the way.

Wading through listings

With Podcast Alley, the results are less detailed because the directory doesn't subcategorize. So instead of being able to separate out investment podcasts from marketing podcasts (as you can on the prior two directories), you have to wade through over 1,000 listings — a less-than-optimal way to browse.

Performing keyword searches

As a fallback — search. It's not elegant, and none of the directories listed in Table 2-1 incorporate advanced search algorithms or provide a way to "search inside these results." And because the keyword you're searching on must be contained within the show title or description, plan on doing a few different searches of different-but-related keywords to find more content.

Successful Searching Strategies

While the search capabilities of podcast directories leave much to be desired, you can employ some more advanced search options to focus and enhance your results. Some options are familiar . . .

Google

Yep, you can use Google to search through a directory's information to get more detailed results. To perform such a search with Google, use the following syntax:

```
"keywords" site:[URL]
```

For example, if you enter the keyword phrase `"sports marketing"` in the search box at Podcast Alley, the results show 200 listings (as of this writing). With Google, you can request the exact phrase `"sports marketing"` — and restrict the search to pages on Podcast Alley — with this query:

```
"sports marketing" site:podcast
   alley.com
```

And you only get back seven results, which is much more manageable.

Of course, you can use Google to search more than specific Web sites for content. In fact, Google will likely lead more listeners to your podcast than any podcast-specific directory. (We cover that topic in detail in Part V of the book.)

The true power of Google comes into play with its advanced search features. You can find them by clicking the More link after you've done a search, or by visiting

```
www.google.com/intl/en/options/
```

You'll probably find plenty of interesting ways to search for shows similar to yours in these options. And if you are open to suggestions, try these:

- ✔ **Alerts:** By setting up an alert, you can receive updates as Google finds and indexes sites, blogs, groups, and information relevant to your search and e-mails the results to you in a simple text format. Who has time to search for `"sports marketing podcast"` every day? Well, Google Alerts does — so you don't have to.

- ✔ **Blog search:** Not quite as comprehensive as Technorati (discussed next), but still very useful. Because most podcasts have accompanying blogs where the notes about the episodes are posted, limiting the search to the blogosphere can further refine your searching.

Speaking of those blog-specific search engines . . .

Blog-specific search engines

In Practice 26, we talk about why so many podcasters use blogs to accompany their podcasts' episodes. For now, it's enough to point out that they do — and that this easily enables some specialty search engines to locate and index content you may find relevant to your search.

By far, Technorati (`www.technorati.com`) is the leader of the pack when it comes to blog searches. Of course, you can do a standard search on the site by typing keywords in the search box. But the key difference with this search is the way it's specialized: to return results *only* from blogs and other independent and user-generated-content sites. This naturally limits the search results to a more manageable list than what you'd get from using a conventional search engine like Google.

 Google has made lazy searchers out of all of us. If you want Technorati to return *only* matches to *all* the keywords you enter, you have to type the word AND between your keywords. In our working example, that might be `sports AND marketing AND podcast`. When all else fails, look at the Advanced options of the search engine in question.

Because Technorati limits the results returned to blogs and bloglike content, you can cut through a lot of the clutter you find on other search engines and concentrate on finding other blogs and podcasts only. Of particular use is the *authority* given to a particular search result. Figure 2-3 highlights this listing on a search for `sports AND marketing AND podcast`. Technorati gives authority to blogs based primarily on how many other blogs link to that blog.

Click to access Watchlist

• **Figure 2-3: By showing the authority of a blog in your search results, you can determine how relevant it is to your needs.**

Technorati's Watchlists work much like Google Alerts: You let Technorati do the searching for you, returning relevant results when its index changes. But rather than cluttering up your e-mail with notifications, Technorati provides an *RSS feed* (a summary of updates in a special format) for your Watchlists. So now you can get updates right in your newsreader! See Figure 2-3 for a Watchlist link.

Technorati doesn't reign supreme over the blog-search tools, though the authors of this book are quite enamored with its power and use it almost exclusively. There's always someone trying to build a better mousetrap (or, in this case, blog-search tool). Here are a few other contenders:

- ✔ **Bloglines:** `http://bloglines.com`
- ✔ **Feedster:** `http://feedster.com`
- ✔ **IceRocket:** `http://icerocket.com`

As with many of the sites listed in this book, your mileage with each will vary depending on many factors, including what you search, how you search, and how well that which you are looking for is indexed by the search engine in question.

Podcast-specific search engines

It stands to reason that you may have the most success searching for podcasts not with an all-purpose search engine, or even a blog-specific search engine, but with a *podcast*-specific search engine. Yeah . . . that makes sense.

Or does it? It's fair to say that the technology required to decipher spoken-word context is nowhere near as reliable as that required for text. Searching electronic text is easy, but searching an audio file is hard. We don't have the time to go into the nuances of what makes it so difficult, but it's probably not too difficult to imagine why. Voice-recognition software is getting better all the time, but still has much room for improvement.

A few companies are pushing the envelope and investing in innovative technologies to get better audio-search results. Notably these:

- **Ooyhaa:** `http://ooyhaa.com`
- **Podscope:** `http://podscope.com`
- **Yahoo! Audio Search:** `http://audio.search.yahoo.com`

 The tools listed here search through the audio files in an attempt to find matching conversations. Just because the *theme* of a show is (say) "sports marketing" doesn't mean that exact phrase crops up in narrative; these engines provide a hit only if the words *sports marketing* are actually *said* in the program. It's a good idea to draw the keywords for your search from among the things you'd expect to hear *about* — for example, a sports-marketing show is a good bet to discuss "two-year exclusive contract" — rather than from the larger theme of the show.

Managing Information Overload

By now you've probably found quite a few Joneses out there to keep up with — each talking about similar topics and areas of interest for your show. But unless you have a penchant for repetitive tasks, you can easily grow weary of searching, reading Web sites, and downloading whole episodes manually just to check out the content. We'll go so far as to say you can't keep up with everything this way; what's needed is a healthy regimen of subscribing, tagging, and skimming to get a taste of the content — else ye go mad!

 Many of the search engines we've listed here — including Google — allow you to schedule automatic searches and have the results e-mailed to you. That's a great idea and highly recommended; after all, most of us check our inboxes on a regular basis.

Using newsreaders

Do you ever wonder how the prolific posters at your favorite news sites can synthesize so much information? Or maybe how the top users on social news sites like Digg.com manage to break stories moments after they have been released? Sure, having the right contacts, insider information, and more free time than your retired grandmother certainly helps. But in almost all cases, these information mavens share a common tool — an RSS subscription tool.

 While we're doing our best to be technology-agnostic in this book, Evo feels the need to put forth a recommendation for the Newscaster suite of RSS-management products. He relies on NetNewsWire (`http://newsgator.com`), the Mac desktop client, to manage hundreds of podcast and blog feeds. NewsGator makes RSS-management tools for your inbox, smart phone, and more. It even offers a free Web-based aggregator to get you hooked.

Your choices in *feed readers* (applications that read RSS feeds, also called *aggregators*) are legion. Table 2-2 lists some of the more-popular feed readers. Many are Web page–based (Google Reader and Bloglines). Some work directly with your browser (Sage and Pluck), while the new Internet Explorer 7 browser comes with native RSS support built in. Many people prefer to integrate their RSS subscriptions with their e-mail clients; power users tend to prefer to install specific applications to get the most control possible.

TABLE 2-2: POPULAR FEED READERS

Reader	URL	Use as
Bloglines	`www.bloglines.com`	Web-based
Google Reader	`www.google.com/reader`	Web-based
Newscaster	`http://newsgator.com`	Application
Pluck	`www.pluck.com`	Browser plug-in
Sage	`http://sage.mozdev.org/`	Browser plug-in

Regardless of which method you choose, remember that it takes dedication and discipline to manage your subscriptions effectively. After all, it's too easy to let hundreds (or even thousands) of news posts pile up. You aren't doing yourself any favors when that happens; the whole idea is to keep updated in as near an approximation of real time as possible.

The key to managing RSS feeds lies in finding the delicate balance between obsessively refreshing to check for new items and leaving that chore until the end of the week. And while neither extreme is likely to benefit you much, every individual has an RSS-feed comfort zone — a check cycle that fits into daily life with minimum fuss.

Keeping your feeds from overflowing

When all else fails, use the thrice-a-day method. When you sit down in front of your computer in the morning, make a habit of going through all of the news items in your reader from the night before. You don't have to read whole articles at that moment. Instead, save 'em for later — but specify a time. In some readers, you can click the headline, and it will spawn another window. Others may open a Web browser with the page loaded. Fine. Your primary goal is to separate the wheat from the chaff. If you find a story that isn't interesting, mark it as read (as in past tense) and move on. Even with a few hundred feeds — and just as many unread news items — this shouldn't take you much more than an hour to do.

Repeat the same process one other time during the day, perhaps at your lunch break or at the end of your workday. Finally, do another pass before turning in. The idea is to keep your feed reader cleaned out, saving the good stuff for a deeper dive later when you have more time.

Tagging with del.icio.us

The concept of *tagging* can be difficult to wrap your head around at first. Not because it's overly complicated, but rather because it's so simple. Many of us were trained in the traditional categorize-by-filing methods. While that's a great way to file last year's tax information, it's less helpful when you're dealing with information that could reasonably fit in multiple categories.

Del.icio.us (`http://del.icio.us`) has become the de-facto standard in *tagging* Web content. Think of it as making your browser's *bookmark this* feature available to you any time you're online from any computer — while at the same time making it a lot easier to find content you've put there. That's tagging the way del.icio.us does it. Follow these steps to get started using del.icio.us:

1. **Go to** `http://del.icio.us` **and click the Get Started link.**

2. **Fill in the requested information to register for a del.icio.us account.**

   Accounts are free of charge, and registration is simple.

3. **Install the browser buttons by clicking the Install Buttons Now link.**

   Browser buttons make it possible for you to tag Web pages and other content you find without having to go back to del.icio.us. Follow the directions for your specific browser.

4. **Start tagging Web content.**

   When you find a page that you want to look at later, click the TAG browser button you just installed. In the pop-up window, fill out the boxes.

Tagging works best when you tag excessively. There is no limit on the number of tags you can put against a single piece of content — so go for it! Use the keywords you expect to use when you look for the content later. Here are some tips regarding what tags to use:

- The name of the product/site/service
- The author of the post, if applicable
- Names of similar products/services
- Keywords found in the article
- Some of the suggestions offered by del.icio.us

Searching your previously tagged items is simple. Assuming you installed the browser buttons mentioned earlier, you can just click the blue/white/gray/ black icon on the toolbar and type in your search terms. Del.icio.us shows you several matches (as shown in Figure 2-4) before taking you to the Web content you select. If you don't have the browser buttons installed (or are on a different computer), log on to del.icio.us and search your bookmarks directly from the site.

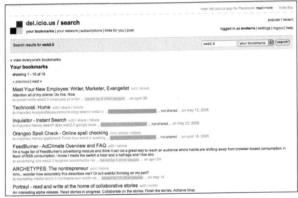

• **Figure 2-4: Results from searching your own saved bookmarks on del.icio.us.**

Subscribing to del.icio.us searches

It should come as no surprise that del.icio.us can also be a great place to find content other users have tagged. In fact, you can set up a del.icio.us search on a given set of tags and then subscribe to that search with your RSS reader. Here's one:

```
http://del.icio.us/rss/tag/podcasting
```

Subscribe to this search in your RSS reader to get a list of the most recent items tagged with `podcasting`. You can modify the URL given here to subscribe to any tag. Just replace `podcasting` with (say) `apples`, and you'll be subscribe to the most recent items tagged with `apples`.

 Join two or more tags together with a + symbol. For example, `sports+marketing` or `horse+carriage` can further refine your results list for that search.

Using del.icio.us to sample media files

Del.icio.us tags Web content, not just Web pages. With some further tweaking and customizing, you can get del.icio.us to create an RSS 2.0 feed of all the neat "found" audio content you discover in your feeds. Yes, you can just download the audio files you discover to your desktop and transfer them to your mp3 player manually. But where's the fun in that? Let del.icio.us do the heavy lifting for you, and you can get back to work faster:

1. **Decide on your trigger word**.

This can be anything you want, but it should be something that you aren't likely to use as a tag on a nonmedia file (that is, something other than audio or video). Evo uses *enclosure* and finds that works well for him.

2. **Subscribe to this feed:**

```
http://del.icio.us/[username]/
    system:media:audio+[trigger]
```

Of course, you'll have to replace `[username]` with your del.icio.us account name and `[trigger]` with the tag you are using to trigger this sequence of events.

3. **Tag a media file with your trigger word.**

Don't tag the entire Web page, but the media file itself. If you have the browser buttons installed, you should be able to Ctrl+click or right-click the link to the media file to do this. If not, here's the drill:

1. Copy the URL of the media file.

2. Log in at `http://del.icio.us`.

3. Post the link to the file manually. Don't forget to add your trigger tag.

4. **Refresh your subscription.**

This may take a few moments, but the feed should recognize the enclosed media file, download it, and then make it available to you as any other podcast media file you are subscribed to.

Skimming podcasts

While all this great content is going to keep you on the cutting edge of what all those podcasting Joneses are up to, it won't do you a whole lot of good if you can't parse all the data in a timely fashion. And as cool as audio and video podcasts may be, they just don't lend themselves to browsing in the same way text does.

Not only that, but sometimes the devices used to listen to or watch a podcast don't make it all that easy to sample different sections of a podcast. Some podcasters use a concept called *bookmarking* (we cover this topic in Practice 33); others are very good at time stamping their show notes, but most don't make it easy.

There are basically three ways to scan podcast content:

- ✔ **Use software to scan the audio file.** We talked about Podscope and other applications earlier in this practice. But as we noted, they're rife with issues. Most notably, they have a hard time deciphering words spoken over background music and aren't too adept at picking out proper names.

- ✔ **Keep your finger on the fast-forward button.** Think of this as skipping forward a few paragraphs or pages. But unless the podcaster uses obvious transition marks (such as sound effects or music beds) when the show switches topics, you'll be hard-pressed to know when the topic has changed.

- ✔ **Skip a bit, brother.** This one is a little more extreme than #2 and should probably not be used if you are looking for something specific. But it can be handy to give you some samples of the show in various forms. It's difficult to get a flavor for a show in the first two minutes, especially if the intro is long. By skipping forward and sampling the show at different time slices, you may get a more rounded picture of the show's overall structure and composition. Of course, it's difficult to gain any meaningful context in 10-to-20-second slices, so use this approach judiciously.

Staying Connected to the Offline World

"There are more things on heaven and on earth than exist inside your podcasts, Horatio." If Bill Shakespeare were alive today, he'd forgive us the poetic license with his quote. And it speaks to the truth: While the amount of information you can gather from online sources continues to swell every day, a significant amount of information — for many industries and professions — lives and breathes offline in that place called the real world. Even for highly Web-enabled content — such as virtual-world development and even the business of podcasting — a significant portion of new developments and opportunities exist in the meatspace.

Take conferences as an example. It's going to be a few years before virtual worlds like Second Life can provide the same level of connection you would find by attending a trade show in person. Cool as VOIP may be, it's no substitute for sitting down with a person for a one-on-one interview where you can read facial expressions and nonverbal clues.

Luckily for those of us who spend an inordinate amount of time online, the Web can help us make real-world connections to other podcasters and to the movers and shakers of our industry (okay, for some it's a hobby, but we're all podcasters here). Here are a few:

- ✔ **Upcoming.yahoo.com:** This site (formerly Upcoming.org) aims to expose more people to conferences, events, and organized gatherings in a social network style. Event organizers (or just interested attendees) list and describe events. Prospective attendees can search by keyword, geography, and other ways to find conferences, conventions, and special events that appeal to them.

- ✔ **Meetup.com:** Similar to Upcoming, but tailored to recurring meetings. It's very good for social activities and has a huge user base. If you are looking for a regularly meeting local group, this should be your first stop.

Practice 3

Staffing Your Podcast for Success

In This Practice

✔ Finding an energetic and enthusiastic host

✔ Seeking out the right support staff

It won't come as a surprise that the host(s) of your show should mean a lot. Duh. But this seemingly obvious statement often goes unchecked. And it can often mean the difference between an okay podcast and a *great* one. This practice will give you some hard-won advice on ways to make sure you have the right staff — from show host to support staff — for your podcast. There are many factors you should consider when you're staffing any one of these positions.

Before we get started, let's talk about existing staff for readers who are already podcasting. Keep those folks in mind as you read this practice, but don't be afraid to make some staffing adjustments afterward. Having said that, don't let your dreams of success cloud your better judgment and potentially jeopardize an existing business relationship or friendship. The main goal of this book is to help you take your show to the next level. But you don't have to be ruthless about it at the peril of others. Some serious thought should be given before reassigning — or (worse) replacing — someone who's been with you from the beginning. Take the time to make sure that your newfound goals and objectives jibe with theirs if at all possible. And never forget the human side of podcasting.

Choosing the Right Host

While your deliberation on who might be the perfect person — or people — to host your show isn't quite as complicated as the astronaut selection process, it should warrant more time than you'd take to decide on pizza toppings. The host of the show will be your audience's primary connection to the content of your show, and his or her interpretation of the topic, content, and/or script will naturally come to the fore.

Here are some basic requirements for good hosts:

✔ They should be experts in the subject matter presented — or at least have more than a passing interest in the material.

✔ They should have a fair command of the language they'll be speaking, a general understanding of grammar and context, and passable diction.

After you get those minimum requirements out of the way, it's time to start looking for specific characteristics in potential candidates.

Taking the host's location into account

We'll refrain from stating the obvious "success in business" joke, but location is also important when evaluating a host. First, the host will need to be physically near the recording studio or location where the recording will take place. If the potential host's proximity is less-than-optimal, delays will crop up at some point. Traffic, illness, or just a general sense of gee-I-really-don't-want-to-drive-down-again will crop up.

Of course, you can mitigate this situation a few ways:

- ✔ **Record remotely.** We live in a world of high-speed Internet access. In fact, podcasting is built on the assumption that listeners are no longer on dial-up connections. This same fact can (and often does) enable a show host to be in a different time zone — or even on a different continent — from that of the co-hosts or the recording engineer. (See Practice 17 for specific applications.)

- ✔ **Record en masse.** For podcasters with a production budget, consider flying your talent in to the studio for a few days and knocking out a month's worth of shows. While this won't work for timely or newsy podcasts, it certainly can work for information-dispersal programs. You can get the recording done ahead of time and add more timely content just before the show release; your audience will never be the wiser.

- ✔ **Satellite recording.** For probably the cost of a single round-trip ticket and a hotel room, you could buy your host a decent microphone and recording interface. And to be extra sure it gets done right, fly your engineer to the host's location to show him or her how to do everything from start to finish. You put the host on a recording schedule and then transfer the files back to your engineer for editing and post-production.

Sometimes getting the right host means you have to sacrifice some convenience. It's a good thing for us that the virtual world is becoming more and more a full-featured model of reality all the time.

Making sure the host has the know-how

Does this guy know what he's talking about? If you haven't bothered to ask yourself that question before selecting your host, it's a sure bet that at least one of your audience members *has*. A podcast needs a host who's a subject-matter expert. Even if he's not world-class adept at the topic, the host should at least profess a working knowledge and show an obvious drive to learn more through the process of doing the show.

Out there in your potential audience pool live some real and undeniable experts, and they can smell someone who's faking it from a mile away. And because podcasting as a medium has an active social dimension, they'll be happy to let the rest of your audience know that your host's opinions and thoughts aren't worth their weight in elephant dung.

Transparency is your best friend in this situation. If your host knows her stuff, shout it to the masses and don't be afraid to stick to your guns when someone with an opposing view starts to question her authority. There are always at least two sides to any argument, and healthy debates by two or more educated parties can make for a great listening experience.

But by the same token, don't get caught making up credentials for your host when he's not really all you've built him up to be. While your audience will likely accept that he may not know everything, they will bail on your show the minute they think you're being disingenuous.

If you find yourself in a situation where you have a host that needs a smidge more education, you have a few choices:

- ✔ **Get that education.** Unless you find yourself in a real-time interview situation, the pre-recorded nature of most podcasts allows you do some (or a lot of) research before you broach a topic that your host is unfamiliar with. And even if it is an interview, your host should be familiar with the guest's background. At a minimum, go find some previous interviews with the guest.

- ✔ **'Fess up to your ignorance.** "Learn along with me" podcasting can be a great way to communicate information. And your audience will appreciate that you're not trying to pull a fast one.

- ✔ **Get an expert to help out.** Some podcasts keep a fact-checker in the wings, always listening for incorrect or inaccurate statements. These are easily removed during post-production editing, but also can make for some interesting and memorable moments if left in on the live-to-tape format shows. That works if your hosts are self-effacing enough to handle it.

Assessing the host's vocal talent

Your final consideration should center around the vocal talent of your host. Note that we did not put this as your primary concern, which will no doubt puzzle those of you who come from a traditional broadcasting background. But the fact of the matter is that a huge set of pipes, while no doubt impressive-sounding, is not the most important consideration for the host of a podcast. The listening audience is turning to a podcast to hear something different from what they get in the traditional broadcasting world; it's okay to have hosts with real voices.

But that's not to say that any podcaster can skip setting a minimum standard level of hosting competence. Someone with a very weak or unconfident voice won't come across as very convincing to your audience. Often people sound unconfident because they lack confidence. (While it goes beyond the scope of this book, there are myriad books and courses to help boost confidence levels.)

Pay attention to the accent of your host and the expectations of your larger audience. Having an accent may lend an exotic sound to your program. But it might also reduce the clarity of your message if the accent is so heavy that only a local audience can decipher the message. Again, this may be a bonus if you are going for the hyperlocalization we spoke of in the previous practice.

Regardless of volume, tone, and inflection, you must pay close attention to pronunciation. Yes, there are local variants, such as the difference between the American and Canadian ways of pronouncing *process* (long "o" versus the short "ah" sound). But few things grate more on listeners' nerves than hearing the same word — for example, *nuclear* (it's "nuke-lee-ar," not "nuke-you-ler") — mispronounced every episode. It's not cute. It's not quaint. It's wrong. Please stop.

Choosing the Support Staff

If you are the host of a podcast, you might want to close your eyes for the next sentence: *The world does not revolve around the hosts, and they are not the be-all-and-end-all of success!* Okay, hosts, you can open your eyes again. We weren't talking about you. Too much.

Many of the more-popular podcasts carry with them a support staff of dedicated individuals with specialized skills who rarely get the credit they deserve. Each of these people contributes much to the show, but usually from behind the scenes and away from the microphone. Much like an exceptional soundtrack to a movie, the more successful they are in their jobs, the less the listening audience will even know they are there.

Producers

You could title this position jack of all trades — because that's pretty much what producers wind up doing . . . everything. In a perfect world, the producer's job is to make sure things run smoothly and that the show stays on track. Hosts can get caught up in the moment, and the producer is there to pull back the reins or gently push things back on course.

Hosts tend to get caught up in the moment and are very close to the action, which sometimes results in too much navel-gazing. A good producer will always take a holistic view of the show and make sound, rational decisions that should (all other things being equal) benefit the show overall.

Good producers have the following traits:

- ✔ **Well-organized and detail-oriented.** The producer tends to be the one in charge and has lots of moving pieces to keep track of. Disaster lurks around the corner for those who try to manage the schedule in their heads or can't find the phone number for the guest when it's time to call.

- ✔ **Responsible and able to follow through.** This is critical whether it's a 2- or 12-person production. The producer assumes responsibility for the actions of the entire team, making sure the rest of the staff has their marching orders correct.

- ✔ **Rather tenacious and goal-focused.** *Ruthless* is another term we could have used. Producers will tirelessly track down leads and call recalcitrant hosts on their mobile phones to make sure they'll be on time, always with an eye on the prize of making the show the best it can be.

- ✔ **Rational and level-headed.** Things can get heated in the studio or in production meetings. And while the producer is required to join in on these conversations, you don't want a hothead in the command chair.

- ✔ **Articulate in verbal and written communications.** The producer often serves as first contact between the podcast team and denizens of the outside world — be they potential guests, prospective sponsors, or listeners receiving a response to their feedback. Producers also tend to draft the press releases and create the show notes, putting their communication skills on the line.

In summary, producers need to be the managers of the whole process, from soup to nuts. Not the pimply faced drive-through manager, but the seasoned and mature professional who is up to the challenge of maintaining the show.

Writers

Not all podcasts need writers, but many podcasts could certainly benefit from having one on staff. That's almost heretical to say, given the anti-establishment nature of podcasting (which assumes more of a do-it-yourself mentality and eschews the conventional media notion that writer and host should be two different individuals). But we're not suggesting you rush off to Hollywood and snatch up a scriptwriter from yesterday's failed sitcom.

The responsibilities of a writer on a podcast will vary depending on the needs of the show. Many podcasts are unscripted and flow from the host naturally. In this case, the writer's job may be to prepare a synopsis or executive summary of the topics at hand that the host can preview prior to recording. This can work in reverse as well: The job of the writer can be to distill the contents of the show into a concise article or show notes for public consumption.

For the more formalized podcast, a writer (or team of writers) may develop a full script for the show that the host will follow. In this case, the writer must be intimately familiar with the presentation style of the host — and adapt the work to the individual. Some hosts will read the script word for word, rarely veering from the script. Others interject their own commentary along the way; some may perform a sort of edit-on-the-fly. Whatever the style of the host, it's the job of the writer to adapt.

There are many differences between effective writing for the page and writing effectively *for the spoken word*. The ideal writer for a podcast will have a mixture of the following traits:

- ✔ **Quickly gets to the point.** Rambling on and on about the color blue may work fine for storytellers, but it's less effective for podcasts (unless, of course, the whole point of your podcast *is* storytelling). Get the main point out first and then add the commentary. Don't make your audience wait for the meat.

- ✔ **Isn't trying to be Shakespeare.** Yes, yes. We're all quite impressed with your vocabulary. But we don't have time to run your show through the thesaurus or Universal Translator, so please use an audience-appropriate language level.

- ✔ **Avoids common grammatical mistakes.** Keep the prior trait in mind, but remember that you should also be able to keep your tense consistent and not abuse proper subject-verb agreement. Rest assured that you have at least one grammarian in your audience. Accurate use of idioms is worth a mention, too; many listeners cringe each time you say "covers the gambit" or use some other mangled figure of speech. Trust us.

Engineers

Talk about your unsung heroes. If anyone deserves a pat on the back or dinner at a five-star restaurant on a regular basis, it's your board monkey. This person wields an unbelievable amount of power, and can have your host speaking with resounding authority or whining pathetically to the masses with a few deft clicks of the mouse or twists of a knob. Don't make the engineer angry.

Audio engineering is one of those avocations that can quickly turn into a vocation — there's just so much to learn! Open up the most basic of audio-recording

applications and you'll likely see a whole host of options and effects with cryptic names such as Nyquist Prompt and Wahwah. Those just sound cool! And they lead you down a deep rabbit hole from which some of the more obsessive never wish to return.

That's fine. We can use them!

A good podcast engineer will need to fully understand the process of editing, mixing, and getting all those cool buttons and knobs to do what they do. She will also need to have a firm grasp of the limits and capabilities of all the equipment used in the recording process — from microphones, effects, and processing boards to the recording device itself. She should also keep up on the latest trends in recording equipment, always on the lookout for acquisitions that might allow her to take the quality up one more notch.

When looking for an engineer, try to a find a good mix of these characteristics:

- ✔ **An exceptional ear.** Some of the best engineers we've worked with have noticed things during a recording session that went unnoticed by the hosts — until the engineer pointed it out.

- ✔ **Obsessive attention to detail.** Remember the last time you edited something until it was good enough? For at least one listener using some high-quality headphones, it wasn't.

- ✔ **Voracious reader.** The world of podcast recoding and distribution is constantly in flux as new listening devices come onto the market. Any engineer worth his salt understands the changing marketplace and how his files will look on the latest (and on legacy) devices.

- ✔ **Budget-minded.** It's no good to you if your engineer constantly laments the lack of a $10,000 mixer that would magically solve all your problems when you are wondering whether you can afford to pay your $30 hosting plan this month. Rather, you need someone who can find creative ways to get that pro sound without putting you in sight of a second mortgage on your house.

Designers

It's highly possible that we have a soft spot in our hearts for designers because all of us, in one way or another, have been responsible for the design of many Web properties over the years. Allow us to recommend that you pay your designer well and buy him or her a new car.

While the other support staffers we've mentioned can have rather unappreciated jobs, that's compounded for designers because they are usually the last ones brought in on a project — if at all. And that's really a shame, because bringing in a qualified designer early in the project can help ensure that the final Web site meets the goals and objectives of the podcast itself. But we're getting ahead of ourselves.

A designer's job is to effectively communicate the ideas, goals, and themes of a podcast in visual form through good Web-site design. With the advent of easily updated Web-publishing tools (such as blogs), designers can modify an incredible amount of built-in functionality, in some cases mitigating the need for a developer.

 We don't mean to imply that there is no role for experienced application developers in the world of podcasting. Quite the contrary, in fact. Our point is that the code that runs WordPress (the engine for many Web-site blogs) is solid and can be extended through the addition of easy-to-install plug-ins, allowing the designer to focus fully on the presentation and layout of the site.

Could your podcast benefit from a designer? Well, we have a quick-and-easy test to help you make that determination. Ask yourself the following questions:

- ✔ What is the single most important thing your site conveys to a brand-new visitor? Chances are, you want to get someone to listen to your show. Or perhaps you want your visitors to read your blog post, or you have a product to sell. Identify the central impression your site should be making.

- ✔ Next, pull up your Web site. How would you, as a brand-new visitor to this site, get the point — that is, how well does the site achieve that goal you just stated? If it doesn't stand out to you, you might need a designer. Or if you thought of three or four other primary goals when looking at your page, then you most certainly need a designer.

We'll talk a bit more about the importance of a well-designed Web site in Practice 26. For now, we cover a few attributes to look for when you're seeking a designer for your podcast's Web site:

- ✔ **Experience with editing templates for your blogging system.** It's not hard to learn how Movable Type, WordPress, or other blogging platforms operate. But experience in the application currently in use goes a long way.

- ✔ **An understanding of complementary colors.** Don't laugh. We've seen purple and lime green combinations from people with design experience. This is easy to verify — ask to see examples of their prior work.

- ✔ **Ability to work independently.** For even the largest podcasting property, the design team will likely consist of a small group — as in, less than two. In that environment, designers need to be able to handle most things on their own without requiring a lot of input.

- ✔ **Ability to adapt quickly.** As previously mentioned and likely to be mentioned again, things are moving pretty quickly. Your designer should be able to put up an idea and then make the changes necessary if and when things don't go as planned.

- ✔ **Understanding of what makes a site search-engine-friendly.** We don't have the space to cover all the ways of making your Web site search-engine-friendly. However, we will tell you that Google and other search engines have the potential to bring you the most traffic — if the person responsible for creating and maintaining your site follows some basic parameters of site design.

Send your designer to `http://cre8asite forums.com` for a crash course in search engine optimization. And have her keep going back; the state of the art changes all the time.

Other roles

We've covered the most important roles in your podcasting organization. There's nothing stopping you from rolling several of those roles into the same person. In fact, it's pretty common for the producer to double as the host, and for the engineer and the designer to be the same person. You have to work within a budget of some sort, so make your decisions accordingly.

Assuming you have more money to pour into this than we do, there are a few other roles you may consider adding in the future:

- ✔ **Personal assistant:** Depending on how much travel or coordination is required, assistants can be helpful to both show hosts and producers.

- ✔ **Production assistant:** If your engineer is working overtime — especially if you do lots of remote interviews or segments — bring on a production assistant. Many PAs work on the cheap just to learn from an experienced engineer.

- ✔ **Public relations coordinator:** Depending on how often you produce a podcast or how many podcasts you are responsible for, your producer could be busy tracking down guests and deciding on show topics. Rather than letting communication with the public slip, find a PR person to take care of press releases and handle much of the show-created communication.

- ✔ **Advertising sales:** Notice how this is last on the list? That's by design. There are plenty of things you need to worry about before hiring someone to make sales for you. But if you have those bases covered, a dedicated person pounding the pavement and making cold calls can sure make the difference in the revenue stream for your show.

Podcast Studio Considerations

Practice 4

Take a look at your recording environment. Does it foster a sense of professionalism? Is it inspirational to your craft and/or set up to help forward your career? Most would agree that the workplace has a significant impact on the final product. Where you produce your podcast is no different. You need a dedicated podcasting studio, plain and simple.

As you'll find out in this practice, studios can and do come in all shapes and sizes. We'll walk you through some things to keep in mind as you start planning, as well as cover some of the innovative ways your fellow podcasters have approached various real-world limitations. We'll also give you a quick overview of equipment choices and soundproofing ideas, though those topics (and more) get more detailed treatment later on in the book.

Designing a Studio with Built-in Flexibility

We're working on the assumption that you don't already have a fully stocked and staffed audio-production facility at your disposal. Furthermore, we're going to assume that this podcast studio you're putting together will need to serve more than one purpose. To that end, your converted space will have to fit a variety of needs — for podcasting as well as other activities.

Planning for hosts or guests

Many podcasters start out their careers solo. At that point, a decent headset microphone and a laptop computer mean that the world is your studio — giving you the ultimate in flexibility and convenience. While others lament their microphone choice or latest aural enhancer, you sit back in puzzlement because everything you need is right there in front of you, often for free.

But that all changes the minute you decide to add someone else to the mix. What are you to do? Share a headset? The addition of a co-host or a guest is the most compelling reason podcasters decide to build a studio.

In order to capture audio from more than one microphone at a time, you need a *mixer*. Mixers allow you to plug in and blend the sound from more than one input, sending this mixed audio signal to your computer or other recording device. You can get more information on selecting mixers in Part II of this book. For now, we'll look at it holistically.

If you plan on having guests or co-hosts on the show, consider the fact that you may want to bring in more than one guest or host at a time — and not too far off in the future. And while you can save money by buying a cheap two-channel mixer, how long will that last you? Good quality multichannel mixers can be found for a few hundred dollars, so make sure you buy equipment that will handle the additional inputs when you decide to do more with your show.

Investing in gear that will serve you well today — and tomorrow

Acquiring new podcasting equipment is a disease with no cure. (Well, other than bankruptcy and threats of divorce. The mere thought of these can be a significant deterrent.) Regardless, there will come a day when you will want the latest and greatest gizmo that'll make you sound like James Earl Jones or Terry Gross — pick your poison.

To our concept of flexibility, make sure the things you buy are not only compatible with one another, but also don't take you down a road that limits your choices in the future. Yes, that $200 plug-and-play USB microphone may fit your needs right now, but it's totally worthless the minute you start using a mixer with no USB inputs. Oops. Money down the drain. Be careful.

 Don't get us wrong. We have nothing against using USB microphones. But it's hard — bordering on the impossible — to get multiple USB mics recording on a single system simultaneously. For all practical purposes, it takes a mixer and conventional microphones (non-USB) to get more than one mic input recording at the same time.

It's hard to plan for every possible turn of events, but you can be smart about your purchases. Start by making sure that the new gizmo works with your existing equipment *and* your work flow. In late 2006, mixers that integrated to computers via FireWire (as opposed to USB) were all the rage. But many podcasters had a rude awakening when they discovered that they could not record Skype calls. That was a *very* big problem for those who were doing interview shows and relied on this VOIP application. Many returns ensued. (See Practice 17 for more on Skype.)

Offering additional services from your studio

As you set up your studio, consider what else you might do with your investment other than podcasting.

Huh? Yeah, that bears restating.

It's possible to find creative ways to offset some of the costs of your equipment by selling your services to those willing to pay. Now, we're not suggesting that you'll be in a "if you build it, they will come" situation. Far from it. Selling your services in audio production, editing, voiceover work, or (for that matter) any other line of work takes time, energy, and connections. But it is a possibility — and one way to help pay off those future equipment investments.

Location, Location, Location: Podcasting from a Room in Your Home

You've been doing a lot of pre-planning for your podcast at this point. The support staff is in place. Your hosts are all geared up for your podcast's topic (or topics), and your current rig stands poised and ready to record. It's all about upping your game, right?

Then you suddenly take a look around your audio equipment. You have upped your game but haven't thought at all about the studio itself. You need to decide where the studio will be located, consider what kind of surrounding noise you'll be dealing with, and think about what you can do to make the most of a good (or bad) situation.

So, how do you improve your studio without major redecoration? Can you tear down a wall and remodel your house to accommodate your audio setup? Well, if you are *Podholes'* Michael R. Mennenga, you can tear down, remodel, rewire, and customize your home to meet your acoustical needs. (And yes, Mike hires himself out for this kind of contract work.)

However, if you cannot fly Mennenga out to where you live and put him up for a few months while he tears your house apart and you explain to your significant other or landlord, "But it's for my podcast!" then we've got a few options (along with pros and cons) for you to consider.

Studio in the upstairs office

At the time of writing this, the audio sanctuary of *Imagine That!* Studios is located on the second floor of Tee's house. It's not a bad location — you can always clear your head with a moment or two of staring out the window, and keep an eye on outside traffic, weather, and any foot traffic that might be making noise.

Here are some of the advantages of setting up shop upstairs:

- No concern for foot traffic on the home's main floor
- View of the outside world so you can pause in time to avoid heavy traffic noise
- Ease of access between bedroom and studio

Here are some of the disadvantages:

- Heavy ground and air traffic are easily picked up by microphones.

- Air-conditioning vents contribute to ambient noise.
- Noise from other rooms on the floor (television, music, children, thundering herds of elephants) is easily picked up by microphones.
- Soundproofing tiles are difficult to mount because wall studs may not be in the best locations.

It makes practical sense to turn your home office into your recording studio — and there's nothing wrong with that — but when upgrading and updating your studio, you will notice more ambient noise around your setup and will want to consider the advantages and disadvantages you face.

A second floor studio can be great if it's just down the hall from the bedroom — spend a night editing, stumble down the hallway, and fall into bed. Easy. But if your house is located only a block away from (say) abundant noise sources as an elementary school, a home day-care across the street, or air traffic from nearby airports, you have to face long pauses while recording and lots of post-editing. (This is the voice of experience speaking.)

Studio in the basement

The studio home of the Billibub Baddings podcast recently moved downstairs to a finished basement. The subterranean studio is a popular option with podcasters like Phil Rossi (*Crescent, Filling the Page*). Ducking underground to avoid noise has some practical appeal.

However, the basement studio is not always the magical answer to achieving a pro-studio sound at home.

First, here's a rundown of the advantages:

- Cooler temperatures mean less wear and tear and a better environment for your audio equipment.
- The foundation of the house creates insulation from most outside traffic noise.

✔ The foundation of the house and surrounding property assist in deadening room noise.

✔ A concrete foundation offers more options for soundproofing tiles.

✔ A/C vents create less to no noise (depending on their design).

Next, consider the disadvantages:

✔ All in-house traffic, both on floors and in stairwells, can be picked up by microphones.

✔ Some A/C vents are direct shafts between a room and the downstairs area, allowing all noise directly outside the room to filter in.

✔ Studio location. (Long walks topside to the bedroom, bathroom, and so on.)

Some of the disadvantages may seem trivial, but they will play a factor in the overall quality of your podcast's sound.

A different kind of floor for your studio

You may hear some audiophiles and sound engineers refer to something in a studio called a *noise floor*. A studio's recording quality is judged by how "low a floor" is achieved. The "floor," in this case, is how much ambient noise is left after you've filtered out every stray sound that you possibly can, and all that remains is the audio produced by voice, instruments, or both. A recording studio, for example, will have an extremely low floor on account of soundproofing tiles, construction, and door seals, isolating all outside noise. A stadium where a concert takes place will not have a noise floor of any kind on account of all the ambient noise, echo, and other acoustic junk bouncing around. When you upgrade your home studio, try to reduce the noise in your room as much as possible before recording. This will help you create a close-to-studio-quality sound for your podcast from home.

Unconventional Options for Your Studio

The options described in the previous section work great for a new-and-improved studio — provided you're recording in a house and can customize it to meet your audio-recording needs. But what if you're podcasting from an apartment or you're constantly on the go? How can you improve the sound quality of your recording when you're working in a living environment owned by someone else?

Podcasting in a closet

The force of nature that is Scott Sigler (*EarthCore, Ancestor,* and many others) brought podcast novels to new media heights when he was featured in *The New York Times.* This article also revealed one of Scott's podcasting secrets (and quickly became a far-too-overdone punch line to a far-too-obvious joke): Scott Sigler records his heavy-metal-steel-tipped-boot-across-the-throat splatter fiction . . . from his apartment's walk-in closet.

It may appear a little odd being surrounded by your wardrobe and speaking into a microphone propped in the midst of shoes, underwear, and sweatshirts, but what Scott is doing is an old broadcasting trick: The fabric surrounding Scott works like an insulator, absorbing much of the ambient noise. Perhaps, on rare occasions, you might pick up the passing ambulance or air vent kicking in, but you can cut out what's happening around you by podcasting from a closet.

This kind of podcasting setup works best for the solo podcaster. If the closet is wide enough, you could try for a two-person cast, but the space limitations of an in-the-closet podcast will work against you. However, if you're working solo, perhaps the closet *is* the best place for you and your podcast to record from.

Podcasting to the blanket

Another couple in the podosphere who are synonymous with the words *podcast* and *top-notch productions* — Paul Fischer and Martha Holloway of Dancing Cut Studios — make the most of their townhome studio. With an extra room converted to house their recording facilities, Paul and Martha face the challenge of working in a room with a lot of echo. Sure, they could try remodeling this room, but because their townhome is the end section of a row of other townhomes, the neighbors probably wouldn't appreciate that. What to do?

With a few hooks secured high into the wall and a strong wire suspended between them, Paul and Martha record episodes with a large blanket suspended in front of a window. Because they and their *Serve It Cold* vocal talent direct their voices into such a heavy, thick fabric, the noise surrounding them is dramatically reduced.

And if they happen to have house guests, their improvised acoustic tile is released from the hooks and returned to its normal duties (keeping their friends warm).

Podcasting in the great outdoors

Romance author Mary Winter decided the best thing to do about her ambient noise is nothing at all.

Her podcast, *Seasons of Passion* (`http://podcasts.marywinter.com`), is recorded at her home, and if the weather is suitable, she records it out on the patio of her home. In the background, you hear birds chirping, a spring breeze rustling through the trees, and perhaps any nearby traffic from her neighborhood.

While some podcasters strive to reach a studio-quality noise floor with their podcasts, Mary has chosen a casual setting for her podcast. The ambient noise of the outdoors establishes a more intimate setting for her listeners, as if they truly are sitting with her on the deck or porch of her home, talking about the craft of writing and just how tough it is to write romance. This disarming approach to podcasting provides not only a terrific atmosphere for your show, but also an easy solution to ambient noise creeping into your audio.

Sometimes, the best way to solve a problem is to simply make it part of the show.

 Although recording outside or allowing the ambient noise to become a co-host in your production is a very cost-effective way to handle excess sound, make sure your podcast lends itself to this approach. If you're producing a podcast novel, an audio drama, or an independent music show, the background noise may become more of a distraction than an asset. Whether it's an air-conditioning system, your computer, or a busy plaza somewhere in your hometown or city, the podcast — unless intended as a soundseeing tour — is supposed to be about you and your message. Make sure the background doesn't garble that message.

Customizing your space, whether in a house or apartment, is easy so long as you're creative in how you solve ambient noise issues. Some of the solutions you come up with for your podcast may be permanent, quick and temporary, or thrown together like something out of a *MacGyver* episode. However you solve noise issues with your studio, make sure the solution — whether happening in recording or in post-production — works for you and your podcast.

A Professional Look for a Professional Sound

A handful of podcasters — Draco Vista Studios, This Week in Tech, Tiki Bar TV — work in a studio environment. Most podcasters are home-studio audiophiles, surprising even the full-time audio and video professionals with the quality of their results. The efficiency and quality of your studio, however, rests on your overall podcasting and recording environment.

Tidiness in the studio

Okay, we *should* be practicing what we preach here.

This practice was typed in a studio that was a complete and utter disaster area — stuff strewn across the desk, stuff in the guest office chair, and a few bulky odds and ends forming an obstacle course from the office door to the computer, as shown in Figure 4-1.

• **Figure 4-1: Try to avoid letting your studio get this disorganized.**

Truth be told, this kind of disorder drives us crazy.

Now, let's say we're recording and need a sound effect from a specific CD or perhaps a reminder of exactly what to cover today in the podcast. As we rummage through the various piles of stuff around us, we hear one of the most unnerving sounds in the universe: something (no idea *what*) sliding off and landing somewhere other than where we last put it. Chances are, whatever slid out of view will be something we're going to need later on in the recording and editing day. That's just Murphy's Law.

George Carlin says it best: "Find a place for your stuff." An organized and clean recording environment will actually make it easier for you to accomplish what you need to do for your podcast.

Tidiness in the home

So let's say that you have an interview show concerning business technology, and you've found out that Leo Laporte (the biz-tech podcast maven) has heard your podcast, knows you're in the area, and would love to appear on your show. Pretty exciting, huh? He's even agreed to an in-studio interview. Fantastic!

Then you look around you at the previously described studio.

"Ah," you say, *"but I took your advice and now my studio is in tip-top shape! Everything has a place. I'm organized. I'm all set to podcast guests."*

Great. How about the rest of the house? Ack.

Anyone who's a parent knows of the continuing and seemingly eternal struggle to keep the house in some semblance of order. Toys (for example) seem to take on a life of their own and migrate everywhere in the home (and that's not even counting things harried grownups set down on any available surface). So before you agree to host in-studio guests or invite others to record from your home office's podcasting rig, assess — and clear — the home environment around the home office.

Of course you know that the concept of children doesn't just include the human kind. Are the dog's chew toys put away? Has the catnip been vacuumed out of the carpet? How's that fishbowl looking?

It doesn't matter what kinds of wee ones are wandering around the house, you'll want to dismantle the obstacle course in the surrounding environment of your home studio. And if guests are coming by the home, treat them with care and hospitality. Make them feel welcome and (most importantly) at home.

Studio at the ready

A prepared studio means a bit more than just having everything organized and put away. It also means having a podcasting setup ready to go.

When podcasting pals swing by Tee's place, he's usually expecting them. This means the house looks presentable, the studio looks presentable (most of the time), and the podcaster looks presentable (most of the time). Spontaneous podcasting usually isn't the order of the day, but when the offer is made, it's up the stairs to the studio to set up for recording. There's the checking of levels, the tweaking of mic positions, and a final "Mic check, one, two . . ." before hitting Record. (Note the *absence* of several interme- diate steps such as: Trip over the dog's bed, just miss catching a toppling stack of assorted CDs, fumble around in a tangle of unplugged cables . . . you get the idea. *Somebody* got the place ready beforehand.)

When guests are coming over specifically for pod- casting, it makes the experience all the better if your recording setup is ready to go:

- ✔ If you're using a mixer, have it on standby with mics already plugged into their respective channels.

- ✔ Depending on how many voices are coming into your studio, give some thought to exactly where those guests will sit and how the mics will be positioned.

These details may seem like common sense, but if you're podcasting solo (or with a regular co-host), it's all too easy to take your setup for granted. By

the time your guests reach the mic, you should have cables plugged in, tripods positioned (for the most part), and an open space around their mics for scripts, memo pads for any on-the-spot note-taking, or beverages . . . particularly if it's a beercast, winecast, or scotchcast.

Make sure that if you're expecting a night of record- ing, your studio is expecting it too. Be ready to record and be situated for guests. A little prepara- tion makes for a more relaxed and professional set- ting for your guests and yourself.

 When you're shopping for studio furniture, remember that many office sets are easily cus- tomizable. If you find a desk set available in various components, see if an extension is available. If you're upgrading your studio, you can also upgrade your studio furniture with an extension that lends itself to a recording area for guests.

Practice 5 — Stick to the Script!

Formats. Scripts. Formulas. It's enough to make many podcasters dash for the torches and pitchforks, ready to shout, "Death to the confines of traditional media!" as they storm the castle. Relax, enraged mob; we're not suggesting that you fall prey to the tyranny of the radio-show-format clock, the vile 3:05-minute broadcast-friendly song, or the servitude of sticking 15 minutes of commercials in with 45 minutes of content.

Forget all the negative things you've heard about formatting from your anarchistic podcasting buddies. Contrary to popular belief, having a format is a Good Thing. And (surprising as it may sound) some of the most loose-sounding podcasts are *planned* to sound that way. For this practice, we show you how to apply solid formatting applications to your podcast (with the finesse to make them transparent) so you can stop worrying about the clock and stay focused on your topic at hand.

Of Intros and Outros

All good podcasts have a beginning and an end. This helps everyone know when the show is starting and when it's over. Seem a bit basic? Listen to a few new shows, and you'll see that it's far from obvious. In fact, several show hosts themselves don't seem to know when a show is starting and stopping. Imagine what that must be like for the listener!

The following sections give you some tips for creating smooth transitions into and out of your show.

Why intros and outros are important

The key to effective intro/outro segments is consistency. Listening to podcasts is, by definition, an episodic experience. By providing a consistent beginning and ending atmosphere at the appropriate times, you put your listeners in the mood to listen to your show. Similarly, the same music, words, or other audio they heard the last time your show was ending can give them a sense of completion and set up anticipation for future episodes.

If conventional broadcasters of TV and radio have done *something* right, it's the way they've trained listeners to know when a show is starting and stopping. This isn't by accident — it's a gimmick. Think about the last time your favorite TV or radio program started. Your attention quickly focused, shutting out distractions; your heart rate probably quickened (or slowed down, if that's the goal of the show); and you might have found yourself tapping your foot in time or singing along with the opening theme music. That's just a smart producer capitalizing on the herd mentality of the human condition, plain and simple.

A similar experience can be noted with followers of high-energy programs as the show comes to a close. Rabid fans tend to lose track of time when watching a show they love, eagerly waiting for more, even though they know it can't last forever. And when the episode fades to black and hits the closing credit music right at the climax . . . whew!

Finding the right music or sounds

That's the best place to start: the *sounds* you use in your podcast to both lead listeners into and carry them out of your show, each and every episode. For some producers, it's an appropriate piece of *bed music* (background music) that effectively carries a level of energy matching the show's content. Others use a mix of clips and effects, building a soundscape that (again) sets the stage.

 Be sure you have the rights to whatever you use. Your favorite TV show may use a killer track from last year's hip-hop star, and your radio program of choice may use a series of clips from popular movies. You can do this as well — *as long as* you are willing to clear the rights to use these copyrighted sounds. That's not as easy as it sounds, so we highly recommend steering clear and sticking with things you find that are royalty free or otherwise cleared for your use. Better yet — try podsafe music. These are tracks that artists specifically make available to podcasters to use in their

shows. You can start your search at the Podsafe Music Network (http://music.podshow.com), though many other avenues exist.

When you've found the perfect intro, start thinking about and working on your outro. While there's nothing stopping you from using a different piece of music, we highly recommend using the same one you use as your intro. It provides closure and reinforces the signature sound of your show one more time. Go ahead and use a different time slice if you can find one that works for your purposes.

Creating a Standard Voiceover for Your Show

Once you've got the tunes selected, it's time to consider the verbal branding you'll wrap around your show. While plenty of people perform their own voiceovers fresh and live each time they record, you may want to consider putting a standard voiceover in the can and making it a production element you use every time you start and end your show. What should you put in there? Well, it all depends on how much material you don't want to do live each time.

Giving out general show info

Canned or live each time, it's a good idea to get a bit of the administratia right in front of your listeners as soon as possible. Some good basics include

- The title of your show
- The name(s) of your host(s)
- A Web site where listeners can find additional information

If you have a voicemail line, give that number out up front. This lets your listeners know that you accept call-in comments, so they should get ready.

Resist the temptation to talk about all the ways people can find your show, give out everyone's e-mail address, and recap the history of your show since the first episode. The idea here is to give them some branding information and a bit of contact information. That's about it.

It's inside this business section where you'll hear many podcasters place a paid sponsorship announcement. We're torn on this issue, to tell you the truth. While there is no question that a sponsor would like to have the paid spot run as early as possible to ensure that the largest number of ears hear the announcement, you have to decide whether that's right for you and your show.

If your intent is to put in a brief "today's episode is sponsored by *Expert Podcasting Practices For Dummies,* helping podcasters elevate their shows to the next level. Buy it online or at any bookstore near you," then fine. It's short enough that there shouldn't be any problem. But if your intent is to run a 30-second pre-recorded commercial right away — don't. That isn't what your audience came to your show to hear, and you'll certainly lose more than one listener if you do it. Your advertisers should understand; after all, they spend money on your podcast to *reach* your listeners, not to alienate them (and in the process shrink the number of ears that hear their spot).

Handling attributions

But what if your business section isn't brief? People may be willing to sit through a minute of you thanking your sponsor and giving out some contact information before you get to your content, but don't push it. If you have more to say on the subject — or would like to give thanks to the myriad people who helped you with your show — do that at the *end* of your show. Get the content out first; worry about the attribution later.

The end of the show is a great place to

- Cover key contributors.
- Provide additional contact information.
- Solicit feedback or other forms of support.
- Provide other content that doesn't fit in with the main purpose of your show.

Some podcasters use this area to feature select e-mails or voicemails from the listening audience. (We cover more of that in Practice 34.) Others find this a great place to plug other podcasts or give sponsors some extra love (so to speak).

As you decide what attribution elements belong at the back of your show, keep in mind that many of your listeners will opt out of listening once your main content segment is over. We say this not to encourage you to sneak in attributions or commercial drops earlier, but to emphasize that you need to get the important stuff out first. If you have a very special announcement you want everyone to listen to at the back end of your show, be sure to pre-sell that to your audience up front. You can't assume they'll all hang around until the end. In fact, you should assume that they won't.

Providing contact and more information

No podcast is an island. Successful podcasters looking to grow an audience will make sure they give their listening audience every opportunity to find out more information about the show or to reach out to the host or producer. Remember that listeners of your show are probably listening to lots of other shows. You'll need to make sure they know where they can get more from you.

We suggest getting your "contact and more" speech down pat. Once you get it worked out, it should roll out of your mouth in almost the same way each and every time. This may sound repetitive — and it is! It becomes a mantra for you to say — and for your listeners to say along with you as you say it at its proper time during each episode of your show.

What should you say? There are many points of view on this, but our recommendation is to make sure listeners never forget the URL of your Web site. This is a piece of cake for many shows because URLs and show names often go hand in hand. But if not, tell your audience what your Web site address is. Then spell it to them. Then say it again. No, we're not kidding. If you can find a way to make it sing-songy, even better. You're trying to create an "ear bug" that sticks with them.

Why the Web site? Because (assuming it's set up properly) that is where listeners can go to find all sorts of contact information for your show. And trust us — it's a lot easier to put a variety of contact methods on a Web page than to try to cram it into an audio program. Plus, getting listeners to your Web site is a great way to reinforce your brand and show that you are more than just a faceless voice on a podcast. Figure 5-1 shows one possible example.

• **Figure 5-1:** Video blogger Chris Brogan puts contact information in a very obvious position on his Web page.

Okay, before the objection is raised, yes, we realize that many folks are listening to your show on portable mp3 players and probably don't have a Web browser handy. Hence the recommendation to burn your URL into their brains. Your URL, assuming it is a true domain and not some odd subdomain with that squiggly line (that's called a tilde) in it, should be fairly easy to remember. Even more so if you repeat it. Again.

And don't be afraid to include your contract mantra at the front and back of your program. Nor should you be afraid to list a whole bunch of other contact methods — such as giving out your voicemail number, reminding listeners to go post on your show's notes, giving out your Skype address, or asking them to add you as their Twitter (www.twitter.com) friend. All these things are fine, but we recommend doing all that *after* you've reminded visitors to check out your Web site.

Middle Management: Planning the Main Part of Your Show

When you've got the front and back of your show figured out, it's time to fill up that big space in the middle. With what? Content!

In the first practice of this book, we give you some pointers on selecting the right topic for your podcast. For the remainder of this practice, we give you some tips on structuring your primary content so it's enjoyable for your audience to hear — and for you to create.

Sticking to a theme

It may seem an obvious point, but you really should have complete command of what you plan on saying during your episode before you sit down to record it. Although a stream of consciousness program may sound appealing, it's usually more cathartic for the host than effective for the audience.

It's possible — likely, even — that you'll have quite a few things you'd like to say or talk about when you sit in front of the microphone on any given recording day. But while you are assembling your script or your notes (more about that in a moment), ask yourself a single question: *What is the one thing I'm trying to communicate today?*

Your show itself should already have a well-defined topic. That same amount of focus should flow through to your episode creation. Let's take a show about sports marketing as an example. In a perfect world, a single episode would cover a single topic — sports-arena advertising, for example. If your perfect world includes giving your listeners more than a single topic inside each episode, then select (if possible) similar topics that are logical companions to one another.

This theme-building idea serves several purposes:

- ✔ It assures your audience of an easy-to-follow listening experience; it won't have them bouncing around or trying to figure how all these things tie together.

- ✔ It allows you to talk to points that crop up in *this* episode instead of mentioning that you'll cover similar topics on future shows.

- ✔ It allows listeners to opt out of shows altogether. That's not a bad thing — the more you respect your listeners' time during a single episode, the likelier it is they'll be willing to stay subscribed to your program.

How do you ensure that your audience gets the theme you are presenting? Different podcasts approach themes from various angles, and the true deciding factor comes down to personal choice. There's nothing wrong with stating your intentions for the episode right away: "On today's show, we'll cover a few approaches to sports-arena advertising." That way your audience knows exactly what to expect.

However, your show may not be nearly that cut-and-dried. If you have a monologue or storytelling podcast, stating your intentions up front may be tantamount to giving away the punch line prior to the setup. In these cases, it may be even more important to work toward a particular theme, because your audience will be looking for you to wrap it all up in the end.

Writing a script or preparing show notes

Regardless of whether you choose to be subtle or blatant about the theme, you'll find it helpful to give yourself a roadmap to follow as you work through the show. Without a script — or at least some pre-planned show notes — your show may wander around aimlessly for a while, causing you to do a lot of work in post-production or (worse) put out an inferior episode or even (worse still) decide to scrap the episode altogether.

Another decision you'll face is how much to commit to paper before your show. (Just so you know, many successful podcasts are nearly 100% scripted.) The benefits of writing a script include having no surprises, accurately estimating the clock-time of an episode, and reducing the amount of post-production editing. The downsides include a requirement for a significant amount of pre-show planning, a reduction in the spontaneity of the program, and the dreaded monotone reading that plagued many a student in ninth-grade literature class.

Alternatively, many podcasts take the show notes or outline approach to planning. The complexity of show notes can range from hastily scribbled highlights on a single sticky note to a well-defined outline of topics, complete with an estimate of how much time to spend on each section. We're fans of this more elaborate approach; it allows much more flexibility than the fully scripted model. Note, however, that you only get as much out of this approach as you put in. If your shows tend to ramble, outline more. If even that doesn't put the stream of consciousness in check, try a fully scripted episode and see how you sound.

Be sure to include consideration of additional elements (such as music, clips, and even promos for other podcasts) in the scripting process: How long do they take? How well do they fit with the theme? How many do you include?

Of course, all this assumes that you currently are (or would like to start) including these elements in your show. If you have a six-minute show covering career opportunities in the IT-consulting world, you probably don't (and probably shouldn't) include too big a dose of these elements.

All too often, these extras are dropped into the show without giving them too much thought. But remember that you're working on building a theme; all the elements of your show should work toward that theme. If the tie-in to the piece isn't immediately apparent, introduce the element and *tell* the audience how it relates. Keeping the idea of relevance first and foremost in your mind ensures that you're adding *supporting materials* to your show, and not fluff.

One final note on themes — be sure to establish, and stick with, some sort of theme. When in doubt, go for an obvious linear theme. Set up the expectations by telling your audience what you're about to do, and then do that in the exact same order. If you are a bit more *avant garde*, take the Quentin Tarantino route: Weave a complex and nonlinear route to the conclusion. (Just don't get too convoluted; how many people do you know who just didn't "get" *Pulp Fiction*?)

Setting time limits for segments

Consistency is important in converting casual listeners to loyal fans. One way to give them this consistent experience is to set time limits on your content segments. Only have a single content segment? Great. Make it as close to the same length as you can for each and every episode. Have five or six? That's okay, as well. And while you don't have to make sure that each episode follows the same clock time each week (not that that's a bad idea), the *total elapsed time* of all of those elements should cover a similar chunk of time for each episode.

Making the case for consistency

We can hear many of you screaming out there right now about time limits. While it is true that many of your more outspoken loyal listeners are begging you for *more* content each week — or they tell you it's okay to put out a five-minute episode instead of your normal hour when you're out of topics — you and they are missing the point. Your rabid fan base isn't threatening to abandon you if you don't give them more. (At least we hope they aren't. They're loyal, right?)

But it is highly possible that a listener who was considering adding your show to his or her podcatcher will take a pass if you put out a show with widely fluctuating lengths. It's about building an expectation and converting those who just discovered you into subscribers. Your loyal and vocal audience will understand, trust us.

If your podcast is of the long-form variety (over 30 minutes), you may want to try breaking up your content into sections. Breaks between the sections give both you and your audience a chance to regroup, and they have the added benefit of helping with clock management.

Segments don't have to be self-contained, each with their own intro and outro. They could be subtle transitions on your part, as you ease from covering the latest news in your sector to an essay about a growing trend. Then again, there's nothing wrong with hard and obvious transitions either. We cover ways to make transitions in Practice 6.

Working with co-hosts provides additional challenges. Unless you plan your show out meticulously in advance, you may not know how much content your co-hosts have to contribute to a given topic. That's a sure-fire way to wipe out your time management.

One way to avoid this problem is to designate one person as the clock master. This person contributes to the conversation, but also gets to rule with an iron thumb. All other hosts should key off of this person, paying attention when he starts gesticulating wildly as the end of the segment approaches.

And of course, don't forget about the magic of post-production. If a conversation is going really well, but getting really long, and you don't want to pull out the aforementioned iron thumb, just let it continue. You can always cut out the boring parts or just limit the time in the next segment. Again, the idea isn't to be a total slave to the clock and hit your internal numbers as a radio show host might be required to do. Just be respectful of your listeners' time, and you should be fine.

Incorporating interviews

Interviews are often added as content elements, and in some cases they're the main content elements. There are dozens of fine books on the art of interviewing, so this book won't dig too deeply into that topic. But a few pointers can't hurt:

- ✔ **Set your guest's expectations before you hit Record.** Take a few moments to tell the guest about your interview style, how long you expect the interview to take, and (of course) what you plan on asking about. No one wants to be uncomfortable.

- ✔ **Keep the questions relevant.** It's okay to break the ice with some small talk. But if you find yourself interviewing an internationally renowned author, refrain from asking (for example) whether she caught last night's episode of your favorite reality program (probably not — and your audience doesn't care).

- ✔ **Keep the questions short.** The idea is to get long responses from your guest — not to take three minutes to ask a question. Avoid things like "That reminds me of a question I was about to ask you about . . ." and just get on with your question, please.

- ✔ **Ask open-ended questions.** It's frustrating for your listeners — and for your guests — if all they can do is answer with yes or no. The same holds true for long praise statements where the guests can only say thank you. Ask about *why* they did something, what was happening when they were doing it, and where they are going next. You'll get quality answers there.

- ✔ **Follow Evo's 3:15 Rule: Fifteen minutes is a good length for an interview.** That's a whole lot longer than your McNews station will ever give you, yet considerably shorter than what you get with public broadcasting. (In our opinion, it's the perfect time. Your mileage may vary.)

That's the 15; here's the 3: Over that last five years, Evo has learned that *three* well-thought-out and open-ended questions (everything we said prior to this) will usually fill up those 15 minutes nicely. As your guest answers, go ahead and ask a few follow-on questions as they come, giving you and the guest plenty of time to fully discuss each question you have. Then move on to the next. Rinse. Repeat. And take a look at the time. Hey! 15 minutes. . . .

Something to consider

There are two styles of interviewing out there: *serious editing* and *record-and-release*. Both have their fans and detractors; they're used about equally. All you need to decide is which approach you plan to take — *before* you get the guest on the phone.

The serious editing crowd (Rob Walch from Podcast411 fits this profile) enjoys letting a conversation develop naturally. The recording may go on for an hour or so, with the host, producer, or engineer spending a lot of time getting to the good stuff and cutting out the rest. Easy to overdo? Sure. But these interviews tend to sound very polished and professional. Who couldn't do with the removal of a few ums and stutters?

Those of the record-and-release persuasion (Evo likes this style) tend to have a bit more practice at interviewing and a lot less time to spend in post. These conversations get minimal editing, usually only to correct miscues and sound levels (more on that in Practice 18). Pitfalls include sounding rushed and missing out on longer conversations.

Writing for Your Podcast

Writing for a podcast (or any type of spoken-word distribution) is a lot different from writing for print. Take it from some guys who have done both — with varying degrees of success.

The biggest thing to keep in mind is that podcast *listeners* tend to do other things while they're listening to a podcast. That's significantly different from someone who is reading a book or an article. It's no problem to listen to a podcast when driving down the road, washing the dishes, or cleaning your office. Try doing those activities when reading. (Come to think of it, don't even try reading and driving at the same time. Not safe.) See the difference?

The best way to avoid running afoul of this difference is by following the K.I.S.S. principle: Keep It Simple, Silly. Stay away from long and complicated sentences in favor of shorter, more concise statements. While the ability to string together clauses and phrases might indicate your strong command of your native tongue, it'll probably leave your audience wondering what the heck you just said and reaching for the Rewind button — or (worse) the Unsubscribe feature.

And don't be afraid to repeat yourself to drive the main points home. If something bears repeating — repeat it! While almost all mp3 players have a Rewind feature, that's not how the public has been trained to consume audio. Don't make your listeners wonder *Did I get that right?* Give it to 'em again!

If you find yourself writing out more than show notes for your podcast, then you may have caught the writing bug. In that case, we highly recommend finding a writing for broadcasting class at a local community college. Say what you will about traditional media, the radio industry has learned a lot over the years about how to grab and keep people's attention. If your local community college doesn't offer a course, head to the bookstore or library and grab a short stack of books to glean for pointers. Your content will be the better for it.

Practice 6

Transitions, Timing, and Cues

How easy do you make it on your audience to listen to your show? Leaving aside the topics of finding your show and filling it with great content, what about the physical activity of listening (or watching, if it's a video podcast) that your audience goes through each time they consume your program? What may seem like a very passive activity is actually anything but, and producers who understand the listening process — and what listeners have been trained to expect — will create a better show.

Consider (by analogy) reading: Text is easier to read when the writer uses correct punctuation, groups related content into paragraphs, gathers paragraphs into sections, and then combines paragraphs into chapters as the final book is assembled. A good author (or editor) uses various techniques to segue from one segment to another at each of those transition points.

In this practice, we show you how to apply that same philosophy to your podcast — including ways to make good transitions during a live recording session and how to add them in during the post-editing process. Consider it "packaging" — and understand that it can make your show dramatically more listenable.

Making Transitions with Bumpers and Rejoiners

Unless your podcast episode is about a single self-contained topic, you will likely cover multiple topics or have more than one segment during your show. These different sections can be thought of as scenes inside of a television show or movie. You need to get your audience through all of these segments in a smooth and orderly fashion.

The primary method of making a transition inside a podcast is with a *bumper* or a *rejoiner*. Consider these the conjunctions of podcasting. Other names are often used, such as sweepers, tags, and so on. But all of them are used as obvious clues that signify something has changed or is about to change in the podcast. And bumpers and rejoiners aren't exclusive to podcasting. Heck, no — we stole the idea from mass media such as radio and television.

Rejoiners

Rejoiners are probably the easiest elements to add to your show. The name *rejoiner* implies that the listening audience went somewhere else (perhaps listening to a commercial or a special content segment) and are now coming back to rejoin the host or main content of the program.

Producing these elements can be as simple as selecting an appropriate piece of bed music or a snippet from a song. Of course, you can also use sound effects as well, either in conjunction with the song or by themselves. Many podcasters will also add voiceover elements, sometimes even falling back on an old radio standby: "And now . . . back to the show!"

Bumpers

In contrast, a *bumper* usually leads in a new segment and pays less homage to the content that came before. For example, a self-contained segment within a show may have its own specialized introductory bumper that gets played before the content is added. Let's say our fictitious sports-marketing podcast has a regular segment that recaps the major sponsorship deals announced since the last recording. A pre-produced clip, complete with the sounds of cheering crowds and cash registers ringing, is played right before the start of this segment.

 Stay legal, okay? Make sure any clips, sound effects, and music you use for your bumpers and rejoiners are in the public domain or have had their rights cleared for you to use. Contrary to popular belief, there is no five-second rule — or any time-frame rule — of how much copyrighted material you can use legally. For a great list of the ways U.S. copyright laws apply to podcasting (and some lists of places to find elements you can use legally), we highly recommend spending some quality time with the Podcaster's Legal Guide (`http://wiki.creativecommons.org/Podcasting_Legal_Guide`).

Using them in your show

Coming up with ideas for bumpers and rejoiners can be a lot of fun and a great way to express your creative side. But don't get carried away with the production; keep 'em short — very short. Your listeners don't want to hear the complete bio of a frequent guest every time the bumper plays, and they'll be less impressed with your mad editing skills if the rejoiner plays longer than the content segment that follows it.

As a rule, bumpers and rejoiners should play for no more than five seconds, though it's acceptable to have them play longer — provided the real content starts inside that five-second time frame.

Pauses Are a Good Thing

Radio has trained us, both as listeners and as producers, to be wary of *dead air* — the condition where no discernable sound is being recorded or transmitted. Back in the days when radio and television stations were discovered by turning a dial, eliminating dead air made obvious sense. Silence (or static) meant nothing existed at this point on the dial, so potential listeners would keep turning in their quest to find a station that *was* transmitting. This is less of a problem today with better feedback mechanisms on radios and televisions that let you know you've actually found a transmitting station. Yet, if you sat for a moment in front of a television or listened to a radio station that was broadcasting dead air, even today, you'd wonder.

Podcasting isn't plagued by that problem, and silence (not static) can be used as an effective tool in the presentation. If the host of a podcast takes a few moments to digest the last answer the guest gave before moving on to the next question, it's a stretch to think someone will chose that point to abandon the show. And because podcasts all start at (well, yeah) the beginning, there is little chance that someone will discover your show during a moment of silence.

Broadcast media aside, pauses are a natural part of the communication process. They can be used to drive a point home or to signify a change in mood or topic, or simply used as an effect. Take the pauses out and you can significantly change the message. Here are some tips on keeping the pauses in your podcast:

- ✔ Think about the value of pauses both while you are recording and editing your content.

- ✔ During the recording process, talk slowly. Slower, in fact, than what you think sounds good. When it sounds like you are going too slow, you're probably getting just the right pacing.

- ✔ If you're speaking off the cuff, don't be afraid to take a breath between sentences or to gather your thoughts when moving to a new topic.

- ✔ It's simple enough to remove pauses in post-production, but much more difficult to add them if they are missing.

- ✔ When you are editing your file, be wary of chopping out all those blank spots in the wav form, even if you need to cut for time. Some engineers out there may argue with us and swear they can cut down the length of a pause without listening — but allow us some polite skepticism: They're wrong.

There is no perfect length for a pause; the appropriate length of a pause is determined by a complex mixture of pacing, diction, content, and a host of other factors. Our point? Don't edit out a pause without listening to it in its full context.

By *full context,* we mean listening to more than a few seconds of the podcast before and after the pause. Okay, if you're familiar with the content (for example, if you just laid down the track moments ago), you can probably get away with doing that. If that's not the case, your best bet is to back up 10 to 15 seconds (and an entire minute may be a better idea) and listen from that point. That way you're more likely to get the point and purpose for the pause.

Using Signals and Signs to Keep the Conversation Flowing Smoothly

In two-party conversations, if one party pauses, it's often an invitation to the other party to start talking. While this is a natural condition and may lead to a fine-sounding recording session, it can also cause things to sound a bit disjointed — especially if the first party wasn't finished and comes back to the point later.

To combat this potential confusion, everyone should fully develop excellent listening skills and learn to play nicely with others. Okay, once you've stopped laughing at that suggestion and can resume reading, we invite you to consider an alternative: developing a set of signs or signals to use with your co-hosts to keep from stepping on each other's toes conversationally.

This system need not be as complicated as the U.S. Navy's semaphore flag system. Many podcasting teams get along fine simply by stepping up to or moving away from their respective microphones to indicate their desire to chime in. If you need more than that, it can be as simple as agreeing on the following signals:

- ✔ I'm next

- ✔ Your turn

- ✔ I'm not finished

- ✔ Wrap it up

Do you need more than that? Go ahead and develop those signals — but you probably won't need to go *much* farther than that. And before you start developing overly complex systems, remember that you can always either stop recording and discuss it, or discuss what needs to be covered and then edit out the discussion in post-production editing.

If you and your co-host(s) are recording in the same location, we submit the following Universally Accepted Podcaster Signaling Conventions (yes, we just made up that title):

- ✔ **"I'm next."** Index finger raised vertically, just off to the side of your microphone in easy view of your co-hosts. Should you feel the need, wave the finger in a slight side-to-side motion to capture the attention of your companions. Increase the frequency and magnitude of said waving as necessary.

- ✔ **"Your turn."** Index finger leveled on the horizontal plane, with a line-of-sight directed toward another host, usually one who has given the "I'm next" signal already. If no one has indicated a desire to go next, use both index fingers to reference yourself and then flick the fingers out and away from your body to indicate another host should be preparing to go next.

- ✔ **"I'm not finished."** Raise the hand, fingers together, palm facing out to the other hosts of the program. This is most commonly used when another host has prematurely given the "I'm next" signal or the current speaker is about to make a dramatic pause, yet has additional information to present.

- ✔ **"Wrap it up."** Both index fingers extended along the horizontal plane, pointing slightly above and below the other. Rotate each finger (or each wrist, depending on your level of manual dexterity) in a barrel-roll fashion, each around the other, as if you were wrapping string around both. This signal is most often used by the host (who's watching the clock near the end of the prescribed time), or to indicate to another host that once again he or she has been rambling non-stop and enough is enough.

Signals such as these are quickly adopted by the staff and can prove very helpful in making the show sound "together." But what if one host is in Madison, Wisconsin, and the other is in Madrid, Spain? While videoconferencing software can solve this problem rather nicely, the bandwidth restrictions of such a connection have a negative impact on the audio recording (assuming you're using the same pipe to pass the video as well as the audio stream).

For remote applications, we suggest keeping an instant messaging application, such as Skype (`http://skype.com`), open between all parties during the conversation. The same signals can be used, either by typing them completely or by an agreed-upon shorthand convention, such as Me/You/Not Done/Wrap.

 You can use instant messaging (IM) applications to make it seem like you are in the same room with your co-host. But the illusion is broken if you allow the audio notifications from that IM application to make it into your recording. First, make sure that the audio notifications for your IM application are disabled so these sounds don't make it into your recording session. In most programs, you can access this feature in the Preferences or Settings menu; look under Audio, Alerts, or Notifications.

Second, do your best to make sure you won't be disturbed by others who may also know your IM handle or screen name. In Skype, you can change your setting to Do Not Disturb — which also turns off any audio notifications. More popular-with-the-masses podcasters may decide to utilize a private screen name known only to their co-hosts, or to use a different application altogether that is not frequented by their adoring fans.

Fade In, Fade Out

We saved the best — and perhaps most important — transition for last. And oddly enough, it's the one we have the least to say about. The other transitions we've discussed in this practice will help the various segments of your podcast flow together. But how will your podcast itself flow with your listeners as they make the transition from one podcast to another? We know it's difficult to imagine, but people listen to more shows than just yours. In fact, they may listen to some of those shows *more often* than they listen to yours.

As an expert podcaster, you owe it to your audience to not only let them know when you've started and are stopping, but also make those things happen *gradually*. While it's important to get to the point quickly, make sure you give the audience an adequate setup before you launch into your topic. If your audience has to play catch-up as they work on digesting the end of the last show they were listening to, they might miss some of what you've worked so hard to present. And by the same token, wrapping up your show with a simple "the end" and hitting the Stop button may sound a little harsh.

Practice 5 gives you many ideas on coming up with effective intros and outros for your show. But as you are deciding how to best implement them, try and look at the situation as if your entire show were a single segment in someone's overall listening day. Here's a great place to take more cues from broadcast media, who spend lots of time making sure that transitions from one show to another are as seamless as possible. While you won't have a lot (read: any) control of how the next show comes up in the listening queue — or of how the previous show was ended by its host — you can do your part by being a good contributor to the podosphere.

Here are some pointers for intros:

- State the name of your show and the day you recorded it before anything else happens. If your show isn't date sensitive, an episode number will suffice. Then play your opening music.

- Keep your canned intro to less than a minute.

- Don't keep us in suspense! Tell us what we can expect out of this program today.

- Keep the chatter to a minimum. Too many hosts engage in a silly amount of meaningless banter at the start of the show in some strange attempt to fool the audience into thinking it's the first time the shows have come together. Please. Get that stuff out of the way before the show starts (or take it out in post-production).

Likewise for outros:

- Thank the listeners for their time and invite them back for more. Common courtesy.

- Tell your listeners when they can expect a new show. Remember: It's the first-time listener you are trying to win over.

- Roll your ending bed music 30 seconds before you finish talking. This gives an easy audio cue that things are wrapping up.

- When you're finished talking, let your outro music continue for around 15 seconds. Fade the last five.

As with all rules in podcasting, these are made to be broken. In fact, call 'em guidelines — they're designed to be modified to fit your needs. The goal of this practice is not to give you hard-and-fast rules, but to foster a sense of continuity and consistency for your podcast — which helps you create a better show for you and your listeners to enjoy.

Reviewing Your Podcast with a Critical Eye

Y ou are a podcaster. You care about your work. You've poured your heart and soul into the script, carefully enunciated every word during the recording, agonized over the decision on various effects and aural enhancements, and spent meticulous hours in post-production. It is a thing of beauty, worthy of both recognition and praise from your peers — nay, the entire world.

Hold on a minute, hotfoot. You may have missed a critical step in this process: listening to what you have done.

"But wait," you exclaim in frustration. "I just spent the last three hours of my life editing this file. Trust me, I've listened!" And we'd agree with that statement. But we'd also argue (and we'd win, 'cuz we're the authors and we RULE) that the ears you listen with differ at each one of the various stages of production.

In this practice, we discuss a new set of ears (and eyes) that have to be utilized after all the other ears (and eyes) have been satisfied. These are the ears and eyes of the Self-Critic, a persona you will need to adopt and modify over time as the goals and objectives for your podcast change. The Self-Critic has to be detached, clinical, and even cold. He's not a very nice person and is all business. Those other eyes and ears utilized in other stages all work *for* this guy, and he's quite the taskmaster.

 Keep this guy locked up in a tiny box until you're completely done with the show, from pre-production all the way through post. In fact, get some sleep, dinner, or at least a cup of tea before you let this guy out of the box to wreak havoc on your final product. You're more likely to get an honest opinion out of him if you give yourself some time to gain a little perspective. (Oh yeah — getting some sleep beforehand is good.)

Accessing Audio Quality

Every single episode of your podcast should be reviewed for audio quality from start to finish after you've finished all post-production.

Yes, from the beginning.

Yes, through the ending.

Yes, every time.

We understand that you're in a hurry. But we really don't care. The only way to make sure that all those transitions, edits, fixes, and segues sound as good as you thought they did is to listen to all of them together as a whole — and in one sitting. So don't try to pull this off in chunks. If your show is 30 minutes long, find a block of time during the day when you won't be interrupted for 30 minutes, and just listen. You are about to release your show to dozens/hundreds/thousands of listeners, many of whom will be listening intently to what you have to say. You do them a disservice if you don't listen with the same intensity prior to letting them hear it.

 Invest in a pair of good-quality studio headphones. (See Practice 9 to find out what to look for.) While many of your listeners will probably listen with ear buds, through built-in computer speakers, or through their car stereo systems, others will not. If you do your critical review (and probably even your editing) with a pair of great headphones, you'll hear your show in the best environment possible and have the chance to catch details (and tiny flaws) that *might* go unnoticed by your audience — but why take the chance?

Finding problems

For now, you'll just be focusing on the quality of the audio. Depending on the content of your show, there could be any number of issues to watch out for. Here are a few of the more-common audio problems to listen for:

- Mic pops
- Background noise
- Really loud spots
- Really soft spots
- Obvious edit marks
- Abrupt edits
- Missed edits
- Bed music that's too loud
- Bed music that's too soft
- Weird noises (unintended)

When you find these problems, we recommend that you don't do anything immediately. Instead take note of them by following these steps:

1. **Pause the playback, and then jot down the time stamp and a quick description of the problem.**

2. **Back up a few seconds before the error and resume your critical review of the audio quality.**

3. **Repeat these steps as necessary until the very end of the audio file — no cheating!**

Deciding whether to fix them

When you've found all the problems with the file, it's time to determine what to do about them. You'll want to go back and fix most flaws. They are errors, after all. But some podcasters deliberately leave some flaws — from stumbles to paper shuffles — intact to emphasize the reality quotient of their program.

 There exists a difference between "letting the reality of the recording process come through" and "just being lazy." Your audience expects a certain amount of professionalism from you, but we'll not presuppose to tell you where that level lies. Having said that, we can't think of a good reason to let the bed music overpower your content, or to let an added effect blow out your audience's eardrums.

If you decide to leave in an error you noticed in your show, cross it off your list. At the same time, decide whether there's anything you can do to future recordings to stop that from happening in the first place. (If you'd like some pointers, we get into quite a few ways to improve the recording and editing process later in this book.)

For those remaining issues you have decided to fix, head back into your files and start tweaking. (Check out Practice 21 for tips on effective editing.) It's highly recommended to have a dedicated *issue edit* session where you take care of all the issues on your list. When you're finished with all your edits, finalize your episode and listen to it — from start to finish — again. No, we're not kidding.

Finding the Perfect Length for Your Show

Forget about the philosophical debates on the nature of existence, the meaning of life, and how many licks it takes to get to the center of a Tootsie Roll Tootsie Pop. Podcasters know of the eternal question that rises above all others: *What is the perfect length for a podcast?*

As we remove our firmly planted tongues from our cheeks, we recognize that there have been many opinions put forth on this topic. But that's not going to stop us from staking our own flag in the ground over this perennial issue. Heck, we wrote the book, so our answer is correct by default! (If only this were true for other things in life. . . .)

Actually, there are three different answers, and all require a bit of explanation.

Easy answer: 20–40 minutes

If you genuinely have no opinion on the matter and are willing and able to create a show independent of time constraints, then shoot for 20 minutes, giving yourself some time to run long. Within the podosphere, there exists a highly questionable (yet ingrained) collective wisdom that defines the average commuting time as between 20 and 40 minutes. And while none of your authors strive to be average with anything that they do, they are willing to pay homage to that particular figure — the idea is for your podcast to get the listener from door to door.

This range also fits in with our history as media consumers. Most television shows — at least those broadcast in the U.S. — clock in at the 30-minute or one-hour mark. Take out the commercials, and you are down to about 20 minutes or 40 minutes (respectively) of show time. It fits nicely with the time frame in which we've all been trained to give our attention to our media programs.

Hard answer: As short as it possibly can be

Notice how we change the operative word from *long* to *short*. When people talk of length, they're thinking in terms of making something *long*. It's a form of the word, so it makes sense. But that sort of thinking can (and often does) slip into padding the podcast with filler; podcasters get hung up on a predetermined length for their 'casts, and wonder what to do to stretch the content to fill up the time.

But if you turn that concept on its head and start thinking about how *short* you can make your show, you'll do a service to both your audience and yourself. What is this service of which we speak? Respect. Respect for everyone's time, because we live in a busy world and have little use for superfluous content.

 Apply this advice judiciously. We never recommend the sacrifice of quality content for saving a few minutes of time. Talk as long about a topic or to a guest as is necessary. Just don't feel the need to stretch.

Short shows don't have to *be* short, but long shows always *feel* long. You're going for that "lost time" feeling, where your listeners get so wrapped up in the content of your program that they literally lose track of the time. NPR calls this driveway time — listeners are so interested in what they're hearing that they don't want to get out of their cars to go inside. (It's a bonus for us podcasters that our content is available on a portable player; listeners can take us inside with them.)

Bite-size, snack-size, and meal-size content

When trying to find the perfect length for your show, consider the *bite-size, snack-size,* and *meal-size* content idea, which we first heard about from Chia-Lin Simmons from the *On Digital Media* podcast (http://ondigitalmedia.com). The concept is pretty simple to grasp, and it may open new avenues for your show.

Bite-size content is short — very short. It may be as short as a single song but up to a few minutes in length. Obviously, there isn't a lot of time for up-front setup or a sizeable credit roll at the end of each podcast. Get in quick, deliver some quick content, and get back out so your listeners can move on to other things in the playlist or go on about their day. Notable examples include *Five Minute Memoirs*, (www.fiveminutememoir.com), *Career Opportunities* (http://welchwrite.com/dewelch/ce/), and the *One Minute How-To* podcast (http://OneMinute HowTo.com).

This format is great for daily programming. Everyone is busy, and they sure would like to consume more podcasts. Shows with a high frequency of updates are often on the chopping block as listeners start looking for more variety. It's a lot easier to decide to keep a show that updates frequently if it only takes a couple of minutes to listen.

Snack-size content fits in the 10–20 minute range. Like their bite-size brethren, snack-size shows are easy on the listener, yet give the content provider a little more room to work. Music podcasters can fit two or three songs in while still leaving room to discuss the story behind the band, song, or whatever. This length is also great for single-interview programs that don't need to go too in depth on a topic. You'd be surprised how much great content you can fit into a 15-minute interview. See Practice 5 for Evo's 3:15 rule.

Anything that goes over the 20-minute mark falls into the *meal-size* category. As the name implies,

they take longer to consume — and prepare. The shows that fit well into this format run the gamut, and it's likely that the majority of podcasts fit this time frame. And while many listeners enjoy these longer-format programs, they do lead busy lives. Keep that in mind before you decide to launch another hour-long program.

It's your show, and you get to decide how long the show should be to be perfect. But think about your content, the larger podosphere, and your potential listeners' time before you rush headlong into a decision, or automatically assume a particular episode length. You aren't stuck with any preset format clock, and variety is the spice of life.

Strive for consistency in whatever standard length you choose

When evaluating your episodes for the perfect length, keep consistency in mind. We're all creatures of habit, and we like our established expectations to be met each time. As you're planning out your show, do your best to fall within a standard length for each episode.

This standard length rule was meant to be broken. From time to time, and if you have a really-great-but-a-little-long piece of content, break it. But please let your audience know up front that the show will be a little different from what they've come to expect from you.

Consistency helps your listeners figure out when they can listen to your program. Consider the commuter who knows that she has a 10-minute wait when she switches trains each morning. She knows she can fit in an episode of *Ask a Ninja* (http://askaninja. com) and *Happy Tree Friends* (http://happytree friends.com) because they usually clock in at less than four minutes each episode. But she probably knows not to start *For Immediate Release* (www. forimmediaterelease.biz) because she'll be at the office in 20 minutes, and Shel and Nevil almost always talk for about an hour.

Working toward the same length for each episode will also help your show grow. Many listeners will try out a few episodes, either by downloading a few or by listening on the Web site, before subscribing. Providing episodes of a uniform length conveys some sense of assurance to the new audience; variable-length shows may cause potential listeners to back off from making your show a regular listening habit, or even assume a lack of attention to detail on your part.

Critiquing the Content of Your Show

If you thought that audio quality and length weren't hard enough to view with a critical eye, you also need to critique your content. As the two prior sections mentioned, you need a certain amount of detachment and objectiveness to effectively evaluate the chosen content of your program. And yeah, that's going to be a challenge to cultivate.

We're going to go out on a limb here and assume that you really like the content of your podcast episodes and you feel that they're worthy of distributing to the larger world — even it that larger world is a small group of dedicated listeners. If you are jaded, the obvious choice is to go outside of yourself and ask for somebody else's perspective on your podcast's content. Well . . .

We highly recommend that you *avoid* doing this.

Getting a slew of opinions is a slippery slope that we really don't want to see you take. The most important person in the world for your podcast content to please is *you*. If living on the Internet has taught your authors any one thing, it's that no matter how strange your tastes, there exists at least one other person with the same proclivities. Podcasting is about serving the needs of niche audiences, not pandering to the whims and desires of some imagined mass audience. If you podcast with a group of folks, then by all means get their opinions and come up

with a collective decision on the content for your show and whether or not any particular episode is up to par.

 Beware of fans bearing advice. We love fans, but we also understand that fans are about as far from objective as anyone. Some fans will want you to focus on one show. Others will lobby for a particular show length; still others will suggest that you avoid particular topics. This is often great advice, but understand that these individuals want their needs served over all others. For examples of why that isn't a good idea, listen critically to any run-of-the-mill top-40 music artist. Doesn't the music all sound the same? A little too safe? A little too predictable?

Most podcasters start questioning their content because of what they perceive as a small audience size. Granted, sweeping changes to your show might attract more listeners. Of course, those same changes might also drive away those who have been with you for a while. Deciding whether to make changes is difficult, and there is no absolute right answer that works for all podcasts. However, we offer you this perspective: If you had a weekly talk scheduled in the real world every single week and 100 people showed up to listen to you *every time*, would you be disappointed? (*We'd* be thrilled.)

Evaluating Your Supporting Materials

A good critique of your own podcast doesn't end with a thorough analysis of the audio file. That might work for radio-show hosts, because they have little control over how the entire station is run. Podcasters usually have more to worry about than that, because listening to the show is only a part of the experience. We concede that it is the most important part, but you have to make sure your supporting materials — the messy parts — are all in top working order to allow your show to reach its full potential.

Here are a few questions to ask yourself about three critical components of your podcast:

mp3 files

We cover the mp3 angle in full detail in Practice 23, but here are the starting points:

- How do your files display in various mp3 players?

- Is the sample rate constant so that the files play properly in Flash-based players (and you don't sound like Alvin the Chipmunk)?

- Did you take the time to fill out your ID3 tags — complete with an image — and do you know how iTunes will be changing tags on your episodes? Yeah, iTunes does that.

RSS feed

Practice 27 will help you make sure these bases are covered for your RSS feed, but here's what they look like:

- Does your feed validate? In other words, is it free of errors, and have you checked? Practice 27 covers this.

- Are you providing adequate information about your episodes and is the iTunes Music Store updated with your most recent episodes?

- Do people have a way to contact you from your feed?

- Is your copyright statement accurate and reflective of your desires?

- RSS means Really Simple Syndication and inherently assumes that someone, somewhere will repurpose that feed. Do you make it easy for that to happen? And are you okay with that?

Web site

Here are some Web site basics to nail down. If you aren't sure they're secure yet, Practice 27 will be your friend.

- Will visitors to your Web site have any idea that you are producing a podcast?

- Do you make it easy for them to listen and (hopefully) subscribe?

- Does the presentation of your site convey what your program is about with graphics and supporting text?

- Have you made it easy to read your show notes and for people to help promote your site with various social-media applications?

These points demonstrate the need for a critical eye on various aspects of your podcast. Some chores (such as checking the final audio quality) simply must be done with each and every episode. Others (such as checking your supporting material) should be done on a regular basis; still others (in particular, decisions on content and length) are probably best done infrequently. Be your own *best* critic; there are always plenty of others waiting in the wings to tell you what they think. Make sure you know what *you* think before that happens.

T-Minus Five Episodes . . .

Practice 8

I t's so exciting when you come up with that idea for a podcast. You could be driving home from a workshop on how to podcast, working out at the gym, or just enjoying some quality time at the playground with your kid, and suddenly the idea strikes you — and whether it's in your iRiver, on a cocktail napkin, or on the back of an envelope, you start jotting down what you want to rant about. Your message is beginning to take shape, and you want to share your idea with the world.

Now you decide to start telling friends, acquaintances, and other podcasters that yes, you have a show in the works, and you cannot wait to get things underway. The questions "How often will it post?" and "How long will the show be?" start filtering in, and then you sit down to record the premiere episode . . .

. . . and this is when you discover that the *real* work has begun.

The Blog: Your Personal Hype Machine

There is nothing wrong with a little bit of hype. Hype is what gets people talking, and it can make incredible things happen. The force-of-nature in podcasting that is Scott Sigler proved that by generating incredible hype for the release of his book, *Ancestor,* using his feed (and others' feeds) to distribute a digital version of the book. That hype was instrumental in taking *Ancestor* to the top of Amazon's Science Fiction and Horror charts, and up to the Top Ten–ranked books alongside the *Harry Potter* series and a few of Oprah's picks.

So how can you make hype happen? The first thing you can do is set up a blog for yourself.

Setting up a blog

While we recommend WordPress as your blogging interface of choice, your blog can really happen just about anywhere, such as MySpace, Blogger, or LiveJournal.

Follow these steps to set up a blog with WordPress.com:

1. Go to www.wordpress.com **and click the link to start your WordPress blog.**

The signup page appears, as shown in Figure 8-1.

2. **Enter a username.**

This name is going to be how you are listed by WordPress. You can always set up your own URL through GoDaddy.com or a similar registrar service; but if you want to stick with the WordPress URL, decide if you want to use your name, a keyword from your show's title, or an acronym of your show's title.

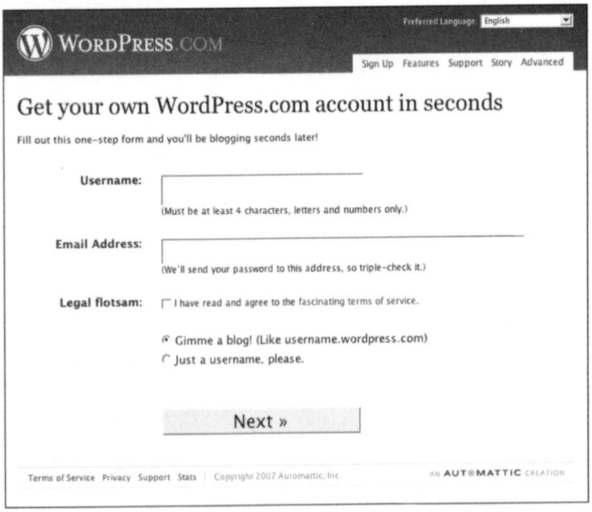

WORDPRESS.COM

Preferred Language: English

Sign Up Features Support Story Advanced

Get your own WordPress.com account in seconds

Fill out this one-step form and you'll be blogging seconds later!

Username: _____
(Must be at least 4 characters, letters and numbers only.)

Email Address: _____
(We'll send your password to this address, so triple-check it.)

Legal flotsam: ☐ I have read and agree to the fascinating terms of service.

⦿ Gimme a blog! (Like username.wordpress.com)
○ Just a username, please.

Next »

Terms of Service Privacy Support Stats | Copyright 2007 Automattic, Inc.   AN **AUT⦿MATTIC** CREATION

• **Figure 8-1:** WordPress makes blog registration a one-step process.

3. **Enter your e-mail address.**

This will be your contact e-mail for WordPress and for people who want to contact you through your blog.

4. **After reading the Terms of Service, select the Legal Flotsam check box.**

5. **Leave Gimme a Blog! selected and click Next to obtain your blog.**

Selecting the Just a Username Please option gives you an account with WordPress. This will grant you access to the Web site's various features. You can start up and shut down as many blogs as you like, but your username and password will always be part of the WordPress database.

Posting about your podcast on your blog

So now you have your blog up and running. Next you're going to want to make a post introducing yourself and your future podcast. It can be as detailed and as informative as you like; this is the foundation for your podcast. This initial post is also a chance to get accustomed to the blog interface (especially if you've never blogged before) and make sure your post shows up without fail.

Follow these steps to post on a new WordPress blog:

1. **Click the Write tab, and in the Title field, enter the headline for this blogpost.**

This is the headline for your blogpost. Starting off, you should say something simple like "Welcome to the podcast" or "Hey, you found us!"

2. **In the Post field, enter whatever you want to say in this blogpost.**

This is where you compose a welcome message and say whatever you like about your upcoming podcast. Again, it can be as detailed or as basic as you want.

3. On the right-hand side, you will see a listing of different categories (see Figure 8-2). Either create a category called Podcasts and then select that, or just select the various check boxes that best describe this blogpost.

Categories are the different filters you create in the WordPress Dashboard that allow you to create search filters. So if you tell the WordPress search engine on your blog to show only the Podcast posts, the other posts are temporarily hidden.

Categories list

• **Figure 8-2:** Your host blog's first posting, filed under different categories.

4. Check for spelling and any additional content issues, and then click Publish.

If you click Save and Continue Editing — or Save — your blog entry is saved but not published. The entry is saved as a *draft,* and you can access it either at the top of a new blog entry interface or at the top of the Manage list in the WordPress Dashboard, as shown in Figure 8-3. The Save and Continue Editing option allows you to save the entry, but it leaves the draft open so you can finish up or make additional changes. No blogpost will go live until you hit the button labeled Publish.

Click to access drafts

• **Figure 8-3:** Access drafts of blogposts at the top of the Manage page in the WordPress Dashboard.

When you have the blog up and running, you can post any particular thoughts or notes while you put together your podcast. You can direct FeedBurner to your blog's location (as described in Practice 27) and get your online hub of activity ready for traffic. You can even let a few friends, neighbors (the tech savvy ones anyway), and family members know about this host blog while you're tending to all the different administrative tasks necessary for your podcast. You can even upload the first five episodes to your server.

But *stop there.*

Make sure your first five episodes are done and ready to go before setting up your podcast on Podcast Pickle, verifying your feed for Podcast Alley, and submitting your feed to iTunes (as described in Practice 28). Posting episodes on your server gives you a visual confirmation of progress, whereas posting on your blog helps you get familiar with what your blog can do and can even generate hype for the actual podcast's release date. Offer text and images all pertaining to your podcast (and, if applicable, produce show notes and save them as drafts on your blog so they're complete and ready for posting later) — but do *not* submit your feed to directories until you and your five episodes are ready to go.

Then — and only then — should you kick off your podcast.

Does It Have to Be Five Episodes?

The question put to us quite frequently is why five episodes? Why not three? Why not just create one episode, whip up a promo, and then go for it?

Because not all episodes of a podcast are created equal.

That may sound like a throwaway answer, but nothing could be further from the truth. Podcasts vary in production demands and effort, even if you have their format set, a boilerplate beginning and ending, and a good idea how you want them to go. Interviews, for example, may be a simple matter of tacking on an intro at the beginning and then an outro at the end. Roundtable discussions may not only need editing, but also require some post-production level-setting. Solo efforts may need severe cleanup in post; you may even have to re-record certain segments. The production demands vary based on whether you want to stick with the basics of recording and mixing, or exercise your creative muscles in the realm of audio. By editing five episodes before officially launching your podcast, you not only develop your approach to podcasting but also get a good idea how long it will take you to record and edit a single episode.

Before putting together the first of these five episodes, you can do a few things to get an even better idea of how much material you will need to have on hand:

A podcast not necessarily in that order

Just because you have five episodes done and ready to go does *not* mean you have to post those five in order (unless your show material is time-sensitive or sequential, as in a novel or play). Flexibility is a good thing; there's nothing wrong with holding the last two shows of your first five if you record an interview that's too good not to post right away. These five recorded episodes can always be renamed, updated, or simply put on hold until you need them.

And don't forget those show notes — your guidelines through the beginning stages of your production. Give yourself a bit of wiggle room and don't worry about sticking rigidly to what you've produced. In the end, this is your podcast; those first five shows are merely your measure of how much time, effort, and material you have for your show's topic.

- ✔ **Outline the first five episodes of your show.** Make up full show notes so you can gauge exactly how much material you intend to record.

- ✔ **If you still have a head full of ideas for episodes, continue to brainstorm.** See if you can outline up to *ten* episodes.

- ✔ **Depending on the ease of producing your show notes (and how much material you plan to record), consider how often you will want to post a show.** If you struggle in planning the first five, aim for a monthly or bimonthly schedule. If you have plenty of material extending across ten (or more) episodes, a weekly schedule could work for your show.

 The more extensive the show notes you produce, the more accurately you can plan how long your episodes will be. If you're planning to keep your show under 30 minutes per episode, and your show notes run longer than two pages, it might be a good idea to find a breaking point in the show notes and make one episode into two. By generating show notes you can gauge exactly how long your show will be.

- After you've created show notes to cover the first five episodes, script a one-minute promo for your podcast. This should be the first thing you edit and record and release in your podcast feed.

- After recording the first five episodes, have them tagged, compressed, and ready to go. You can either post them as needed, or post all of them and simply provide links to them when needed. (See Practice 25 for more on tags.)

Producing five episodes will give you a good idea of exactly how much effort you can expect to put into this podcast on a regular basis. Knowing that is a key to a podcast's success. Regardless of whether the production values are high (adding in special effects in post-production, incorporating vocal talent other than your own, and so on) or kept to the basics (one voice, one mic), knowing how much work goes into the podcast will only help you to plan and prepare more efficiently. One way to do that is to know exactly how much of what goes into each episode of your podcast. As long as the amount of effort suits your purpose and doesn't strain your resources, you can't go wrong. You'll also find that having five episodes all set and ready to go is a terrific security blanket when you're launching your podcast.

Part II

Going for a Professional Sound

Practice **9**

Upgrading Your Headphones

If you ever see *Escape Pod*'s Steve Eley at a podcast camp or at a science fiction convention, you will discover he is a man of conviction. In other words, he's got an opinion on everything!

There is a bit of advice he gives again and again, on panel discussions, on speaker talks, and on the show *Podholes* (http://www.podholes.com), which he co-hosts with Michael R. Mennenga:

> "Get good headphones before a better microphone."

We have always found this advice and his reasoning behind it to be rock-solid, but because our own headphones were doing just fine, we never really considered the investment.

When we finally did, we asked ourselves what took us so long.

Why Focus on Headphones?

When podcasters want to upgrade their studios, usually it's the mixer board or the microphone that's the first accessory targeted for improvement — but (along with Eley) we recommend that you take a good, long look at your headphones. They're an aspect of the studio easily overlooked but perhaps the most important add-on to your studio.

Think about it — the headphones are telling you how you sound.

As with microphones, there are different kinds of headphones out there, different styles and different makes. Shopping for decent headphones can be intimidating. But just like with any audio gear, if you know what to look for, the intimidation factor is removed completely from the equation.

Shop safe. Shop smart. Shop S-Mart.

Before You Jump for Those $300 Headphones . . .

Another way of shopping with a strategy is to know what *not* to look for in headphones. High up on the list of what not to look for is *noise reduction.*

Noise-reduction headphones review an incoming audio signal and block what is designated as unwanted ambient noise. Bose brought this technology to the consumer with several models of *noise-canceling* headphones. Other manufacturers have been developing headphones with similar (if not identical) technology, promising the listener a superior audio experience.

So, let's review: Noise-reduction headphones are, without a doubt, the best investment for *listening* to audio. What you want, though, are headphones geared more for *recording* audio.

What's the difference? When you are recording with noise reduction, unwanted ambient noise is filtered out at the headphones. You don't hear it. It's still there, and it makes it on to your recording, but you think the audio is clean as can be because the noise-reducing headphones are filtering out what you'd want to eliminate *if you could hear it.* If your audience listens to you with noise-reduction headphones, they too will enjoy a relatively clean, crisp recording and terrific audio quality.

If your listeners lack noise-canceling technology in their speakers, car stereos, headphones, or earbuds, they may be asking their mp3 players, "Don't you hear *that?*" Or they may leave comments on your blog, asking you to do something about the background noise.

You want to be able to hear in your headphones all the actual sound coming into your mic and mixer. When it comes to reducing unwanted noise, that should happen either during the recording process or in post-production. Noise-reduction headphones give you an inaccurate representation of how you sound and where your noise floor is, so we recommend avoiding headphones with this feature.

I used noise reduction . . . but I still hear something!

You can reduce the amount of surrounding ambient noise either during the recording process or in post-production by applying noise-reduction filters. However, keep in mind that "noise reduction" is not the same as "noise *eliminating.*" Post-production filters, external compressors, and noise gates can only do so much with sound before the audio begins to distort. The best way to make sure you have little (if any) ambient background noise is to reduce (or attempt to completely eliminate) any *outside* noise. In some recording environments, this may be a simple exercise of finding the best places to put the components. Other recording environments may be harder to rig to reduce the amount of incoming noise. For more on how to eliminate potential noise, see Practice 12 on creating suitable recording settings and Practice 13 on compressors and noise gates.

Just remember: Post-recording noise reduction is not always the best answer. Try to get as much ambient noise out of the recording environment as you can.

What to Look for in Headphones

You have a lot of headphone options to choose from. It's no surprise that headphones are like microphones in the sheer range of manufacturers — and price (from the economical to the equivalent of a down payment on a car). How do you narrow down exactly what you need — and what "a *good* pair of headphones" should have going for them?

Closed-ear headsets

Headphones best suited for recording purposes have earpieces that fit completely around the ear, as shown in Figure 9-1. Other kinds of headsets rest on the outside of the ear or fit inside the ear canal *(earbuds).* While earbuds may seem preferable for recording use, they're not ideal for podcasters. Closed-ear headphones allow just enough sound in (and isolate you from just enough of the other sounds around you) so as not to interfere with the incoming audio signal.

By narrowing your search to closed-ear headsets (and avoiding noise-canceling headphones), you've narrowed the playing field considerably.

 When shopping at BSW, zZounds, or other vendors — be it online or a brick-and-mortar store — you might see different kinds of headphones, such as *semi-open ear, closed-back,* and *open-back* headphones. These variations on a theme are not the same as *closed-ear* headphones.

Frequency response

You'll also hear the term *frequency response* bandied about for microphones in this practice; that's because frequency response is something that mics and headphones share. *Frequency response* is a measurement of how headphones respond to audio signals. Audio frequencies are either *exaggerated* or *reduced* during recording and playback, so audio engineers look — or rather, listen — for equipment that is equally sensitive to all frequencies (a *flat* frequency response), creating a more accurate representation of the original audio source.

In our experience, a flat frequency response produces the purest audio overall; but because podcasters focus on voice, headphones that can pick up low-frequency noise are better than those that pick up a true flat-frequency response. That's because the human voice tends to produce sound and audio nuances in lower frequencies than those of musical instruments.

Impedance

An *ohm* is a unit of measurement for electrical resistance. *Impedance* is the resistance that audio equipment produces to the alternating current coming from an amplifier. The lower the impedance, the more power that's required to reproduce audio. The average pair of stereo speakers produces an

impedance of four to eight ohms. If headphones use high impedance (more ohms), it not only takes very little power to get them working, but also means more power is available for additional mics and input devices. The preamps in your mixer will not be taxed as hard on account of that.

Listen Up!

Now that you've absorbed some terminology about what goes into a solid set of headphones, it's time to go shopping. Take a look online or in your neighborhood store for different headphones, and — if possible — listen to various kinds of audio through them. Ask other podcasters what headphones they use and make a list of a few brands to consider. Then do some careful testing to find out which ones work best for you.

Samson CH700 ($40 USD)

Samson Technologies (www.samsontech.com) has been busy building products for podcasters, including the C01U, the H4 Zoom, and most recently the G-Track USB microphone. Along with microphones, compressors, and other studio accessories, Samson also makes various closed-ear headphones, offering solid sound quality within an affordable price range.

Samson's CH700 Studio Reference Headphones, shown in Figure 9-1, are a reasonable step up from a pair of Radio Shack 33-1225 headphones ($25 USD) or similar models. The CH700 headphones offer these features:

- Closed-ear design
- 20 Hz–20 kHz frequency response
- 64 ohms impedance
- ⅛-inch connector (with ¼-inch connector adapter)

• **Figure 9-1: Samson CH700 headphones.**

The CH700 headphones are good headphones to offer guests and show co-hosts because they provide an accurate and fair representation of the recorded audio. They may lack the range of the Audio-Technica DH40f headphones (described later in this practice), but they do very well in keeping other studio participants in the know on how everyone sounds and what is happening around them in studio. If you're working on a tight budget or unsure how much you want to invest in your headphones, the Samson CH700 headphones are a good, sure investment.

Expecting a few friends to come over to podcast?

If your podcast has a single host (*Moldower in the Morning, Random Signal, Jack Mangan's Deadpan*) or a crew of two (*Two Girls and A Podcast, Technorama*), the investment in headphones is hardly a concern. However, if you start building a motley crew of podcasters (*Wingin' It 3D, Fear the Boot, The ADD Cast*) and suddenly have a cast of thousands, you will need to invest in multiple pairs of headphones, which can start to burn a hole in your wallet.

Fortunately, the best friend of the podcaster — the online audio software and hardware vendor BSW (www.bsw usa.com) — offers an economical solution for podcasters who like their productions super-sized. For $50 USD (at the time of this writing), BSW sells the AKG Acoustics K44 headphones in a convenient pack of three. For $90 USD, you can also pick up a five-pack of Sennheiser HD202 headphones. These models may not give you the superior quality of the other headphones described here, but they will do the job of bringing everyone into the podcast without breaking your bank.

Koss UR-40 Collapsible Headphones ($50 USD)

For Tee, Koss holds a very special place in his heart as he recalls quite vividly growing up in the '70s and listening to his Disney albums with a pair of Koss headphones. (In fact, the model was close to the current Pro44AA headphones still sold today!) Sure, they were heavy and the coiled cable didn't give you much mobility, but they had volume control on the outside and sounded great.

Now in 2007, Tee returns to that manufacturer with the Koss UR-40 headphones, shown in Figure 9-2. Along with a bit of nostalgia for their maker, the Koss UR-40 headphones attracted Tee's attention on account of the following features:

- Closed-ear design
- Lightweight design
- 15 Hz–28 kHz frequency response
- ⅛-inch connector (with ¼-inch connector adapter)

• **Figure 9-2: Koss UR-40 headphones.**

The main selling point of the UR-40 headphones, though, is the *collapsible* feature. When podcasting on the road, headphones are tough to pack, and finding good *collapsible* headphones (not only for good sound quality, but also for just being able to collapse easily) that are closed-ear can prove to be a challenge. The Koss UR-40 provides both good audio quality and convenience of storage, and with the included ¼-inch connector adapter, the headset can easily float around from MobilePre to H4 Zoom to Tee's studio rig. Durable, reliable, and ready for travel, the Koss UR-40 headphones are a good purchase for the portable podcast.

Audio-Technica ATH-D40fs ($71 USD)

After hearing Steve Eley say it again and again (and again!) about upgrading headphones, Tee started shopping. He found the Audio-Technica ATH-D40fs on BSW (www.bswusa.com), and after reviewing his budget, the features, and the set itself (in image only), he went ahead and upgraded from his modest Radio Shack 33-1225 to these.

Tee was simply blown away by the Audio-Technica headphones, both in a wonderful and regretful way. The D40fs headphones (shown in Figure 9-3) are built to the following specs:

- ✔ Closed-ear design
- ✔ 20 Hz–28 kHz frequency response
- ✔ 66 ohms impedance
- ✔ ¼-inch connector (with ⅛-inch connector adapter)
- ✔ Rotating earpieces (for easy one-ear monitoring)

The headphones reproduce a crisp, clear reproduction of vocals. Every detail of your speech, every note of background music, and even the tiniest of special effects come through these headphones. Tee finally understood Steve's mantra of good headphones as the first studio upgrade.

• **Figure 9-3: Audio-Technica ATH-D40fs headphones.**

Dude, this time I get to wear the headphones!

If you like having guests in studio or have launched a show sporting a posse of podcasters, it's a little weird to be the only one all wired up with headphones to the mixer. You want everyone to be in on the fun, especially if you're dropping in sound effects and voicemail calls. You want the in-studio crew to hear what's going on, but your mixer board has only one jack.

An easy solution that will bring everyone into your podcast is adding a stereo headphone amp to your studio.

Guitar Center (www.guitarcenter.com) is not just a haven for guitarists, but for podcasters as well. (In fact, it's an authorized Apple Audio Reseller, so for all your Apple audio needs. . . .) The Guitar Center folks are also quite knowledgeable on what you need. Before Tee could even get out the words "stereo headphone amp," an employee handed him a Rolls HA43 Stereo Headphone Amp ($50 USD, pictured here). Along with a ¼-inch male-to-male stereo cable ($15 USD), the Rolls HA43 connects to the Phones jack of your mixer, and then you can connect up to four headphones, all of them with their own individual volume control, bringing you and your co-hosts or guests in on the audio recording fun.

Tee also understood what some listeners told him about his studio's ambient noise. Along with the details of his own voice, the D40fs also picked up loud and clear the PowerMac G4 *underneath* his desk! He was mortified at how loud his computer's fan was, and soon discovered that his early podcasts were unknowingly graced with a touch of Macintosh ambiance.

That doesn't mean Tee regrets his purchase. The Audio-Technica D40fs headphones were not just a fantastic investment for his studio. Those headphones made Tee a better podcaster.

A common thread with all the headphones mentioned in this practice, from the Radio Shack 33-1225 to the Audio-Technica D40fs, is their design: All these models are closed-ear headphones. Regardless of what financial route you take in your shopping, you will want to find a good, comfortable pair of closed-ear headphones to catch all the nuances of your recording sessions.

Another lesson to learn from this practice: If *Escape Pod*'s Steve Eley gives the same advice more than three times, it's tried and true. Run with it. When upgrading your studio, invest in a set of headphones that works best for your rig, your needs, and you.

Selecting the Right Microphone

Practice 10

In This Practice

- Shopping for a microphone
- Looking at some recommended models
- Taking a mic for a test drive

John Belushi and Dan Ackroyd, on teaming up with director John Landis for the 1980 film, *The Blues Brothers,* created comedy gold. The humor in the film still stands the test of time, but there was always one exchange early in the film that never *really* made sense to Tee:

> *"Where's the Caddy? The Bluesmobile?"*
>
> *"I traded it. For a microphone."*
>
> *"You traded the Bluesmobile for a microphone?! Okay, I can see that."*

Tee never did get that joke. At least not in the first few (hundred) times he saw it. Then he got into podcasting. A few months into *Morevi,* he was watching *The Blues Brothers* once again, and when that moment came up, he guffawed so loud that his wife was wondering if they were watching the same movie.

He *finally* got the joke.

Microphones are a great mystery in podcasting. There are so many to choose from — and they vary in price, some going well beyond the $1,000 mark. Which one works for you? If you ask a podcaster, brand names will come flying at you from every direction. Along with the brand names, you get *types* of microphones. It can be a bit daunting. It can be a bit frustrating.

It can also be a lot easier to find the right mic if you know what to look for and how to shop.

Choosing the Best Microphone FOR YOU

Microphones to podcasters are what shoes are to *Sex in the City*'s Carrie Bradshaw. You see some of the particularly pretty microphones, USB-powered, and looking all slick in their shockmounts, and a voice in your head whispers, "Soon, my Precious . . . soon." It is very easy to fall under the spell of high-tech audio toys. (We can still find the drool stains we made during the Podcast and New Media Expo in 2006.)

However, our opinion on a $1,000 microphone is the same opinion we have on Prada shoes: If we pay $1,000 for a microphone, that puppy is going to make us sound like James Earl Jones when we speak into it, edit out any mistakes in real time, cook us breakfast, give us foot massages, and pay our bills to the online audio mega-supermarket, BSW.

The shoe analogy works when breaking consumers into the microphone market because microphones share a lot in common with shoes. Not everyone is suited for Nike. A lesser-known brand, like Saucony, may shave off 10 or 20 seconds off your lap time. The same thing can be said for mics: Shure microphones are considered the industry standard — but does that mean you should ignore the other mic vendors out there? Is a state-of-the-art USB the way to go, or will XLR give you better sound and flexibility? Where do you draw the financial lines for acquiring microphones?

So it's worth taking some time in this practice to cut through the confusion surrounding what to buy — and set out to find the right mic for you.

Taking into account where you'll use the mic

Shopping for microphones is a science, and its methodology involves asking yourself a lot of questions. The first question is, "*Where will you be recording your podcast?*"

On location

If you're working outdoors or remotely, taking your microphone to a variety of locations, fielding comments and questions, and need a microphone to pass around from person to person, a *dynamic mic* may be best for you. In a dynamic microphone, as shown in Figure 10-1, sound manipulates a thin metallic diaphragm and coiled wire. Behind this

array, a magnet, in concert with motion coming from the coil, creates an electrical current. Dynamic mics work by the same principle as a loudspeaker; the sound is incoming (as opposed to outgoing), but the anatomy of the two devices is so similar that intercom systems use their speakers as microphones.

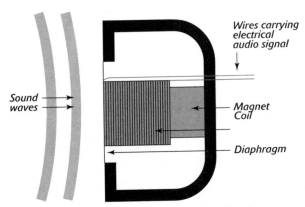

• **Figure 10-1: Cross-section of a dynamic microphone.**

Dynamic microphones are built to be durable (you can manhandle them, pass them around, and in some cases — though it's not recommended — drop them). They're terrific for portable rigs and question-and-answer sessions with audiences, and they can work in any recording environment.

Built-in microphones (such as USB headsets, an iRiver, and iPod's iMic) are common examples of dynamic microphones. Dynamic microphones range in price from a Radio Shack *unidirectional* (which picks up sound from only one direction) for $20 all the way up to the Sennheiser E945 *supercardioid* (which picks up sound in a heart-shaped pattern that isolates the sound you want from background noise, as Figure 10-2 demonstrates). One of Sennheiser's supercardioid mics will set you back $300 or more.

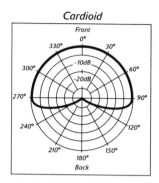

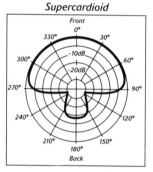
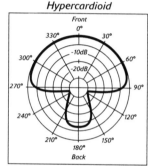

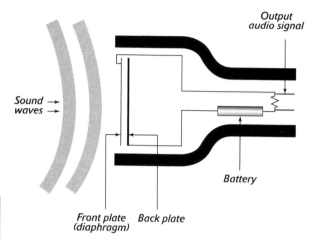

• **Figure 10-3: Anatomy of a condenser microphone and how it works with sound.**

• **Figure 10-2: Pickup pattern of a supercardioid microphone.**

In the friendly confines of a studio

If you know your podcast is going to happen in-studio, then you need a mic that is sensitive to the subtleties of the human voice. *Condenser microphones* are a different breed because the diaphragm is mounted close to — without touching — a backplate. As depicted in Figure 10-3, a battery connected to both the diaphragm and backplate produces the electrical current. The amount of charge you get is determined by the voltage of the battery, the area of the diaphragm and backplate, and the distance between the two. Power for the microphone comes either from a battery or something called *phantom power* (a current coming directly from a mixer board or preamp). Condenser mics, on account of this setup, create the truest reproduction of sound.

However, the relatively delicate construction (and fragility) of condenser mics means a trade-off: They are not built for durability. Sure, you can use them for question-and-answer sessions on your podcasts, but passing them around from person to person will be a pretty heavy test of how well the diaphragm and backplate work to re-create all that shifting sound. Also, unlike a dynamic microphone, if you talk on the wrong end of a condenser mic (say, from the top, or with the microphone label pointing away from you), your voice will vibrate the diaphragm improperly — creating interference in your recording.

And if you happen to drop a condenser mic, you'd better start shopping for a new one.

Condenser mics produce a fantastic sound on account of their *frequency response* (graphically represented in Figure 10-4) — essentially how a microphone responds to sound. Microphones, depending on their design, will amplify higher-frequency sound and then *attenuate* (or exclude) audio of lower frequencies.

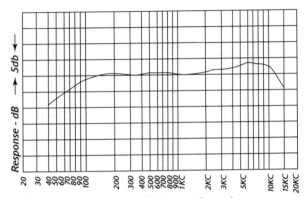

Frequency – Cycles per Second

• **Figure 10-4: Measurement of a condenser microphone's frequency response.**

Perusing consumer product reviews

Before making that purchase online at BSW (www.bsw usa.com) or Musician's Friend (www.musicians friend.com), take a few minutes to read the product reviews. These reviews are posted by customers (many of them professionals who have a track record of repeat business with this online vendor) who express praise or disdain for their recent investments, provide in-the-field reports, and even offer insight into what they're doing with the equipment. With some merchandise, the opinions may be unanimous or strongly divided. You may need to read between the lines and find the common thread among product reviews.

The best microphones produce a *flat* frequency response — the microphone is equally sensitive to all sound, whether the frequency is high or low. With no signals exaggerated or attenuated, the end result is clear, pure audio.

A perfect, flat frequency response in any microphone is difficult (if not impossible) to reach. But understanding frequency response will help you shop for the microphone best suited for you and your podcast.

Doing your research

Podcasters (and other people interested in podcasting) are always curious about what kinds of mics we're using — and we love talking up what works for us. Tee, for example, doesn't shy away from the $30 Radio Shack special when he finishes talking about the $160 AKG Perception-200 because both have their jobs; for what they do, each one performs admirably. So it's worth listing the tasks you want your mics to perform before you go shopping. After you've compiled a corresponding list of possible mics to buy, the next step is to check out reviews and gather feedback from other podcasters.

Chatting up fellow podcasters

Along with product reviews, you also have a fantastic resource to tap into that can really enlighten you about how a product works for podcasting — *other podcasters*. Podcasters *love* to talk about their equipment. If you find one — or several — podcasts whose sound quality you want to emulate, drop a line to the hosts to find out what they're using. Trust me — they will *love* to tell you!

For tips on how to connect with the podcasting community, take a look at Practice 32. Or check out the last section of this practice ("Can I Take This Mic for a Test Cast?").

And if you think podcasters are passionate when they fire up a mic, just wait until you ask them for their opinions on various recording equipment.

 Podcasters can provide a wealth of feedback and critical reviews of microphones, but when podcasters blast a particular model of microphone, take the dissing with a grain of salt. It doesn't necessarily mean they got a bad microphone; it was just a bad mic *for them*. When searching for product reviews from other podcasters, ask why a certain microphone works for them and their production — or doesn't.

Okay, it's true: Reviews and specs won't tell you how a particular mic works with *your* particular voice. So while you're at it, ask around at your local pro audio stores to see whether you can *try* the microphones you're most interested in. Although many places won't allow you to return microphones after you've bought them, they may have demo models that you can try out in the store. It can't hurt to ask.

Staying within your budget

Going back to the original *Blues Brothers* joke (and our own opinions on the $1,000 microphones), you might get the impression that we're not all about the price tag. The $1,000 microphone has a lot going for it, sure, but if a pricey microphone isn't in your budget, that should not deter you from getting into podcasting.

After you decide what kind of microphone will do the job for you, you should take a look at what you can afford. From there, you can then decide what to begin with or what you expect to upgrade to. Cost isn't everything. What is crucial in your podcasting setup is what you'll be using the microphone for — and whether it's best suited for that job as you do it. Collect feedback and reviews, look at your budget, and then make the investment (not purchase, mind you, but investment). While you probably *could* trade a car for a microphone, it's an option that we do not recommend.

What we *do* recommend comes later in this practice.

My Mama Told Me, "You Better Shop Around"

So what is out there? How does it measure up and why would you want it? These are all valid questions — and we're more than willing to share with you a short list of tried-and-true products that have been terrific investments for us. Along with the recommendations, we give you a look at how a particular mic works in our respective rigs — and where you can hear it in practice. These are just a few recommendations; what you find can either be the magic mic you're looking for or a starting point in your quest for the microphone best suited to you and your podcast.

Radio Shack Unidirectional Dynamic Microphone ($30–$40 USD)

This microphone is Tee's workhorse. With its 25-foot cable (the $30 model), an XLR connector to the mic itself, and a quarter-inch jack plugging into his M-Audio MobilePre, Tee can pass this microphone through an audience for any question-and-answer sessions he hosts when his podcast is on the road and recording live. The frequency response ranges between 60 Hz and 16 kHz — okay, not a particularly sensitive microphone, but its unidirectional pickup pattern makes it easy for anyone to use. Tee just boosts the MobilePre a bit and perhaps does some tweaking in post-production.

If you want to hear how the microphone sounds in practice, take a listen to any of Tee's *Microbrewed* segments with Phil Rossi on *Speaking of Beer* (www.speakingofbeer.com) or Special Edition #006 on *The Survival Guide to Writing Fantasy* (www.tee morris.com/blog).

Marshall Electronics MXL990 ($60 USD)

Farpoint Media's Michael R. Mennenga, when Tee asked for his help in setting up his first rig, recommended many different components for a beginning studio. When it came to microphones, he recommended the MXL 990, shown in Figure 10-5.

• **Figure 10-5: Marshall's MXL990, a reliable, affordable, and versatile microphone for podcasting.**

With its 30Hz–20kHz frequency response and XLR inputs and outputs to carry the signal, the MXL produces a far cleaner, more accurate reproduction of his voice than its Radio Shack counterpart. Tee was quite pleased with the sound of the 990, but even happier to find he got a *shockmount* (an apparatus that holds the mic in a specific, isolated grip so it won't pick up sound from the stand) — and even a carrying case — with the mic. The 990's durable build also makes it ready for travel, so Tee has no problems taking it with him on the road. The MXL is reliable, sturdy, and a terrific investment.

It's worth repeating: The more elaborate condenser mics just aren't made for roughhousing. Don't pass them around or submit them to too much jostling. (You may want to use a cheaper, more robust mic to cover that regional wrestling match.)

To hear what the MXL microphone sounds like, take a listen to Chuck Tomasi and Kreg Steppe on *Technorama* (www.chuckchat.com/technorama), or *Morevi: The Chronicles of Rafe & Askana* (www.podiobooks.com/podiobooks/book.php?ID=23) available on Podiobooks.com.

Sounds like a deal!

Always keep an eye and an ear out for sales and special deals. Often they include sweet microphones as part of the investment. When hired to record a podcast for both Wiley Publishing at BookExpo America 2006 and the NIST 2006 National Conference (both in the same week!), Tee had to put together a high-quality — yet still portable — recording rig. Imagine his delight when Musician's Friend was offering a free MXL 900 with the M-Audio USB MobilePre. And just before starting work on this book, BSW offered — with the purchase of an Alesis MulitMix-8 FireWire — a free AKG Perception 100, shown in the following figure. So, when you're shopping for a new microphone or for an upgrade, keep an eye out for deals.

AKG Perception 100 ($100 USD) and 200 ($160 USD)

When it was time for Tee to upgrade his studio this year, he (once again) turned to his audio oracle, Mike Mennenga, this time asking him for a mic best suited for his voice. (Keep in mind that shoe analogy.) Without hesitation, he recommended the AKG Perception: "I use a couple of AKGs in my studio, and you sound great in them."

Mike Mennega uses the AKG Perception 100 at Draco Vista Studios. With its large-diaphragm condenser (yielding low distortion and sporting a frequency range between 20 Hz and 20 kHz), Tee felt like he was hearing himself all over again. You wouldn't think the extra 10 Hz would make a difference — but did it ever!

The model Tee purchased was the Perception-200. Unlike the 100, the 200 comes with two extra features:

- **Bass Cut filter:** The Bass Cut reduces low-end distortion (footfalls, wind noise, and so on) and minimizes clipping and popping problems in close mic situations.

- **Switchable Preattenuation pad:** The Switchable Preattenuation pad allows you to safely increase the frequency range by 10 dB for close-in recording, preventing overloading transformers in mixer boards.

Tee has been thrilled with the performance of the AKG Perception, and he highly recommends it. His most recent podcast, *Billibub Baddings and the Case of the Singing Sword* (www.podiobooks.com/ podiobooks/book.php?ID=131), can give you an idea of how it sounds, especially with close-in recording. You can also have a listen to *The Dragon Page: Cover-to-Cover* (www.dragonpage.com) with the aforementioned Mike Mennenga, and authors Summer Brooks and Michael A. Stackpole.

As tickled pink as Tee is with the AKG mics, he still uses the MXL 990 for his portable recordings. Just because you invest in new and higher-grade equipment does not mean you must stop using the reliable gear you've already implemented.

Speaking of portable options . . .

Samson Technologies C01U Recording Pak ($170 USD)

Samson Technologies (http://samsontech.com) was first on the scene with a mic geared specifically to podcasters: the C01U. Priced under $90 USD, the C01U was a big hit; condenser microphones could only interface with a computer through third-party audio interfaces, a mixer board, or specific cables and adapters. The C01U provided a USB connection — the first mic to interface directly with the computer. Audio cards, adapters, and other hardware were no longer needed.

This innovative mic also offered some very podcast-friendly capabilities:

- Cardioid pickup pattern

- A smooth, flat frequency response between 40 Hz and 18 kHz

- Ability to record at 16-bit sample resolution with support for five different sampling rates: 8 kHz, 11.025 kHz, 22.05 kHz, 44.1 kHz, and 48 kHz

The C01U led the charge for other USB condenser microphones such as the Blue Snowball ($100 USD), the Røde Podcaster ($161 USD), and most recently the MXL 990-USB ($100 USD) to meet the demands of podcasters.

 USB mics are terrific options for solo podcasters, but just because you can take two USB mics and plug them into your computer's available ports doesn't mean you have Channel One and Channel Two covered. We're not talking stereo here. You have dedicated USB ports, so you can use *either* one USB mic *or* the other — not both at the same time.

With newfound competition like this, how could Samson keep the C01U in everyone's sights?

Simple — Samson created an easy-to-transport, all-in-one kit (that's it in Figure 10-6).

• **Figure 10-6: The C01U Recording Pak, podcasting gear packed up in one suitcase. All you need is a laptop and a voice.**

The C01U Recording Pak is Samson's travel-ready podcasting solution. Along with the popular C01U, the Pak also includes

- ✔ USB cable for the microphone
- ✔ Two-part microphone stand and base
- ✔ Microphone clip
- ✔ SP01 Shockmount for the C01U
- ✔ Cakewalk's Sonar LE (DAW)
- ✔ Aluminum suitcase with a foam-padded interior (Not only does it cradle the gear, but it also really projects a James Bond kind of aura around you!)

Tee took the C01U out west to Phoenix, Arizona, and then to Tuscon (a major Arizona science-fiction convention) as part of an on-the-road podcasting

rig. He was impressed as the ease of setup and strike, no-hassle transporting of the equipment, and high performance on the road. If you're a podcaster in need of portability, the C01U Recording Pak is a must-have.

For other portable solutions in podcasting, take a look at Practice 16.

 A problem the C01U and other USB mics have encountered (and still struggle to overcome) is the issue of *latency* during recording. Latency is when you begin to notice a slight delay between your voice and what you hear over the monitor while recording. The longer you record, the more latency that builds up — until finally what you're saying and what you're hearing sound more like a distracting echo. A common cause of this latency is lack of RAM and too many applications running at the same time as your DAW. Make sure you have an ample amount of RAM installed in your computer before recording — and be sure to restart your computer before starting up a new recording session. You can also choose not to listen to yourself as you record, an option many podcasters practice.

Final thoughts

Again, these suggestions are just that — suggestions. The more you can find out about a mic before purchasing it, the better the investment for your podcast. If these recommendations provide you with solutions, fantastic! If these recommendations lead to other microphones, even better. What matters, in the end, is finding the right microphone for your voice.

So how do you go about getting the right microphone for your podcast? Keeping with the shoe analogy, the best way to find the mic that works best for you is to try it on, as detailed in the next section. Record something somewhere with the recommended microphone and then compare it to your current recordings.

Can I Take This Mic for a Test Cast?

Perhaps the best way to test a microphone is to record with it first. While it might be hard to find a vendor (especially an online one) who will *loan* you a microphone so you can get a feel for it, you might be able to find a local podcasting group in your area whose members would be happy to talk with you about investing in a microphone. They may even invite you to their recording studios or bring their equipment to a meeting for you to take a look at, up close and personal.

Here are some suggestions for seeking out fellow podcasters:

- **Local podcasting groups:** Do a search online for *podcasting meet up groups* in your area and find out when and where they will meet. Attend that first meeting, introduce yourself, and make a few contacts.

- **Podcamps:** You can also network with other podcasters at *podcamps* — open workshops and panel discussions on how to podcast and how to improve the sound of your podcast. You will find a podcamp wiki (featuring locations of podcamps happening across the country) at `http://podcamp.pbwiki.com/`.

- **Conferences:** Conferences of all kinds, ranging from science fiction and fantasy conventions (Balticon, Dragon*Con, and Hyperion), feature podcasting tracks in their programming. Additionally, the Podcast and New Media Expo (`http://newmediaexpo.com/`) features audio vendors, show hosts, and various online services geared to podcasting. These events are all opportunities to network and even test-drive new products.

These podcaster get-togethers are great opportunities to find deals on used equipment. If you feel a bit gun-shy about picking up audio equipment from eBay, ask around at these get-togethers, podcamps, and conventions to see if anyone has equipment for sale. You may find some very good deals and reliable equipment there.

If you do get a chance to try out someone's rig, keep the following points in mind:

- **Talk normally into the microphone.** This is not *Good Morning, Vietnam,* and you are not Robin Williams. Avoid shouting into the microphone you are currently testing. Talk normally, and take notes on the model of microphone and what kind of mic it is — dynamic or condenser.

- **Ask as many questions as you can think of.** Ask about the microphone model and manufacturer, any special features, whether it's still being made (so you can get parts), where the mic was purchased, and any deals the podcaster may know of. With a list of mic vendors, comparison-shop both locally and online before purchasing.

- **Be respectful.** Remember that this is someone else's rig. Treat the equipment with respect. Heck, treat it as if it were a newborn: Use tender, loving care and slow, gentle movements so you don't startle the podcast gear's parent who's watching over you.

Turning to Podcasts for Insight into Mics (And Other Audio Gear)

If you are looking for more on mics, how to shop for them, and what to listen for in their performance, there are plenty of podcasts currently running about microphones (and other audio equipment ideas). Here are a few you may want to check out:

- The earlier- (and often-) mentioned Michael R. Mennenga and *Escape Pod's* Steve Eley host *Podholes* (`http://podholes.com`), a podcast about the engineering that goes into a podcast; their topics cover everything from mics to mixers to mp3 compression.

- ✔ *Inside Home Recording* (`http://insidehome recording.com`), hosted by Paul Garay and Derek K. Miller, also offers insight for home-studio recording and gives tips on how to keep your sound up to professional standards.

- ✔ *GearCast* (`http://gearcast.blogspot.com`), hosted by Cal Mazzarra, is a weekly audio magazine for enthusiasts of audio and video. Alongside product reviews and commentary, *GearCast* also hosts roundtable discussions covering various issues and topics in digital audio and video production.

Your options among information sources, much like your possible selections in shoes — er, microphones — are many. With just a bit of research and patience, you'll find a microphone that makes you sound like gold.

Just for the record, if you *are* searching for that one microphone that makes you sound exactly like James Earl Jones or Kathleen Turner, sorry. You, my friend, are going to be searching for a good long while. We're talking technology here, not magic.

Not all mics are created equal

When shopping for equipment, always keep an open mind. Just because you strike audio gold on the first purchase does not always mean that a particular vendor or manufacturer is for you. For example, Thomas of *The Command Line Podcast* (`http://thecommandline.net`) upgraded from a simple headset mic to an Audio-Technica 3035. The 3035 was his first cardioid, phantom-powered mic. "It was much better for midrange response than the headset mic I tried using. I now have two 3035s and absolutely love them."

In need of a third mic (Isn't success in podcasting grand?), Thomas tried the same vendor where he picked up the 3035 and was talked out of buying a Shure SM-57/58 mic in favor of another Audio-Technica microphone: the Pro24. The A-T Pro24, unlike the 3035, is not phantom-powered and produces a weak signal when running on his iMic or Microtrack. Also, the frequency range is far narrower in comparison to the 3035. "When I move it more than 8 or 10 inches from the sound I am recording," Thomas comments, "the signal basically fades to nothing." Same vendor, same mic manufacturer, but the microphone didn't fulfill Thomas's production needs.

Practice

Upgrading Your Software

In This Practice

✔ Deciding whether to step up from Audacity or GarageBand

✔ Examining professional applications across both platforms

Making the jump from one software package to another can only be described as nerve-wracking. An application becomes an old and *trusted* friend when you're podcasting. You know every nook and cranny of the application, and swear by it even in the face of doubtful comments from other podcasters.

Whether you're using something along the lines of Audacity (where the capabilities stick to the basics) or perhaps something like Pyro 5 (where you have multiple tracks and extra features not found in free, open-source software), your software is the not-so-silent partner in your audio production. You have developed a bond with it and have accomplished great things with it as part of your team. But as with your favorite party shirt or the trusted coffee mug that was always within reach during the long nights of editing, you are ready to move on. Perhaps you feel a sense of betrayal, or guilt? Why discard the ally who has worked so hard to make you sound so good? Doesn't the application that helped you develop your voice in the podosphere have a say in this sudden parting of the ways?

Of course not. It's a piece of software. Get over it.

Time to play with the Big Kids' Toys.

Working Beyond Audacity

For many podcasters, their first audio editor is the open-source software Audacity (`http://sourceforge.audacity.net`). Audacity is a good starting point for podcasters because it is a safe investment (The software is free. You can't get any safer than that!) and works on a variety of platforms. If you're uncertain if podcasting is right for you, starting off with Audacity is far less intimidating than firing up Soundtrack Pro (with its many windows of options, add-ons, and the like). And if you find that playing with audio isn't for you, then the only thing lost in the Audacity investment is time — nothing more. So why decide to step up from

Audacity to another software package? If the system ain't broke, why fix it? Here are a few reasons why you may want to make a switch:

✔ **Stability:** Audacity users have been on the fence about this issue since the open-source software began to gain popularity in the podosphere. We have heard podcasters swear up and down that this application runs true and reliably, and that stability is what compels them to keep Audacity as part of their podcasting setup. We have also heard of (and experienced first-hand) some users who can only record so much on Audacity before the application crashes so hard that it takes the audio with it, leaving frustrated podcast hosts to start over once again.

The stability issue of Audacity is a giant question mark. Some podcasters are willing to deal with it, but others find that game of chance a little too daunting — especially when, after recording several lengthy episodes, they lose the audio completely and have to start again.

✔ **Operating-system compatibility and conflicts:** Because Audacity is open-source software, there is contention that some of its extra plug-ins and user-developed (and user-approved) extensions don't play well with applications from Adobe, Microsoft, and other major software developers. Computer-conspiracy theorists may cry foul, but open-source software can create problems with other applications.

✔ **Lack of backup in case of a crash:** As mentioned previously, when Audacity crashes, it takes everything with it — and we do mean *everything*: original audio, edits, effects, and any recent imports. When you reopen the project, you either start from the last save, or from scratch. There is a slim chance you can piece a lost audio recording together out of the work files Audacity generates (usually kept in a folder identified by the project's name), but that's a painstaking process that may not sit well with your production schedule. Re-recording, while equally gut-wrenching and frustrating, is far easier. In other applications, recording sessions are saved intact elsewhere on the computer — a far more desirable solution in case of application or system failure.

✔ **Lack of extra features:** Unlike Soundtrack Pro, Adobe Audition, Steinberg Cubase, and others, Audacity does not come with any free music loops or royalty-free sound effects. Some would argue this keeps the application streamlined, but for podcasting use, it does limit any possible out-of-the-box solutions. Additionally, *ducking* — a popular feature in GarageBand that automatically takes another track down in volume when another begins its audio — is not available in Audacity. (For more on ducking, jump ahead to Practice 24 on enhanced podcasting.) Again, the out-of-the-box solutions that these other programs offer are appealing and can assist you in improving your podcasting productivity.

✔ **Free only goes so far:** If you want to do multiple-track recording, employ industry-standard noise-reduction filters, and have deeper control over the various audio effects that an audio application offers — even after the effect has been implemented — you're going to have to shell out the bucks. A free application won't do all that for you. While the expensive applications and Audacity do have similar effects, filters, and editing tools, you get better audio results from the built-in effects and far more control and flexibility with the professional applications than with the open-source software.

Working Beyond GarageBand

GarageBand (`http://apple.com/ilife/garage band`) is the other popular first-time audio editor, usually installed with new Macs and available as part of iLife. Tee used GarageBand (Version 2) for *Morevi: The Chronicles of Rafe and Askana* and pushed its recording limits as far as he could. The end result was a first podcast he is still very proud of.

With the changes in GarageBand since Version 3, the Mac-centric application remains a very popular choice with both new and established podcasters. It has even been a selling point that swayed some PC users to purchase Mac Minis.

GarageBand, even before podcasting came along, had developed a good reputation in audio-recording and editing circles, but podcasters embraced it so passionately that Version 3 was released with out-of-the-box podcasting solutions. With such advanced features, solid stability, and even a backup of recorded audio in case of an application crash, why would you want to upgrade to a more-expensive application (also known as *digital audio workstation*, DAW for short) like Soundtrack Pro, for example?

Well, here are some points that may make you consider upping your game with Soundtrack:

- ✔ **Limited number of built-in sounds:** GarageBand comes with hundreds of royalty-free sound loops and effects, but eventually — depending on your production demands — your show's needs can easily go beyond what those loops can do. Expanding the basic sound library is possible with GarageBand Jam Packs, but those additional loops and riffs are $100 per pack, which can get costly in a hurry. Other professional applications come with *thousands* of sound loops, and you can get more mileage out of those bigger libraries than from the hundreds of loops that come preinstalled with GarageBand.

- ✔ **Technical limitations:** GarageBand offers some clever workarounds with a recording-playback issue. After 30 minutes, we have found that simple features like dynamic volume control and even horizontal scrolling shut down, making the editing process a challenge.

  What makes GarageBand a preferred tool (apart from the ease of its interface) is its multitrack recording capabilities, which give you up to eight separate inputs. For some podcasters, that's plenty; but if you're doing roundtable discussions, eight channels of input aren't enough.

- ✔ **Time-consuming editing process:** Later practices in this book get into the difference between *destructive* and *non-destructive* editing, but here's the quick-and-easy explanation of the non-destructive variety: GarageBand allows you to edit the audio you've recorded without editing

the *original* audio file. So if you ever want to restore audio that was removed earlier, you can simply go back and restore it from the original recording.

While non-destructive editing may seem like a superior way to edit audio, it can add a lot of time-intensive hassle if you make a change early in the timeline and then you have to shift later clips backward a second or two. The option to edit the original audio is usually reserved for higher-end applications — but it can cut your post-production time considerably.

 Editing audio in a *destructive* manner is a commitment. You are saying "I don't like this take" or "I don't think I need this segment." When the audio is removed, it may either remain in a History (similar to the History palette in Adobe Photoshop) or in your application's Undo menu until the audio is *flattened.* (When you dramatically change the state of an audio clip such as mono-to-stereo or resample, the history of previous edits goes away, similar to the way the layers merge into one when you flatten a Photoshop document.) Remember that when you are editing audio destructively, you are changing the *original* recorded audio. Any segment lost that you may find necessary later on in the project will have to be recorded again.

- ✔ **Limited control of filters and effects:** While GarageBand does provide more control over various audio effects than Audacity, even more control and flexibility is available with higher-end applications like Cubase, Peak, Audition, and Soundtrack. How closely you want to control your audio in post-production will be a factor in whether you want to jump from GarageBand to one of the professional audio applications.

Okay, you may never have to touch some of the professional filters and effect applications built into these DAWs — but other such high-end capabilities may offer you a solution to some long-standing production problem. Figuring out what your podcast requires in post-production editing will help you decide whether to stick with GarageBand or step up to a bigger player.

Looking at the Major-League Players

In no way, shape, or form are we dismissing Audacity or GarageBand; both applications are terrific starting points — and if they meet your podcast's needs, an upgrade may not make practical sense yet. But if you're looking to expand your options so you can get more flexibility in how you create — and more efficiency in how you record — consider the following software packages for your podcast studio.

Adobe Audition

Adobe Audition (`http://adobe.com/audition`), the digital audio workstation formerly known as CoolEdit, continues to be a favorite application in the audio and video industry. Audition (shown in Figure 11-1) is not for the faint-of-heart Windows user or the casual podcaster; but it is an Adobe product, so the interface is easy to navigate and understand. The application offers podcasters a wide array of features:

• Figure 11-1: Adobe Audition survived the changeover from CoolEdit and remains an audio standard in the industry.

✔ Unlimited number of available audio tracks

✔ Capacity to record 80 live inputs (just in case you have 80 people in your home studio!)

✔ Over 50 real-time audio effects (including echo, flange, and reverb), allowing you to listen to the effects as you work with the audio

✔ Over 5,000 performance-based, royalty-free music loops, ready-to-play music beds, and Audition *sample sessions* you can edit easily to create your show's music

✔ Real-time control in your project's timeline over volume, pan, and effects

✔ External device-control options you can use to adjust the mix and effects in real time with your own equipment (such as mixing boards, compressors, and so on)

And for those of you who are really into high-end audio production or venturing into video podcasting, Audition offers even more creative capabilities:

✔ A Surround Encoder outputs multitrack into 5.1 surround sound.

✔ A Quick Punch feature allows you to rerecord errors over existing audio — in real time.

✔ Output audio at high-resolution (24- or 32-bit files) with sample rates up to 192 kHz. Result: HD- and DVD-quality audio.

✔ With looping tools, Audition can create royalty-free looped music for soundtracks. User-created loops can automatically match your project's tempo and key.

✔ For video podcasters, Audition can edit and sweeten soundtracks and Foley (sound effects made live by actual people — such as walking in sneakers across wooden floors, turning pages in a book, lighting a match, and so on) for videos from After Effects or Adobe Premiere Pro.

✔ Audition supports AVI, MPEG, DV, and WMV video formats, giving video podcasters more options for post-production audio editing.

Apple Soundtrack Pro

Apple Soundtrack Pro (`http://apple.com/soundtrackpro`) is the up-and-coming software in the industry and one of many incredible applications that make up the Apple Final Cut Studio. In its latest incarnation, Soundtrack Pro (shown in Figure 11-2) has been given vast improvements, many of which Mac-based podcasters will find extremely beneficial:

✔ Soundtrack Pro now supports multitrack recording.

✔ Soundtrack's Multitake Editor displays multiple audio takes in a single window. After you select the best ones, Soundtrack Pro compiles them for a final composite — complete with *crossfades* (fading down one audio source while fading another one up simultaneously) — creating seamless playback for the end result.

✔ Soundtrack's Lift & Stamp tool copies audio effects and EQ settings from another clip — setting them on an audio clipboard for quick access and application or you can save the settings as a preset for future use.

✔ Soundtrack Pro now features specific functions for producing podcasts, including audio-only, enhanced, and video podcast formats. You can place chapter, artwork, and URL markers without leaving Soundtrack Pro, and output your files with Compressor 3.

✔ Similar to Audition's Surround Encoder, Soundtrack outputs multitrack audio projects into 5.1 surround sound. Additionally, with Space Designer, Soundtrack can render sound effects and music beds that cater to 5.1 surround-sound mixes (in addition to the thousands of sound effects and loops already installed).

✔ For video podcasters, Soundtrack now automatically updates any changes made in Final Cut Pro, using its new Conform feature.

✔ Crossfades between edited clips are now given options and the ability to be customized in a visual interface to suit your project's needs. Additionally, rolling edits similar to working with video in Final Cut Pro can be applied to projects.

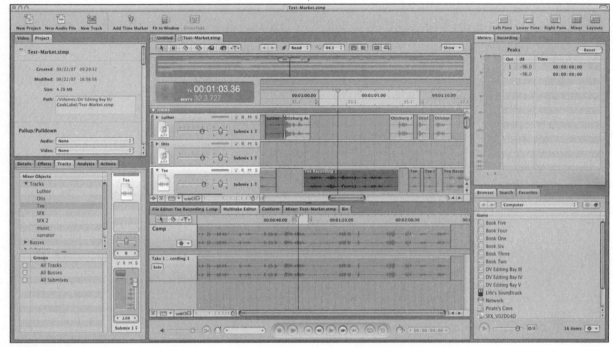

• Figure 11-2: Apple Soundtrack Pro is coming on strong as the must-have DAW for podcasters.

This DAW sounds like a podcaster's dream come true, but here is the reality in this fantasy: Soundtrack Pro is no longer a standalone purchase. It only comes bundled with the Final Cut Suite. While the other applications bundled with Soundtrack are power-houses (Final Cut Pro, Motion, DVD Studio Pro, Color, and Compressor), Soundtrack is a serious investment at $1,300 USD.

Bias Peak Pro

Another player for the affections of Mac users is Bias Peak (http://bias-inc.com/), shown in Figure 11-3. This application comes in two flavors — Lite Edition (LE) and Professional (pro). While dramatically different in price, both applications offer similar features to help make your podcast sound as professional as possible:

✔ Support for 24-bit/96 kHz digital audio

✔ Support for synchronizing QuickTime DV clips

✔ An Auto-Define Track feature that separates audio input (LP, cassette, CD, and so on) to independent audio tracks for transfer to iPod, CD-R, and other audio output media

✔ Unlimited Undo/Redo commands and Edit History window

✔ Capability to create, edit, and read region, loop, and reference markers in user-generated and imported audio

✔ Software bundled with VST and AU audio effect plug-ins for expanded capabilities

✔ Support for reading and rendering the following audio formats: mp3, AAC, AIFF, WAV, SDII, QT, JAM, and many more

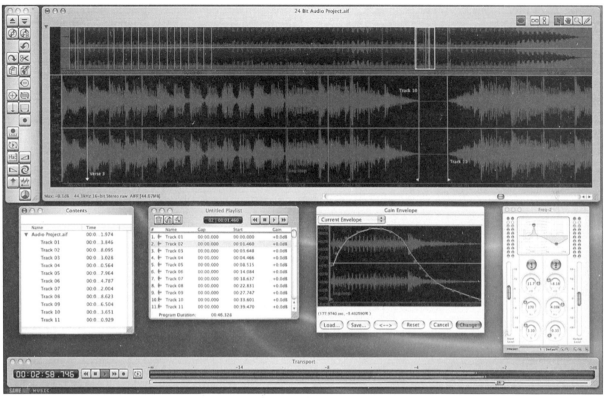

• **Figure 11-3: Bias Peak proves to be an alternative to both GarageBand and Soundtrack Pro.**

✔ Port that enables a Mac keyboard to be used as an external control device for the software, including its audio playback and editing features

Bias Peak Pro, however, does offer some tantalizing extras that its younger sibling does not:

✔ SFX Machine LT plug-in with 21 real-time special effects

✔ ImpulseVerb, giving ambient room to any audio file in order to equalize recording conditions for all audio imported into a project

✔ Added versatility: Use it as a standalone application or integrated with other audio- and video-editing software (such as Deck, Live, or Final Cut Pro)

✔ Over 300MB of high-quality sound loops from PowerFX and Sound-FX-Design

Adobe Soundbooth

We round off this list of major-league digital-audio applications with another Adobe product — a brand *new* Adobe product, in fact.

Adobe Soundbooth (http://adobe.com/sound
booth), the latest creation and newest edition to
Adobe's Creative Suite (the Premium or Master
Collection Edition), is the cross-platform solution for
audio in film, video, and Adobe Flash presentations.
Offering seamless integration between itself and Flash

Professional and Adobe Premiere Pro, Soundbooth
(shown in Figure 11-4) offers many functions that
used to be available only to Windows users through
Audition — as well as a few new features not found in
either Audition or Soundtrack Pro:

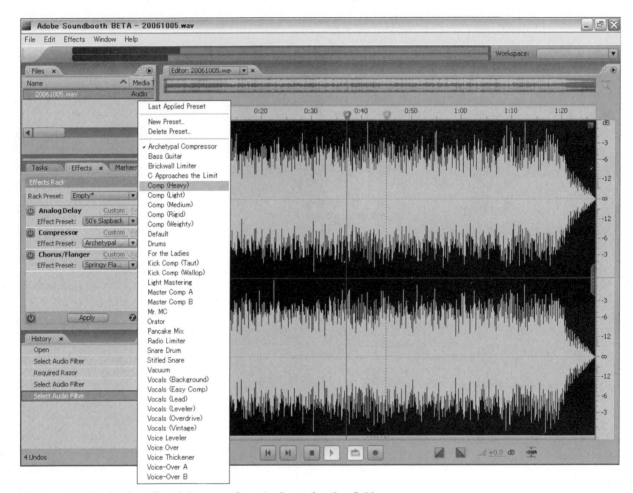

• **Figure 11-4: Adobe Soundbooth is a new player in the podcasting field.**

Before you produce plastic, think about the podcast

Designed for the Mac, Bias Peak LE and Pro offer a podcaster many more options for editing projects. However, before you whip out the Visa or MasterCard for the Professional Edition over the Lite, consider your podcast's specific production needs. It's nice to up your game from Audacity or GarageBand to something more polished or high-end, but ask yourself whether your podcast's production values really need such a major upgrade. It is important to remember that you should invest the time, effort, and finances *appropriate for your podcast*. Will you want (or even need) the extra features in the Professional Edition of Peak? (Unused features are pretty expensive as mere status symbols go.) Does the interface look intuitive and easy to work with?

Always review the Features pages and screen captures of software you are considering; find out whether the application offers something truly essential to your podcast's production values.

✔ Built-in filters and options for detecting and removing audio flaws such as hisses, hums, cracks, and pops

✔ Pre-installed audio filters (such as reverb, echo, EQ, time and pitch stretching, distortion, and chorus). You can use an Effects Rack feature on individual tracks, combining up to five effects in real time.

✔ Soundbooth integrates smoothly with Adobe Premiere Pro; Premiere even offers an Edit in Soundbooth command. When your edits are complete, the audio in the Premiere sequence's timeline updates itself automatically.

✔ You can set and export markers as part of XML or FLV files, and then access them using ActionScript for timing and cueing when you're creating Flash presentations.

✔ As with Audition, Soundbooth can show audio signals on-screen as a *spectral frequency* display so you can analyze waveforms in detail — and edit them — using Adobe Photoshop–style tools.

✔ The AutoComposer feature allows Soundbooth users to create customized music from dozens of included scores for individual projects. You can stretch these royalty-free compositions automatically to match the length of your video clips or desired running time for your audio.

✔ The included Adobe Media Encoder can export audio to video formats such as MPEG-2, H.264, RealVideo, FLV, and more. Using the built-in export functions, you can save your files in WAV, AIFF, mp3, and WMA formats.

What's in a name?

Although Adobe Soundbooth is pretty impressive (even out of the box), it seems geared more to video post-production than to audio engineering — especially in comparison to Adobe Audition. Adobe Systems gives a nod to that difference on its Web site (www.adobe.com/products/soundbooth/compare/):

✔ **Soundbooth** is aimed at "video editors, designers and developers who work with Flash, motion graphics artists, and other creative professionals without a background in audio." Translation: If you're a video podcaster and looking for a less-daunting tool for sweetening your audio in post-production, Adobe Soundbooth would seem to be your best choice in software.

✔ **Audition** is designed for "audio-centric professionals such as sound designers, recording and mastering engineers, and musicians." Translation: If your podcast does not deal with video or Flash in any way, then Soundtrack Pro may not be the right option for you. Check out Audition instead.

Deciding Whether to Upgrade

Let's talk realistically about the *U* word for a moment. It's true — upgrading your software requires a lot of patience. If you want to upgrade your studio and the sound of your podcast and are caught up in the complexities of production, that patience is hard to find. You'll want to install the new digital audio workstation as soon as possible, and then begin the arduous process of figuring how everything works in this new application so you lose as little production time as possible. Before making that online purchase or heading to the cash register with credit card in hand, take a moment to consider the features this investment carries with it.

- What will this new application bring to your podcast?

- Will its features help or hinder your production — enhance or confuse the way you work?

- How easy or intuitive will this interface be in comparison to your original DAW application?

Remember that what you invest in your podcast — finances, time, and effort — should suit the demands of your podcast. Don't saddle yourself with a big investment and learning curve just because "all the cool podcasters are using it, too."

Creating a Quiet, Happy Place

Practice 12

Podcasting is all about the moment, about the spontaneity of life, and about the world around us. Ambient noise, particularly in soundseeing tours, is not only welcome but also encouraged. Podcasters set out with every episode to capture a slice of life or give the audience a peek at their lifestyle or environment, if the show is more formal in nature. Podcasts about writing continue their discussion of world-building or character development as birds chirp or dogs bark happily in the backyard. Cooking podcasts press on in their recipes as the radio plays softly in the background. The ambient noise bleeding into a podcast becomes less of a distraction and more of an added dimension to your production.

Atmosphere like this works for some podcasts, but not for all. Ambient noise is generally unwelcome in, say, podiobooks, formal business presentations, and news reports. The content in podcasts like these would lose some of its momentum and impact if distractions — such as the garbage truck, the neighbor's kids playing in the sprinkler, or a lawnmower — make it into the recording.

So now you take on one of the biggest challenges for podcasters — controlling the sound that comes into your home studio. Piece of cake, right?

Well, you can't make batter without breaking a few eggs first. . . .

Common Sources of Unwanted Ambient Noise

Practice 4 briefly talks about creating a *noise floor*. No, we're not talking about carpeting here (though that may be part of the solution). A studio's recording quality is judged by its lack of sound and echo; the *floor,* in this case, is defined as how much ambient noise is filtered out of a studio so all that remains, audio-wise, is voice, instruments, or both.

When upgrading an office to a recording studio, podcasters aim for the *floor* — as low a noise floor as possible. Deadening the room — depending on what your indoor sources of ambient noise are (computers, office accessories, household pets, whatever) — can be an easy process, but other sources of outside noise might also come into play.

Unwanted noise can be created by anything, at any time, by anyone. Even something as harmless as a stress ball can make noise if passed casually from hand to hand (or if it rolls off a desk and strikes the carpet).

Common sources of unwanted ambient noise bleeding into a podcast are described in the following sections.

Planes, trains, and automobiles

The "quietest room" in your house may suddenly reveal that your neighborhood is not as quiet as you initially thought. Traffic of all kinds can make enough noise to be picked up by your microphone; and if you can hear that noise in your headphones, then most assuredly your audience will hear it as well.

Don't be surprised if you suddenly notice the commuter train's horn from 7 miles away, the air traffic of the regional airport 7 miles away, and the international airport over 20 miles away. You may also notice passing automobile traffic, especially trucks, school buses, and the occasional hip-hop/rap/metal fan who has the bass turned up too high. The low-frequency intensity of that noise sends it right through walls, where it can creep into your recording.

Creature comforts

Podcasters on the whole are able to stay in great shape. How, you ask? Simple — during the summer, they sweat off unwanted pounds because the air-conditioning system is disabled during recording sessions. Not only is the air conditioning cut off, but any ceiling fans are turned off as well. The little things that make life easy (and comfortable) can make podcasting very hard. No matter where you locate your home studio, the washer and dryer,

dishwasher, shower, and plumbing can make your home or apartment ping, groan, creak, trickle, or pop while the mics are up and recording.

Children

Well, people in general can cause noise issues as they're outside enjoying the sunny weather, grilling sausages for the barbecue, or hoisting a soda or microbrew with friends to toast a baseball victory. Just as the heavy bass of a large vehicle can bleed into your audio, the high shrill of children at play easily slips through walls, windows, and any other barriers. (What is it about kids and screaming? Even those of us who are parents still don't understand that!) So if the weather is particularly sunny outside or you see the neighbors inflating a moon bounce in the backyard for their kid's birthday party, you might want to reconsider recording.

Computer equipment and accessories

The new Windows and Mac machines, even with their jacked-up and tricked-out processors, are whisper-silent. These state-of-the-art scream machines of number-crunching capabilities are extremely cool . . . but unless you're in the market for a new computer, you are podcasting with a computer that is far from the consistent state of stealth mode.

Your computer may seem to be developing an unfriendly form of artificial intelligence — waiting for that key moment in your podcast (be it an affected pause or dramatic tension) to kick in the fans and stay on until you decide, "We're done until the fan is done." Older computers need to stay cool; it's a fact of technology. Along with the computers, external drives also need ways of beating the heat. Any computer accessory reliant on fans or motors of any kind (and that covers just about everything) offers a risk of creating noise. While hardly as sudden or intermittent as children at play or the passing UPS truck, the noise is constant and can be a distraction.

Much like the unassuming stress ball, some noise can be managed. Eliminated completely? Maybe not. But managed? Absolutely. Reducing the noise enough so the microphone does not pick up the sound or eliminating the noise with audio-dampening tricks is very possible. It's all a matter of strategy.

The Podcaster's Feng Shui

From the land of silk, tea, and really cool Jackie Chan and Jet Li movies comes the (peaceful) art of *Feng Shui,* defined by the *Oxford Dictionary* as "a system of laws considered to govern spatial arrangement and orientation in relation to the flow of energy, and whose favorable or unfavorable effects are taken into account when siting and designing buildings."

According to the laws of Feng Shui, everything follows these laws — and if you obey them, you enjoy a much healthier life. We didn't really grasp how much this discipline works until we applied it to our podcasts.

So when it comes to a good recording environment and a podcaster's personal energy management, obey Feng Shui. It's the law. . . .

Relocating your computer

Okay, suppose your computer hasn't yet made it onto the list of noise generators — until the minute after you upgrade the microphone and headphones of your studio. Now you discover it's making quite the racket. How do you remedy this?

Easy. Find the closest closet in your home office.

While some podcasters (such as Nebula winner James Patrick Kelly and superstar Scott Sigler) take advantage of their own walk-in closets by recording in them, you can simply move your computer in there, as shown in Figure 12-1. You may need to invest in 15-foot (or longer) cables for your DVI or VGA monitors, USB devices, and FireWire devices. You can find these extensions at any retail computer

• **Figure 12-1: One way to reduce noise: Isolate the computer from the recording area. Here the computer hangs out in the office closet.**

 Make sure you close the closet door before recording, as well as *open* the closet door after your recording session is done. Heat can build up in and around your computer, and although the computer may be in a cooler location now, the tight confines of a closet can warm up quickly. So to avoid any overheating issues or fire hazards, make sure you open the closet door after recording ends.

If your office does not have a closet or storage area, consider investing in an extension cable and moving your computer to a corner opposite of where the mic and mixer are located. Or if you're in a small alcove of a one bedroom-and-study apartment, put the computer outside the study.

Before you ask: Yes, if you need to swap out DVDs or CDs or any other removable media, you will have to get out of your chair and walk over to the computer. Is that a hassle? Actually, no. It gets you out of the chair and gets blood flowing back into your legs, for starters.

Reducing your desk accessories

Before Tee plunged into podcasting, his desk was a collection of knick-knacks ranging from New Age to flat-out geeky. There was also a tech corner full of external drives and almost no flat surface.

Shortly after making his third episode of *Morevi,* he cleared off the desk — and immediately noticed a difference in the recording quality.

The habit of having a variety of gadgets and gizmos within reach is convenient, but fidgeting with whatever widget is in reach can be noisier than you think. When you relocate the computer, relocate the collection of external drives as well, which should help minimize the additional noise from them. You can easily rest your external drives on top of the computer's housing, or invest in a small shelf unit and store the drives there.

Keeping your desk clutter-free and sticking to only what you need for podcasting will give you a more manageable and noise-free environment to work in.

Well, maybe this isn't a secret — but it's definitely an idea. Some podcasters who don't have a closet for their noisy computers often do have a wide, two-level shelf unit. The computer is situated underneath the shelf that holds external drives; the top shelf above the drive remains empty. When they're ready to record, the podcasters cover the entire shelf unit with a comforter — deadening the sound. As with the closet door, that's temporary. When the recording session is done, the comforter is removed.

Trying a "comforting" solution

When Tee relocated his studio to the basement, he had to consider where to put the recording gear and in what direction the recordist should face. After figuring out those two issues (and establishing the direction of the desk), it was time to put the curtain rod in place.

These particular draperies, however, were not intended to keep sunlight out (because the only window in this room was behind the recordist); they were meant to absorb sound. The curtain rod was used to suspend three comforters in front of the recordist. This idea (illustrated in Figure 12-2) comes from podcasters Paul Fischer and Martha Holloway of Dancing Cat Studios (http://www.dancingcat studios.com) who effectively deadened a second-story room of their townhome with two small comforters.

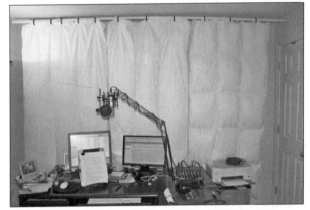

• **Figure 12-2: Comforters help deaden the sound of the home studio Tee records from.**

So how does this work? Well, when you record in a room with only carpeting for sound control and very little (or nothing) adorning the walls, you may notice that your voice sounds hollow. There may even be a slight echo in the room when you record. The hollow sound is *reverb* (the natural equivalent of the familiar echo effect produced by an amplifier or an amplified musical instrument); that brief echo is produced by *reflection* (sound waves bouncing off hard surfaces like light off a mirror). As you speak, the sound waves you produce go past the microphone and bounce off the walls and other reflective surfaces in the room; the more hard surfaces, the more reflection. Hanging comforters in front of your recording rig puts up a soft barrier that catches the sound waves. The fabric and stuffing soak up what would otherwise be potential reflection or reverb — essentially stopping the waves there and reducing the ambient noise around you.

Timing Is Everything

Something to consider before you record is the time of day you're recording. During the summer, in particular in the afternoon or early-evening hours (and on Saturdays), you may find that more people are out and about. Kids are playing in backyards. Cookouts are happening all around you. Teenagers are working on the latest skateboarding or inline skating stunt as seen on the *X-Games*. With that much activity in your area at this time of day, perhaps it isn't the best time for recording.

In many neighborhoods, Friday and Saturday nights (all year 'round) tend to be bad times to record. In a word, the issue is *traffic.* Whether it's people going to and from the happening party in the neighborhood, or people breezing (and thumping) through on their way somewhere, cars will be coming and going well into the wee-small hours of the morning.

Anytime is a good time to edit, of course, but for recording, listen for some good times in the day when activity around your home, apartment, or office is at its lowest. You might luck out and find a few pockets of time on a weekday evening or a quiet Sunday afternoon that are perfect for recording. Try to schedule your recording around these times, but keep your mind — and your schedule — open for opportunities. (That's another reason to keep your recording area neat and your equipment ready to run — you can seize the quiet!)

 Before you consider doing an early-morning recording session, however, be forewarned about that bird who's up at the crack of dawn to get the worm. It's not easy to record when you have feathered backup singers chiming in their two chirps' worth.

Patience, Patience, Patience: Waiting Out the Noise

We've been taking a look at all kinds of ways to soundproof your office without major renovations.

All right, maybe not sound*proof* your office so much as make it *noise-resistant;* you can reduce the noise enough to give your podcast as close-to-studio quality sound as you can get. You can move your computer, move your office, or hang comforters to deaden the ambient noise creeping into your podcast. But of all the different options covered in this practice, there is one more option — definitely the most cost-effective method covered here, but not necessarily economic when it comes to time — to consider:

Wait out the noise.

When it comes to passing traffic, be it air or ground, your microphone and headphone combination will pick up the approaching sound. The moment you hear the offending ambient noise, stop speaking. Leave the recorder going, but you (and your co-hosts, if involved) stop speaking. When the noise subsides, pick up from a logical point in your discussion, and continue forward.

When Tee was asked why it took so long to produce a single episode of the *Billibub Baddings* podcast, he always replied that two things caused the most delay: post-production time and waiting for school buses to pass by. There will be some ambient-noise issues that you might not be able to wait out (such as people walking around on the other floor, parties next door, household appliances, and computer fans), but when it comes to intermittent sounds (internal plumbing in a house, air traffic, ice cream trucks, little sonic surprises that normally take less than a minute to go away), the most cost-effective way of dealing with these issues is to simply stop talking, wait the sound out, and then continue. Not only is this a thrifty way of dealing with ambient noise, but these points are very easy to edit out because they appear as gaps of silence in your recording session's waveform. And your recording level stays consistent, which makes the edits a lot less obvious.

Practice 13

Eliminating Ambient Noise

The quest for the perfect home studio is a challenge that many podcasters attempt to conquer after the monkey that is *audio* grabs hold and finds a good grip. True, some podcasters simply don't care about things like ambient noise, and they record regardless of the air conditioning, the dogs barking outside, or the like. Other podcasters solve the issue of a quiet environment with a recording setup in a walk-in closet (as described in Practice 12). And then some ambitious ones invest in acoustic tiles, remove the wall between a guest room and an office, and create a mega-studio worthy of professional productions.

Sometimes you can find the solutions in a single piece of hardware or an unassuming filter in Audition or Soundtrack Pro. It all depends on the approach you adopt for reducing noise in your recording sessions.

Removing Unwanted Noise with a Noise Gate

In Practices 4 and 12, we talk about achieving a *noise floor,* the sound of a room after steps are taken to filter out ambient noise, leaving only voice, instruments, or both with little or no echo.

Hardware is available that gives podcasters the ability to tone down some of this ambient noise. In Practice 12, we recommend hanging up comforters, finding pockets of quiet time, and trying to take advantage of every acoustical trick in the book — but your recording may still struggle and long for that noise floor. This is why podcasters choose to invest in a *noise gate* — a piece of hardware (usually included with a *compressor,* which we talk about next) or a filter included with audio-editing software that removes noise bleeding into microphones.

The best way to think of how a noise gate works is to imagine your studio as a fortress. To keep an invading audio signal out, you have a gate that closes automatically when sound of a particular decibel level is detected. Your microphone and recording equipment record absolute silence while the gate is closed. When you resume talking, the gate swings open, allowing live audio into the microphone.

This is a pretty simple, tech-free analogy behind the function of a noise gate and how it works. If you want to find out more about gates, compressors, limiters, and how they all fit into the grand scheme of podcasting, take a look at *Home Recording For Musicians For Dummies,* 2nd Edition by Jeff Strong (Wiley). Jeff features detailed and easy-to-follow explanations of how gates and compressors work, what they do, and how to best set them for your needs. While his book is geared primarily for musicians, the recording principles remain the same; they apply to podcasting without fail.

Setting up

Before you apply the noise gate to your recording equipment, you need to incorporate the *compressor,* which is part of the component featured in this practice. In this practice, we work with the Samson Technologies S-com Stereo Compressor (shown in Figure 13-1). This particular model functions both as a compressor and a noise gate. (While noise gates and compressors can be purchased as standalone components, many compressors are also built to work as noise gates.)

 A bewildering array of hardware is out there, so the steps offered here are for setting up and working with one particular make and model: the Samson S-com. While this compressor may look identical to others (such as the Alesis 3630 or the Rane DC22), they may not hook up in the same way as the Samson S-com. We have tried to make the steps here as broad and generic as possible to fit compressors of all kinds — but always defer to your compressor's user manual if you have questions.

• **Figure 13-1: Samson's S-com Stereo Compressor also offers an expander, gate, and limiter, all in one unit.**

The compressor's purpose in a recording setup is to help normalize levels and prevent *clipping* (where power output of an amp exceeds the speaker's power, and the audio is abruptly cut off — clipped) when capturing louder-than-usual audio. Along with setting limits for the loud sounds, compressors can also improve softer dB sound quality. What you'll be doing with *this* compressor is taking advantage of its built-in noise gate and reducing the ambient noise in your studio.

In this section, you go through the process of connecting a compressor that also offers the options of an expander, a gate, and a limiter.

 In this practice, we connect the S-com to an Alesis MultiMix-8 FireWire mixer board. As we stated earlier about the differences from compressor to compressor, this setup procedure may have some subtle differences from the one your specific equipment needs. When you're hooking up unfamiliar equipment, *always* have the user manuals (for both mixer and compressor) on hand to aid in the installation process.

Here's how to connect a compressor to a mixer:

1. **Make sure the mixer is turned off before connecting the compressor to it.**

   Having the computer running during this process is fine.

2. **Plug the compressor into an electrical outlet.**

   Don't turn on the compressor yet. Get everything hooked up before you turn the components on.

3. **Connect the compressor to the mixer.**

   You may need to consult your mixer's user manual to check to see whether your mixer has *inserts* (connectors for quarter-inch jacks).

   If your mixer *does* have inserts . . .

1. *Make sure you have a standard insert (two mono connectors to one stereo connector) quarter-inch-jack cable, male-to-male.*

   Just ask for *insert cables* at a music store or Radio Shack; the folks there should know what you want.

2. *Connect the stereo plugs into the mixer insert port on the channel through which you want to run the compressor.*

3. *Connect the two mono cables into the available unbalanced input and output connections on the compressor.*

   The compressor may refer to the red cable as the *tip* and the white cable as the *ring*.

If your mixer *does not* have inserts . . .

1. *Confirm that your mixer has auxiliary sends.*

   On the Alesis MultiMix-8, we're using Aux Send A.

2. *Use a mono-to-mono quarter-inch jack cable, male-to-male, and plug it into Aux Send A.*

   This cable is shown in Figure 13-2; it's available at any music store or Radio Shack.

3. *Plug the other end of the cable into an available unbalanced input connection on the compressor.*

   For this example, our available unbalanced input is Channel 1.

4. *Take a second mono-to-mono quarter-inch jack cable, male-to-male, and connect it to the channel with a quarter-inch input jack.*

   In the case of the Alesis, we're using Channel 5.

5. *Connect the other end of the cable to the unbalanced output on the compressor.*

   Again, this is Channel 1 on the Alesis.

The male-to-male cables discussed in this exercise are *not* part of the compressor when you begin pulling stuff out of the box. If you are rummaging through the contents and reviewing the box contents as featured in the owner's manual, you won't find some of the cables mentioned here. You need to take a trip to your closest music store or Radio Shack.

4. **On your mixer, find the channel strip for the microphone you want to use with the compressor. In that strip, you should see a knob or slider for *Aux A*. Turn it up all the way to its maximum setting.**

For the Alesis MultiMix, this knob is red and labeled *Aux A Pre*. The maximum setting reads *10 dB*. The setting of the auxiliary lets you control how much of the mic's audio signal runs through the compressor. Do you want half the audio's signal to pass through the compressor (50%), a slight adjustment of the incoming audio (25%), or all the mic signal (maximum setting) running through the compressor?

For the example, we want to run the whole microphone signal through it.

5. **Turn the compressor on.**

6. **Turn the mixer on.**

You may need to check the user manual for your compressor model (and that manual is going to be your best friend, so keep it close). After you've turned everything on, make sure the controls are at the *neutral setting* (or *default* if you want to put it in computer terms) where the compressor is operating but not doing anything to the signal.

Setting your gate

When the compressor is connected to your mixer and both components are running, it's time to set your gate. This is, by no means, your one-and-only solution — but it is a start.

Follow these steps to set your gate:

1. **Turn down the fader on the channel that your mic is directly plugged into.**

For the example, this channel is Channel 1, where the mic (in this case, an AKG Preception 200) is plugged into the Alesis.

2. **Turn up the fader on the channel you have the compressor plugged into.**

If everything is working properly, you should have levels on both your mixer and the compressor, and you should hear your voice.

So, using the Alesis setup, how is it that your voice is coming through Channel 5 but your mic is plugged into the (now silent) Channel 1?

Figure 13-2 shows how the compressor is connected to Channel 5 of the Alesis MultiMix. That is where the signal is coming out (as in unbalanced *output*). The signal is coming in (as in unbalanced *input*) through the Alesis' Auxiliary A, the auxiliary that you have just told Channel 1 to send all of Channel 1's signal through.

Get it? Got it? Good. (Thanks, Danny Kaye!)

3. **Look at your compressor's control panel and find the Expander/Gate section of your compressor. Press the button marked Gate to put the Expander/Gate into Gate mode.**

When the button isn't lit up, the Expander/Gate is in Expander mode (discussed later in this practice). When it is lit up, you're in Gate mode.

4. **Use the knob labeled Trigger to adjust the *decibel trigger* (the sound level above which you're telling the gate "allow audio over this decibel level through") for the gate. Set your trigger point by talking into your mic as you normally would while podcasting; monitor yourself with headphones.**

• **Figure 13-2: Even though Channel 1, where the mic resides, is turned down, you can still hear yourself as you're utilizing the Auxiliary Sends and Channel 5.**

When setting your trigger, don't cut off the A/C or silence any other devices (ceiling fans, second computers, whatever) that may be making noise. Leave everything running and then *slowly* turn the Trigger knob up. At one point, you may hear an *audio flutter* — the sound of ambient noise and silence. This dB level is right on the cusp of what will and will not trigger the gate. Go on and read something — a newspaper, the owner's manual to the compressor, anything that you are comfortable with — and play with the Trigger settings.

What you should notice here is that in between your thoughts and your voice, background noise disappears. This is because you are telling the compressor's noise gate to remain closed until audio at a certain dB level is detected. The softer the noise, the less likely the microphone picks it up.

Right now the audio situation feels extreme — either you get your voice coming in (along with the ambient noise) or extreme silence — and you may notice that when your volume dips to a certain level, the microphone doesn't pick up the sound. That's because your voice is under the trigger point you set. You can either adjust the way you speak or fine-tune the settings of your noise gate (which is next).

What we are about to do in the next section is one of the hardest things to get right. When noise gates are not set properly, the end result is worse (and more distracting) than a podcast with ambient noise rumbling in the background. If the trigger is set on the cusp of that earlier-mentioned audio flutter, that can create an odd skipping sound in your audio. If your gate is set too high, you may actually draw attention to the ambient noise behind you as the silence between points of audio are so extreme. Be patient with yourself, have something to read so you can listen to what you sound like coming through the gate, and give yourself some time to set levels and be happy with the end results.

Adjusting the gate

At present, your gate is active on its most basic settings. You now have to adjust those settings to what you want for your podcast, and here's where you explore the other features of your compressor.

An *expander* does the opposite of a limiter: Any audio *below* the dB level set by the engineer is cancelled out. In effect, an expander makes soft sounds softer. The difference between an expander and a noise gate is that the expander still allows the audio to be picked up. The noise gate removes the sound completely.

Upon reading that the noise gate removes sound and the expander simply reduces it, you may think it's best never to use the expander. Well, that depends on the settings of your compressor and what happens during the actual podcast. If your voice goes soft, the noise gate may shut it out completely; the expander just filters out the noise you don't want while preserving the softer vocal nuances of your podcast. Just remember: *Absolute* does not always mean *better*.

Your compressor also works as a *limiter*. A limiter does exactly what it says: It limits the peaks in audio. Therefore, if your volume reaches above 10 dB, the limiter stops the signal. Not all compressors have limiters built into them, but it's a good feature to look for when you're shopping for compressors.

You can also use settings of your compressor to gain more control over your noise gate. For example, the Samson's S-com offers these settings:

- **Threshold:** The Threshold setting looks for a maximum dB level that you set. After the audio signal reaches that level, the compressor's volume reduction sets in. If the threshold setting is high, reduction is never triggered. If the threshold is low, any signal triggers the reduction.

✔ **Ratio:** The Ratio controls the proportion of gain reduction needed against a signal. For example, if you set your ratio to 4:1 (the halfway point on most compressors) and your signal crosses the level set using the threshold, audio 4 dB above that ceiling only produces 1 dB past the threshold at output.

✔ **Attack time:** After a strong audio signal runs through gain reduction, *attack time* is the time your audio takes to return to normal levels.

✔ **Release time:** *Release time* is the opposite of attack time — that is, the time your audio takes to return to normal after a signal has come in *under* the threshold level. For spoken-word projects, faster release times are preferred.

 Some of the latest compressors reaching the market have an *Auto Attack and Release* function: The compressor adjusts attack and release times in real time, according to the dynamics of the incoming audio signal. It's a neat concept — but bear in mind that if your podcast plays with voice inflections and various levels of intensity, an automatic approach may not be the best option here. It does, however, allow your podcast some audio flexibility. If you know you're going to have voices of varying dynamics, different emotional levels, and moments of variable intensity, then fixed attack and release times may not show off those qualities to the best advantage. Still, experiment and play with this new option if your compressor offers it. Automatic attack and release may be a workable solution for your podcast.

Grab some material to read aloud and position your mic. Then you can put some final touches on the compressor's gate. Here's how that process looks for the S-com:

1. **Look for the Release button. There should be an indicator that shows a setting for Fast and Slow. If it's set to Slow, change that setting to Fast and take a listen between the two. Select the setting you prefer.**

This option is different from the Release knob on your compressor. *This* release is specifically for the Gate mode:

▶ If the Gate release is slow, the return to absolute silence is gradual.

▶ If the setting is fast, the Gate "closes" quickly.

2. **Look for the knob labeled Threshold. Begin increasing the Threshold level as you talk into your mic, and listen for a healthy balance between the silence and your voice.**

3. **Set your attack time at just past the 50 mSec mark, or at a level you find comfortable for recording your podcast.**

 The attack time is for louder dB levels; if your voice isn't that powerful and your audio isn't all that strong, keep the Attack below 50 mSec.

4. **Set your release time at its lowest setting.**

Because your podcast is primarily voice (unless you have live musicians in-studio for a visit), you may not need slower release times, so set this at its lowest setting for the fastest release time.

At present, you should have a compressor normalizing your audio signal in real time. You may want to tweak and adjust your settings for a while before you feel comfortable with them. After you have your settings the way you want them, the compressor is much like working with an automated mixing board — you won't need to fiddle or tweak. Your audio limits are set, and now the compressor takes care of the rest.

Now you move on to the next microphone.

Yes, the real shock about all this is that you have effectively applied the compressor to one channel — only one. If you want to have *two* microphones running through your compressor, you must repeat these steps for the compressor's next available channel — and the settings are different for each make and model of compressor. Some compressors handle only one channel at a time; the Samson S-com can handle two microphones at once.

We've focused on condenser microphones as our in-studio microphones of choice, but one disadvantage of condenser microphones (compared to dynamic mics) is that *condensers cannot plug directly into compressors*. (Dynamic mics can.) If you decide you have to plug a condenser mic directly into a compressor, you have two options, and both do the same thing: provide power. Remember that condenser mics need it — usually in the form of phantom power (more about that in Practice 10) — to run. You can either install a battery inside the mic, or buy an external power source that connects between the mic and the compressor.

Reducing Noise in Post-Production

Perhaps you don't have an unlimited budget right now (as many podcasters will attest without hesitation), so a compressor may be temporarily out of reach for your ever-growing studio. However, when you listen to your recording sessions, you realize that even after all that hard work to eliminate noise (hanging comforters off curtain rods, banishing the computer to the office closet, or recording only when the noise in your neighborhood is down to a dull roar), you still have a hint of distraction: just enough ambient noise to bother you.

Now the good news: Applications such as Audition and Soundtrack (shown in Figure 13-3) come with fully working compressors, noise gates, limiters, and expanders. A whole digital toolbox awaits on your call to work a little post-production magic.

Open your Noise Gate filter in Audition or Soundtrack, and you see many of the same options discussed here. Open the compressor, and you see features such as Threshold, Ratio, Attack, and Release — all of which behave identically to their hardware counterparts.

We use Adobe Audition or Soundtrack Pro for this portion of the practice. The first order of business, however, is to find the file and preview it in the DAW of your choice:

1. **From the book's DVD, import the audio file** `Billi-Ch14-Cabbie.aif` **into either Audition or Soundtrack Pro.**

2. **Press the spacebar to play the clip.**

   Because the loop playback is active, the clip of the audio loops.

3. **Open the Noise Gate window in whichever digital audio workstation (DAW) you currently have running.**

The voice talent for this audio file was recorded in a room with very little acoustic dampening, so you want to use the Noise Gate in your software to remedy that problem. The following sections show you how to improve the sound in Audition and in Soundtrack.

Using Audition

With Audition running, we run this example through the built-in compressor filter. To improve this audio in post-production, we perform the following steps that work like gangbusters for us:

1. **Drag the audio file to the main multitrack window, drop it there, and then select the Edit mode to edit the selected audio clip.**

2. **Go to the Effects panel (nested behind the Files panel), expand Amplitude, and double-click the Dynamic Processor option.**

   Alternatively, go to the Application Menu and choose Effects⇨Amplitude⇨Dynamic Processor.

3. **From the presets, select Noise Gate @ 10 dB for your starting point of adjustments.**

   If you want to hear the audio as you change it, click the Play button in this interface.

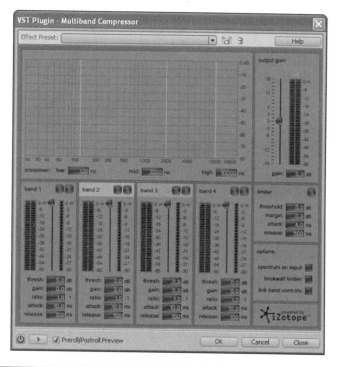

• **Figure 13-3:** Audition (top) and Soundtrack (bottom) have built-in compressors that work with the audio after it's recorded.

4. **Click the Traditional option in the Dynamics Processor and set the following:**

Under Ratio for Expand: 6

Under Ratio for Compress: 6

Under Threshold for Expand: –10 dB

Under Threshold for Compress: –10 dB

Under Attack/Release:

  Gain Processor

  Output: 0

  Attack: 1 ms

  Release: 2000 ms

Under Level Detector:

  Gain Processor

  Output: 0

  Attack: 1 ms

  Release: 2000 ms

5. **Click OK.**

6. **Still in the Effects panel nested behind the Files panel, expand Amplitude and double-click the Multichannel Compressor option.**

Or go to the Application Menu and choose Effects⇨Amplitude⇨Multichannel Compressor.

7. **From the Compressor's presets, select Hiss Reduction as your starting point.**

8. **Toggle the Limiter button (located to the right of the Compressor window), and then set the following:**

Threshold: –10.0 dB

Margin: –5 dB

Attack: 20.0 ms

Release: 50–0 ms

Output Gain: –5 dB

9. **Click OK.**

10. **Toggle your audio changes on and off; listen to the difference.**

When you're editing audio in this manner, keep in mind that you're editing destructively; when you apply the changes you've chosen, you can't revert to the original file.

Using Soundtrack Pro

If you are using Soundtrack Pro, follow these steps to take advantage of your built-in compressor filter:

1. **Drag the audio file to the main multitrack window, drop it there, and double-click it — or just double-click the file in the Browser menu.**

2. **Choose Process⇨Effects ⇨Dynamics⇨Noise Gate.**

3. **From the Noise Gate interface, set the following:**

Threshold: –10 dB

Reduction: –15 dB

Attack: 78 ms

Release: 10000.0 ms

Hysteresis: –3.0 dB

4. **Click Apply.**

5. **Choose Process⇨Effects ⇨Dynamics⇨ Compressor.**

6. **From the Compressor interface, set the following:**

Threshold: –11.0 dB

Attack: 1.0 ms

Release: 2000.0 ms

Gain: –9.5 dB

Ratio: 6.6:1

7. **Click Apply.**

8. **Toggle your audio changes on and off; listen to the difference.**

Using built-in noise-reduction filters: Too good to be true?

With post-production noise gates and compressors, you have a built-in option to deaden echo and reduce some ambient noise that has bled into your recording sessions. Or you can adjust the dynamics of audio signals sent in by others for your podcast.

You can add these filters destructively to audio sources, or you can apply the noise gate and compressor to the track itself, adjusting the ambient noise evident in a clip in a non-destructive manner.

You can find the Noise Reduction filter in Soundtrack under Process. In Audition, the filter is under the Restoration submenu of Effects. (Both filters are shown in Figure 13-4.)

While both DAW applications accomplish the same goal, Audition and Soundtrack go about attaining that goal in two different ways:

- With Soundtrack Pro, you control the noise threshold, adjust the amount of reduction to apply to the audio, and tell the filter to preserve either the bass or the treble.

- With Audition, you create or use a *sound profile* from a built-in library. From here, the Noise Reduction filter adjusts the results to fit both that profile and your changes.

When using Noise Reduction filters, you want to avoid overcompensation. Too much noise reduction in post can muffle the sounds you want to keep or create *artifacts* — unwanted audio side effects, such as a clipping or a flanger-like effect on your voice that's usually associated with too much compression in your final mp3. While the Noise Reduction filters *can* improve the quality of dodgy audio, they can't turn lead into gold. Use them with an alert ear and a clear head.

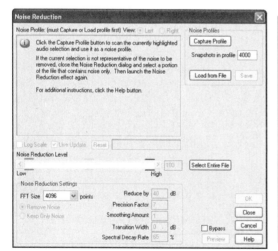
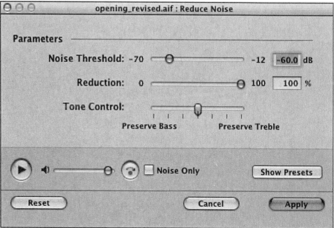

• **Figure 13-4: Audition (left) and Soundtrack (right) offer noise reduction, but each has a different way of achieving the same goal.**

Finally, accept that the powerful tools technology provides aren't miracle workers. Sometimes you will have unwanted noise in your audio. Ambiance happens.

The Best Noise-Reduction Device: You!

There's a reason why it's called noise reduction — realistic expectations. Noise *reduction* does not mean noise *removal*. You cannot have a fan running or the vents open in your office and expect the noise-reduction features of Audition or Soundtrack Pro to pick them up and say, "Not a worry. Let me take care of those for you." Noise-reduction devices — compressors, noise gates, and filters — do not discriminate between you and the offending ambient noise. It's *all* noise to the hardware and software.

Your best option for noise *removal* is to create a quiet, happy recording place for yourself. The devices and filters we cover in this practice are tools to help you create the ultimate home studio, but they won't do it for you. Some of the sharpest wits and most professional voices in podcasting — the likes of Leann Mabry, Phil Rossi, and George Hrab — all use compressors and noise-reduction tools in both the recording and in post-production, but what these podcasters share in common are the steps they take to create a near-ideal recording session. Read on.

Take control of what you can

Before recording, listen to what's around you. If the air conditioner is running, turn it off. Fans, space heaters, or ionizers should also be powered down. Now listen for any other devices in your office that make noise — external drives, clocks, fluorescent lighting, or other office accessories. The only thing left to do is check the sound quality of the room. Is there still too much echo in the room? Do you need to adopt the comforter-and-curtain-rod trick mentioned in Practice 12? Before investing in new hardware or

exploring the more obscure software options, work on getting your recording environment as quiet as possible. Basics first.

Noise reduction in recording versus noise reduction in post-production

Compressors, expanders, and noise gates can help reduce the unwanted ambient noise of your recordings, but they can't magically project Maxwell Smart's "Cone of Silence" around you while you're recording.

"What, Chief?"

We said, these devices are *not* built to make your recording environment *perfectly silent!*

Your goal, as you improve the sound of your podcast, is to create a quiet-as-possible recording environment for you and your show. The compressor hardware helps you with that before you hit Record — but the cleaner the audio you record, the easier you can edit it later in post. Post-production should be a time for final touches, flourishes, and the last-minute edits, but many podcasters find that the lion's share of their work has somehow wound up here. They toil for hours to clean up audio from other sources or spruce up their own recordings.

Does this mean you can't improve your recordings in post-production if your budget does not allow for a Samson S-com Stereo Compressor or similar unit? Sure, you can still improve the signal with software plug-ins and filters, but a lot of that work is taken care of already if you eliminate the noise *before* it reaches the microphone. The software can reduce any noise *left over* after you create your dead audio room, but keep in mind that the background noise isn't all these filters are working on. They also affect the voice in the foreground. It's all noise to them.

Filters are terrific tools, but they can't differentiate between your voice and the air conditioning. The best noise reduction is all that careful listening and preparation you do before a single syllable is recorded.

One-Take Wonders

Podcasting is all about the impulsive moments in life, the raw and unedited perspectives of hosts on the world around them. Life is captured in the moment, thoughts are from the heart and soul, and the listenership dives deep into the show host's id — all thanks to a podcast episode recorded in *one* masterful take.

Sure, easier said than done.

Recording in one take does sound as if you're throwing caution to the wind; and while podcasting is associated with audio productions peppered with stammers, flubs, and moments of brash honesty, a science is behind the spontaneity. Podcasts can be recorded in one take and can sound polished and refined. One-take recording takes a bit of planning, though, and some forethought before hitting that Record button.

And You're Recording! (Good Luck. You'll Need It.)

Simply sitting in front of a microphone, hitting the bright red button of your DAW (digital audio workstation), and talking is truly an affirmation of self-confidence. You're stating to yourself and to the world that your message is ready to be heard, and there is no need for show prep, editing, or even session planning. Just your voice and a microphone are all that's needed.

To accomplish this feat for five minutes — recording thoughts in a coherent manner — is something to be proud of, but try it for *ten* minutes, and it becomes a bit more daunting. Go ahead and give it a whirl. Fire up your studio or portable rig and try talking with no notes, no prep time, and no inhibition about something you're passionate about. Sports. Religion. Politics. Movies. Just try to *coherently* talk into a microphone for ten minutes off the top of your head. Hey, that's okay, we can wait. We'll be right here when you get back.

Welcome back. Your head hurts a little bit, doesn't it? And we wouldn't be surprised if your tongue feels like it's been lifting barbells. Trying to carry on a ten-minute unscripted conversation isn't easy, is it? Now maybe the thought "This is a lot easier when I'm out with friends . . ." or "Man, I can type out ten minutes of material on my blog easier than this . . ." might have crossed your mind, but podcasting isn't the same as a social gathering with friends or a sit-down at the blog where ten minutes pass by in a blink. This is, simply put, improv.

We're the first to agree that improvisation *of any kind* isn't easy. Improvisation and fast thinking may come easier to some than others, but even the brightest and most intelligent can't sit behind a mic and go on a whim. It's a challenge to sit behind your rig and produce a show in one take. It puts a great amount of pressure on you, especially if you haven't given yourself time to think through what you're talking about in this week's or this month's episode.

Recording a show in one take, however, is not impossible, as we explain next.

The Method in the One-Take Madness

No matter how brilliant you may think spontaneous podcasters sound, a science is behind what they do. Even these improvisational hosts themselves may not think they do anything special beyond firing up their recorders and going for it — but there is. No matter how basic or organized the method is, it's a method — a plan for what they're about to say.

So what *are* you going to say?

If you're working alongside a co-host or several hosts, the conversation tends to record a little better when you discuss the ideas and direction you want your podcast to follow *before* you start recording

that particular episode. Canadian podcasters Chris and Eliza do just that as part of their show prep for *Two Girls and a Podcast* (`http://twogirlsand apodcast.libsyn.com`; see Figure 14-1). Their show takes a cue from Jim Henson's legacy, *Sesame Street*, by "sponsoring" their various episodes with letters (D is for *Doctor Who*, S is for Summer Movies, and so on). The show then follows the topic with copious amounts of speculation on why Canadians get their science fiction at different intervals from their U.S. counterparts, what they are currently geeking over, and why *Stargate: Atlantis'* Rodney McKay (David Hewlett) isn't arrogant, just misunderstood.

Oh yeah, and there's giggling. Lots and lots *and lots* of giggling. (And for us, that's part of *Two Girls and a Podcast's* appeal.)

• **Figure 14-1: From Canada, Chris and Eliza keep the chat lively with their slice-of-geek-life offering, *Two Girls and a Podcast*.**

"We are very much the one-take recording podcasters," Elisa admits. "We would never intentionally record a show twice. 'Show prep' is one of us has an idea for a show, and we mention it to the other to see how they feel about talking about it. Some topics we can discuss right away; some need to be postponed until we are both up to speed."

The show's spontaneity comes in deciding not only what they talk about, but also *when* they talk about it. "Once decided, we don't overtalk the topic beforehand, usually just some points that we think we should discuss during the show. Sometimes we hit those points during recording, but oftentimes, we go in a different direction altogether."

Where *Two Girls . . .* succeeds so brilliantly is that with just an idea of what they want to talk about, Chris and Eliza create a charming half-hour chat that the world is invited to listen and even give feedback on through voicemail, blog comments, and e-mails. No script, no notes — just an understanding of the topic they need to stick to as best as they can (amidst the giggling, of course). On occasion they manage to surprise one another, but the surprises are in tune with the podcast; neither host tries to one-up or outdo the other. This show is a great exercise in host chemistry and teamwork, creating a delightful sit-down with two friends from the Great White North.

Working with notes and scripts

Perhaps the easiest way to make sure you get your message across in one take is to write down what you want to say, read it aloud a few times, and then record it.

Notes and scripts (discussed in detail in Practice 5) guarantee you that your thoughts are down on paper. If your notes or your script are detailed enough (but not *too* obsessively so), you shouldn't have a problem remembering what you want to say and how you want to say it. Then all that remains is for you to express it however you wish.

If you try to script your show, you're committing to a certain level of development and writing, and steering the course of the show. There's nothing wrong with scripting a podcast, but when you do, you face a large amount of pre-production work. Even if you save time by getting your podcast recorded in one take, you wind up investing more time in writing your episode.

 Writing show notes takes far less prep time than a fully scripted show, and these notes can be as detailed as you make them. While not as thought-out or developed as scripts, show notes can help you keep the show on track. They also give you room to improvise and explore tangents on the topic your current episode is about.

Pacing your podcast

Podcasting in one take can be tough when you're trying to get on the same train of thought with your show's co-host, but nailing that one take can feel even more daunting when the only voice in the room is yours. How do voices like Nicole Simon (http://usefulsounds.com), Mur Lafferty (http://murlafferty.com), and Dan Klass (http://thebitterestpill.com) manage to sound so good with only one take under their belts?

When you listen to solo podcasts, listen to how they sound when speaking. You may notice that their vocal patterns and pacing are, on the whole, very deliberate. Not slow, but deliberate. These podcasters take their normal, everyday speech cadence and relax their delivery by a second or two.

Recording at a deliberate pace offers many advantages. You may sound slower-than-normal when recording, but what you don't hear is that subconscious excitement — that podcaster's passion — creeping into your voice. This passion tends to tweak up your adrenaline levels; while subtle, it does affect your voice and diction. Slowing down your delivery improves diction, keeps you relaxed, and gives you a moment or two to think about what you want to say next.

Recording in segments

Another smart approach in one-take podcasting is to record your show in segments as opposed to one-take, beginning-to-end, 30-minute marathon recording sessions. For the earlier-mentioned podcasters, their shows — whether clearly by a title or going from one topic to another (simply by saying, "Something else I wanted to talk about . . .") — break up the podcast into individual sections.

In her writing-and-cultural podcast, *Whispers at the Edge* (`http://whispers.libsyn.com`), New Zealand author Philippa Ballantine offers a section called Pip's Picks, where she offers book reviews. In Mur Lafferty's *I Should Be Writing* (`http://ishould bewriting.com`), Mur features a section where she discusses what she has done to further her career, whether with agent queries or publisher submissions. (See Figure 14-2.) And then there is the popular "Whiskey Tango Foxtrot Moment" (from *The Survival Guide to Writing Fantasy*) where authors, agents, and publishers are asked, "What were you thinking when you did that?!"

• **Figure 14-2: Pip Ballantine's *Whispers at the Edge* (left) and Mur Lafferty's *I Should be Writing* (right) are writing podcasts that use show notes and segments to pace each episode.**

It may not seem exhausting, but recording nonstop for 20 minutes, 30 minutes, or (yikes!) an hour can tax you. Your brain is firing on all cylinders, and your voice hasn't let up since you hit that blinking red button. Instead of pushing yourself to an extreme limit or trying to complete the show in one massive, mammoth weeknight (or weekend afternoon) of recording, why not break your show into segments? Record 10 minutes here, and 10 minutes there. The post-production time is manageable, and you also leave room for promos (described in Practice 29) and listener-produced contributions.

By pacing the delivery and the production of your podcast, one-take recording is an easier feat to accomplish. Remember that no one, save for you, is keeping time. Find logical breakpoints in your show and use them to pace your delivery. From there, you can make the one-take podcasting happen.

Author, podcaster, and monotone voice-talent-extraordinaire Jack Mangan, in his appropriately titled *Deadpan*, has one-take podcasting down to a science. He is able to consistently produce a 30-to-40 minute show without breaking a sweat. His two-part secret: (a) do the show in segments, and (b) incorporate listener contributions.

Jack's show segments are as various and random as his show's content. You never know what's coming at you with every new *Deadpan,* but when you hear the show segment's intro, you smile because you have an idea. Jack's vignettes include "Highbrow, Lowbrow" (a sophisticated moment of humor, coupled with a juvenile joke), "Unrelated Thought" (the unexpected left-field comment Jack has filed away at that particular moment), and "Interviews with Famous People" (where we hear Jack typing on a keyboard, a pause, and then more typing — comedy gold!). Jack also features listener content, ranging from serialized fiction to "The Contents of My Fridge," leaving Jack to provide vocal bridges from one segment to the next.

Between the contributions, his own segments, and a razor-sharp, bone-dry wit, Jack to produces a weekly podcast that is nothing short of brilliant . . . in a deadpan sort of way.

What You Gain with One-Take Recording

On the surface, podcasting in one take can seem out of the realm of possibility unless you hire seasoned, experienced radio personalities or one brilliant stand-up comedian for your show host. With a bit of planning, some rehearsal, and one deep breath (to start with, anyway), a podcast can happen in one take. Sure, there's some pressure to deliver once the mic goes hot, but it is possible.

But why subject you or your show hosts to that kind of stress? Recording in one take isn't as stressful (or as difficult) as it appears on the outside, listening in.

There are also some real perks:

- **Economy of time:** When you plan your episode, you have a roadmap to follow to reach your destination. That takes you roughly an hour, maybe two. Then, when you hit Record, you're off and running — pacing your delivery, taking your time to talk clearly about the episode's topic, and allowing yourself, your co-host, or your guest a little time for some fun on the podcast. Ten or 20 minutes later, that segment or episode is completed. Now comes the time invested in ID3 tagging (see Practice 25) and posting show notes. Your podcast is ready to go in three hours.

  One-take podcasting is a terrific way to produce multiple segments or shows in one day. If you need to economize your time, getting good at one-take podcasting can help you make the most of the time you have.

- **Spontaneity:** Podcasting, no matter how you edit in post-production, is all about the moment you record — capturing life in audio or video as it happens. The best way to keep that spontaneity — as heard in *Fear the Boot*, Christiana Ellis' *Hey Wanna Watch a Movie*, and Ronald D. Moore's *Battlestar Galactica* podcasts — is to hit Record and let fly. How brash and honest your podcast is when you post

it depends on how much you want to edit in post-production. However, even with minor cuts here and there, the moment between you and your show's hosts or special guests — or those moments of unabashed honesty spoken with your microphone taking it all in — are preserved for your listeners to appreciate.

 Take a moment, remember why you're doing this podcast, and then start talking. And allow yourself to enjoy the ride. The enjoyment comes out in your podcast, and your audience catches it from you.

- **Quick post-production work:** If you record an entire episode or show segment in one take, your final editing and post-production can be measured in fast mouse clicks. Drop in your introduction segment, position your latest episode accordingly, and then drop in your outro. Your podcast is now ready for exporting, compression, and tagging.

  If you want to check any segments for *ah*s and *um*s that might detract from the confidence of the podcast's message, then you can go back and remove them, along with any unnatural breaks or pauses in your podcast. Instead of requiring hours dedicated to editing, your podcast is prepped and ready for the final steps in a matter of minutes.

One-take podcasting is not a secret, but a skill — just like anything else in this medium. The professionals make it look easy, but even for them it isn't. How seasoned and experienced broadcasters, voice talent, actors, and comics make this process look as easy as taking a breath is they do just that: They take a breath. Give your episode (and yourself) a direction and have a little fun following that direction. After you get used to taking just a moment to think about what you're going to say before you hit Record, you'll probably find that one-take podcasting cuts your editing time dramatically, and you can produce segments and shows efficiently, even effortlessly.

Practice 15

Multiplicity: Recording Multiple Takes

In This Practice

- Getting the benefits of multiple takes
- Recording segments efficiently
- Rising to the demands of multiple takes

A little bit of editing goes a long, long way in podcasting. It's debated that once editing and post-production occur, the podcast *really isn't* a podcast. It's no longer that spontaneous, impulsive slice-of-life captured in audio, and nothing different from what you'll find in radio, television, or other mainstream media.

Why can't podcasting meet those standards?

Spontaneity, impulsiveness, and the "Fireside Chat" nature of podcasting can still be there; but depending on the project, you may need (or want) multiple takes to choose from. Sure, it's going to demand more work from you, and it will also test your editing skills, but the end result may be that your modest podcast turns the heads of industry pros and broadcast veterans.

Challenge yourself — see what your creativity can yield.

Multiple Takes: Variety Is the Spice of Life (And Podcasting)

We truly admire one-take podcasting (see Practice 14) — that incredible (and somewhat daunting) ability to hit Record and create a podcast. It really does take a fair amount of bravery, skill, and just plain *chutzpah* to pull off a podcast like that. In many instances — interviews, symposiums, seminars, and speaker panels, you name it — you're given no other option; you have to capture the audio as it's happening.

Some audio projects, though — training sessions, dramatizations, formal readings, and promotional pieces, for instance — may work best if you take the opportunity to record the same thought or expression with a different intent, correct a mispronunciation, or smooth a slip-up. Recording multiple takes provides you, the editor, with a wider variety of options for you to build your podcast on and around. The more raw material you have to pull from, the more polished and refined you can make your podcast.

Learning Tricks in the Take

The *take* (just so we're clear on what it is) is the recording of a segment followed by a marker in the audio or video, and then the segment is recorded again (sometimes in the same recording session) to see whether it can be done better or differently.

For example, if you're recording a scripted segment of a podcast and you read, "Now is the time for all good podcasters to stand up and be edited," that would be considered *Take One*. When you repeat the line a moment or two later, your emphasis on *good* as opposed to *podcasters* would be considered *Take Two*. And so on. You then compile these multiple takes into the final production; your editing makes the thoughts appear continuous and flowing.

 From Hollywood comes the concept of a *safety* take: An actor or a group of actors can shoot the same scene from various angles until the producers, directors, or both are satisfied. Even after a specific take feels right, a director — or in some *rare* cases, an actor — will ask for a safety. The scene is set up again and shot *one more time* as a backup in case anything is discovered that cannot be remedied (a lighting problem missed during shooting, background interference missed by the sound guy, whatever) in post-production. Podcasters, when working with multiple vocal talents, should consider safety takes. You may not need them, but in many cases, the safety takes outshine the takes you initially thought were right for the production.

One problem in working with multiple takes is knowing where one take stops and another one starts. Without proper markers in the audio, it can be easy to skim by two takes and leave a repeated phrase or expression in your editing wake *(D'oh!)*. Therefore, you need quick-and-easy ways to leave notes for yourself in your audio to let you know when a take begins and ends.

Audio and video podcasters have a few simple tricks up their sleeves that help make their editing sessions more efficient and productive, even with so much audio to listen to and evaluate. Here are some in-studio and on-location methods that may help you:

- ✔ **Pause for a moment.** In between takes, simply wait five to ten seconds and then resume your thought from the point of the mistake or from the beginning of the segment. In your audio, these quiet moments appear as long, flat lines. You can then easily hop between segments of audio, find the takes you prefer, and then compile them into the final version.

- ✔ **Create audio markers.** Some podcasters will snap fingers; others use a click of the tongue. You can even make a trip out to the local pet store and pick up a dog trainer's clicker, as shown in Figure 15-1. The intent of an audio marker, no matter what makes the sound, is to create sharp spikes in your audio. This makes searching for takes easy.

• **Figure 15-1: Dog clickers like these create spikes in audio, making edit points (and mistakes) easy to find.**

✔ **Record in segments.** You record a segment, mistakes and all, until you reach its end. You stop recording. You then begin recording again. In digital audio workstations such as Audition, Soundtrack, GarageBand, and Pyro, these sessions appear on your track as segments of audio — all independent of one another. You can then check each take for quality and compile them like a jigsaw puzzle.

 When you're doing multiple takes, there's nothing wrong with combining half of one segment and another half of a later segment. However, if you stumble in the middle of your take and then pick up the second take from the moment of the mistake, editing the segment becomes far more difficult. Words can easily run together, even with the best diction. If you're recording multiple takes, it's better to start from the beginning of the material (or a logical break between two phrases). The priority here is to make the edit practically unnoticeable; the goal is a smooth and continuous end result. Make your editing easier and find logical editing points within your takes.

The Demands of Multiple Takes

While you're working on giving your editor and your podcast a wide range of audio to choose from, it's time to consider the way this approach to podcasting changes your in-studio procedures. Editing needs change dramatically between the one-take podcast and what you're doing now, but that's only a part of how your podcast is put together.

With multiple takes, you must now take these points into account:

✔ **File storage:** With every take you record, another part of your disk space is taken. Whether it's one long take with audio markers or a series of takes broken up into smaller segments, your recordings will take up space. How much space? Well, consider that every minute of uncompressed audio equals 10MB (give or take a megabyte). If you have recording segments totaling up to a running time of 1 hour and 30 minutes, you're inching close to 1GB of uncompressed audio. These sessions can quickly stack up on you if you're recording multiple takes.

✔ **Timing multiple takes together:** As mentioned earlier in this practice, timing together two separate sessions takes practice. You want the segments and sessions you edit together to sound like one cohesive recording, one concise expression. Sometimes editing your sessions together is merely a matter of timing the breaks between words and phrases. Other times, you're editing audio beat for beat. And then there are those edits that sound seamless out of sheer luck. No matter your skill level, editing your takes together requires a lot of patience and time to get it right.

✔ **Editing time:** Editing multiple takes together takes time. Recording segments two, three, or more times over and over again takes time. Reviewing edits so you don't have any repeat statements or missed mistakes takes time. Unlike the one-take podcast, the multiple-take approach increases your editing workload exponentially. It's a trade-off you make when you go beyond the simple podcast: To get more variety in the audio you create, you have to invest more time in listening, editing, and reviewing it for timing, flow, and continuity, as shown in Figure 15-2.

Understanding the Advantages of Multiple Takes

We can imagine the interior monologue at this point: "More editing time? Skill? Practice? Wait a second — I thought I was *podcasting!* You know, what Steve Jobs described as the *Wayne's World* of audio and the media professionals huff at as being amateur hour. This is starting to sound as if there's a lot of *work* involved in engineering audio at home (or at the office)."

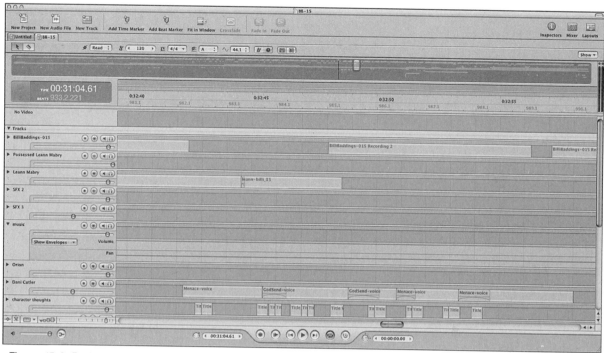

• **Figure 15-2: Projects using multiple segments (like this in Soundtrack Pro) increase the time demands on you as a podcast producer.**

Podcasting is like any creative endeavor: You get what you put into it. Podcasting can be the low-budget, economical investment of finances, time, and resources that it continues to be portrayed as; but it doesn't have to stay on a shoestring budget if you don't want it to. Modest purchases, a dedication to the project's audio quality, and a bit of clever thinking can help you develop and engineer a podcast that rivals studio-quality productions.

So now that you've had a look at the costs of working with multiple takes, here is what you gain from this increased workload:

- ✔ **Variety in audio and vocal range:** Unlike the one-take wonder, you have a choice of line readings. Even if your material is far from high drama, you can try difference paces with your script, emphasize certain words in the material, and play around with different volume intensities.

You can now give your material an aural texture that may not be present in a one-take podcast.

- ✔ **Polished product:** What's considered the "charm" of one-take podcasting consists of the unedited stammers and stumbles that some show hosts make when recording. With multiple takes, *ahs, ums,* and repetitive words — such as *but, so,* and (of course) *and* — are easily removed from the beginnings of thoughts and snipped out of the middle of long replies or commentary. Result: The whole thing sounds more impressive.

Using the multiple-take approach, you can also clean up the time between thoughts, shorten (or, for some tension, lengthen) pauses in your show hosts' comments. When you can control the timing and variety of the final work, the end result is a refined podcast, featuring only the best takes and the sharpest timing.

✔ **Editing education and practice:** Practice makes perfect, and perfect practice makes for incredible podcasts. With every editing challenge, you will learn skills that only help your productions mature and evolve into something better than the afore-mentioned *"Wayne's World* of audio" that podcasting still tends to be regarded as. There will be moments of trial, and a few errors should be expected, but each edit is practice for a future situation: Before long, you'll have the confidence and finesse to think, "I've done this before. No sweat."

Deciding Whether the Investment Is Worth It for You

Creating podcasts with multiple takes requires a serious time commitment, but the end result is a production easily ranked with the most polished and professional of audio offerings. By having a variety of samples to choose from, you can do a lot more than create a podcast. You can create an *exceptional* podcast.

But before working in this edit-intensive state of mind, it's worth asking whether your podcast warrants — or really needs — this kind of time and effort. Perhaps the one-take podcast and 10 minutes of quality time between you and the microphone is all you need; or maybe you want to consider allotting more time and resources to your podcast. The question you should be asking yourself is, "Am I investing the *right* amount of time and effort for this podcast?"

Not all podcasts are created equal. Each podcast, depending on its ideas, execution, and post-production needs, will demand your time, effort, and (to some extent) emotional wear and tear. When you begin planning out those first five shows, take a moment to ask yourself, "Does the investment match the basic needs and direction of this podcast?" By taking a good, realistic look at what you want to do with your podcast, you can get a good handle on how to proceed.

Practice 16

Podcasting from the Road

Recording in your own studio is a lot like being Batman. You retreat into that section of the house or apartment reserved only for you or your closest companions, surround yourself with high-tech equipment, and test your skills before an audio rig and computer eagerly awaiting input. When Tee was moving his studio from the upstairs office to the basement, he asked the wife if he could build a slide-away bookcase in the foyer with either a high-speed elevator or a fireman's pole to slide down into the heart of the recording sanctuary.

That idea was quickly shot down. The jury is still out on the underground garage, its entrance concealed by either a waterfall or a folding *Danger: Dead End* sign. (No, really, podcasters *need* that.)

Why, you ask? Because sometimes you need to take your show on the road. In this practice, you assume the journey of an audio ronin, facing the challenge of capturing quality sound *outside* the studio. You've worked very hard to achieve a solid noise floor from within the confines of the studio, and now you step out into the wide expanse of the real world with all its air traffic, chirping birds, enthusiastic audiences, and general noisy ambience. How do you quell that, or should you even try? Is it possible to take your show on the road and produce the same audio quality as your home studio? Well, just as Batman has various options and remote locations of his own Bat Cave, you as a podcaster have choices for taking your sanctuary of sound to the sidewalk.

(Geeky? Us? Why would you say that?)

Portable Podcasting: The Good, the Bad, and the Ugly

Any time you step out of the controlled environment of a studio, there is the unknown element to consider. Sometimes the unknown element can add an entirely new and welcomed dimension to your podcast. Other times this element can work against your episode and either slow its pace or completely unhinge it, sending you and your show out of control.

You have a lot of issues to consider when you're recording *live* (or what may be better described as recording *remotely*); live recordings are usually posted later in the same week or month.

Seizing the podcasting opportunity

Whenever you're on the road, it's hard to fathom who or what you will encounter beforehand — an impromptu musical performance by another podcaster, or a representative of a group, corporation, or perhaps a trade-show vendor that is of keen interest to you and your podcast (as shown in Figure 16-1). This moment could be a serendipitous opportunity that may not repeat itself anytime soon. On such an occasion, you have two options:

- ✔ Exchange contact information, go home, and try to figure out the best time to schedule a sit-down and record either over the phone or through Skype.

- ✔ Ask this individual or group what their schedule is, lock down a time, and record. The sooner you can do it, the better.

• Figure 16-1: At the Podcast and New Media Expo 2006, Tee secured an interview with PR Web's Andrew Schlicktling shortly after meeting him on the expo floor.

You never know when your paths will cross again in something like the situation you currently find yourself in; having a recording device or rig on hand can provide a fantastic opportunity for your podcast.

However, an opportunity presented isn't always a good one if you find yourself unprepared or lacking direction.

Before grabbing a moment to gab, consider what you want to talk about *and* (this is a harsh truth you'll have to deal with) what to do if the recording or the interview doesn't go quite the way you hope. True, the audio you get will be superior to a Skype or telephone recording; but we're talking about a trade-off between convenience and opportunity versus preparation and environment. Depending on how quickly you set up the recording rig or audio device, you may not be able to scout out a quiet place fast enough to minimize ambient noise.

Finding the right setting

A very cool thing about podcasting remotely is the lively and fun settings you can use — a bookstore, for example. In 2006, New Zealand author Philippa Ballantine allowed Tee to arrange bookstore signings for the two of them. They hopped between Baltimore, Maryland, and Harrisonburg, Viriginia, in a matter of four days — podcasting every step of the trip. In their visit to a Harrisonburg bookstore, as shown in Figure 16-2, the microphones were live, and the audience asked questions ranging from their writing processes to a Kiwi's perspective on Americans. It made for some fun and informative podcasting.

• Figure 16-2: Authors Philippa Ballantine and Tee Morris, podcasting an evening at Barnes & Noble, Harrisonburg.

With interaction and reaction from the audience, the setting of this *Survival Guide to Writing Fantasy* (www.teemorris.com/blog) episode took on a more personal, less-sterile atmosphere. The audience took part in a virtual question-and-answer session with Pip Ballantine — an opportunity hard to come by because her trips to the United States are limited.

Sometimes a lively setting can get a bit *too* crazy. For the same podcast, Tee attempted to interview Hugo and Nebula Award winner Robert J. Sawyer at a science-fiction convention. The first attempted recording location — a corridor in the host hotel — erupted suddenly into activity, effectively drowning out the interview. Moving to a hotel room provided a less-frantic location for the interview, sacrificing some on-location ambiance for clarity.

The hotel-room solution was an easy fix for the setting, but other such fixes may not always be so easy. If you're recording an interview with a celebrity or authority in your podcast's focus, an offer to "hold the interview in my hotel room" could easily be misconstrued. If a public setting seems less productive for an interview, offer to have your interview subject *and* his or her assistant(s) join you for the interview, if that would be more convenient. If this is not an option, lock down a time later in the day — and then take a moment to scout around for a quiet area. (These spots are out there in convention and conference settings; you may just have to ferret them out.) Keep a professional attitude and always seek out an amicable solution.

The trade-off between recording in studio and recording remotely

The three types of portable rigs discussed in the next section enable you to expand their built-in recording capabilities. From the iRiver to the Zoom H4, the portable digital recorder can do much more than the simple handheld microcassette recorder that many people still consider the norm for portable recording. The technology of built-in microphones has also greatly improved with time, providing better recording and pickup capabilities than ever before.

A drawback in portability is the consistency of those built-in microphones, pickups, and (if applicable) pre-amps. One recorder (say, an Olympus digital) may yield fantastic results in one setting, but changing that remote setting to someplace else may produce audio that's harder to engineer up to your normal audio standards. The inconsistency could be the result of anything from freak weather to weak batteries. There's also a certain built-in risk factor: Most of these portable recorders can't monitor incoming audio, so the quality of what you get is usually evident only *after* the recording session.

One way of improving the quality of the built-in microphone is to employ an accessory such as an external mic — but the more accessories you plug into your handheld, the less portable you become. So if you want better audio quality, you begin with a tradeoff: How much mobility do you sacrifice in your mobile podcasting rig?

Taking Your Show on the Road

You have various ways to take your podcast mobile. Some podcasters like to travel with a gig bag that can hold cables, a mixer board, headphones, and maybe the kitchen sink. At one time that was as portable as recording rigs got, but with the popularity of podcasting and advancements in digital recording technology, the new portable is now more portable than you might think.

iRiver: The podcaster's necktie

If you have ever attended a podcasters' convention (or are sitting in on the podcasting track of a science fiction convention), you might notice a few of the panelists and other participants wearing things around their necks that look like bulkier versions of the first-generation iPod Shuffles. They may come in a variety of colors, and at the right time, you might even see some of the podcasters talking into them. These devices from iRiver (http://iriver america.com) are known as the Ultra-Portable iRiver Players.

Pictured in Figure 16-3 is the 800 series, the iRiver that remains a popular model with podcasters because of extremely reliable built-in mics (with fantastic pickups), available mic jacks for external microphones, and stereo mp3 recording (with bit rates up to 320 kbps and sampling rates up to 44.1 kHz). iRivers also come in a variety of sizes (256MB, 512MB, and 1GB) and can record hours of audio, powered by a single AA battery. Weighing no more than a set of car keys, this accessory remains vital to any podcaster because the iRiver 800 (and even the older models) can interface seamlessly with both Mac and Windows platforms. Later versions of the iRiver (from the T-series) support only Windows XP, shutting out many other podcasters. Another problem with the iRiver is its interface, which its users hardly describe as intuitive.

 These iRivers, while not available at your local Best Buy and Circuit City stores, are readily available online at eBay and other online vendors. (Simply do a search for iRiver Portable players and hit results should pop up.)

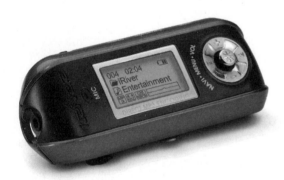

• Figure 16-3: The iRiver Ultra-Portable 800 series mp3 player and digital recorder.

A squid even Captain Nemo could love

The iRiver 800-series Ultra-Portables could brag with confidence that their built-in microphones were (and still are) very good microphones, considering their size and construction. However, in interview situations (and some sound-seeing tour settings), the built-in microphone's limitations show up right away. From overmodulation to sudden drop outs, the iRiver microphone can be a bit unpredictable from situation to situation.

However, with the 800-series comes a Line In jack that gives users the opportunity (provided they can navigate through the user-unfriendly interface) to plug in other audio-input devices. And from Giant Squid Labs (www.giant-squid-audio-lab.com/) comes an economic and reliable alternative to the iRiver's built-in mic: the Podcasting Omni Stereo Microphone (shown below). Tethered to a 5-foot cable, its two dime-size lavalier mics provide some nice specs for podcasters:

- ✔ Frequency response: 20–20,000 Hz
- ✔ Sensitivity: rated at -35 decibels +4 decibels
- ✔ Sound-to-noise ratio: > 62 dB
- ✔ High-quality 1/8-inch (3.5mm) stereo mini plug

From *Escape Pod's* Steve Eley to *Hey Wanna Watch a Movie* and *Christiana Talks About Stuff's* Christiana Ellis, podcasters are giving high marks across the board for these mics. Durable. Affordable. If you have an iRiver (or any digital recorder for that matter) with a Line In option, then give Giant Squid Lab's Podcasting Omni a look. It may be one of the most versatile and reliable accessories in your portable podcasting arsenal.

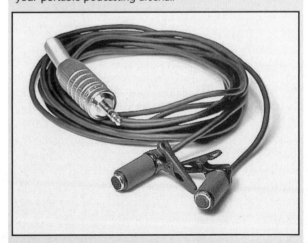

The M-Audio MobilePre: Your recording studio as carry-on luggage

The iRivers are excellent portable devices, providing you with quick podcasting solutions, but even their built-in microphones have limitations. You want a studio-quality sound, but you would also like to take your setup on the road as needed. M-Audio (online at www.m-audio.com) offers an option that answers the call: the USB MobilePre (shown in Figure 16-4).

• **Figure 16-4: The M-Audio MobilePre USB preamp.**

This compact recording solution, priced at around $150 USD, fits in the palm of your hand and is completely USB-powered. After its drivers are installed, setup is a snap:

1. Plug your MobilePre's USB cable into your computer's USB port.

 Install the drivers for your MobilePre USB in your computer *first*. Drivers are available for both Mac and Windows platforms at www.m-audio.com/index.php?do= support.drivers under the option of USB Audio Series.

 As you're working with audio, we recommend plugging into a USB port directly, not through a USB hub. While the M-Audio component will probably work, there may be a loss of recording quality or data transfer issues when working through a hub.

2. Plug in your microphones' XLR or 1/8-inch connectors.

The MobilePre USB has several Line inputs, but the preamps there are built for instruments, not microphones and vocals. Any signal you get if you use the line inputs will be weak at best.

3. Press the button labeled *Phantom Power* to supply power for your XLR microphones.

4. Launch your audio-editing software.

Your MobilePre has to be up and running before you launch your digital audio workstation (DAW). Otherwise, the software won't see the device, or you may get a software or system crash. (For more on the various DAWs out there, see Practice 11.)

5. Set your levels by adjusting either the Channel 1 or Channel 2 knobs.

Keep an eye on the lights to the right of each knob. The signal light is telling you that the MobilePre is receiving an audio signal, which is always a good thing. The blinking red light labeled *clip* is an indication that your incoming signal is too loud — the nuances of your sound are being cut off *(clipped)* by the MobilePre to keep the overmodulation under some kind of control.

6. Record your podcast, adjusting Channel 1 or 2 as you see fit.

 The third knob on the MobilePre is for your headphone volume. Adjusting this setting won't affect your input signal, but make sure that you're adjusting either the volume of your headphones or increasing the signal coming into your DAW. Don't lose track of what you're adjusting. If your headphones are all the way up, you might need to adjust your channels. If you are noticing a lot of clipping, check your headphone volume; the signal may be blasting in at a higher level than you know. And try to keep both the input level and the headphone volume down to a comfortable level. Your ears are easier to damage than you might think.

The MobilePre, along with being extremely mobile, is extremely versatile for podcasting purposes, offering to your rig these extra bonuses:

- **Hookup for third mic:** The MobilePre not only allows for two XLR mics, but also has a Stereo Mic jack in the back all set up and ready for a third microphone. For a two-person podcast, the third mic can provide a terrific opportunity for live audiences to interact with you and your co-host or interview subject. The third mic can also open up your show for more participants. If your podcast features music, you can take advantage of the MobilePre's instrument line inputs.

The more stuff you plug into the MobilePre, the more you are splitting the incoming audio signals. You may need to readjust the levels to keep volume levels of the podcast audible and constant.

- **Top-notch sound quality for portable device:** Another terrific advantage of the MobilePre is that it provides you with as close-to-studio-quality sound as you'll find with portable recording devices. If you're a podcasting newcomer, the MobilePre is an excellent, inexpensive way to give podcasting a try without having to invest in heavy-duty equipment.

M-Audio offers other portable solutions similar to the MobilePre USB, but for the expandability you get for the investment, the MobilePre is hard to beat and a great way to test the waters. Then if you ever upgrade your studio, hang on to the unit and use it for recordings from the road.

The Zoom H4: The best of both worlds

Introduced at the Podcast and Portable Media Expo in 2006 — and quickly becoming the must-have accessory for podcasters — Samson (online at www.samsontech.com) combines the power of the MobilePre USB and the portability of the iRiver.

The designers made this gizmo look like something Jack Bauer would use on *24* when interrogating bad guys. It's not a Tazer. It's not a tricorder from *Star Trek*. It's not a dimensional rift-maker from *Sliders,* either. It's the Zoom H4, a new all-in-one, portable recording device designed for podcasters, audio professionals, and recording enthusiasts (see Figure 16-5).

• **Figure 16-5: Samson's Zoom H4.**

At around $300 USD, the Zoom H4 rests comfortably in the palm of your hand, but comes with an optional tray and two Velcro straps that secure the device and allow mounting on an optional tripod for live settings and musical performances. The Zoom also comes with a windscreen designed for the two stereo mics built into the top of the unit, a free 128MB flash card (where your audio is stored), a USB cable to make the transfer of audio simple, a handy carrying bag, and finally, a copy of Cubase in case you don't have Soundtrack Pro or Audition handy.

Running on two AA batteries, the Zoom can record in four modes:

- ✔ Track 1: WAV format at 96 kHz
- ✔ Track 2: WAV format at 48 kHz
- ✔ Track 3: WAV format at 44.1 kHz
- ✔ Track 4: mp3 format at 44.1 kHz

Recording

When you load up the Zoom with batteries and the flash storage (128MB gains you roughly two hours of recording time when you're recording directly to the mp3 format), the interface may be a little intimidating at first, but it's easy to navigate one you get past the learning curve.

To make your first recording on the Zoom:

1. **Turn the Zoom H4 on by flipping the ON/OFF switch located on the left side of the unit.**

2. **Select your mode of recording.**

For this example, let's work with recording directly to mp3. Press the **4** button on the left side of the screen. It lights up green, and the screen gives you a summary of what mode you're recording in.

3. **Press the Rec button on the right-hand side once.**

The Rec light blinks until you press the button again. Figure 16-6 shows what you see on-screen.

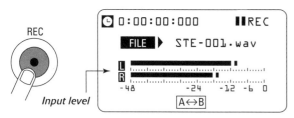

REC

Input level

- Figure 16-6: When you press the Record button, you see your Zoom picking up sound — but you are NOT recording yet.

Pressing the record button once does not mean you are recording. Unlike the iRiver, pressing the Rec button puts you into a Level Test mode. Only on the second pressing of the Record button do you start recording audio.

4. **Press the Menu button located underneath the readout. From the options offered in the Zoom's interface window, select File by using the small wheel on the right-hand side of the device. (This will move the cursor up or down.) When you have the cursor next to File, push the wheel to select that option.**

In the top-right corner of the interface window, the REC indicator is set to pause even though you see the sound in a range that registers on the Zoom's VU meter.

5. **Set your levels by adjusting the placement of the Zoom in the vicinity of your recording subject.**

6. **Record your podcast by pushing the blinking Record button a second time.**

The button is now a solid red, indicating that the device is recording sound.

7. **To stop recording, press the solid red Record button.**

The Zoom stops recording and the red light turns off.

Transferring recordings to your computer

When you've bagged that recorded sound for your podcast, follow these steps to get the sound off the Zoom H4 and into your computer for editing purposes:

1. **Located next to the ON/OFF switch is a USB input port. Plug in your USB cord there.**

Turn off the H4 Zoom before plugging the USB cable into the unit and the computer.

2. **Plug the Zoom H4 into a USB port on your computer.**

You're asked on the Zoom interface either to use it as an Audio I/O device or Connect to a PC (see Figure 16-7). Move the wheel located on the right side to scroll between the two options.

```
   USB MODE SELECT
  ─────────────────────
 ▸AUDIO I/O
  CONNECT TO PC
```

• **Figure 16-7: When initially plugged into a computer, the Zoom can work as an audio interface or as a flash drive.**

3. **Move the tiny arrow indicator to Connect to PC and then push the wheel to select this option.**

 It says *Connect to a PC,* but the Zoom interfaces seamlessly with a Mac *or* a PC.

4. **The Zoom will appear on your desktop as a removable drive. Double-click the drive and look for the directory marked Stereo. Your recordings are kept here. Drag and drop the audio files onto your hard drive.**

The files remain on your Flash memory card until you clear the card. Simply drag the audio files on the card to your Trash or Recycle Bin, drop them there and empty the bin, and your Flash memory is ready to go.

5. **Safely eject the Zoom, either by right-clicking it and selecting the Eject option or by selecting the drive and ejecting it from your computer as you would other removable media.**

6. **Go out and record again.**

The recordings you make off the built-in microphones are clear and clean, but the Zoom H4 has a further bonus: two XLR inputs for mics or instrument pickups. It also has jacks for output devices and headphones; this recorder has the same

expandability that the M-Audio MobilePre offers, only now you have everything — microphones, recording software, preamps, pickups, the works — in one device. Copy the files from the Zoom to your computer (much the way you would with the iRiver), and you're all set to go.

Exploring the Zoom

The Zoom has many, many other features and capabilities, but you may have to do some experimenting to find out everything this incredible piece of audio technology can do. So, for other functions (such as activating phantom power, utilizing the Zoom's compressor/limiter, and using the multitrack recording capabilities), keep the operations manual close at hand. Some afternoon or evening, you may be playing with the higher functions, only to discover that one function that unlocks the full potential of this fantastic recorder. (Hey, it beats watching reruns, and it helps your podcast. What's not to like?)

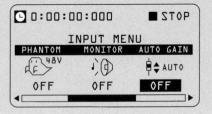

While a heftier investment than a MobilePre or the iRiver iFP model, the Zoom does offer a lot of possibilities for the podcaster, and its cousin the Zoom H2 also promises to be a terrific portable option for your audio.

When you've chosen your remote-recording option and spent some time getting to know it, it's time to take the show on the road!

Could You Keep It Down?! I'm Podcasting!

No matter how you choose to take your podcast to a live setting, you're going to face some unknown elements that are easily filtered (and in some cases, edited) out. When you have the microphones out and nestled in their respective shock mounts, curious individuals will wonder what's going on. If you're in a festive setting where bystanders are enjoying a drink or two, often people will summon up the courage to come on mic (or *on pod,* as some people are now coining the phrase) and ask, "What are you all doing over here?"

Not all mics are created equal; it's a good idea to have the right mics for on-the-road-podcasting. To find out more about what mics are best for you and your podcasting demands, jump back to Practice 10 for all the details and a few solid recommendations.

It's a real challenge to maintain a focus with so much outside stimulation, and it can be a real testament to the engaging nature of your content. Can you keep your focus, or is it easy to just let the coherence of your podcast fall by the wayside and let the environment distract you?

When you're recording remotely, keep the following points in mind:

- ✔ **Make sure that recording in a live setting is right for your show.** Does the podcast really need this extra element? If you are doing it primarily for crowd reaction, then run with the environment and don't worry about the challenge acoustics are going to pose. In fact, enjoy the hollow, echoing sound a live setting gives your voice because it adds to that live sound all the more.

  That said, the live setting of your recording should have a purpose behind it. Otherwise your podcast is taken out of its element for no real reason other than to say, "Hey, we're live!" Have an answer in mind for this question of purpose.

- ✔ **Plan out your live show.** It is always a good idea to have a plan for your episode, be it a full-out script or an outline. Having a game plan before a live recording is paramount, though. We've seen experienced podcasters try to fly by the seat of their pants while putting together a live recording. Sometimes the spontaneity works. Other times, it's a painful and laborious ride.

The best approach to mobile podcasting is to have an idea — a direction — for the live recording. Keep in mind that when you're in a live setting with unknown elements in the mix, your plan may become more like a guideline; allow the direction of the episode some wiggle room so it can change course a bit if necessary.

- ✔ **React *and comment* on distractions.** The second-worst thing we've seen podcast hosts do in live settings is pretend that nothing is happening in front of their recording session. If the setting is (say) Dragon*Con, with costumes galore passing by, this is a tragedy — those individuals are interviews (and instant content) waiting to happen. Or if the Elvis Chicken is walking by at the Podcast and New Media Expo, why not comment on it? It's hard to miss it.

  The *worst* thing we've seen at a live recording is when another host or guest comments on a distraction, only to have the host completely blow off the comment with, "Don't pay any attention to that. We were talking about. . . . " The activity around you is fantastic fodder for your podcast. Let the setting carry your conversation or interview onto interesting tangents. Tying them back into the main theme may challenge your creativity, but it is a credit to your podcasting skills when you do pull that off.

- ✔ **Don't let the distractions dictate your podcast.** This may seem contradictory, but always keep it in the forefront of your mind: While the live setting can provide a lot of fun topics for your episode to explore, the podcast should still keep a sense of focus about itself. If you rely on distractions to provide your episode with content, or if your engaging discussion suddenly diverts into talking about a particular car that just drove by the window, you run the risk of losing the focus and intent of your podcast. Invite some stimulus from the outside world, but never lose sight of your podcast's goals. Figure 16-8 shows Tee making the most of a live setting.

• Figure 16-8: **Tee (far right) captures the liveliness of four authors (from l to r: Tony Ruggiero, Kristy Tallman, Mark Wildes) podcasting at Chester Perk coffeehouse in Chester, VA.**

There are good reasons to podcast from live settings, but do your best never to shy away from what the live setting throws at you. Otherwise why leave the comfort zone of your studio? Embrace the space around you and your mobile recording rig; enjoy this new and exciting avenue of podcasting. The more fun you have in your outdoor, away-from-studio environment, the more your audience will feel as if they're right there, enjoying the afternoon with you.

Part III

Post-Production Approaches

THE PODCAST "LAMP TALK" WAS ABOUT TO BECOME "EXPLICIT."

"Sometimes these sockets need cleaning. First, make sure the lamp is unplugged, and then ..."

Practice 17
Interviews from the Road

Working remotely has its advantages and disadvantages over working in a studio. Although something can be said for the ambiance of passers-by and sounds of activity around you while you record a podcast on the road, you can also make a strong case for having the control over your surroundings that a studio offers: You know how your studio sounds, you keep the undesired noise to a minimum, and you can set up the best kind of background (a quiet one) for recording your content.

In some situations, though, you have no choice but to record remotely — and that's often true of interview settings. If you incorporate guests into your podcast's format, you may not always be able to do interviews in your home or studio. You may need to conduct phone-in interviews, make use of online communication options like Skype, or work with a portable rig (more about that in Practice 16) — none of which is necessarily a bad thing; it's often good interview etiquette to bring your recording equipment to your interview subjects rather than make them come to you. In this practice, we cover the ins and outs of taking the show (in this case, the interview) on the road.

Introducing a "Live on Location" Interview

Say you have your laptop equipment or your portable digital recorder set up and ready to go. When you're recording interviews from the road, you can either launch into your interview or regard your guest as part of that particular episode show. Find out what the subject's schedule allows for and then record accordingly.

While you're pondering which approach is likely to work best, think about how guests are worked into the shows *Late Night with David Letterman* and *The Tonight Show*. At the opening of the show, Dave does his monologue and the goofy segments such as the Top Ten List or what's on the menu at local delis. For Jay, it's roughly the same thing: opening monologue followed by segments like "Jaywalking" or offbeat classified ads.

What both formats have in common are that the guests are not present initially.

Unless the guests become an active part of these segments, they are usually being prepped for their appearance in the Green Room, or on the way to the studio while the opening skits are going on. The skits are treated as independent spots, distinct from the sit-down interviews. Therefore, after these segments occur, the host usually creates a bumper that leads to a commercial, saying (for instance), "When we get back, an interview with so-and-so."

Generally, it's bad form to keep guests waiting or sitting next to you saying nothing while you do the opening banter for your podcast (or hit the news and interesting sidebar tidbits) before getting around to the interview. Instead, treat the interview as an independent segment. Unless the guest is a part of the introduction banter, news segments, or other content, conduct the interview first; you can record the other segments later.

Recording your interview's intro

After you're all set up for the interview, record an introduction that brings you into the discussion with your guest. Here are a few examples:

- ✔ **"And welcome to another episode of (*your podcast*). I am your chief drill instructor, (*your name*), and I am here with (*your guest's name*)."** This sort of introduction launches your show right into the interview — no introduction banter and no opening news segments.

- ✔ **"We are recording live from (*your location*), and I am here with (*your guest's name*)."** This approach gives you a little versatility. You can have an opening show segment bring you into an interview, or you can record a brief introduction that segues into the interview.

- ✔ **"And welcome back to (*your podcast name*). I am your chief drill instructor, (*your name*), here with (*your guest's name*)."** By opening your interview with this kind of introduction, you now have set up the interview as a segment of your show. You open with your show's introduction banter, perhaps a news segment or what's going on around the studio, and then you transition into a break by saying, "When we return, an interview with. . . ." You then play promos and return immediately with your interview.

All three of these interview introductions are intentionally brief. You don't want to keep your guests waiting. You want to give them as much time on-mic as you can. Many guests, whether they're recording on location or even phoning in for an interview, have allocated a specific period of time for your interview. So before you begin recording, ask your guests how much time they have. Your intro should take up as little time as possible, giving you more time for questions and answers. Your time with guests is very valuable — make it count!

Recording the segue to the introduction

If you've decided that the sit-down with your guest is going to be a show segment, you should still record a brief transition, or *segue,* from the flow of podcast banter into the interview. The segue brings you and your listeners into the discussion and can even provide a bit of background for why this guest is appearing on your show. For example, you can say right before your first break spot, "When we return, an interview with. . . ," or "Coming up next, an interview with. . . ." These are examples of segues.

With your segue, follow these tips in putting it together:

- ✔ **Let your listeners know what's coming up.** Interviews may not be the norm for your show, and if this guest is particularly special, the segue is a good opportunity to let your subscribers know what's coming up in this episode or (say) after the next break. An introduction like this is just a friendly heads-up.

✔ **Provide some background on your guest.** Never assume that everyone listening knows your guest — not even if the guest is someone often seen in the media spotlight. Fill in some of your guest's background, the company or organization he or she represents (if that's relevant), and what brings this person to your podcast. Keeping your audience in the know is a nice touch.

✔ **Keep the introduction *brief*.** Once again, there's that B-word. You want to build up expectations in your segue, not paraphrase the interview that is coming up. Keep your segue under five minutes (two to three minutes is best). Keep the facts quick, concise, and clear. Then you go into the interview and let the discussion speak for itself.

Working with VoIP: The Voice of a New Generation

You will likely hear the term *VoIP* quite a bit from podcasters when they talk about recording interviews from various locations. VoIP stands for *Voice over Internet Protocol,* but it's also called *IP telephony* or *Internet telephony.* VoIP is a combination of software and hardware that makes audio conversations happen over the Internet.

So why is VoIP so important in remote recording? Podcasters can take advantage of the ease and accessibility of VoIP in a variety of ways, but the two main reasons are audio quality and cost. Many conference-call services offer a free option for you to set up hard-line-based conversations, but if you want to *record* those meetings, you have to pay a steep fee. Additionally, the call itself is coming in at a mere 8 kHz quality — and that's if the quality of the phone service is top notch. With mobile phones becoming the primary phones (both at home and on the road) for many people, the connection you get can be somewhat dodgy.

Dodgy phone service is enough for you to consider a VoIP solution. But many VoIP solutions (described

next) offer recording capabilities ranging from free to under $20 USD for a one-time purchase of the software. With a dramatic boost in the audio quality of VoIP (32 kHz or better), the cost-effectiveness of the recording software, and the ability to hold conversations in any Wi-Fi hot spot, VoIP is an essential tool for interviewers.

Using Skype

Skype (www.skype.com) is the most popular VoIP solution for recording conversations and interviews. The application is safe, offered as a free download, and is available for Mac, Windows, and Linux platforms. The audio quality of Skype improves if the application is running through an audio card different from the one preinstalled in your computer. (Many of the manufacturer's internal sound cards handle the basics, but audio cards from vendors like M-Audio may offer more power for the audio signal, allowing for better reception.) You can use the computer's existing audio card, but your performance may vary.

For the best audio quality, you want to use Skype-to-Skype connections, where all parties involved in the recorded discussion are using Skype.

Before you can use Skype, you need to download and install the software from www.skype.com and create a Skype account. After Skype is up and running, follow these steps to add contacts:

1. **In the main Contacts window, click the plus sign in the lower-left corner; or choose Contacts↷Add a Contact.**

The Add a Skype Contact dialog box appears, as shown in Figure 17-1.

2. **In the top field, enter a Skype Name (the account nickname you created when registering with Skype), a legal name, or an e-mail address of the individual you want to add to your contacts. Then click the Search button.**

Search results appear below the search field.

• Figure 17-1: To begin building your list of contacts, simply
let your fingers do the walking through the
Skype directory.

3. Click the desired name in the Search Results
and then click Add Contact in the lower-right
corner of the dialog box.

If you are asked to request authorization, per-
sonalize the message offered and click OK.

Now with approved contacts in your Skype contacts,
you can begin making Skype-to-Skype calls. To make
a VoIP call using Skype, simply click the name of the
Skype user to expand the user details and then click
the green phone icon to make a call. You then see
one of the two windows shown in Figure 17-2.

It's just that simple to call someone on Skype. You
can also double-click the contact in your Skype window to make a call, or if your Preferences pull up the
Instant Message interface, click the green phone
icon. That's it!

But what if you are hosting several individuals in this
interview? Skype can handle conference calls as well:

1. Contact your first interview subject in your
Skype contact window by placing the call.

2. After the call is established, find the other parties involved in this interview or discussion on
your Skype contacts.

3. Click and drag the desired Skype IDs from
the Contact window into the active Skype call
window.

The names then appear in the active Skype call
window, and your conference is underway.

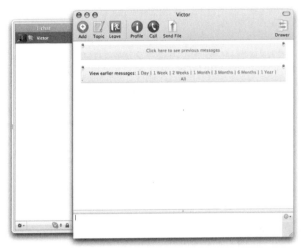

• Figure 17-2: Depending on how you have set up your
Skype Preferences, double-clicking a contact
either produces an instant message interface
(top) or automatically makes a Skype call to
that contact (bottom).

Unlike text chats on Skype, the only person who can add people to a Skype VoIP conference call is the person who initiated the call.

Using SkypeOut

SkypeOut is just one of Skype's many features. While Skype-to-Skype conversations are far from the norm, you can take advantage of SkypeOut for those guests who are still not certain about using VoIP on their own computers. With SkypeOut, you can make telephone calls to users anywhere in the world, to any telephone in the world. For the people who aren't on Skype, SkypeOut is your option.

At the time of this writing, here's what the SkypeOut nationwide plan offers:

- 12 months of unlimited calls to any phone within the U.S. and Canada
- No connection fees charged for calls to U.S. or Canadian phones
- Only $29.95 for 12 months, or $8.85 for 3 months

Here's how the SkypeOut international plan currently works:

- 2.1¢ per minute to more than 30 global destinations
- Rates based on destination country
- Connection fee of 3.9¢ charged for each call
- Buy Skype Credit to pay per-minute. The credits are deducted as you make your SkypeOut calls.

Skype users can buy time (credits) to make calls to hard lines from coast-to-coast or around the world. After you have your credit in place, place your call through Skype:

1. **In the main Skype window, click the telephone icon in the lower-left corner.**

   The icon is labeled with the words Call Phones or Send SMS.

2. **From the Select Country or Region drop-down menu, shown in Figure 17-3, select the country you want to call.**

3. **With your country zone selected, enter the phone number and make the call.**

With Skype, you've sidestepped the need for complicated (and expensive) phone patches that might not yield the same quality as a Skype call. You can now have calls, both Skype-to-Skype and Skype-to-Phone, running digitally through your computer.

All that remains is recording your calls, as described in the next section.

• Figure 17-3: Skype makes international calls simple by plugging in country zones.

Using Skype and third-party recorders

When recording interviews with your guests while on the road, you could try to bring with you hardware that "plugs" into your friend's telephone or utilizes the hotel's telephone . . . and pay for it later when it's time to settle the bill. The complicated solution is not always the best one, so why not invest in a simple one-button recorder installed into your laptop for your needs? Mac and Windows both have these third-party solutions that perform admirably and do not break the bank. In the next sections, we talk about two: HotRecorder (Windows) and Call Recorder (Mac).

HotRecorder

HotRecorder (http://hotrecorder.com) allows you to record conversations running through Skype along with other applications like AOL Instant Messenger and Google Talk. HotRecorder (shown in Figure 17-4) can record and export your Skype chats by recording all connected parties through two separate channels, merging them into a single file at the end.

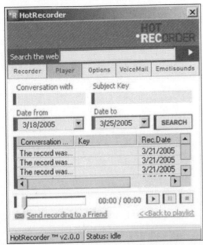

• Figure 17-4: HotRecorder is the cost-effective solution for recording Skype chats using Windows.

This quick and easy Windows solution costs $15 USD at the time of this writing. If you've invested a lot of money in microphones, headphones, compressors, and other audio toys, the cost of HotRecorder is

hardly anything to give you pause. For a mere $15, your interview is captured (on both sides) and ready for editing and posting.

Call Recorder

ECamm's *Call Recorder* for the Mac OS (www.ecamm. com/mac/callrecorder/) is the recording solution for both Skype audio *and* video, capturing your conversations and allowing you to turn them into podcasts.

Features of Call Recorder, shown in Figure 17-5, include

- ✔ Manual start, stop, and pause

- ✔ Preferences that allow you to auto-record all calls

- ✔ The capability to record and save your voice-mail messages

- ✔ Control over file size, quality, and compression to mp3, H.264, or AAC file formats

• Figure 17-5: Mac users can easily incorporate Call Recorder with Skype.

Priced at $16 USD at the time of this writing, Call Recorder has established itself as a Mac podcaster's essential asset when recording interviews via Skype. Audio and video can be captured either uncompressed or already compressed and ready for posting.

Many audio recorders have preset compression settings for formats like mp3 and AAC, giving you little if any control over how the audio or video is compressed. Provided you have the disk space, capture the video or audio in its raw, uncompressed format and then compress it with the application of your choice. By compressing the media from a raw format, not a compressed one, you have more versatility with the media and are less likely to overcompress your interview.

Whether you are using Call Recorder or HotRecorder, interviewing guests over Skype gives you, the podcaster, an inexpensive option for bringing guests from all parts of the world into your studio.

Improving Sound Quality on the Road

With portable recording rigs like the M-Audio MobilePre and Samson's H2 and H4 Zoom, you can take your act on tour. Two microphones, a portable recorder, and mic stands can now all fit into an over-the-shoulder gig bag, turning the world (and wherever you happen to stop) into your own personal recording studio.

However, as we've discussed in other practices, ambient noise may provide a challenge when you're recording on the road. *Ambient noise* should not be confused with *white noise;* often these two terms are used interchangeably when they shouldn't be.

Ambient noise is background noise that comes from the immediate surroundings, used to create or enhance a mood or atmosphere. If (say) you're recording a podcast with a friend in the park, then the sounds of traffic, people passing by, dogs barking, and birds chirping are considered ambient noise; they set an atmosphere or mood.

White noise is a wash of noise, pure and simple. White noise contains many frequencies (as ambient noise can), but these frequencies are all heard at equal intensities. Static is most commonly identified as white noise, but a crowd at a rock concert, the sound of a train passing by, or traffic on the tarmac of an airport can constitute white noise.

When recording interviews remotely, take a look at where you want to record and run down a checklist of variables:

- **Does the ambiance remain in the background, or overpower the interview?** Where you decide to record directly affects the interview, both in its flow and in its recording quality. You want the atmosphere to add something to the interview, not detract from the message or intent of the interview (or the episode) itself.

- **Regardless of the ambiance, does the setting of your remote interview remain conducive to your interview?** High-traffic areas, though they provide terrific backdrops for your interviews, may prove counterproductive when you're recording. Too much traffic, too many simultaneous conversations, and occasional interruptions can disrupt the pace of your interview or drown out the interview subject altogether. Larger rooms — even if they're quiet — can provide challenges because sound travels differently within their cavernous confines. Get a sense for how you sound in the room of choice; from there, you can decide how you will proceed.

- **What kind of microphones are you using?** Dynamic microphones are best for field recordings, but they vary in quality from manufacturer to manufacturer — and can demand a lot from the interview subject (for example, speaking louder than normal). Condenser microphones are optimal for studio use but should not be used out in the field. Due to their sensitivity, condenser mics pick up far more sound from the background.

So you have found a good place to record, but now you're looking for balanced audio levels between you, your interview subject, and your background. The solutions happen either during recording or in post-production. The following sections explore your options.

Riding the board

Keeping your audio at levels that make everyone happy — and (more importantly) keep everyone sounding professional — means getting a good balance from both (or all) voices involved. As you and your interview subject (or your podcasting crew) gather in a central location, you or one of your crew members can focus attention on the mixer or preamp and *ride the board* — adjust channel settings during the recording session. When a voice suddenly picks up in volume, the levels are adjusted to compensate, and then readjusted to the original setting when the voice returns to its original decibel level.

Riding the board may sound easy to do, but if you are the interviewer, your attention is divided between your subject and your levels. You want to focus on the reactions of your subject to gauge the pace of the interview. Are you and the subject making a good connection or creating chemistry? Is the subject comfortable with the line of questioning and the direction of the discussion? Is the level of interest with the interview subject still there? This kind of consistency is difficult to achieve when your attention hops between the subject and your mixer or pre-amp levels. So here's another relevant question: Are your multitasking skills fluent enough to chance jeopardizing the quality of your on-site interview?

Handling audio levels during the recording session does give you an advantage in that you spend less time in post-editing and production. Also, riding the board (provided you're comfortable with managing levels in real time) can give you a better-quality recording that's easier to edit in post-production.

Using Levelator

The Conversations Network has developed a quick post-production solution for making your interview subject and yourself match aurally: the Levelator (`www.conversationsnetwork.org/levelator`), shown in Figure 17-6. This free download is a popular audio solution for podcasters, and no wonder: Podcasters developed it, and it is available for Mac, Windows, and Linux. The Levelator adjusts audio levels within a recording session, offering the most sought-after qualities of a compressor/limiter.

• Figure 17-6: The Levelator is a quick post-production solution to set levels of all audio signals in a recording session.

The Levelator has been called everything from *efficient* to *magic* in how it works (and it doesn't hurt that it's free). Designed specifically for recording settings such as interviews and panel discussions, Levelator balances all sounds in a single audio file, boosting fainter frequencies and clipping louder frequencies when needed.

The Levelator is better as a "post-treatment" than as a "post-production" tool. After your session is concluded, go on and run your audio through Levelator. When doing so, be sure you:

- ✔ **Save your Levelator-treated audio under a *different* filename.** By having the original audio to go back to, you haven't lost the interview if Levelator turns out to be the wrong answer.

- ✔ **Review your Levelator-treated audio after you're done.** As mentioned in this book repeatedly, you should always review your podcast before posting it. Take a listen to the Levelator's treatment of your audio to find out what it has done to the audio.

- ✔ **Mix in bed music, sound effects, and opening and closing themes *after* using the Levelator.** Now that the Levelator has evened the audio playing field, take this audio and give it a solid post-production treatment.

 Although it's a quick and easy solution, the Levelator is (of course) neither magic nor artificial intelligence and therefore does not discriminate on audio signals. It looks at all the incoming signals and attempts to boost or reduce *all* audio levels in order to maintain the same level; all noise, including bed music and background ambiance, is *balanced* to peak at the same level. The end result resembles less of a podcast and something more like a medley of competing audio. When using Levelator, make sure subtleties (such as fade-outs, bed music, and so on) are added in after Levelator is applied to the audio.

Inserting Breaks into an Interview

When an interview is taking place, often such niceties as show format, spot breaks, and IDs are forgotten — especially when the interview hits its stride and the chemistry between show host and subject is evident.

This means that you insert your breaks in post-production. Where are some good places to work in spot breaks? Here are some ideas:

✔ **Halfway through the interview.** During your interview, you should always be aware of the time. When your interview is done, look at its running time and simply place your break at or near the halfway point. You can fade out during a question and then fade up before the break point in order to hear the initial question — or break before your next halfway-point question is asked.

✔ **Brief pauses within your interview.** Many interviews or discussions have natural breaks in their flow, where you're reviewing your questions or the interview subject is thinking about the next answer. These natural pauses in the flow of discussion, provided they land in the right places, can provide equally nice places for podcast IDs, spot breaks, or quick announcements that are independent of the interview.

✔ **Break the interview across two (or more) shows.** Depending on the running time of your show and the recorded interview, you can simply make the interview a single segment of your show and then break the interview to cover multiple shows. This method can keep the format of your show intact. You can also get several shows out of one good interview.

Wrapping Up Your Interview

If the answers start to slow down or the pace of the interview is not as rapid-fire as in the beginning, take a glance at the time. Whether you're recording

with hardware like an iRiver or a Zoom, or software like Soundtrack Pro or Audition, you can keep track of how long you have been talking with your subject. The average interview can run 10 to 15 minutes, but if an interview is moving along on track with terrific synergy, it's not unheard-of to record 30 to 40 minutes of discussion.

But to quote actor John de Lancie from the finale of *Star Trek: The Next Generation:* "It's been fun . . . but all good things must come to an end."

Especially if you are just kicking back with friends (like an evening with *Fear the Boot* in a cigar bar) or with someone you admire (like a sit-down chat with fantasy author Terry Brooks), you don't want to overstay your welcome. Watch the time spent with your guest. Regardless of whether things are going well in your recording session, look to wrap up your interview efficiently if you happen to pass the 30-minute mark. Here are some good transitions to wrap things up:

✔ **"And finally, I'd like to ask. . . ."** This signals to your interview subject or to your crew that there is time for one more comment or tangent to explore and then you're bringing the recording to a close. Give the subject or discussion time to wrap up after the question is asked. Anywhere from five to ten minutes (and if the discussion is lively, ten minutes will go by *fast*) should be a good pocket of time to grant to the final question.

✔ **"In closing, is there anything you'd like to promote or talk about. . . ."** Most interviews are part of a promotion and marketing plan, or an "awareness tour" that brings attention to an event or cause close to the speaker. This opportunity gives the subject time to plug the event they're attending, mention upcoming appearances, or expound a little more on what's happening in the live setting where you're recording.

✔ **"Thanks so much for joining me on (*your podcast name*)."** Before completely closing up your production, make sure that you thank your guest for taking time to talk to you. Especially if this interview is in a live setting where your guest has made prior commitments, consider that you may be taking time that he or she set aside for others. Don't take that kind of attention for granted. Give a sincere thank you (and a firm handshake) to your guest. It's a really nice way to end an interview.

Recording on the road is not an impossible feat — but it does serve up a fair share of challenges. Applying some of the tips and approaches offered in this practice, you can give your studio-quality recording a new perspective with a nice backdrop of a live setting.

Setting Acceptable Sound Levels

Practice 18

In This Practice

✔ Understanding gain staging

✔ Using an external preamp

✔ Avoiding distortion

Recording studios and broadcast facilities have rack after rack of equipment, all designed to change, alter, and enhance audio for presentation to the public. Chances are, you don't have access to that kind of equipment — and you might not know what to do with it if you did. One of the great things about podcasting is that you don't need that kind of facility to create a show. All you need is a computer and a decent microphone that can connect to your computer. The headset microphone you use for chatting with your video game's strike team probably won't work, but plenty of other low-cost options will.

No matter what equipment you use, however, you need to make sure that you get the proper volume levels for your recording. Levels that are too low could allow static and other noise into the recording, and your listeners will be forced to crank their volume knobs in order to hear anything at all (providing a rude awakening when the normal volume recording up next blasts them out of the room like a Schwarzenegger stunt). Crank it up too much, and it's going to sound distorted no matter what you do to it later. It's impossible to fix that kind of a problem during mixing. The best practice is to record at the right level the first time.

Controlling Volume: All the Gains in Stages

The first step in getting good sound levels is understanding *gain-staging.* Between the microphone and the computer can be several levels of equipment designed to raise the volume, or *gain,* of the audio signal going through it. Each stage is capable of hurting or helping the audio as it goes along; you want to be careful as you move through each stage of the recording process.

When gain-staging your equipment, the most important step is the first volume control encountered in the chain. This control has the most effect on how the signal sounds throughout the process. If the signal is too low at this point, noise creeps in, and that noise becomes amplified as the gain-staging continues. If the signal is too high, nothing can remove the distortion.

The first stage is the distance between you and the mic, and the volume at which you or another person speaks into the mic. Make sure that you speak into the mic from about 3 to 4 inches away, and that you speak in a clear and precise voice. Watch the levels on the devices you're using to record and make sure that you're staying around the –6 dB level.

Without getting bogged down in a bunch of math and no doubt making your head swim, a decibel (or dB) is a measure of the power of sound. It's based on a logarithmic scale; even though a sound may increase by 10 dB, it represents only an apparent doubling in the loudness. Another 10 dB would double that loudness, though, and so on. Things can get rather loud rather quickly.

The microphone

Most microphones don't have volume knobs on them — that kind of control comes later down the line. Still, controls are on the device that alter how the initial sound is recorded. The most common is an *attenuator* switch, more commonly known as a *pad* switch. This switch automatically reduces the gain coming out of the microphone, in case the signal level coming out of the mic is distorted.

It's going to be pretty hard to get most modern microphones to distort, but some older models or types of mics might cause problems. So this little switch can be a handy tool to use when available — though it's mostly used for loud singers and not spoken word recordings.

Avoid the temptation to use a "radio voice" or affect an accent during your podcast. Unless you're going for a special effect, it sounds unnatural and could turn your listeners off.

Computer mixers

Both Mac and Windows operating systems have volume controls built in, commonly used to control the levels for things like CD audio or sound coming from the Internet. One of the controls affects the volume

of incoming mics — and it demands your attention. If this volume control is the first you have on your setup, a good rule in the digital realm is to set that gain at or below –6 dB to –10 dB. You never want to let the volume on that first control rise above 0 dB, because that's where digital distortion occurs.

Start by speaking into the mic (so *that's* why roadies keep saying, "Check one, check two!") in a clear and even tone, like you would use to actually record the podcast. As you're talking, adjust the volume to the proper range.

On the Mac, the volume control (as shown in Figure 18-1) is found under Applications⇨Utilities⇨Audio/MIDI Control. In Windows, you can access the recording volume control by following these steps:

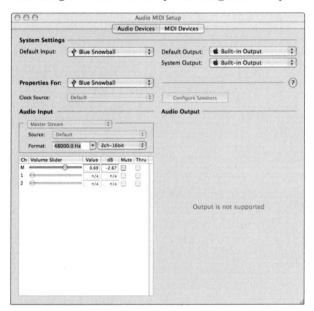

• **Figure 18-1:** The volume control for a Blue Snowball microphone.

1. **Right-click the small speaker icon in the bottom-right corner of your desktop.**

2. **In Windows Vista, click Recording Devices and select the microphone you want to use.**

In Windows XP, click Open Volume Control, choose Options⇨Properties, and click Recording.

3. **Find the volume control in the window that comes up and adjust the volume as necessary.**

Digital distortion is not forgiving, and it never sounds good during a podcast. The best place to start is setting each volume control past the first one at –6 dB and making sure that the level remains constant from there. Depending on the devices you include in the chain, you may have to make slight adjustments here and there. Avoiding large changes in volume late in the chain if possible is best.

Sound-recording program

The final stage of the signal chain is the program you're using to record audio. If you've used gain staging correctly, you should be getting a good, consistent signal without adjusting the volume control for that track. You use these controls later to mix the tracks used in the podcast, so leave these controls alone as much as possible. Large adjustments at this stage might indicate the need to go back and look at previous gain stages for adjustments there.

Working with External Devices

Depending on your equipment budget and needs, you might have some external devices, either hardware or software, that you insert into the signal chain. These devices can either boost or cut the signal gain and change the tonal properties of the audio. Used judiciously, they can make your product sound very professional. But if you go crazy with them, your original signal could get lost in a wash of effects and tricks, lost forever inside an audio morass. Be careful when inserting devices into the signal chain — less can often be more.

External preamps

An external preamp goes between the microphone and the computer, allowing you to boost the signal going into the recording. These preamps are either

in the mixer itself or in a separate box. Some also include analog-to-digital converters that allow you to plug the preamp directly into the computer, using a USB or FireWire cable. Your signal chain looks something like Figure 18-2.

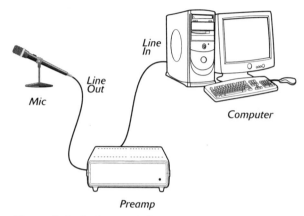

• **Figure 18-2: Audio travels from the mic through the preamp into the computer.**

The normal process to set up a mic preamp uses a few simple steps:

1. **Connect the mic to the preamp, usually with an XLR cable, as shown in Figure 18-3.**

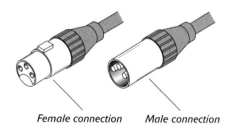

Female connection   *Male connection*

• **Figure 18-3: The XLR jack.**

2. **Connect the preamp to the analog-to-digital converter to the computer, depending on whether the preamp contains converters.**

Figure 18-4 shows what this setup looks like.

3. **Talk into the mic and use the onboard meters to set the correct level, as shown in Figure 18-5.**

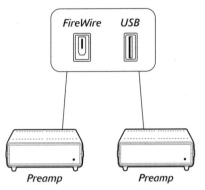

• **Figure 18-4: Analog-to-digital converters can use USB or FireWire connections.**

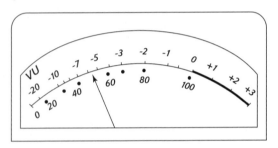

• **Figure 18-5: The preamp meter.**

Some mics designed for computer use already go straight into a USB connection: An external preamp can't be used with that kind of mic.

Compressors and limiters

Compressors and limiters are devices that help smooth out signals and keep levels from getting (respectively) either too low or too high. If used, these are often inserted right after preamps in the signal chain. Concentrate on getting a good, strong signal first, and then use these devices to enhance your sound.

 For more information on compressors and limiters, flip forward to Practice 23.

Software plug-ins

Instead of an actual physical device between the mic and the computer, a *plug-in* is a software-based program inserted into the sound-recording program. Plug-ins simulate physical devices such as compressors, limiters, and other effects units. Just like their hardware counterparts, they can enhance or destroy your audio, depending on how they're used — so you want to be careful when applying them to your podcast. Again, it's best to concentrate on a clear, strong signal at this point — before you start applying effects.

The big advantage to using software plug-ins is the Undo command — which makes it possible to take back a huge mistake if you happen to make one. Just delete the plug-in or use Undo to go back, and there's no harm, no foul. That Undo option isn't available when recording through hardware. Many engineers swear by hardware, however, and maintain that software emulation never equals hardware quality.

The best test is to let your ears decide. Your budget and technical knowledge might have some input here, as well. Above all, remember what your gain-staging technology *should* give you:

✔ A clear, understandable audio signal

✔ A lack of noise

✔ A lack of distortion

✔ A series of meters that allow you to mix and control the audio easily

Level It Out

After the audio is recorded, you can start putting everything in its place volume-wise. Depending on how many voices or music tracks you want to include in your podcast, you may have to move only a couple volume controls — or you might have to manage a multitude of vocal and music tracks. The examples in this section were taken from Apple Soundtrack Pro, but similar controls exist in Adobe Audition, Audacity, Pro Tools, GarageBand, and more. One familiar form is the per-track volume control, where there's a slider on each track (as shown in Figure 18-6).

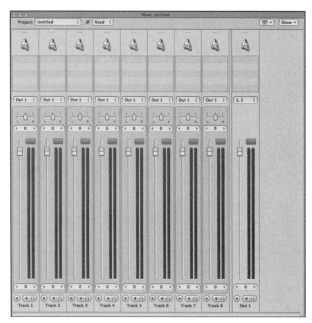

• **Figure 18-6: Track volume controls.**

Another familiar form is the mixer view — the on-screen version of the familiar analog mixer, which has looked much the same since analog mixers were invented (see Figure 18-7).

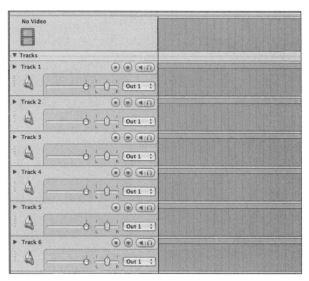

• **Figure 18-7: Mixer volume controls.**

Finally, you can automate the volume level with software controls (Figure 18-8 shows an example). This is useful if you want to have the volume change at different times in the podcast; Practice 20, for example, shows how to do just that when you're setting levels for bed music. You just set the two gain points, and the computer automatically reduces or increases the volume over the length of time between the two points. It's like knowing where you're starting and where you want to end up, and letting the computer take care of the driving.

• **Figure 18-8: An automated volume curve.**

You use these tools to adjust each track's volume in the overall presentation. Fortunately, you won't be tweaking all of them all the time. You probably won't *use* all of them in a normal podcast, and you don't have to worry about what you don't use. And it's easy to categorize the controls according to what you want to emphasize. Read on. . . .

First things first

Decide what is most important for the audience to hear and make sure that clip is the loudest one at all times. In most cases, that's going to be your voice — and the voices of anybody else on the podcast. At other times, it could be the music you're playing or the theme music to your show. In any case, the clip you're emphasizing needs to be the loudest — without creating any distortion.

When you've set a good, strong, clear level for that clip, you can insert the other clips and adjust their volume so they can be heard without overpowering the vocals. As an example, in the next section we take a look at putting some music behind the talking.

Setting music levels

Many podcasts include music under any vocal introductions (or even throughout the whole podcast), so it's important to know how to balance the level of music with that of the spoken word. The trick is to keep the vocals high enough to be heard and understood, but at the same time, let the music provide the atmosphere for the podcast. This section shows you how to balance the levels in Soundtrack Pro, but the concepts and general directions are applicable in many audio-editing programs.

Follow these steps to set music levels:

1. **Launch your audio-editing program.**

2. **Insert the** *Expert Podcasting Practices For Dummies* **DVD into your computer's drive and find the Practice 18 folder. Copy** PodcastIntro.aif **and** PodcastTheme.aif **onto your computer.**

The intro is the spoken word for the podcast, and the theme is the background music. You're going to balance these correctly.

3. **Click the label for Track 1 and rename this track** Vocals. **Then click the label for Track 2 and rename it** Music.

Labeling tracks is a nice way to keep your audio projects organized. Take that extra step and get into the habit of setting up your multi-track projects this way.

4. **Find the location where you saved the two files. Select** PodcastTheme.aif **and import it into the Music track.**

5. **Click the small triangle to the left of the Music label to expand the Music track, as shown in Figure 18-9.**

This is how you access the Volume control on individual tracks.

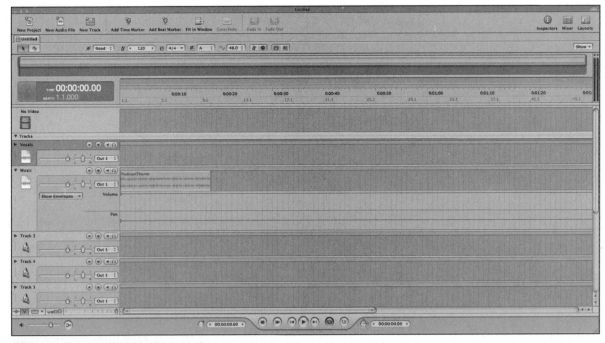

• **Figure 18-9: Expanding the Music track.**

Many audio-editing programs give a variety of options for viewing your tracks. You can make your audio tracks appear larger, making non-destructive editing easier. Another way to view your tracks is by zooming in and out by increments. Check your program's manual for more information.

6. **Pressing the right-arrow key, progress in your Timeline to 00:00:05.00 and double-click the point where the edit line and volume level intersect.**

This intersection is a *control point* that you can designate in any of the various *envelopes* (an audio term that represents an aspect of the audio clip, such as Volume, Pan, Pitch Shifter, and other effects over time). It's a pivot point where you can change values of the effects on the individual track. To affect the entire project,

you can make changes on the *Master Track* at the bottom of the Timeline window.

By the way, you're setting the control point here (as shown in Figure 18-10) because you want the theme to decrease volume at this point.

7. **Pressing the right-arrow key, progress in the Timeline to 00:00:10.00 and double-click the point where the edit line and volume level intersect.**

Doing so creates a second control point, which is the point where you want the volume to end up.

8. **Click and drag the new control point down to –19.00 dB, as shown in Figure 18-11.**

Notice how the level dips down at the first point you created. Now, using the second control point, you set the level for the rest of the music.

9. **Import the** `PodcastIntro.aif` **file into the Vocals track.**

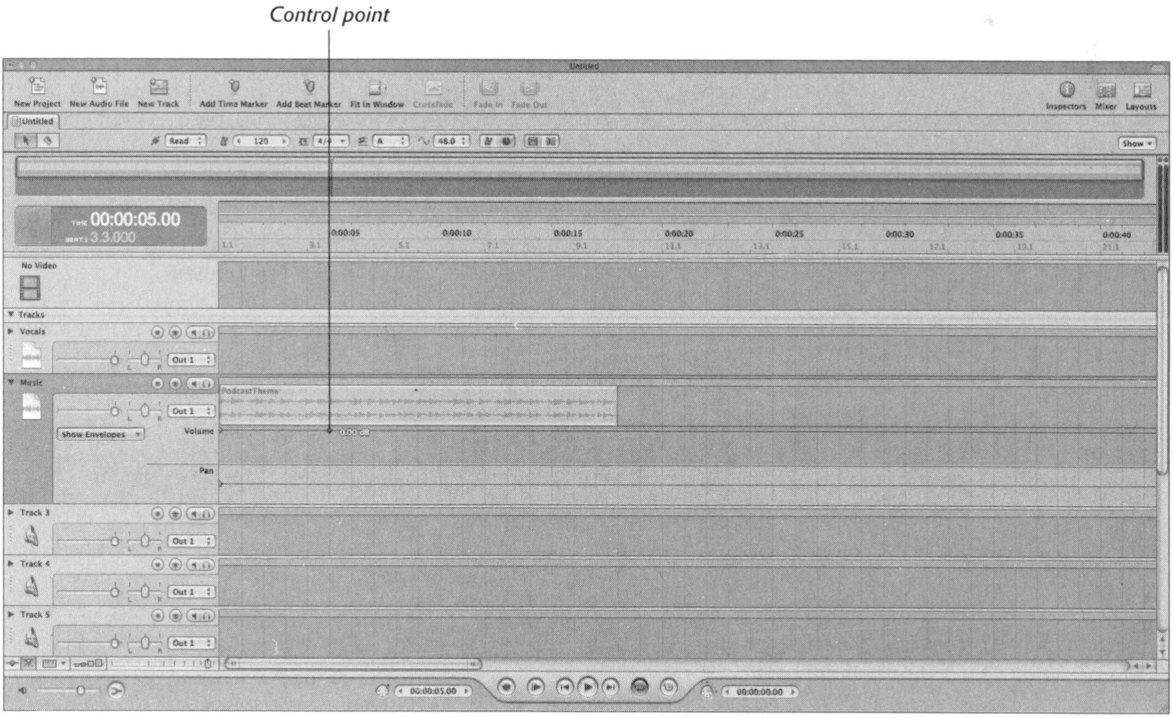

Control point

• **Figure 18-10: Adding a volume control point.**

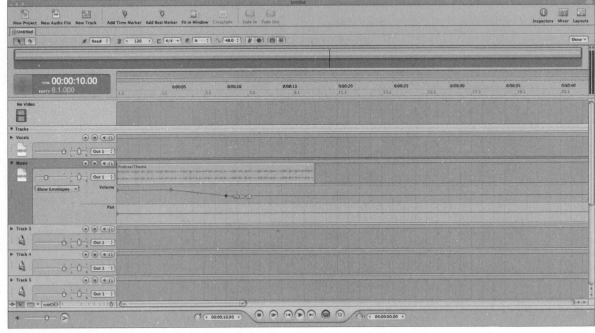

• **Figure 18-11: Using the second control point to lower the volume.**

Here's where you position the voice so the entrance of the podcast's content is smooth and even. Having the voice come in while the music is fading is a nice touch.

10. Return the *playhead* (the line that indicates where the audio will be played, such as the needle on a record) back to the beginning and then review the change. If you need to, add more control points to adjust the levels at critical points.

Note that this music (composed in GarageBand) swells from time to time. You establish the control points to compensate; the last point returns the volume level to –19.00 dB.

11. Return the playhead to the beginning and then review your changes. Find the break in your audio (at the line ". . . the process of podcasting") and add a control point there.

12. Pressing the right-arrow key, progress ten seconds forward in your Timeline and then create a control point here.

Here's where you create a fade-out for the theme.

13. With this new control point in place, click and drag the point down to –96.00 dB.

Doing so fades out your music.

When you've made a lead-in with some music underneath, the next task is mix the outro:

1. Move the playhead to the end of the audio.

2. Move back into the Vocals track to the break in the audio just before you hear, "And if you want to find out more about me. . . ."

This break should happen at approximately 00:03:38.00 in your Timeline.

3. In the Browser window of Soundtrack Pro, select `PodcastTheme.aif` and drag it into the Music track so the clip starts at the control point you established for the edit line.

4. Pressing the left-arrow key, step back in your Timeline to 00:03:35.00 and double-click the point where the edit line and volume level intersect to create a control point.

This control point is where the fade will start.

5. Pressing the right-arrow key, go back to 00:03:38.00 and double-click the point where the edit line and volume level intersect to create another control point. Click and drag this point to –19.00 dB, as shown in Figure 18-12.

6. Play your audio from this point until you hear, "Take care and remember. . . ." Press the space bar after "Remember" to pause the edit line. Double-click to place a control point here.

This point is where the audio will begin to fade up.

7. Pressing the right-arrow key, progress in the Timeline five seconds and double-click the point where the edit line and volume level intersect to create a final control point.

This point is where you want the final audio level to end.

8. Click and drag the new control point up to 0.00 dB.

This takes the fade-up to full. Now the music will finish playing at a normal level and naturally fade out on its own.

9. Return the playhead back to 00:03:35.00 and then play back your outro to review it.

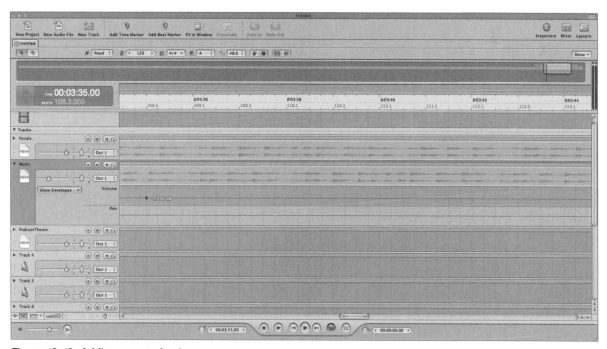

• **Figure 18-12: Adding a control point.**

You have now created an effective fade-in and fade-out of audio, with a segment of music from the DVD providing a background intro and a signal to listeners that the show episode is coming to a close.

Working with audio takes practice, and with every audio project you create, you will develop your own ear for what sounds balanced and level, as well as what may sound too harsh or too soft.

Adding Special Effects

Whearsen you start podcasting, a good rule is to *keep it simple.* That's easy to do, sure, especially if you want to crank out your episodes and spend only a day or two editing and mixing in any music. "Keeping it simple" gets tougher to do, though, when you explore some of the higher-end audio programs and the cool bells and whistles they offer. Filters. Effects. Audio loops. With so many cool toys to play with, your mind begins to get a little crazy mulling over everything you can do with all these extra touches.

That is the trick in mastering all those wacky special effects and royalty-free music loops — playtime. Some of the coolest effects you can come up with for your podcast simply happen from sitting behind the application and playing with it. While we can't teach you how to play with effects, we can take a simple scene from a podcast (provided on the DVD) and dive into your application's filters and effects, and add a new depth to what begins as a very static scene.

Along the way, we also talk about permissions, licenses, and when too much is too much.

Adding in Foley Effects and Filters

Foley effects are studio-quality sound effects of the simple, everyday moments of life captured and then edited or dropped into works of audio or video. The term gets its name from sound-effects pioneer Jack Foley who, in the 1930s, took the art of sound very seriously in Hollywood. His work in getting sound to work with motion pictures set standards still used today. In fact, people who create these sounds and even manipulate them to work for other productions are known as *Foley artists.*

In this practice, you turn into a Foley artist as you add in sound effects. On the DVD, find the file `BilliBaddings_ch8_scene`. This audio is taken from the podcast of *Billibub Baddings and The Case of The Singing Sword.*

What you are going to accomplish here is sweetening up a setting with only a few Foley effects and filters commonly found in pro audio software. You add a door sound effect, and then you slowly build on the effects to create a setting for this scene.

First, listen to the scene as is:

1. **From the DVD, copy the folder marked** Practice 19 **to any location on your computer. Then launch your audio editor and use it to find and import the audio** BilliBaddings_ch8_scene **from the** Practice 19 **folder on your computer.**

   In this practice, we show you how to add sound effects using Apple's Soundtrack Pro (Version 2.0.1), shown in Figure 19-1. The audio is a pretty straightforward read of the moment Billi meets Al Capone face to face for the first time. You want to set the scene by adding in sound effects at key moments.

2. **Play the audio and listen to the five-minute file.**

If you're using a different editing program than Soundtrack Pro, you can easily translate these steps to your application. Before you begin, check the documentation of your application to find out how to import external audio sources.

Applying basic sound effects to audio

Sound effects, or that part of sound design simply called *Foley,* can come included with digital audio workstations (such as Soundtrack Pro and Audition) or can be purchased from places like Digital Juice (described later in this practice). Working with Foley to bring in a sense of realism or put together a "theater of the mind" can be a lot of fun. This kind of post-production can also be just as time-consuming as creating the podcast itself. However, it takes only a little bit of extra effort and strategic placement of Foley to bring a scene to life or add a new dimension to your podcast.

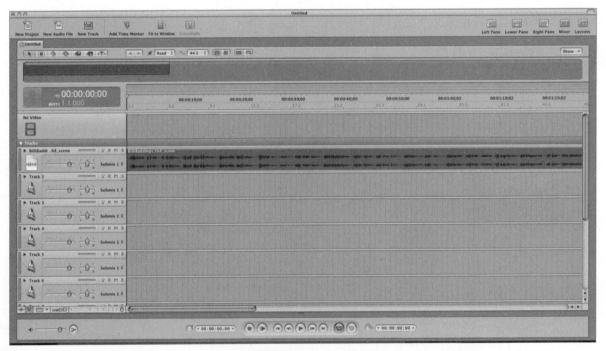

• **Figure 19-1: With the main audio in place, you can now get to sweetening this scene with Foley.**

Follow these steps to add a door sound effect to your scene:

1. **In the audio file, advance 25 seconds in.**

You should hear (and see in the waveform) a break in the audio between " . . . for unscheduled room service" and "the other ogre opened. . . ."

2. **Label one of the available tracks** SFX.

3. **Import the file** Door Opening.aif **from the** Practice 19 **folder, and place it in the SFX track.**

 When you're dropping in sound effects, any breaks you find in the audio are the best places to drop them. If your podcast is scripted, record with these breaks in mind. Make notes in your script indicating where you would like music, sound effects, or anything out of the ordinary.

4. **In the audio file, advance another 25 seconds to the 50-second mark.**

This should place you and your playhead just before " . . . the light behind me dimmed, followed by a soft click."

5. **Import the file** Door Closing.aif **and place it at the 50-second mark in the track labeled SFX.**

6. **Review the scene between 00:00:20.00 and 00:00:55.00.**

Figure 19-2 shows what you should have at this point of the practice. If you're working with Soundtrack Pro or Audition, this should be a close match. If you are using Pro Tools, Bias, or something else, it may not be a mirror reflection but should still be pretty accurate.

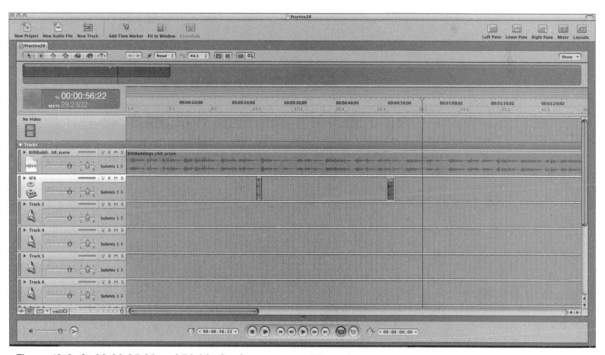

• **Figure 19-2: At 00:00:25.00 and 50.00, the door opens and then closes.**

Many pro applications (such as Adobe Audition and Soundtrack Pro) come with a library of sound effects that are at your disposal. You can incorporate them into your podcast, or go one step further and alter them in playback speed or frequency, creating sound effects custom-built for your production.

Right now the opening of the door sounds great, but you might notice that the door-closing sound effect drowns out the narration (anything but a *soft* click). You can fix that by setting levels, as detailed later on in this practice. However, you need to make a few more changes to this scene first.

Adding ambiance to the scene

Later in this scene, Billi describes the opera music playing on a phonograph. When Tee initially wrote this scene, he pictured a dimly lit dining room with Al Capone at the head of a long table, enjoying his Italian dinner with classical music providing a backdrop. While the narrative already paints that scene, you want to create the setting even more vividly with the sound of a phonograph playing opera music. You achieve this by bringing in some new audio and then applying effects to this audio.

Your audio recorder comes with a variety of *effects* — specific filters that alter or creatively manipulate the audio in your project. Much like that spiffy new mixer board with all its sliders, knobs, and features, the sheer number of effects (not to mention the options for each of them) can appear daunting. What you want to do with these effects so you know what they can do for you is actually pretty simple: You play with them. Experiment, tinker, and go from one extreme to the next, eventually coming up with a sound perfect for the mood, character, or setting you want to create. (For more on audio effects and what you can do with them, check out Episode 5 of *Podcasting For Dummies: The Companion Podcast* on the enclosed DVD.)

With the right application of effects — both Foley and audio — your podcast gains a sense of depth and perspective. Sure, the investment of time grows (exponentially, it feels like), but the end result is well worth it.

That is what you are going to do, right now: Set the scene between the detective and Al Capone with the right application of audio and effects. Here's the blow-by-blow:

1. **Move in your audio project to 00:00:43.00.**

This is right before "Continuing into the next room. . . ."

2. **Label one of the available tracks** Music.

3. **Import the file** `3 Pie Jesu.aif` **from the Music folder of the Practice 19 folder and place it into the** Music **track.**

Vocalist Gwynn Fulcher (shown in Figure 19-3) graciously granted Tee permission to use two selections from her 2002 recital for this lesson. She is the operatic voice in the background of this dinner.

• **Figure 19-3: Vocalist Gwynn Fulcher provides some dinner music for the mob of 1929 Chicago. She is also an artist understanding the benefits of sharing her music with podcasters, as discussed in Practice 20.**

Tee also loves arias by Charlotte Church and Kiri Te Kanawa, especially when backed by the National Symphony Orchestra, but he cannot use those performances on account of copyright laws. Although the *music* may be in public domain, the *performances* are protected — and only the rights-holders can grant permission. Because Gwynn Fulcher owns all rights for distribution of her recital recordings, she can grant Tee permission to use them in this example. (For more on this topic, take a closer look at Practice 20's section on Copyright 101.)

4. Place 3 Pie Jesu.aif **into a new track at 00:00:43.00.**

You don't need to listen to this end result just yet, but if you're feeling brave, you can. You have music against the main audio track and the whole thing sounds like a train wreck; that's because nothing is mixed. All the audio in this scene is competing to be heard, and the current project sounds like a lot of sound files haphazardly thrown together.

Okay, *now* you're going to play around with levels.

Setting levels

So you have the basic elements built into the scene, but right now everything is too loud. So you need to go in and set your volume levels. *Levels* refer to the decibel (dB) level at which each audio track is playing. Depending on which sound you want to have precedence and what sets the background, your levels can vary from track to track.

Follow these steps to set levels to appropriate volumes and make sure everything sounds right:

1. **For your audio editor, find the SFX track's volume control and reduce it to –4.50 dB.**

You could leave the volume level at 0 dB, but for a door to sound that loud, Billi would practically have to be nose-to-nose with the doorknob. Reducing the track's volume down by –4.5 dB mutes the sound enough to make it sound natural.

2. **Still in the SFX track, before the door's closing, reduce the sound even further to –19.00 dB. You can do this by establishing *control points* in the volume track and adjusting the levels. Double-click along the Volume Level to establish these control points.**

Applications like GarageBand, Pyro, Audition, and Soundtrack Pro (shown in Figure 19-4) offer both global control over track volume and dynamic control over volume. In Figure 19-4, you use control points. To find out more about control points and working with them, see Practices 18 and 21.

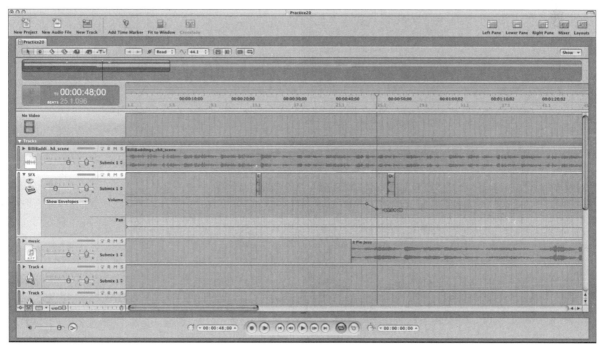

• **Figure 19-4: Adjusting the sound level in Soundtrack Pro using control points.**

Mute the music track and play the clip between 00:00:25.00 and 00:00:55.00. You now hear that the door closing is far softer. This stands to reason because when Billi has entered this room, the door would sound further away, slightly distant.

Now if you muted the music track, unmute it and proceed to the next step to set the levels for Gwynn.

3. **In the Music track, set the track volume to −24.00 dB.**

This may seem like a crime, but remember that Gwynn's talents are (in this case) merely setting the ambiance. So while that volume may seem low, it actually balances out for the rest of the scene.

4. **Save the audio project and then play it for review.**

So where are these numbers (−24 dB, −19 dB, and so on) coming from? Is there a book out there with all the music pieces in the world that state, "If you are mixing Gwynn Fulcher into your podcast, set her levels at −24 dB if she is in the background"? Actually, the level settings are coming from Tee's own preferences and experiences in mixing audio. Feel free to experiment with the levels and find your own preferred balance. You may find that you want some of your Foley to be louder than what is suggested here. You may also discover that no two sound effects and no two music pieces mix alike. You may find you have to adjust throughout some effects and music beds. It all depends on the desired setting you are working to achieve.

Adding the final touches

Listening to this mix, most podcasters would agree it sounds good — and stop here. Something that audiences really respect in their podcasts, though, is an eye (or perhaps *ear,* in this case) for detail. What is tricky here is the narration mentioning that the music is softly playing on a *phonograph.* Even the best gramophone of 1929 (which we're sure Capone had) did not offer a sound comparable to the fidelity you get from an iPod.

In these next steps, you apply some additional sound effects and audio filters to give the background music that scratchy phonograph sound:

1. **In your DAW's documentation, find out where you can apply *effects* on a single track in a project.**

Figure 19-5 shows the option to apply an effect on a track in Soundtrack Pro. Simply select a track, click the Effects tab (or go to Window↝Tabs↝Effects) and then click and drag your desired effect into the window.

2. **Make sure that Music is the selected track where you want to apply the following effect.**

3. **In the Effects menu of your sound application, find the Exciter effect.**

The Exciter effect is a common filter found in many audio applications that changes the texture of an audio signal. It can brighten the treble in sound and mimic the qualities of over-the-phone or walkie-talkie audio. While many applications offer their own built exclusively for effects, some filters (including the Exciter effect) can be found from application to application, program to program:

▶ **Echo:** Applies to audio, based on the *decay* set in the filter, a slight delay, repeating whatever is spoken or recorded. The greater the decay, the greater the delay.

▶ **Reverb:** Similar to echo, reverb adds a booming quality or slight hollowness to audio, mimicking the sound of recording in a large room or concert hall.

▶ **Flanger:** A flanger changes various frequencies found in audio, warping the final audio and giving it an old-style-science-fiction, robotic quality.

▶ **Phase shifter:** Similar to the flanger, a phase shifter not only changes the tone of recorded audio but also layers additional copies of the audio signal on top of it, making it sound like five, six, or seven voices, all speaking at various tones. This effect is reminiscent of 1970s horror-film announcers.

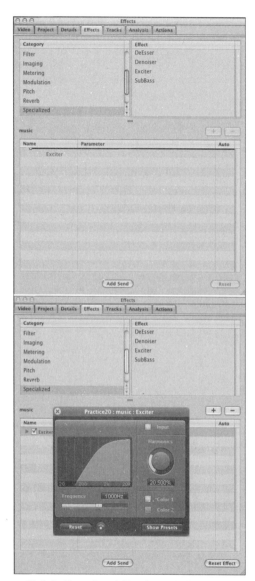

• Figure 19-5: In Soundtrack Pro (or a similar DAW), find
an effect and then click and drag it into the
window associated with the selected track
(top). A control panel for that effect appears
(bottom), allowing you to make adjustments
to the effect's parameters.

Others effects are available, but you can accomplish a lot with these five effects.

Enclosed on this DVD is the first season of Wiley
Publishing's popular podcast, *Podcasting For
Dummies: The Companion Podcast.* Episode
Five discusses some of the different qualities
these various effects have on a recording.

4. **Hit Play on your audio editor and adjust the
Exciter filter to give the music a bright, tinny
sound, almost as if the vocalist is singing over a
telephone.**

The interface may be different from application
to application, but the filter behaves roughly the
same. For Figure 19-6, the Exciter's Harmonics
are set at 169 percent, and the Frequency is set
at 1700 Hz. The quality of Gwen's voice is dramatically changed, making it sound tinny, as if
coming through an old gramophone's horn.
Figure 19-6 shows what the Exciter filter looks
like in Soundtrack Pro.

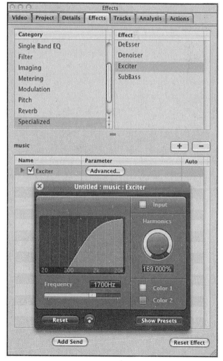

• Figure 19-6: To re-create the phonograph sound, set the
Exciter's Frequency to 1700 Hz and the
Harmonics to 169%.

Next, you give this Foley the last sound effect of a scratchy phonograph.

5. **Label one of the available tracks in your DAW** Record Player.

6. **Import the file** `Pop-Scratch Effect Loop.aif` **from the SFX folder of Practice 19 and place it in the** Record Player **track.**

7. **Place this sound effect to coincide with the beginning of "Pie Jesu" in the Music track. See Figure 19-7 for a reference.**

8. **Continue this sound effect underneath the performance in the Music track.**

Every DAW handles looped SFX differently. The easiest way is to copy the new sound effect and then repeatedly paste it (pressing Ctrl+V or ⌘+V) into the track.

 Many audio applications come with mini-applications that can create *loops* (sound effects or music riffs that repeat so seamlessly you cannot tell where they start and when they stop), making an effect such as this one easy to create and then implement in a project. Check your audio software's documentation to see if it includes such a utility or if freeware is included in the installation.

9. **In the track volume for Record Player, lower the volume to –28.50 dB.**

10. **For both the Record Player and Music tracks, create a five second fade up from –96.00 dB to the current settings by expanding the Track Controls and establishing control points (as described in Step 2 of "Setting levels," earlier in this practice).**

With a five-second fade up for both sound effects, you gradually bring the background into the action, creating the atmosphere. You create a similar fade-out in just a moment. Figure 19-8 gives you a general idea of how this process looks on-screen.

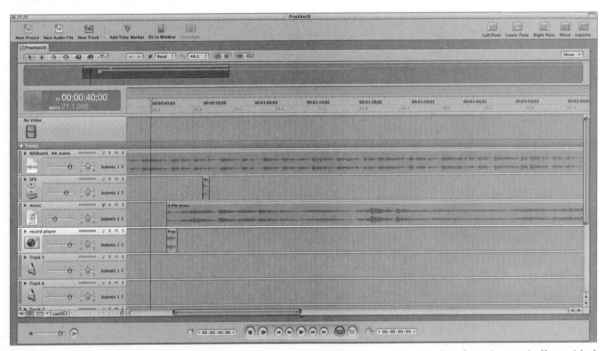

• **Figure 19-7:** This sound effect should start at the same time as the music. Line up the Pop Scratch sound effect with the beginning of Pie Jesu so that both start at the same time.

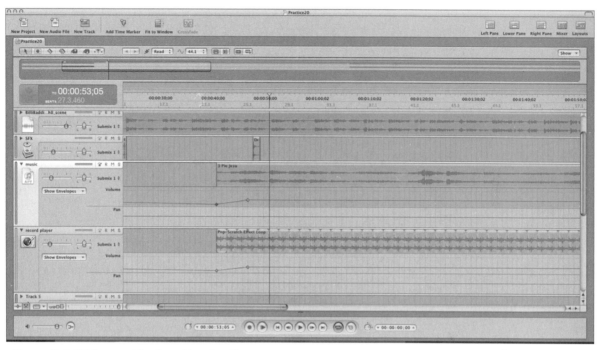

• Figure 19-8: With a combination of levels, effects, and sound effects, the scene begins to take shape.

11. Two seconds after "Pie Jesu" finishes on the Music track, drop in the `6 Biest du dei Mir.aif` file from the Practice 19 folder.

You are bringing in a second track here so it appears as if the record is still playing, and this is the next song.

12. Extend the `Pop-Scratch Effect Loop.aif` sound effect in the Record Player track underneath the performance in the Music track.

You extend the sound effect underneath the new audio to remain consistent in how the songs would sound when playing through the phonograph. Otherwise, the music continues, but the sound of pops and scratches stops. When applying this kind of Foley touch, be consistent.

13. Jump to 00:04:53.00 in your audio project, close to the end of the words "good conversation."

14. In the Track Volume for both the Music and Record Player **tracks, create a control point for the beginning of a fade-out.**

15. At 00:04:59.00, create control points in both the Music and Record Player tracks and fade both tracks down to –96.00 dB, creating a gradual fade-out that draws people into the scene. (See Figure 19-9.)

When you listen to the five-minute scene again, you should notice a depth to it that was lacking earlier. With the application of effects, Foley, and levels, you now have an atmosphere for the upcoming dialogue between dwarf detective Billibub Baddings and Gangland crime boss Al Capone. You can find the final version of the scene in the lesson folder. Look for the file named `Practice19-final.aif`.

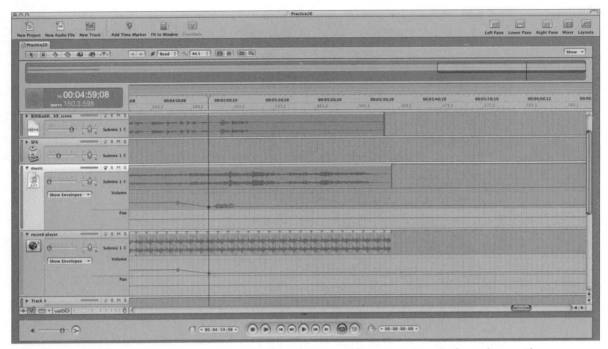

• **Figure 19-9: With this gradual fade-out, the setting is complete, and focus can return to the main narration.**

Audiences appreciate these final touches because there is a thought process behind the application of sound effects and special effects. The "Continuing forward . . ." line ushers in the fade-up into the music. The music is far from perfect; record pops and scratches attest to that. The distance between where Billi stood and the door is also evident here. All these touches indicate the podcaster's care for the production and the intent of the scene being set.

Pretty cool, huh?

Where Else Can I Find All These Cool Special Effects?

Soundtrack Pro, Audition, GarageBand, Peak, and Cubase all come with music loops and sound effects ready for use — but for the previous example, you needed an effect (the record pops) that none of these applications provided.

Sound effects can be found far and wide, and you can find them in a number of ways — online, on CD, on old tapes and records, and in your own imagination. Depending on the venue, what you get varies in quality, but you never have to worry about coming up empty-handed in the pursuit of effects for your podcast.

Online searches and Web sites

Long before the days of podcasting, enthusiastic audiophiles were posting some of their favorite sound effects online and offering them as free downloads. These effects ran the gamut from simple cartoon sound effects to classic one-liners from motion pictures. This range is why, if you embark on a Google-search for sound effects, *be careful.* The range of quality with these AIF and WAV files goes from digital-clear to "What was that again?" Also, you need to worry about licenses and copyrights.

You might not think about copyrights when it comes to sound effects, but the earlier warning about using copyright music also holds true for many sound effects. For example, if you are using the *chirpity-chirp-chirp* communicator sound effect from *Star Trek* in your podcast, you risk Paramount sending you a cease-and-desist because it owns the rights to the effect. The same holds true for the Gate effect from the *Stargate* franchise and the unmistakable sound of that incredible car from *Chitty Chitty, Bang Bang*. These examples of sound effects are copyrighted and trademarked.

Freesound Project

The Freesound Project (`http://freesound.iua. upf.edu`) could be best described as a Magnatune or Podsafe Music Network, only for Foley artists. Working with Creative Commons–licensed sounds, Freesound (shown in Figure 19-10) focuses only on sound effects, not songs. The group strives to offer high-quality sound effects — which you can find easily via its search engines — and cultivates community through forums and awareness. As long as you mention in your podcast that the sound effects are coming from Freesound, you have access to a variety of SFX for free. It's a terrific site and resource.

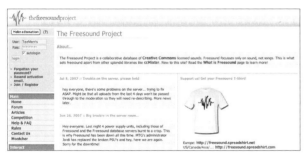

• **Figure 19-10: The Freesound Project — a collection of sound effects, all offered for free under the Creative Commons license.**

SoundSnap

This Web site is a newcomer to the podosphere. SoundSnap (`http://soundsnap.com`) combines creative sound artistry with community by inviting registered users to freely distribute their music loops, sound effects, and production techniques in one convenient location online. In the same vein as The Freesound Project, SoundSnap's sound effects and music loops are all protected under Creative Commons, and it offers its own search engine in order to help you track down that perfect effect for your podcast. While not part of its Terms of Use, make sure you tell people about SoundSnap, either at the end of a podcast episode or on forums outside of its own. If you are working on a budget and need a high-quality sound effect or music loop fast, give SoundSnap a search. This Web site can be a powerful tool in your podcast's production.

SoundDogs

We were in a serious pinch when we couldn't find a vintage camera flash sound effect, and while searching high and low online for one that was royalty-free and of good quality, we came across SoundDogs (`www.sounddogs.com`). SoundDogs is one part database of SFX vendors, one part search engine for high-quality SFX, and a one-stop-shop for high-quality SFX collections. We happened to find the vintage flash effect on the *Dog Pack #3: Mixed Bag* and were so happy with the quality that we picked up *Dog Pack #4* on an impulse. Reasonably priced and easy-to-download collections, SoundDog is a good place to start building your library.

Digital Juice

Tee blames *New York Times* Bestseller Tracy Hickman for turning him on to the Juice (`www.digital juice.com`), shown in Figure 19-11. Digital Juice is hardly cheap . . . at first glance. What makes Digital Juice the podcaster's best friend is how high quality the product is, the professionalism of its tech support, and the versatility of everything it offers in the way of audio and video media. Tee's first purchase was the Digital Juice SoundFX Library, a collection of over 10,000 professional-grade, royalty-free SFX. The package of CDs normally sold for $700. Digital Juice was having a special and selling it for $250.

This is the other reason why Digital Juice is the podcaster's best friend: extremely fantastic deals!

Thanks to the generosity of Digital Juice, Tee now sports a library of royalty-free music (that can be customized to the job in question), and unlike some royalty-free collections where you're lucky if you get one or two really usable tracks, Tee has some discs that are nearly exhausted. Digital Juice is a resource all podcasters serious about their production values should invest in.

• **Figure 19-11: Digital Juice — great deals for great products that help you give the final touches to a podcast.**

D.I.Y.

Necessity is the mother of invention. Sometimes the simplest of sound effects is nowhere to be found, be it among 10,000 on Digital Juice or online as a free download. You can scour the Internet for hours on end, find a collection (which may hit you up for a healthy chunk of change), and then wait for the collection either to download via your connection or to arrive via the post office, but we have an even better idea — a cost-effective one, too: Take two steps away from your computer and look at it. You have recording equipment and audio-editing software. Give it a shot!

Figure 19-12 includes candid shots of the award-winning podcast group, Prometheus Radio Theatre, taking the next logical step: creating their own sound effects.

• **Figure 19-12: Prometheus Radio Theatre (led by Steven H. Wilson, top) creates its own sound effects live with Foley artists (middle) and actors (bottom) during a live performance for podcast.**

Okay, you may feel silly repeatedly opening and closing newspapers, striking two glasses together to make the sound of a toast, sipping loudly on your coffee or iced tea, and then recording yourself swallowing your beverage of choice. But Foley artists do these kinds of things on a daily basis. They create the sounds that add a new dimension to audio and video works, and these small details are what make your podcasts unique experiences. If you have the equipment, take advantage of it and create your own SFX. In a pinch, what you create can work just as effectively as the SFX created by the pros.

Can I See Your License for These Special Effects, Sir?

When you listen to podcasts about how to podcast (such as the *Podcasting For Dummies* podcast, *Podholes*, or Jason Van Orden's *Podcast Underground*), you'll hear all of us talk about royalty-free music and sound effects. Something you might hear us say is, *"When you buy it, it's yours. You own it."*

This is a quick-and-dirty way of saying *"Yes, you have purchased permission to play the music as much as you like,"* but not all royalty-free vendors are created equal, and *licenses* are very important to pay attention to. They help you stay unsummoned and unsued.

End-User License Agreements

An *End User License Agreement* is usually posted or comes with the software you have just purchased. For example, the ten-dollar CD of sound effects that you just bought off the rack may have a few paragraphs on the inside jacket that read, "These sound effects are granted permission for *commercial* use (such as in the office, around the home, and so on) but not for *broadcast* use (that is, television, radio, film — and that means they're taboo for *pod*cast use)."

If you were to purchase a *Star Trek* sound effects CD, its inside jacket uses only one sentence for its license agreement:

> *WARNING: unauthorized reproduction of any recordings contained in this album is prohibited by Federal Law and subject to criminal prosecution.*

License agreements don't get more clear-cut than that.

Demystifying Digital Juice's license agreement

For Digital Juice, the license agreement grants the user a touch more flexibility:

✔ You can use Digital Juice's music (and even sound effects) for opening fanfares, background music, and the like. However, you can't use the music as performance or foreground music (say, music heard over the phone while on hold or as the basis for your own song).

✔ You can use the sound effects and music of Digital Juice as *enhancements* in your media (that is, as a part of your video, narration, slide presentations, radio or television productions, and such). Additionally, you have permission to alter the sound effect or music to fit your production's needs.

So what *can't* you do with Digital Juice's stuff? Just because you bought music or SFX from Digital Juice doesn't mean you own it outright, so you can't do any of the following:

✔ Resell it. (This means burning your own CDs and selling the stock music as is, reworking mixes to create your own and then selling them, and writing accompanying vocals to its music and passing it off as your own.)

- ✔ Post Digital Juice SFX on your Web site for download.

- ✔ Store it on a network server for everyone to use.

That kind of distribution is either prohibited or requires a different license.

For all the details in Digital Juice's license, you can visit the Digital Juice Web site and look at any of its Products windows. In the Overview window is a link for Royalty-Free End-User License Agreement, which explains everything clearly. (That's something else we love about its Web site!)

The point is that while you do own *permission* to do stuff with special effects and music you purchase, there are limits. Make sure you check out the details in all the license agreements, and make sure you're not tempting fate — or someone's legal team, for that matter.

Too Much of a Good Thing Is . . . Too Much

Can you overdo it with special effects and music? Absolutely. In the five-minute sample provided for this practice, you could have added in footsteps and even the sounds of silverware against a plate. There is also the temptation to add in room noise or reverb into a conversation to give it that realistic room echo. There are a lot of possibilities. What you need to ask yourself is whether the production is helping or hindering the intent and message of your podcast.

 Whenever you make changes to audio projects, it's a good idea to back up ten seconds (or more) before the new edit and *then* play it. This way you get an idea of what is happening before the change and get a good handle on the timing heading into the new edit.

Even if you scale back "realistic" effects (that is, sounds of nature, music, outside traffic, and room noise), try listening to sweetened scenes with an objective ear and an open mind. Overdoing it can entail more than just the time dedicated to composing or procuring just the right kind of music. Another real risk is overengineering a podcast until the content is lost in a sea of special effects and post-production smoke and mirrors. The experience of listening to highly produced podcasts like this one should bring a smile to your face, and not give you a splitting headache and make you more than ready to say, "Enough!"

Controlling the inner composer

Tee was working with GarageBand (version 2) when he podcast *Morevi: The Chronicles of Rafe & Askana*. One of many reasons he chose to use that software was because of the hundreds of music loops he had access to. He wanted to use music for themes, bridges between scenes, and setting moods. (Yeah, he likes moods in his podcasts.) In the second chapter of *Morevi* (third episode), he had his first segue. He started playing. He continued to play. And play. *And* play. With GarageBand, he changed pitches, tempos, and instruments in all the various riffs and loops he was playing with. The final composition was (if he does say so himself) an impressive piece capturing the emotion and turmoil Askana grappled with in the moment.

Those ten seconds of music took him only 2½ hours to compose.

When it comes to drawing the line for post-production and adding in the next dimension of your podcast, always ask yourself these questions:

- ✔ Is this extra step really needed?

- ✔ Do I really want to dedicate more time to the post-production of this podcast?

Will listeners appreciate the extra effort? Sure, *provided the content of the podcast is not lost.* No matter how good the production quality of your podcast is, good content is what keeps your listeners subscribed. The content of each episode is paramount, and the amount of post-production you put into the episode should work *with* the content, not compete against it for listeners' attention. Invest the right amount of time and effort

specifically for your podcast, and you will find the balance best suited for you.

Now that you have a taste of what you can do with sound effects, go play! It's the best way to find out exactly what you can do — and what you'll want to do with your podcast's production values.

Adding Music

You're ready to kick off your podcast. You could do what Ron Moore does on his *Battlestar Galactica* podcast and welcome your listeners to whichever episode or special treat he is introducing you to, or you can search for a good opening theme.

But if you want that opening theme to be Bear McCreary's primal, tribal opening to *Battlestar Galactica,* there may be issues. (No, frak that — there *will* be issues, as in *legal* issues!)

This means you need to know where to find good music for your podcast, and while you're shopping around, you may want to think about having the music — especially if you really like it — playing throughout your podcast. This kind of music is also commonly referred to as *bed music* — a track dedicated to providing an aural backdrop for your podcast. Music-as-backdrop can remedy incurable ambient noise and set a pleasant atmosphere for your show hosts and guests — but a little bit can go a long way.

Where to Find Good Music

As mentioned elsewhere in this book, good music that's available free (or at least affordably) to podcasters isn't hard to find, provided you know where to look.

Magnatune

Magnatune (www.magnatune.com) is a favorite site for many podcasts; it offers quality mp3 downloads of independent musicians of all genres, of all backgrounds (see Figure 20-1). Users can perform a search for a style, a specific instrument, or an artist they may have heard on another podcast. All search results appear in a Web page that links back to the artists and the mp3 offerings.

What makes Magnatune a good choice for your podcast's musical demands is that all music featured here is deemed *podsafe* — you can download these high-quality mp3s and use them for your own production, provided you follow the rules and guidelines of the Creative Commons 2.5 License. Podsafe music, contrary to the belief that it features only obscure talent on par with bands like Wyld Stallionz and The Lone Rangers, includes music by professionals. Independent artists have found sites like Magnatune to be the Napsters of the next generation — providing their music (and themselves) free press and publicity, distributing their work worldwide. That's because, as a condition of the Creative Commons agreement, they must be given credit in the podcast for their music.

• **Figure 20-1: Magnatune welcomes listeners with a user-friendly interface and a variety of musical styles, all podsafe and waiting for use.**

Magnatune's other terrific perk is the quality control in its mp3s. This is a vast improvement over illicit Web sites promising free mp3 downloads after an onslaught of flashing banner ads try to snag you into raffles, contests, and the like, only to palm off audio that sounds as if it is being played from the bottom of the barrel (in one of *Titanic's* cargo holds). Magnatune assures listeners that the mp3s are safe downloads and high-quality in their sound, and

that none of the music offered is in violation of copyright laws (as discussed in brief at the end of this practice). So if you need a cool touch for your podcast, check out what waits for you at Magnatune.

Podsafe Music Network

When it comes to 800-pound podosphere gorillas, this site is King Kong. Music found here has been prominently featured on shows like *LoveHouse Radio* (www.lovehouseradio.com), *The ADD Cast* (www.addcast.net), and *The RevUp Review* (www.rev-up-review.co.uk); and has provided themes for popular podcasts like Scott Sigler's *The Rookie* (Lacunna Coil, "Heaven's a Lie") and Phil Rossi's *Crescent* (Chrysalis, "Chrysalis"). This Web site, of course, is the Podsafe Music Network (http://music.podshow.com), a staple in Adam Curry's Podshow Network.

The Podsafe Music Network (shown in Figure 20-2) was the first on the scene that offered podcasters professional, amateur, and somewhere-in-between music for free. Its database of musicians and genres continues to grow, promising the new, the experimental, and the edgy to audio producers everywhere.

• **Figure 20-2: Podshow, the first (and considered by some to be the best) site to offer podsafe music.**

On arriving at the Podsafe Music Network's Web site, take a look at the layout, and you'll find two access points here — one for musicians and the other for podcasters:

✔ **Musicians:** If you have music *that you have all rights and permissions to record and distribute,* then you will want to register yourself and your works. This information includes not only your music, but also your Web site (or your band's Web site), where to find albums for sale (iTunes, CD Baby, and such), and contact information for the band or musician. Shortly after registration, your mp3s become part of the database, and you're given private access in order to update your profile with new music. Podcasters should know about this site in case their podcast features someone *not* registered in the Podsafe Music Network (PMN). Let your music talent know about what this site offers and the potential for publicity.

✔ **Podcasters:** The second entry for podcasters is similar to that for musicians; you register as much information as you have on your show, its feed, and what it is all about. Your Podsafe Music Network profile lets visitors know what your show is all about and also gives others in the network links to recent genres, bands, and interests you've found on PMN. (After all, it's a network. You're helping fellow podcasters by sharing your discoveries.) Musicians can also find out more about your show and its message via your PMN profile.

After setting up your profile, you can surf, sample, and download safely because all the music featured on PMN is completely podsafe, just waiting for you to feature it in a podcast.

Make sure to play by the rules of the Creative Commons License. (For more on what the Creative Commons License is, visit `www.creative commons.org`.)

Digital Juice

Another option (albeit another financial investment in your podcast) is to look into Digital Juice (`www.digitaljuice.com`), the cutting-edge, award-winning production studio that has become a friend to both professional and amateur media studios. Digital Juice produces *royalty-free music* of various genres and of various quality. Royalty-free music

means you purchase the music offered and then the music is yours to use in your podcasts, audio spots, and other media projects. You don't have to pay any additional fees to use this music.

 Just because the music is royalty free and you have purchased the rights to use it does not mean you "own" this music. Don't assume that it is yours to do with as you see fit. You cannot (for example) sell this music track by track to other podcasters, nor is it your right to loan out the music to others. Royalty-free music vendors have terms of agreements that spell out what you can and cannot do legally with their music — ranging from the amount of use (such as "drop-and-pay" royalty-free music) to the circumstances in which the music is used (say, private license versus commercial-use license). Make sure you understand the terms of the agreement before you invest in a vendor's music; also understand that the music — although it's in your library — is legally not *your* music.

So why Digital Juice? True, other royalty-free music vendors are out there, but consistent quality is hard to find. In some cases, the music is all synthesizers and drum machines, and at other times, the music is full orchestration. It's hard to decide beforehand what you need, how you're going to use the composition, and more importantly, whether the investment (CDs of royalty-free music range in the hundreds of dollars) is a sound one. (Pun intended.)

Digital Juice (shown in Figure 20-3) is a step up from other vendors of royalty-free music vendors in what it offers to is clientele: fully orchestrated and professionally produced music pieces.

Digital Juice offers musical beds in the Sound FX Libraries, and various pieces in both BackTraxx volumes and its extensive StackTraxx Series. Very few, if any, of its beds rely solely on synth and electronic percussion. Each piece, whether ten seconds long or the full three- to four-minute suite, is fully stocked with brass, woodwinds, guitar, exotic instruments from world cultures, and even vocal accompaniment. Digital Juice doesn't cut corners in its compositions;

the end result is a DVD of superior music that can be easily applied to your podcast's needs.

• **Figure 20-3: Digital Juice, the podcaster's best friend and second-biggest addiction next to podcasting itself.**

Another advantage of Digital Juice is The Juicer (shown in Figure 20-4), which adds a new degree of versatility to its music.

The Juicer goes through the composition you have selected and separates it into individual tracks. You can then turn off unwanted instruments or effects and export the new piece, or isolate only the tracks you want as separate tracks so that you can mix and match other pieces. This capability lets users customize the music to their specific needs.

 If you are a video podcaster or considering the jump from audio to video podcasting, Digital Juice also offers superior video products. Alongside its audio collections, Digital Juice also offers *Jump Backs* and *Swipes*, stock footage, video animations, and transitions that give your video podcasts that newsmagazine-and-broadcast-TV quality. There are also Editor's Tookits, Motion Elements, and other stock animation — in both standard and high-definition resolution — that can add a final polish and edge to your video podcast.

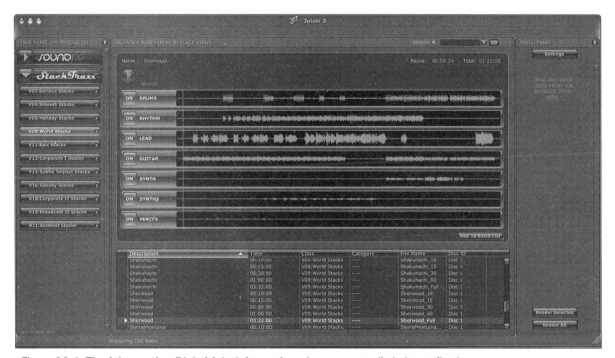

• **Figure 20-4: The Juicer makes Digital Juice's layered music more versatile in its application.**

Independent Musicians: Creating a Synergy

When New Zealand author Philippa Ballantine was planning out her podcast, *Whispers at the Edge* (http://whispers.libsyn.com), her goals not only included giving writing advice but also offering a look at the culture of New Zealand. The song "Southern Gael" from Celtic musician Steve McDonald was her desired opening and closing theme. It was composed and performed by a New Zealand native from her hometown of Wellington, and the song itself set a fun, lively tone. The only problem was that this independent musician was already featured on the Etherean Music label (www.ethereanmusic.com).

Pip sent his label a query, making it a point to mention she was from Wellington as well and that she planned attribution within the podcast because the track would be used for the intro and outro online. Her expectations were realistic: a polite "no thank you" at best — and at worst, a reading of leagalese and statements concerning copyright permission.

The Etherean Music folks did reply. They offered up "Southern Gael," along with *any* of Steve's tracks, and then offered to arrange an interview with him if Pip was interested. Suffice it to say she was.

Pip isn't the only one to offer (and benefit from) this opportunity for both podcasters and musicians. Figure 20-5 shows several musical acts who have introduced their works to new audiences everywhere via podcasting.

In the late 1990s and then in the first year or two of the 2000s, independent musicians were huge supporters of Napster as a means of getting their music introduced to a wider audience. Podcasting offers similar opportunities — a new venue for independent musicians to introduce themselves and find new audiences for their work.

• **Figure 20-5:** Musicians like (top to bottom) Diane Arkenstone, The Beatnik Turtles, and Lisa Furukawa have offered their music to the podosphere.

Podcasters offer an important bonus from the Napster-like music services out there: the personal touch. Show hosts are reaching out to musicians and independent record labels, asking for permission to play music on their shows. The trade-off is typically free promotion on a podcast in exchange for playing the music, but this new distribution method is proving itself to be a platform for independent musicians, showcasing new and aspiring talent. Some musicians like Jonathan Coulton with his *Thing a Week* and Beatnik Turtles' *Song of the Day* have even gone on to launch their own podcasts, producing music for a global audience. The RIAA may be watching (and listening) closely, but podcasters are discovering brighter (and, in many cases, better) voices in music.

Still, there are processes to follow, even on this most casual of approaches.

Ask for permission

Oh sure, this may sound like a no-brainer, but formally asking for permission to play a musician's work is considered good etiquette. If you're considering asking permission from musicians you've found somewhere other than on podsafe music sites, you'll want to set up a dialogue to address some important considerations:

- **Who you are:** "Hi, my name is [*your name*] . . . "

- **What you do:** " . . . and I'm planning a podcast called *How Do I Do This?* It's a do-it-yourself kind of podcast."

- **Why you're talking to them:** " . . . I believe your music would be perfect for this project."

Make sure you cover all these aspects in your pitch e-mail, along with a follow-up (which we get to a bit later in this practice).

Confirm the proper contact

Even with independent musicians, make certain that the *distribution rightsholder* is the one you're talking to. While some indie artists do hold all rights to their music — rights to the music itself, to recordings, and

to performances — some musicians sign contracts with independent recording studios that hold on to the *distribution* rights to the songs. These rightsholders are the ones who grant permissions to play music on podcasts, radio, television, and other such forms of distribution — and they will have the final say on whether (legally) you can or cannot feature the desired music on your podcast.

Ask the artists whether they own *all* rights to their music, including distribution rights. If they don't, then ask them, "Who can I talk to about featuring your music on my podcast?" Once you have the ear of the right contact, there's only one more commitment to meet before you can feature this music on your show.

Pay it forward once permission is granted

Now, there's a basic difference of assumptions here: You've made a conscious effort to give away your podcast's content for free; the indie musician didn't really plan to record an album just to give the music away for people to do with as they pleased. When a musician is donating time, talent, and the result of all that effort to your podcast, you should not take it for granted. As a podcaster with a listenership, you have several ways to compensate the musician's work:

- **Provide links in the show notes and on the podcast's blog.** Give the musicians involved with your podcast active links in your show notes (and on the show's blog) back to their Web sites — or (better still) to their URLs in iTunes and CD Baby.

- **Give pages and brief bios of the musicians on your show's host blog.** Create a page in your blog that's all about the musicians featured in your podcast. Give a brief background on the performers, links to their Web sites, and point out the artists' specific contributions to your podcast (such as opening credits, love theme, or closing credits).

- **Give musicians credit for their contributions in the podcast.** A quick nod to the talent — along the lines of "Theme music by . . ." and "Visit the band's Web site . . ." — means a lot to the artists who graciously give their work to you. It's free advertising, as well as a sincere thank you from the show's host. Remember, they didn't have to give you their music, so step up and give them a shout out in your show's outro.

From behind the drums, it's Geo!

George Hrab (http://geologicrecords.net) is an independent musician who is finding out firsthand the benefits of working with podcasters. After being featured on *Skepticality*, George was invited by the show's hosts Derek and Swoopy to Dragon Con 2006 in Atlanta, Georgia. Geo and his music were soon introduced to podcasters like Mur Lafferty, Leann Mabry, and others. With such a broad range in musical styles, podcasters started coming to him asking for permission to feature his music. George now regards the gamble of his music giveaway as one that paid off.

"There has been an undeniable increase in sales and digital downloads," he says. "More people are going to iTunes and the like, and then end up buying a physical CD from CDBaby." The unexpected windfall is the instant global reach of his music. "Folks from Australia and Singapore who should have no idea who I am have downloaded songs and bought albums. That is purely due to podcasts."

Not only has the podosphere embraced Geo, but Geo in turn has returned the admiration with the launching of his own podcast, the *GeoLogic Podcast* (http://geologicpodcast.com).

The Method to Mixing Music with Dialogue

Striking the right balance between dialogue and music takes patience, time, and a lot of trial and error. At one moment, you may find that your music is right where it should be. Then the quality of the song changes, and now suddenly your voices are competing with the backdrop.

To set the right balance between your music and your show's content, here are a few tips to follow:

- **Consider whether bed music is really needed.** Keep in mind that when you bring music into your podcast, the production demands are stepped up. Is bed music something the podcast needs or lends itself to, and how much bed music will you need? Will you need it for a theme at the beginning and end that lets people know the episode is (respectively) beginning and ending? Or will it need a consistent level of background music to set a mood, tone, or atmosphere?

   When you incorporate bed music into a podcast, you should ask whether the podcast really needs this extra touch. High production values are always appreciated, but if you can keep it to the basics, your listeners will appreciate that, too.

- **Watch and listen to your levels from beginning to end.** Many podcasters set their levels only once and then think the job is done. Music of any kind has a variety of qualities about it, and these qualities become complicated on crescendos and decrescendos.

 After you have brought in the music you want to use for your bed, continue to listen to the podcast with the music playing underneath. When needed, add in volume control points and bring your music only a decibel or two down. A tiny adjustment may be all you need.

✔ **Keep your music above –30 dB.** No, this is not *the* magic number, and all music behaves differently; but *on average* when music drops down underneath –30 dB, it begins to resemble an audio signal bleeding in from some other source. You want the bed music to have a purpose as well as a definitive presence — but you don't want the music to overpower the content or message of your podcast. While there will always be exceptions to the rule, music above –30 dB is a good average to shoot for in post-production.

Fair Use 101: What Is and Isn't "Fair" in Podcasting

Before we get into this, we want to crystal clear about something: We are not lawyers. (But sometimes we play them on podcasts.) This section offers general insights about copyrights and *fair use,* but none of us writing this book are lawyers. So when it came time to write a bit about the laws around copyrights and fair use, we thought, "Why not talk to a lawyer?" And did we ever find the right guy — a lawyer who is also a musician!

And when we asked attorney Robert S. Meitus about copyrights, fair use, and podcasts, he responded with an answer for the ages: "Podcasts are tricky."

Podcasters attempt to stretch the fair use doctrine to its limits and then see if there's just a little more give to it. Fair use is governed by Section 117 of the Copyright Act and is not limited to criticism, education, or noncommercial use, as is commonly believed. This does not mean that you can be doing a podcast, make zero money at it, use your favorite science fiction theme as your theme, and *then* claim fair use.

Robert states, "There are four factors to analyze when determining if something is fair use":

✔ **How is the music being used in your podcast?** Is it *commercial* (as in, is this a money-making

venture?) or noncommercial (not-for-profit, or for fun and no profit at all)? If it's noncommercial, the use is more likely a fair use.

Is it *transformative* or nontransformative? Transformative works usually have a socially beneficial purpose, such as parodies. (A good example of transformative work is the fan film, Troops, where Inner Circle's "Bad Boys" was used but both *Cops* and *Star Wars* were parodied in this work.)

✔ **Is the underlying work a highly creative work, such as a song or literature or a less-creative work, such as a news story?** Fair use is more likely with the latter.

✔ **What is the market effect on the underlying work?** This is probably the trickiest part of fair use. The more effect a use has on the underlying work's marketability, the less likely it is to be a fair use. Insignificant economic impact on the underlying work favors fair use.

✔ **How much of the material is used?** Are you using the whole theme for the podcast, or just a portion of it? The *less* you use the copyrighted material, the more favorably the courts tend to regard that use — and the likelier it will be deemed fair use.

Objective rules — such as the "30–60 second rule" where you are allowed 30 seconds of a song with no voiceover and 60 seconds if a voiceover is applied — are myths. There is no objective way to measure the fair use factors. Rather, courts subjectively weigh all four factors, typically placing the most importance on the first and fourth. Fair use is an affirmative defense, which might help you in court but doesn't prevent you from being sued in the first place.

Robert goes further into the explanation of fair use and copyright protections with a legal look at what some have claimed was the precursor to music-in-podcasting: Napster. "Napster was commercial (proxy for purchases), nontransformative (whole songs), and dealt with highly creative works (the music compositions and sound recordings), and it hurt the market value of the music according to the courts (people were downloading for free instead of buying albums). Therefore Napster lost its fair use defense and, ultimately, the case."

When it comes to podcasting, these rules can still apply. "So let's say you start up a *Sci-Fi at the Movies* podcast. You have a *Star Wars* soundtrack. Your podcast's theme would be repetitive, nontransformative, and could possibly hurt the market by devaluing the license value of the creative music. The podcast might have some luck if it's noncommercial and only a small amount of music is used; but, this is not a strong case for fair use."

The best defense you can implement concerning music for your podcast is to use royalty-free music from the get-go. For maximum legal safety, stick to music from Web sites that promote and offer pod-safe music, or use music from independent artists *only* if you have the *written* permission of the artists and the rights holders. It's best to podcast with a clear conscience — and if you err, err on the better side of caution.

Practice

Editing Audio after Editing the Session

In This Practice

✔ Choosing an audio file format

✔ Exporting your finished product

✔ Making edits in the final file

One of the greatest gifts of digital audio is the ease of creating a final product. Anybody who ever had to take a razor blade to tape in order to splice together a finished master track knows the pain of making an incorrect final cut and ruining the project. In the land of ones and zeros, removing a momentary mistake is just an Undo away. You've also gained a great deal of power over a range of processes — from placing sound clips in tracks to arranging their position and volume to panning their envelopes in just the right way. Once all that's done, you'll want to create a master file of your edited podcast to prepare for release. You may still have to do some editing, but the heavy lifting is done. You're ready to do some precision surgery at this point.

Choosing the Format for Your Audio File

Once your mix is done, you're going to create a final file to use for the rest of the work on your podcast. You're not quite ready to send it on to the listeners yet; you're just going to add the finishing touches to your final mix. The first step is to choose the format of your final file. Many programs have their own default formats — and for the most part they're interchangeable. Your main concern at this point is making sure that all your information is retained during the post-production process — and that requires an uncompressed format.

Keep it uncompressed to make it larger than life

Compression is a word that's thrown about quite a bit in audio production; unfortunately, it can have a couple of different meanings. When applied to audio, as in a vocal track, it applies to an effect that brings down higher volume levels and raises lower volume levels to produce a smooth, even track. When applied to a data file (such as your podcast's final mix), compression means a reduction in the file size without losing a terrible amount of sound quality. You'll compress your file when you create an mp3 or AAC file of your podcast. For now, though, you need to make sure your file remains *un*compressed. You're going to want the maximum amount of audio quality you can get when you make cuts or apply effects to your podcast. These edits will sound better when you're working with a full audio file, and not the digital photocopy you get from a compressed file.

 When you're making a compressed audio file, always start with an uncompressed file. Making a compressed file from an already-compressed file can further reduce audio quality and create *artifacts* (extraneous noises) that can turn off a listener.

Uncompressed file types: Wave and AIFF

There are two main types of uncompressed audio files; either one will give you good results:

- **Wave** files (marked with the file extension .WAV) are often found in Windows-based programs, and this file format is the default setting for Adobe Audition and other audio editors.

- **AIFF** files are traditionally found more on Mac-based systems, but these days it's easier to interchange these formats between operating systems than it used to be.

Using the default for whichever program you choose should be okay.

Sample rates

Both WAV and AIFF files can have different bit rates and sample rates, depending on the capabilities of your audio-editing program and hardware. (See Practice 24 for more on bit rates and sample rates.)

Every audio program you'd want to use with a podcast is capable of CD-quality audio (16-bit, 44.1kHz). If your audio is at a lower resolution, you won't see a benefit from exporting at a higher level. You'll also just end up creating an unnecessarily large file size

because all that extra data has to go *somewhere*. Choose a sample rate consistent with your recording, and you'll be ready to go.

Exporting Your Goods

This process used to be called *mixing down* by music producers in Hawaiian shirts and studio tans. It's received the more computer-oriented term *exporting* now, but it represents the same thing: You're taking the multiple tracks you've put together and converting them into a stereo file. Luckily, you don't have to roll tape and man the mixing board to get everything right. You've already set the levels — and maybe even automated any volume changes — in your music beds and sound effects. You just have to issue a few commands, and everything else is automated.

Exporting with Soundtrack Pro

Let's take a look at exporting a file in Soundtrack Pro. At this point, the mix is finished, and you just want a final file. First, choose File⇨Export from the menu bar, as shown in Figure 21-1. From here you have several choices:

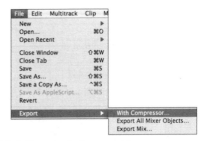

• **Figure 21-1: Export choices start here.**

With Compressor (there's that word again) gives you several presets to choose from when creating your final file, as shown in Figure 21-2. You're going to be primarily concerned with the audio formats, unless you're producing a video podcast. Look at these options:

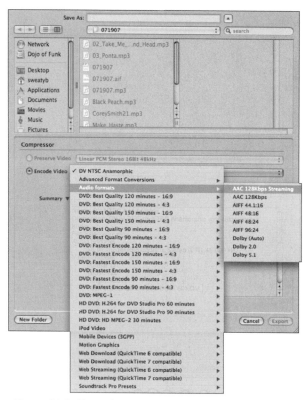

• Figure 21-2: From these export presets, you can choose a degree of compression.

You can also just export selected tracks — the usual option if you're sending individual tracks to be mixed elsewhere. For creating your podcast, the With Compressor or the Export Mix commands are more appropriate. If you've taken the time to create a full mix, you'll want all the ingredients to be in the final product.

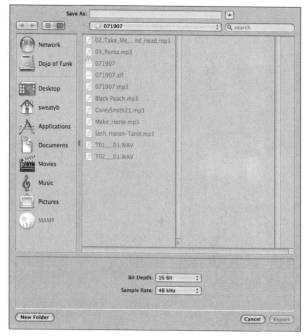

• Figure 21-3: The Export Mix option gives you an AIFF final file.

✔ The AAC formats are already compressed audio, so you're going to want to pass over those.

✔ The AIFF files are followed by their resolutions (sample rate, then bit rate), and you can choose the one most appropriate for your recording.

After you select an AIFF option, just choose what to name your file and where to save it. Your final mix is finished.

Export Mix automatically selects an AIFF file, and all you have to choose are the sample and bit rates. (See Figure 21-3.)

Rendering the file

Don't be surprised if it takes a few minutes to create your final file. This process is a little more time-intensive than saving a text document. The computer is *rendering* (a fancy computer term for creating) all the files and commands in your mix to create the final file, and that can take a little time. It won't take as long as the actual program, though; you may just have time to go grab a cup of coffee while you're waiting instead of making a grocery run. The process will take longer for longer programs or higher resolutions, but it shouldn't take too long.

If you're in a hurry, turn off other programs you're running to ease the load on your computer and get the track done faster.

Making Edits: The First Cut Is the Deepest

There are a few edits that can easily be accomplished on a final file that might be a little more difficult in the mixer view of your project. You can clip out small segments of audio, move sections of your program around, or take out unwanted silence. First, open the audio file you've just exported and listen to it.

Performing a nip and tuck

You should always listen to the file you create *before* you make it available to the public, and you may find places where you want to take out a section of audio. At the very least, you'll want to hear what the file sounds like and make sure it's ready for distribution. Removing those audio sections may or may not be necessary.

If you don't want to stop playback while you're doing this, you can press M in Soundtrack Pro (F8 in Audition) to add a reference marker to indicate where to go back to later. When you're ready to make your cut, highlight the section of the audio you want by clicking and dragging your cursor over what you want to remove (see Figure 21-4).

This kind of work is usually better done before you do the mix. It should only be used to remove audio (or awkward stretches of silence) as a last resort.

Zoom in to make sure you can cut with precision, and play the audio you've highlighted back by clicking the Play button to make sure you're only taking what you want to remove.

Highlighted audio

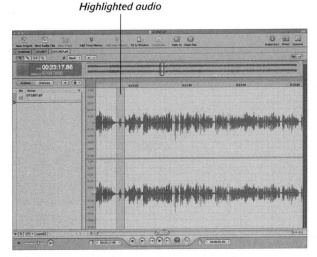

• Figure 21-4: Highlighting audio to snip out is more accurate this way than with scissors.

Press ⌘+X (Ctrl+X in Audition), and the audio is cut and moved to the Clipboard (see Figure 21-5). If you just want to delete the audio without possibly saving it for later, press the Delete key. As always, remember the Undo command is available if you need to go back on your changes.

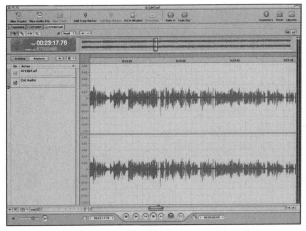

• Figure 21-5: After the cut, the removed audio in the Clipboard is ready to move or discard.

Moving sections around

Perhaps you wanted to move the phrase you just cut to another section of the file. Choose the location you want to move the audio to (as shown in Figure 21-6), and press ⌘+V (Ctrl+V in Audition).

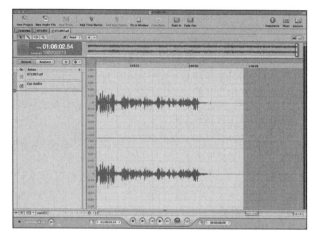

• **Figure 21-6: Finding where to put your cut audio phrase.**

The audio will appear wherever you placed the cursor, as shown in Figure 21-7. Again, remember to zoom in and make the cuts as precise as possible.

• **Figure 21-7: Inserting the new audio.**

This function can be extremely helpful if you want to move segments of your show around — or remove entire sections entirely.

 If you're using bed music or any sort of background effects, make sure your cuts don't throw anything off the beat or make your effects sound unnatural. If that's impossible to do in the original audio file, you may have to go back to your original session and make some edits there.

Erasing the silence

Depending on how you've put together your show, you may have some silence at the beginning, the middle, or the end of the file. This is basically adding more data to the file (the computer has to use more file space to tell the file to remain quiet), and long pauses can be annoying to the listener if they're not an integral part of the show. It's just as easy to remove silence as audio, though. Just highlight the section you want to remove — in this case, at the end of the file, as shown in Figure 21-8.

Highlighted silence

• **Figure 21-8: Highlighting the silence for discreet removal.**

Then, either cut or delete the audio as you did before. This will dramatically *tighten up* your podcast (as shown in Figure 21-9) and make it seem more professional. There's very little that's more annoying than dead air (although infomercials do spring to mind as a candidate for that honor).

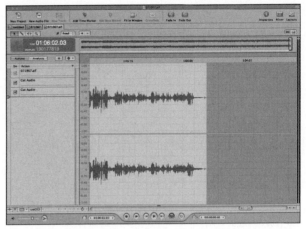

• **Figure 21-9: Removing the silence leaves more room for content.**

Practice 22

Taking Your Audio File into the Home Stretch

A t this point, your podcast has been mixed, exported, and maybe even cut and rearranged. Considering the care you've put into it up until now, it also probably sounds pretty good. However, you may want to go back and look at a few things. Think of this as the few subtle brushstrokes and blends you perform before hanging your Mona Lisa in the Louvre of the Internet. (And yes, that may be the first time the Internet has been compared to an art museum. Okay, maybe not. But what the heck, aim high.)

Listening with a New Ear

You've spent a lot of time with the file, and you're hyperaware of everything you've had to do to make your podcast sound good. It's started to sound so familiar that you can practically recite everything word for word from memory. Still, it's important to put all this aside and listen to the podcast again — as if you've never heard it before.

Of course, barring access to a personal time machine, you can't really do that. It does help, however, to put some distance between yourself and the episode to gain some perspective. Before you shotput your laptop, we're talking about *mental* distance — spending some time away from the podcast. Go and take care of the other things in your life, and come back to it in a few hours, or even the next day if you have the time (this is one reason it's a good idea to give yourself plenty of time before your deadline). Come back and listen to the episode later, and you'll notice things you may not have noticed before. True, all the heavy lifting should be done by now — but be prepared to alter the file a little bit if you notice anything you need to change.

 At some point, you have to turn the file loose and stop tweaking and adjusting. There may be some things you're never quite happy with (say, the way your co-host breathes weirdly sometimes), but it's not something you can fix without having to put in hours and hours of work. And it probably only bothers you, really. When it's done, it's done. Let it go.

The Finishing Touches

The final project is probably the wrong time to start adding most audio effects (reverb, delay, and the like). Such johnny-come-lately additions can make the audio unlistenable at worst, and they just don't make much sense at best. There are, however, a few functions that could help you improve the sound with just a few subtle tweaks. Even so, it's best to leave major audio surgery to earlier work with the session file and not try to cram it into the final project.

Even out the sound with gentle compression settings

We've already looked at compression several times in this book — but it's not always a good idea at this stage, especially if you apply it too heavily. It can be useful if you're just evening out the levels a little in the final file (say, speech levels that come across as too low compared to the music) — although this is also something that's better handled in the mix before you get to the final-episode stage. If you find such subtle tweaks necessary, though, use a compressor with a gentle setting (around a 2:1 ratio with a high dB threshold setting); it could help even out the sound of the file and raise the overall volume a bit.

 It may be tempting to use more extreme compressor settings to raise the volume level of the file to high levels. That's because reducing volume peaks and raising the lower volume levels means you can make your files louder without distortion. But resist. Audio engineers, mixers, and other aficionados decry the loudness of modern music as exhausting to the ear (and terrible-sounding, to boot). Make sure the file sounds good *first;* make sure it's safely loud — audible and clear — but don't push it.

Controlling high peaks with a limiter

If you just want to squash some loud and transient peaks of volume (and you can't just cut them out of the file without disturbing the bed music or sound effects), a limiter might be helpful. This plug-in doesn't raise the lower volume levels; it just stops the louder sounds from exceeding a certain level. Again, trust your users — use gentle settings on the limiter. Set the threshold to affect just the highest peaks in the audio, and let everything else go.

 If you've managed the levels on your audio and music well up to this point, you probably won't have to mess with this step. It's better to handle these kinds of things before you mix than after. This should be a final option for your audio.

Pump It Up

You don't want your listeners turning off your podcast because it sounds distorted and loud, but you also don't want them reaching for the speakers to crank it up and then losing their eardrums when they go on to a track at normal volume. It's just not polite. There are a couple of ways you can achieve the right balance, and both Soundtrack and Audition provide similar functions. Look at the menu in Soundtrack Pro, as shown in Figure 22-1, to see what's available.

• **Figure 22-1: Volume options in Soundtrack Pro:**
Use with taste.

Normalization

This function, shown in Figure 22-2, analyzes the overall volume of the file, gives you its findings, and asks how you want to proceed. Remember that a widely accepted convention of –6 dB is a good setting for final audio files, so that's a good place to start.

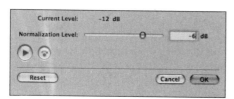

• **Figure 22-2: Normalization gives you a look at your file's overall volume level.**

Once you choose to process the file, the highest volume peak in the file will be raised to –6 dB, and all of the other volume levels in that file will be raised by the same ratio. It's a good way to raise the level of your file somewhat and still keep your file from clipping and distorting.

Adjust Amplitude

This function, shown in Figure 22-3, is basically the same thing as normalization, except you don't get the information about the file in the plug-in. Instead, you get a volume slider and a read-out of the adjustment. You can use this tool on the entire file, but it's probably better to select a portion of the file by highlighting the section (using the mouse) and just amplifying a section of the file.

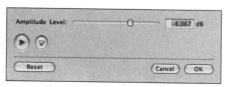

• **Figure 22-3: The Adjust Amplitude function is appropriate for adjusting sections of the file.**

One More Time, with Feeling

What, yet *another* listening? Yes, it's time. After this, you'll convert the file to other formats, so this is the last chance you'll have to actively control the quality of your sound (programs that create mp3 or other lossy formats don't take user input too well, really). You might as well make sure the file sounds as good as possible before it goes that route. Listen for the following:

- ✔ Clicks
- ✔ Pops
- ✔ Distortion
- ✔ Anything else that doesn't sound right

After you've done the last run-through, your audio has passed through some rigorous quality control. Have a congratulatory cup of coffee and get ready to turn your project loose on the world.

Practice 23

Creating a Perfect mp3 File

In This Practice

- ✔ Choosing a conversion program
- ✔ Making sure your file sounds great
- ✔ Keeping your file size down
- ✔ Considering other formats

Like a true artist or craftsman, you've analyzed, poked, prodded, and nursed your master audio file into a perfect podcast episode. It sounds fantastic, and you can't wait to turn it loose on the masses and bask in their approval. The problem is that your file is still an uncompressed audio file — it hasn't been modified or made smaller in any way. All the data that was recorded is still in that file, and it carries quite a lot of heft. These files are great for editing purposes, but they're far too large to post on your Web site or through your RSS feed. The Internet would get bogged down, valuable birthday e-mails would be delayed, and somewhere a child would cry. Avoid that if at all possible.

That's where compressed audio comes in. Even if you've never heard the term *compressed audio* before, you know what it is. The most popular example is the venerable mp3 format. Think of it like the tube that allows you to fit a T-shirt into a smaller space and send it hurtling into the stands at any major sporting event. You could adjust the size of the tube for faster and easier flight, but you'll also want to make sure you don't mangle the T-shirt inside.

The mp3 format also allows you to include a great deal of information embedded directly into the file, including title, copyright, year of creation, and more. (We look more closely at that information in Practice 25.)

Crunching the Numbers

All mp3 files are not created equal. You've probably heard this principle in practice if you've listened to a lot of podcasts. Some files may sound quite good, while others seem to have crawled forth from the sonic space occupied by old AM radios and Edison wax cylinders. This quality (or lack thereof) could be traced back to the audio-production skills (or lack thereof) of the person who put together the podcast, but it might also be the responsibility of the mp3 file settings. There are three main characteristics that define an mp3 file, and their values help you determine the right mix of file size and sound quality.

Bit rate

The bit rate of the mp3 file determines how much audio "information" is captured in the file. A higher bit rate means you'll capture more information, and a lower bit rate means you'll get less information (as well as a flat, tinny sound with glitches and pops). Think of it as the difference between a picture of a black cat and a picture of a long-haired black cat with green eyes lying on the floor of a decent-size living room. The bit rate is measured in kilobits per second (kbps) — the widely accepted rate for music files is 128 kbps — although you can cheat a *little* with a lower bit rate for podcasts that use only spoken-word voices. (A good setting for that would be 96 kbps.) For higher-quality music podcasts, you might want to increase the bit rate, even though doing so will result in a larger file. Bit rates can range from 32 to 320 kbps.

Sample rate

If the bit rate is the amount of information in a picture, the sample rate is the amount of times a picture can be taken. The sample rate of an mp3 file is measured in how many thousands of samples are taken each second. Available rates include 32 kHz, 44.1 kHz, and 48 kHz. You'll find most mp3 files at 44.1 because that's the standard established for CD audio; you can go higher or lower, depending on the quality of audio you desire. A higher sample rate means the file can include higher frequencies (44.1 kHz files can hold frequencies up to 22 kHz, which is roughly the range of human hearing).

 There's a known bug in Flash-based players that causes audio voices to sound like cartoon chipmunks (think Alvin, Simon, and Theodore to get the right idea) when using non-standard sampling rates. Stick to 44.1 kHz (or, failing that, to any multiple of 11) to keep that from happening. You want to make sure your audio can be heard by the greatest possible number of people — and that means playing nice with all kinds of programs.

Constant and variable bit rate

There are two ways to send audio information down the pipeline:

- ✔ A **constant bit rate** means that the bit rate stays the same no matter what. Even if there's three seconds of total and utter silence in the file, you'll get that three seconds in all the glory that file's bit rate can provide. And at 320 kbps, that's a considerable amount of glory.

- ✔ A **variable bit rate** is a conversion process that looks at the audio files, predicts where less information (and smaller file size) is necessary, and converts the file accordingly. That means you get only the silence at a lower bit rate, but everything else will come through in better quality. This approach can save some file size here and there and make the files sound better, but you might run into hassles with incompatible players — even (sometimes) the iPod.

Preaching to the Converted

It's like finding a long-lost and extremely useful tool during the otherwise-tedious cleaning of your basement: More than likely you've already got a program on your computer that can compress your audio file. File compression is a built-in function for most media players, and there are several free or low-cost programs available for download that are built specifically for file conversion. Some editing software can save you a step (and some space on your hard drive) by saving or converting your completed audio folder inside the program.

Media players

Here's where we take a look at the common media players available to the public, just so you can understand how easy file conversion can be. For openers, just about every computer user has access to iTunes — it's a free program and easy to download. Because most folks with computers use PCs (sorry Mac fans, this is just quantity, not necessarily quality), the Windows Media Player (currently on version 11) is also a common feature. Both players start out saving files in their default formats (M4A for iTunes and WMA for Windows Media Player) and to default locations (the users' Music folders), but this can be tweaked easily to save the file format you want wherever you want.

Here's how to convert a file to a different format in iTunes:

1. Open iTunes, select the iTunes option in the top menu, and click Preferences.

2. Click the Advanced tab and select the Importing option.

3. Select the encoder you want to use (mp3, AAC, and so on) and the bit rate you want. You can choose either a preset or the custom settings.

4. Open iTunes and choose File⇨Add File to Library and navigate to the file you want to convert.

The Add to Library dialog box appears, as shown in Figure 23-1.

5. Find the file you want to convert in the iTunes library and select it.

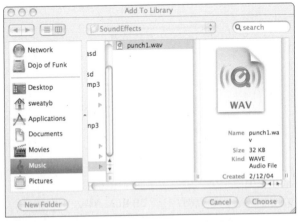

• **Figure 23-1: The Add to Library dialog box in iTunes.**

6. Choose Advanced⇨Convert Selection to mp3, as shown in Figure 23-2.

 This option might be called Convert Selection to AAC the first time you use it. We look at how to change this feature later in this section.

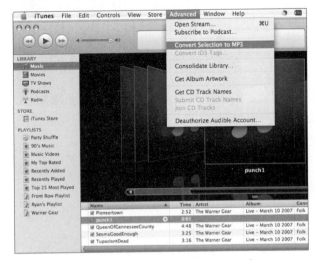

• **Figure 23-2: Converting your selection to mp3.**

The file is saved to your default folder (usually the My Music folder on the PC or Music on the Mac).

If you want to alter the default settings of iTunes, either to raise or lower the bit rate and sample rate, here's the process (tweak it to your heart's content):

1. Open iTunes and choose iTunes⇨Preferences, as shown in Figure 23-3.

2. Click Advanced and select the Importing tab.

3. From the Setting drop-down menu, choose Custom to see all options available to you.

The mp3 Encoder dialog box opens, as shown in Figure 23-4.

• Figure 23-3: Here's where you set preferences in iTunes.

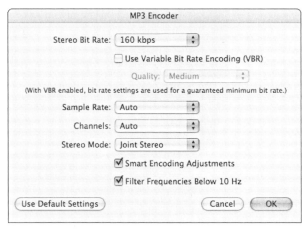

• Figure 23-4: The mp3 Encoder dialog box in iTunes.

4. Select the stereo bit rate, the sample rate, constant or variable bit rate, stereo or mono, and other options, as desired. Most podcasters will want to go with a stereo mp3 file at 128 kbps. When you're finished, click OK.

5. To change the default folder for the files, select the General tab and click Change next to the default library location.

The Change Music Folder Location dialog box appears, as shown in Figure 23-5.

6. **Navigate to wherever you want to save the file and choose that location.**

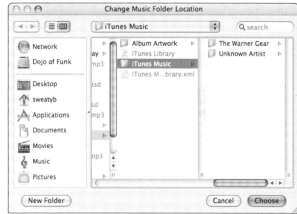

• Figure 23-5: Changing the location of a music folder in iTunes.

This last step will change the location of *all* the files you convert in iTunes from now on. Choose wisely or be prepared to change it back.

Specific conversion programs

There are just too many programs available that can convert files from any format to mp3 to consider each one individually. They can use a variety of methods to perform this conversion, although quite a few use the LAME encoder (great program, unfortunate name) to make the transition. This encoder is available free of charge at `http://lame.sourceforge.net/`.

Exporting your goods to an mp3 file

Programs like Adobe's Audition and SoundBooth and others can export your mix directly to an mp3 file, should you desire that bit of magic. This step essentially allows you to skip the creation of a *master* file and go directly to your final product. It does save time, but it takes away some of the mastering and customizing options detailed in Practice 22. You have to have a lot of confidence in your mixing skills to take this step.

Examining Other Formats

Creating an mp3 file isn't the only way to compress audio, although it's probably the most universally accepted. That's why it's so commonly used for podcasts — you can be reasonably sure that everybody who downloads it will be able to use it. If you're going for the widest audience, mp3 is probably the way to go. If, however, you have a specific audience in mind and want to add some capabilities to your podcast, you may want to consider a different format.

AAC

This format was popularized by Apple and is used as the default setting for the iPod and the iTunes Store. It can be played on both PC and Mac, but not many media players outside of the iTunes program will play these files. Using the AAC format will give you better sound quality — at lower bit rates — than mp3, and it can also contain embedded photos and bookmarks to give the listener more control over the podcast.

WMA

WMA is the preferred format for Windows Media Player, and it also offers quality and bit-rate savings over mp3. It can also add the images and bookmarks that AAC offers, but Windows Media Player doesn't allow these scripts to run by default. It's still possible to run them, but if some of your listeners don't know how to enable scripts in WMP, they're in for a bit of a hassle.

Switching back and forth between formats

Imagine that you are making a series of copies of a painting. If you're using the original of that painting, the copies you make will probably look pretty good. If you start copying the copies, though, you'll notice the picture degrading. Pretty soon, you're left with shapeless lumps that look more like abstract art than the Mona Lisa you started with.

Starting with an uncompressed file format and then compressing it ensures that you get the most quality at the smallest possible file size. If you go from one compressed file to another, though, you'll notice that things start sounding worse. Remember that mp3, AAC, and WMA files (among others) are *lossy* compression schemes — information is lost in the conversion process. It's information that the coders believe you won't miss, but it's gone nonetheless. Start trying to make copies from incomplete sources, and you'll see where this is going. That's why it's always better to start with an uncompressed file.

There are several *lossless* compression schemes available, including proprietary Apple and Microsoft formats along with the open-source FLAC (Free Lossless Audio Codec) format. These give you smaller files sizes without losing any information, but they're still usually too large to send down the podcast pipeline.

Enhanced Podcasting

In the summer of 2006, a new kind of podcasting introduced itself to the podosphere. This new approach to podcasting breaks the "fourth wall" (non-existent in *Ferris Bueller's Day Off*), bringing the audience into the action by offering images, links, and some ways and means of becoming part of the podcast. Because this podcast offered features beyond those found in standard audio productions, creators deemed this kind of podcast as *enhanced*.

While an enhanced podcast appears very slick and complicated on the outside, it's actually a lot of fun and very easy to create. In this practice, you find out all the details behind an enhanced podcast, helping you understand what you have created, what it can (and cannot) play back on, and how to promote this kind of podcast.

What Is an Enhanced Podcast?

With enhanced podcasts, the audience members are no longer spectators but active participants in the episode. They can click individual images for a closer look, follow hyperlinks to additional resources cited in the episode, and even hop back and forth to the beginning of a section in the podcast, as if they were surfing a DVD for a specific moment in a film.

Enhanced podcasts can feature

- Chapter markers
- Changing images
- Hyperlinks
- E-mail links

As you already know, traditional podcasts consist of mp3 files automatically distributed to a list of subscribers via an RSS feed. So what happens when you "enhance" a podcast? Well, the good news is that the feed itself does not change. The iTunes tags stay the same; ID3 tags are still very much the norm.

The media file itself, though, changes dramatically.

Instead of creating an mp3 file, you create an *M4A* file. This format is slightly different from the typical mp3 compression, designed to provide lossless encoding using less file space. This audio compression also allows for image compression and some HTML coding, putting even more distance between it and mp3.

Enhancements with a Cost

There's no denying that enhanced podcasting is very, very cool. It is also very, very easy to do . . . for Mac users. You can still make enhanced podcasts on Windows; but for ease and simplicity, the Mac OS is in the forefront in creating enhanced podcasts (as you find out later on in this practice).

The enhanced podcast truly merits its name; it allows a stronger connection between the podcast host and audience. In effect, you have a captive audience awaiting your instructions and watching iTunes or their iPods for the next image or hyperlink.

With that said, already a few downsides of working with enhanced podcasts become evident:

- ✔ **Enhanced podcasts play back only on iTunes (for the desktop computer) and iPods (portable players).** Although the operating system doesn't matter to a podcast, the playback device *does.* When it comes to enhanced podcasts, only iTunes and iPods serve as playback devices. Your audience can listen to your podcasts only if they have access to iTunes/iPod technology.

  According to some statistical programs, over 70 percent of podcast audience members listen to podcasts using iTunes — which means you're excluding about 30 percent of your potential listenership. Are you sure you want to do that?

- ✔ **Enhanced podcasts can be tricky for Windows users to create.** With a Macintosh, creating an enhanced podcast is simply an issue of dragging

and dropping images and URLs. For Windows users, something as simple and elegant as GarageBand 3 or Podcast Maker (both of which are designed for the Mac OS and covered later in this practice) doesn't exist.

 Perform a search on Google for *creating enhanced podcasts using Windows,* and you'll discover links to many online discussions but only one tutorial. *Jake Ludington's MediaBlab* (www.jakeludington.com/project_ studio/20051004_windows_media_ enhanced_podcast.html) offers a lesson (complete with screen shots and reference links) on how to create enhanced podcasts using Windows Media. If you use Windows, you can give this lesson a go. Alas, the software options are Mac-only.

- ✔ **Your audience loses the ability to multitask or work on something else while listening to your enhanced podcast.** In the same vein as a video podcast (covered in Part VI), subscribers to the enhanced podcast will want to pay close attention to their iPods or iTunes to take in everything you're offering them. Listeners must focus all their time and attention on the imagery and possible reference links. The "captive audience" factor, at least in this case, may deter listeners from subscribing to your podcast.

 While Macs make it easier to create enhanced podcasts, the process can be an issue in GarageBand. When you launch GarageBand, you have a choice of what media to produce, as shown in Figure 24-1. Selecting the New Podcast Episode option may seem like a no-brainer, but the documentation (and the books available on enhanced podcasting) fails to mention a significant little detail: By making this selection, you have committed to creating a M4A file and not a simple AIFF file that can be exported in iTunes as an mp3. GarageBand, by default, assumes you want to create enhanced podcasts. The best way to avoid hopping in and out of Preferences is to select the New Music Project option for standard podcasts and New Podcast Episode for your *enhanced* episodes.

• **Figure 24-1:** GarageBand 3 offers several options for recording and scoring, but just because you want to record a podcast doesn't mean you'll want to use the Podcast option.

Before launching your podcast and taking full advantage of the possibilities that come with enhanced podcasting, take a look at the pros and cons in this approach. True, an enhanced podcast is dynamic and engaging, but are you trying to reach people in a multitasking environment, or are you out to keep your audience's eyes (or should we say "i's"?) glued to their iPods, iTunes, and now iPhones? (Ay-yi-yi!) So long as you're aware of the trade-off and the available compromise with enhanced podcasting, you can decide whether enhanced podcasting is for you.

Reasons Why You May Want to Enhance a Podcast

You have a new level of podcasting to explore, a way of making a tactile (well, through the mouse, anyway) connection with your listenership. Keeping in mind that enhancing your podcast may limit your audience to iTunes and iPod users, you may still have some compelling reasons that make up for the reduced audience size.

So the question remains: Why would you even want to enhance a podcast? Well, for openers . . .

On-the-job training

For podcasts in the corporate, not-for-profit, and government sectors, enhanced podcasting is a fantastic way to associate images and hyperlinks with audio training sessions. Instead of working just with commentary, you can showcase specific images in the podcast, displaying *how* Widget A fits with Socket B. Subscribers can also pause the podcast on images and diagrams for prolonged looks, and if they need more information, they can e-mail the contact at the link provided or go straight from the podcast to the Web site.

Education

Duke University is now requiring iPods for specific classes in order to bring lectures and additional classroom material into the semester's curriculum. With enhanced podcasting, visual aids, additional URLs (approved by the professor), and e-mail contacts can be provided. Duke's Continuing Education podcasts — such as the *K9cast with Tara and Walter* (www.k9cast.com) — offer specific topics for college graduates and take advantage of enhanced podcasting features, such as images of proper procedures, hyperlinks to other noted resources, and e-mail contacts — all approved by the professors.

Soundseeing tours with visuals

Tim Burgess of *Kyoto Podcast* (http://homepage. mac.com/japanpodguides/) was an early adopter of the enhanced podcast. His soundseeing tour of Kyoto, Japan, went one step further, offering listeners informative links and breathtaking images of the Land of the Rising Sun.

Other soundseeing podcasts have posted special editions that feature accompanying images to their captured moments of culture. Whether you decide to do your entire soundseeing tour as an enhanced podcast or simply post special editions, enhanced podcasting can bring your listeners into a truer, more complete virtual visit to where you are in the world.

Seminars and guest symposiums

Provided you get permission from the speakers at a conference or symposium, podcasting a presentation *with the accompanying slides* can be a real boon to your subscribers. On cue, in the enhanced podcast, images progress with the audio, making it possible for anyone who missed the talk to attend virtually. Those participating in this recorded seminar also benefit by going back and reviewing the presentation, pausing at specific slides for any details they might have missed the first time around. For the speakers themselves, their talks can be reviewed with the slides, making enhanced podcasting an excellent tool for improving the flow of presentations.

Product reviews

As featured on Adam Christensen's *MacCast* (`http://maccast.com`), users (and Adam himself) will reference many products and links throughout the show. In the enhanced version of the podcast, Adam also features an image of the product, podcast, or Mac-centric accessory so listeners can see what the user's review is talking about and know specifically what to look for when shopping for it.

Maintaining Two Feeds to Reach a Wider Audience

The previous section gives several valid reasons to try out — or, if you're sold on it, commit to — the enhanced podcast approach. Keep in mind, however, that reaching the widest audience possible with an enhanced podcast may require you to make a compromise:

> Create two feeds.

It may sound complicated and perhaps a bit time-consuming, but maintaining a second feed for the same podcast is actually fairly easy (compared to the production time required for the podcast itself,

anyway). You may have to put some time into posting show notes, but even that can be easily managed.

Here are a few tips for running both an enhanced *and* a standard mp3 podcast:

- ✔ **Produce the audio-only version first.** Record and edit your audio first. As a general rule, try to avoid (if you can) directly referring to images and links in the audio. By keeping your audio independent of the imagery and the link you'll be using in an enhanced version, your mp3 can stand alone. The mp3 can then be easily converted (complete with URLs and images) into an enhanced version.

- ✔ **Produce show notes for the audio-only version first.** Similar to the media file, you can produce the detailed show notes that include links to various resources mentioned in the podcast. After you've got your show notes proofed, all linked up, and ready to go, simply copy and paste your show notes into the enhanced podcast's host blog. Result: The show's content has not changed from the standard to enhanced version, and the links are included in the show notes as an extra courtesy.

- ✔ **While planning your podcast's next episode, collect images and links for the enhanced version.** You'll have to do some pre-production work, compiling show notes, looking over links to reference for your next podcast, and even getting images you might want to showcase on the host blog. This is the time to compile images, resize them, and get them ready for your enhanced version. You can also compile e-mail addresses and URLs, and double-check them before recording to make sure the Web sites and contacts are still valid. Then when your audio-only version of the podcast is ready, just drag and drop your new images into place for the enhanced podcast.

The main reason to maintain both feeds is maximum coverage. While the standard podcast gives you the widest listenership, an enhanced podcast offers a new level of participation for your subscribers.

A good idea from the SciFi Channel

The SciFi Channel has offered a variety of science fiction programming over the years, but recently an unassuming show with boatloads of charm and wit has come on the scene, and now this "small town with big secrets" steps into the podosphere with its own official podcast.

Colin Ferguson (Sheriff Jack Carter) is host of *The Eureka Podcast* (`http://scifi.com/eureka/downloads/podcast/`), a behind-the-scenes look at SciFi's popular comedy, *Eureka*. Each episode is a candid moment with the actor's opinions and perspectives on a particular episode. He also invites guests to chime in, the additional voices ranging from creators Andrew Crosby and Jamie Paglia to fellow actors like Ed Quinn (Nathan Stark) and Jordan Hinson (Zoe Carter).

The Eureka Podcast offers more than just audio. With the enhanced version, accompanying images of scenes and characters appear as they are discussed. These little touches help the audience see what the actors, writers, and producers are talking about; or provide reminders of what specific scenes are being referred to. Other times, the images serve as chapter markers, allowing you to skip back or ahead between commercial breaks, making it easier to keep pace with the commentary as you watch the show.

In the same vein as *Battlestar Galactica*, *Eureka* provides an intimate link between artists and audience. The podcast is a lot of fun to listen to, either with the show or on its own. The *Eureka Enhanced Podcast* is definitely affirmation that while Sheriff Carter may not be the sharpest tool in this small-town shed, he's definitely the coolest. Why? He's hosting his own podcast.

Hosting two feeds may split your statistics in two, but you don't need higher math skills to add those numbers together later for a total count. Some audience members may even listen to both (say, when the audio-only piques their curiosity to check out the visuals).

 Try *special enhanced editions* first if you're unsure about enhanced podcasts. If your listeners like what they hear and see, launch an independent enhanced feed and see what happens.

Creating Enhanced Podcasts in GarageBand 3

Upon launching GarageBand 3 (`www.apple.com/garageband`), Mac users are greeted with several options (see Figure 24-2) that show what this component of iLife has to offer.

After you click Create New Podcast, GarageBand creates an interface with the following tracks already in place:

- ✔ **Podcast Track:** Here is where you drag in images and establish markers for your podcast.

- ✔ **Male Voice:** This is a basic vocal track (created from the Real Instrument settings of GarageBand) and optimized for the average male voice.

- ✔ **Female Voice:** Same as above, only optimized for the average female voice.

- ✔ **Jingles:** This track has presets for the already prepared, mixed, and ready-to-play looped *jingles* (short pieces of music) included with GarageBand.

- ✔ **Radio Sounds:** This final track is optimized for sound effects and a feature called *musical typing*, where GarageBand turns your alphanumeric keyboard into a sound effects machine, playing drop-in audio bytes provided by the application.

Ducking switch

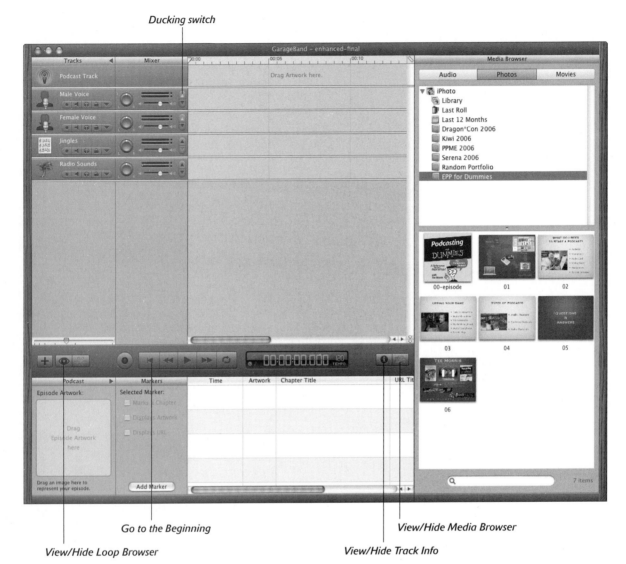

Go to the Beginning

View/Hide Loop Browser

View/Hide Media Browser

View/Hide Track Info

• **Figure 24-2:** GarageBand 3's interface for Create New Podcast makes enhanced podcasting a breeze.

For this practice, you will focus on creating an enhanced podcast using the Podcast, Male Voice, and Jingles tracks. You can find out more about the rest of the features in *GarageBand For Dummies* by Bob LeVitus (Wiley).

Prep work for the enhanced podcast

Before you can start creating the enhanced podcast, you need to gather your resources, including your images and audio files. As explained earlier, this is a Mac-centric process; you'll need to be using (well, yeah) a Macintosh. You'll also need the *Expert Podcasting Practices For Dummies* DVD, iPhoto, and iTunes at the ready.

In the following steps, you gather the media you're going to use for your enhanced podcast:

1. **Copy the Practice 24 folder from the DVD onto your Macintosh.**

2. **Open iPhoto.**

3. **Choose File⇨Import to Library (Shift+⌘+I) and import the following files from the Images directory:**

▶ 00-episode.jpg

▶ 01.jpg

▶ 02.jpg

▶ 03.jpg

▶ 04.jpg

▶ 05.jpg

▶ 06.jpg

You'll use these seven images for the chapter markers that you'll create a little later in this practice.

4. **Choose File⇨New Album (⌘+N) and create a new album called** EPP For Dummies.

5. **Select the seven images you just imported into iPhoto and drag them into the** EPP For Dummies **album.**

6. **Launch iTunes.**

7. **Choose File⇨Add to Library (⌘+O) and import** P24-audio.aif **and** enhanced-audio.mp3 **from the** Practice 24 **directory.**

These files are your audio, both music and voice, that you will drop images and links around and build your podcast on.

8. **With the new audio files selected, choose File⇨New Playlist from Selection (Shift+⌘+N) and name the new playlist** Podcast Files.

Now that you have what you need for this podcast, you're ready to put it all together.

Building the basic podcast

With the resources you need at the ready, follow these steps to use GarageBand to create the podcast:

1. **Launch GarageBand and select the Create New Podcast option.**

2. **After the interface appears, click the Jingles track.**

You're going to drop in music for your podcast's theme in this track.

3. **Click the View/Hide the Loop Browser button (refer to Figure 24-2) to turn the Loop Browser on.**

The Loop Browser window allows you to scroll through all the different fully mixed, fully orchestrated jingles and suites that GarageBand 3 offers. Some are labeled "short," setting them at around 10 to 15 seconds, while the "long" versions run past the 1-minute mark.

4. **In the Loop Browser window (currently on the default setting of Jingles⇨All), find the song marked "Gelato" and click it.**

GarageBand plays the song for you before you drop it into the project. We're suggesting "Gelato" because it's a fun ditty for this podcast.

5. **Click "Gelato" again to stop this preview. Then click and drag "Gelato" to your Jingles track.**

6. **Check to see whether the Media Browser is in view. Click the View/Hide Media Browser button (refer to Figure 24-2) to view your media elements in the Media Browser window, shown in Figure 24-3.**

The Media Browser appears blue when active.

7. **Click the Media Browser tab for Audio. Expand iTunes and then click the Podcast Files playlist.**

You see P24-audio in your Media Browser.

8. **Click and drag P24-audio into the Male Voice Track. Place it at the beginning of the track.**

9. **Preview the track.**

Press the spacebar or the Play button to preview it. Press the spacebar or Play button again to stop.

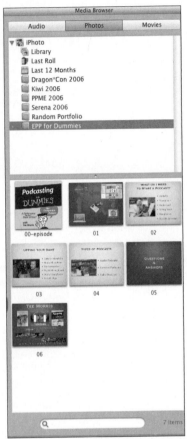

• **Figure 24-3:** The Media Browser allows you to view all the media (music and audio) available for your enhanced podcast.

10. **Click the Go to the Beginning of Song button (refer to Figure 24-2) and then turn off the Ducking feature for the Male and Female Voice Tracks.**

Ducking is a built-in GarageBand 3 feature that takes down the volume of the music in a designated track the moment another track comes in. Although this feature is often a convenient

step-saver, it lacks subtlety. In the next few steps, you'll be setting levels manually (with a lot more nuance).

11. **Click the Show Volume Track or Pan Curve option (the small triangle in the track options) to expand the Track Volume.**

In the following steps, you'll be creating *control points* along the Track Volume Level. These points act much like the control points created in Soundtrack Pro and Audition, allowing you to change the volume of the music. Unlike the Ducking feature, control points give you full control over levels. From here to Step 19, the steps guide you through mixing audio and voice in GarageBand using control points.

12. **Move your playhead to 00:00:02.000 in the timeline and click at the intersection between the volume level and the edit line.**

This operation creates a control point.

13. **Using the right-arrow key on your keyboard, advance to 00:00:05.000; then click at the intersection between the volume level and the edit line.**

Doing so creates another control point so you can set the volume of your music.

14. **Click and drag the new control point down to –22.9 dB, as shown in Figure 24-4.**

For this particular piece, this dB level makes the music soft enough to still be heard without overpowering the voice.

15. **Click and drag the audio in the Male Vocals track toward the right. Time the vocals to start after the fade down of music.**

By moving the audio in the Male Vocals track to the right, the voice starts closer to the end of the fade-out in music.

16. **Click the Podcast Track and then click the View/Hide Track Editor button (the scissors icon) in GarageBand.**

Clicking this button opens the interface needed for incorporating images.

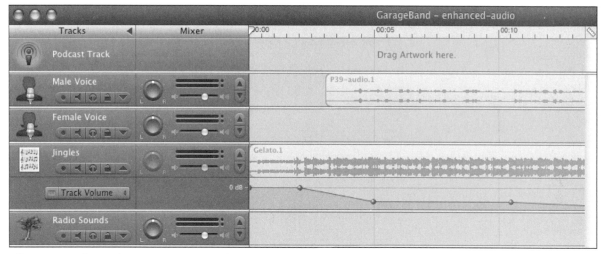

• **Figure 24-4:** Setting levels in audio using GarageBand's control points.

17. Click the Media Browser tab for Photos; then click and drag the `00-episode` image into the Episode Artwork area.

The Episode Artwork is the main logo for the show. This image appears in iTunes and other directories, as well as at the beginning of the show, by default.

18. Click the Jingles track. Advance in your timeline to 00:00:10.500 and create a control point here.

19. Create another control point at 00:00:15.000. Click this last control point and drag it to its lowest setting to fade out your theme.

20. Save your project.

The basics of your podcast are in place. Now, with just a few clicks and drags, you're going to turn this podcast into an enhanced podcast.

Enhancing the podcast with images

The foundations of your podcast are established. You have the audio and the mood-setting theme in place, along with professional fade-ins and fade-outs. You even have the show logo in place.

Now you're ready to enhance the podcast with images. Follow these steps:

1. Click the Podcast Track and listen for the break between " . . . talking about enhanced podcasting" and "But since we have taken. . . ." Click and drag the image marked 01 from the Media Browser into the Podcast Track where the playhead resides, as shown in Figure 24-5.

You have just added your first image (for Chapter 1) to the podcast. Now when users listen to the host suggest that a review of the podcasting process is in order, an image of how podcasting happens appears on-screen.

When selecting images for your enhanced podcast, try to choose relevant images for what you or you and your guest are talking about. The more relevant and helpful the image, the more you are taking advantage of the enhanced podcast.

 Another way to add an image to your enhanced podcast is to click and drag the image marked 01 from the Media Browser into the Podcast Track Editor window.

Drag image

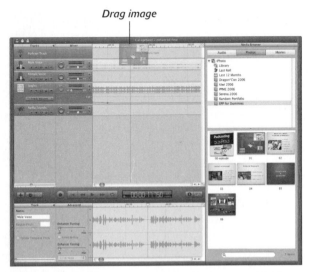

• **Figure 24-5:** Click and drag the image from the Media Browser to the Podcast Track.

2. Next, you want to add a title for your image. In the Podcast Track's editor window, click the grayed-out words `Chapter Title` and type in `The Podcasting Process`.

Although it's called a "chapter title," this label can be anything you want it to be. A caption for the image works well here.

3. Now you're going to mark an endpoint for this image. Listen in the voice track for the break between " . . . is that you'll sync it up with your computer" and "another quick review. . . ." With your playhead resting in this break, click the segment titled `The Podcasting Process` in the Podcast Track; then choose Edit⇨Split (⌘+T).

Doing so marks an endpoint for this image.

4. Click the second `Podcasting Process` clip in the Editor window and then press the Delete key.

You delete the second instance of the image so that you can make a place to drop in your second image. From here, you will repeat these steps for other images throughout this enhanced podcast.

5. Repeat Steps 1–4 to add the remaining four images. Place them at the following breaks with these chapter titles:

Adding Image 02:

Location: Between "Another quick review . . ." and "And finally, portable recorders like the iRiver."

Title: What Do I Need to Podcast?

Adding Image 03:

Location: Between "But let's say you want . . ." and " . . . like the M-Audio Mobile PreAmp."

Title: Upping Your Game

Adding Image 04:

Location: Between "In the next few episodes . . . " and ". . . and Video Podcasting."

Title: Types of Podcasts

Adding Image 05:

Location: Between "Now, if you have any questions . . . " and ". . . at Tee at Tee Morris dot com."

Title: Contact Tee

Adding Image 06:

Location: Between "And if you want to find out more about me . . . " and ". . . w-w-w-dot-Tee Morris dot com."

Title: More Information on Tee Morris

6. Save your project.

7. Click the Go to the Beginning button. With the Podcast Track still active, click the View/Hide Track Info button (refer to Figure 24-2).

A window opens that will allow you to review the podcast.

8. Press Play or your spacebar to begin the review.

The images you're working with are taken from a presentation concerning podcasting. Because of the screen resolution of the presentation, the graphics are 1024×768. These images work fine, but larger images bulk up your enhanced podcast and make it unnecessarily large. When creating graphics — either for your podcast's primary graphic or for your enhanced podcast — follow these specs, which are perfect for podcasting:

72-ppi resolution

JPEG format

300-pixel width by 300-pixel height

As you review your podcast, watch how it plays back with each image appearing and changing on cue, ending with the Episode Graphic (the *Podcasting For Dummies Podcast* artwork).

Adding final touches to your enhanced podcast

You have given your audience something to look at. Now you need to give 'em somewhere to go from your podcast. Follow these steps:

1. With the Podcast Track still active, go to the editor window and double-click the *chapter marker* (yellow diamond) next to the time code for the `More Information on Tee Morris` slide.

In your timeline, you hop directly to that point.

2. Scroll *horizontally* to where you see the grayed-out sections for `URL Title` and `URL`, as shown in Figure 24-6.

• **Figure 24-6:** Scroll to the right in the editor window to find fields where you can enter URL titles and links.

3. Click URL Title and type in `The Official Website of Tee Morris`.

4. Click URL and type in `www.teemorris.com`.

GarageBand will add in the `http://` for you.

5. Scroll horizontally in the editor window and double-click the chapter marker next to the time code for the `Contact Tee` slide.

6. Scroll to where you see the grayed-out `URL Title` and `URL`. Click URL Title and type in `E-mail Tee`.

7. Click URL and type in `mailto:tee@ teemorris.com`, **as shown in Figure 24-7.**

GarageBand won't add the `http://` here; that's because you're *hard-coding* (typing in) the `mailto` link.

• **Figure 24-7:** When you drop in a URL or e-mail link, the link appears at the bottom of the graphic to indicate an active link for this slide.

You have now incorporated e-mail and hyperlinks into your presentation. These links are active and can be tested in GarageBand by previewing the finished episode in the Podcast Preview window.

You may notice in the preview, however, that some of the images are cropped too tightly. Follow these steps to remedy that situation:

1. Go to the Editor window and double-click the Artwork icon for the slide titled `The Podcasting Process`.

The Artwork Editor window, shown in Figure 24-8, appears.

• **Figure 24-8: Use the Artwork Editor to resize, crop, and reposition artwork in your enhanced podcast.**

2. Drag the slider in the Artwork Editor to the left so the slide fits in the boundaries of the wireframe box; then click Set to resize the image and close the Artwork Editor window.

3. Repeat Steps 2–3 for the slides titled What Do I Need to Podcast?, Upping Your Game, and More Information on Tee Morris.

4. Go to the Editor window and double-click the Artwork icon for the slide titled Types of Podcasts.

5. Drag the slider in the Artwork Editor to the right so the slide increases in size.

Continue to drag the slider to the right until the image stops increasing in size.

6. With your cursor outside the wireframe box, click and drag.

Your cursor now becomes a *Move* tool (it will look like a hand).

7. Reposition this slide inside the boundaries of the wireframe box so that only the photo of the two podcasters is visible. If needed, reduce or enlarge the image with the slider. When you're ready, click Set to resize the image.

8. Save your project.

9. Click the Go to the Beginning button. Review the podcast.

10. When you're satisfied with the podcast, choose Share⇨Send Podcast to iTunes.

Your enhanced podcast is exported to iTunes.

Your enhanced podcast is now complete. The only tasks that remain are ID3 tagging, uploading to your host server, and then finally adding show notes — and the podcast itself — to your blog.

 You have an option to turn Displays URL off of any enhanced podcast slides that have a URL plugged into them. If you hide the URL, the URL link becomes inactive. When designing slides or capturing images for enhanced podcasts, note that to keep the URL active you should leave the Displays URL active.

Creating Enhanced Podcasts in Podcast Maker

Podcast Maker (www.lemonzdream.com/podcast maker/) from Lemonz Dream is similar to GarageBand in that enhanced podcasting is a simple process of dragging and dropping images. This independent Mac application also offers an RSS Feed Generator and seamless interaction with .Mac and FTP client programs.

This application, however, does not allow for audio editing. You'll have to import a completely edited audio file into Podcast Maker before you can enhance it. Podcast Maker isn't a standalone application for recording and editing — but it *is* a terrific tool for turning any audio file into a podcast (hence its name).

Similar to GarageBand 3, Podcast Maker pulls media from iPhoto and iTunes. Additionally, it pulls bookmarked links from Safari — *and only from Safari* — making this application (believe it or not) even more Mac-centric than GarageBand.

If you have jumped to this section of this practice, follow the earlier steps in the "Prep work for the enhanced podcast" section before proceeding. From here, you will build the enhanced podcast, starting with the basics and working your way up.

Building the basic podcast

Your files are all set up and ready for implementing into your enhanced podcast. Follow these steps to get started:

1. **Launch Podcast Maker.**

2. **In the Media window, click the tab for Audio. Expand iTunes and then click the Podcast Files playlist.**

Similar to GarageBand, the Media window (shown in Figure 24-9) keeps track of the mp3 versions of the episodes.

• **Figure 24-9:** After creating the mp3 audio, you can access it in Podcast Maker's Media window.

You see the `enhanced-audio.mp3` file in the selected playlist. This file is already mixed down, fully edited, and even has the episode graphic of the *For Dummies* cover. This is a perfectly good mp3 file that you are about to enhance using Podcast Maker.

3. **Click and drag the** `enhanced-audio.mp3` **file into the Episode window, shown in Figure 24-10.**

You are now ready to start "enhancing" it.

• **Figure 24-10:** Simply click and drag the file from the Media window for your podcast.

4. **In the Episode Name, type in** `Episode 2.01: Welcome Back!`. **In the Description box at the bottom of the Episode interface, type in** `Welcome to Season Two of the Podcasting For Dummies` podcast.

Podcast Maker allows you to create some of your ID3 tags before posting.

5. If you want to give this episode an Explicit tag of *Clean* or *No,* select the appropriate option from the Explicit drop-down menu.

Some podcasts individually tag episodes as either Clean or No (the latter option leaving the episode untagged), flagging only certain episodes as Explicit. When tagging your episodes, be honest. Directories reserve the right to yank your show out of their database if you misrepresent the show's content.

6. Click the Edit Podcast button located at the top of the Podcast Maker interface.

7. Enter the information that you want to appear on the iTunes page for your podcast.

For this example, please type the following information:

▶ **Podcast Title:** Podcasting For Dummies, Season Two

▶ **Author:** Tee Morris

▶ **Description:** This is the official podcast of the books *Podcasting For Dummies* and *Expert Podcasting Practices For Dummies* from Wiley Publishing.

▶ **Website:** ForDummies.com

▶ **Explicit:** No

▶ **Where it says Drag & Drop Image:** Go to the Media window, click the Photos icon, select the EPP For Dummies album, and click and drag the *Podcasting For Dummies* cover into this space.

8. Click Preview in the upper-right corner of Podcast Maker's interface to get an idea of what your iTunes Directory window will look like.

What you see should resemble Figure 24-11.

• **Figure 24-11:** Podcast Maker gives you a sneak peek at how your podcast will appear in iTunes after it's online.

Creating chapters and adding images

Next, follow these steps to add artwork to the podcast:

1. Click the Chapters button in the lower-right corner of the window and then select the Enhanced Podcast check box.

The Artwork and Chapters window appears, as shown in Figure 24-12.

2. To create the first break, click the Play button and listen for the break between " . . . talking about enhanced podcasting" and "But since we have taken. . . . "

You can also click and drag the *playhead* (the black line in Podcast Maker's timeline ruler) back and forth to find the break. (The break is approximately at 0:00:17.5 in the timeline. Reference the time code located above and to the left of the timeline ruler.)

3. From the Media window, select the Photos icon; then click and drag the Preview slider (located at the bottom of the Media window) to the left until your slides form a single column.

The slides should be easy to see, as shown in Figure 24-13.

• **Figure 24-12:** By clicking the Chapters button, the episode's timeline is given a graphic representation and is ready for images.

4. Click and drag the podcasting process diagram from the Media window into the first row of the Artwork and Chapters window.

5. In the Artwork and Chapters window, double-click the Chapter column's first cell and type in The Podcasting Process.

6. To add the second break, click Play (or press your spacebar) and listen for the break between " . . . is that you'll sync it up with your computer" and "Another quick review . . . " (approximately at 0:01:37.6). With your playhead resting in this break, click and drag the image titled What Do I Need to Podcast? from the Media window into the second row of the Artwork and Chapters interface.

• **Figure 24-13:** You can either view artwork in several columns (left) or as a single column (right).

 A bonus of Podcast Maker is that clicking and dragging the playhead while the Play button is on gives you the ability to scrub through the audio. *Scrubbing* is a quick and easy way to zip through your audio, allowing you to hear various snippets of the audio as you move forward or backward. This is an easy way to listen for a specific moment of your narration, breaks in the audio, or when music begins or ends in an episode.

7. Double-click the Chapter column's second cell and type in What Do I Need to Podcast?.

8. Repeat Steps 6–7 to add the remaining images. Place them at the following breaks with these chapter titles:

Image: Upping Your Game

Between "And finally, portable recorders like the iRiver" and "But let's say you want . . ."

Title: Upping Your Game

Image: Types of Podcasts

Between ". . . like the M-Audio MobilePre Amp" and "In the next few episodes . . ."

Title: Types of Podcasts

Image: Questions & Answers

Between ". . . at Video Podcasting" and "Now, if you have any questions . . ."

Title: Contact Tee

Image: Tee Morris

Between ". . . at TeeMorris.com" and "If you want to find out more about me . . ."

Title: More Information on Tee Morris

9. Save your project as Enhanced-PM and then click and drag the playhead back to the beginning of your podcast (see Figure 24-14). Click Play to review the podcast.

 Whether it's a bug in the software or just a problem with our installation, the chapter markers you create in Podcast Maker might not match up with your playhead. If this happens, the remedy is simple: Click and drag the new marker in the timeline ruler back to your playhead. That's all you need to do to fix this glitch.

• **Figure 24-14:** When completed, you can click and drag your playhead back to the beginning and preview your enhanced podcast.

Adding e-mail and Web links

As the final step for creating your enhanced pod-cast, add e-mail and Web site links by following these steps:

1. **Double-click the Link Title cell associated with the More Information on Tee Morris slide and type in** The Official Website of Tee Morris.

2. **Double-click the Link cell associated with the More Information on Tee Morris slide and type in** http://www.teemorris.com.

Note that Podcast Maker will not add in the http:// for you.

3. **Double-click the Link Title cell associated with the Contact Tee slide and type in** E-mail Tee Morris.

4. **Double-click the Link cell associated with the Contact Tee slide and type in** mailto:tee@teemorris.com.

5. **Save your podcast and then choose File⇨ Publish (⌘+P) to render a preview for iTunes. Set up this publishing process as follows (see Figure 24-15):**

▶ **Protocol:** Folder

▶ **Display Name:** Enhanced Podcast-PM

▶ **Base URL:** http://mywebsite.com/podcast (This is a mock URL for this exercise. When you are using Podcast Maker to create your own podcast, enter the URL on your server where you want files to reside.)

▶ **Folder:** (Select Choose and then find a local folder for you to keep your podcast files on your computer.)

6. **Click Publish.**

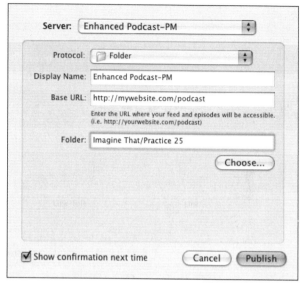

• **Figure 24-15:** Podcast Maker gives you options to either set aside your podcasts for review or upload them directly to your server.

Podcast Maker now generates the XML and the M4A media file. Find the M4A file in the directory you designated; double-click it to preview your enhanced podcast in iTunes.

Podcast Maker will want to *publish* your pod-cast and feed straightaway, making the episode live immediately. This may be a time-saver, but nothing beats previewing your work first before you make it a live podcast episode. Listen for any missed cues, bungles, or fluffs in your audio, double-check your ID3 tags, and make certain that images are where they should be and that links take viewers where you want them to go. Bottom line: Although the automatic FTP and Publish capa-bilities are great shortcuts that Podcast Maker offers, they may not be the best way to go for you.

Part IV

The Final Steps Before Episode #0

The 5th Wave
By Rich Tennant

"It's like any other pacemaker, but it comes with an internal iPod docking accessory."

Creating and Editing ID3 Tags

In This Practice

- ✔ Understanding why ID3 tags are important
- ✔ Examining critical tags you won't want to miss
- ✔ Looking at other tags you may want to include

If you attended primary school in the States, you probably encountered your first truly draconian teacher somewhere around the third grade. She may have been some gnarled woman with a beehive hairdo and horn-rimmed glasses who demanded that all assignments be complete with your name written in the upper-left-hand corner of the page, followed by the date and perhaps even subject. For kickers, you also had to include the class period and perhaps even the number of your seating assignment. To make matters worse, if you neglected to complete any one of these descriptors on a paper, you ran the risk of having the paper returned to you, a reduction in your overall score, or possibly even getting a zero on the whole thing. Yes, just because you left off the date or used your nickname.

Mrs. Crabtree (substitute any name here) didn't do this because she was a horrid person. No, she required this of you — and every student — so she could easily identify the papers by student, assignment, subject, and period. While you were off to attempt your mastery of the teeter-totter at recess, Mrs. Crabtree was busy sifting through the homework and class-work of 350 other students, and the only way she could do this with any sort of efficiency was to require this descriptive data on each and every paper, test, or project. (Just imagine how cranky she would have been without it. . . .)

Nostalgia aside, we certainly hope *some* of that experience was ingrained into your behavior patterns — because mp3 tags have an identification schema that serves almost the exact same purpose. In this practice, we describe a system of tagging inherent to mp3 files called *ID3 tags.* Proper tagging of files ensures that any listener or consumer of the mp3 file knows what it is, where it came from, and where it belongs. It's an elegantly simple system to use that is, quite frankly, overlooked (or considered superfluous) by many — but it can help stave off podcasting chaos.

The Miracle of ID3 Tags

As a podcaster, you should already be familiar with ID3 tags; it's likely you've been using them since your very first episode. We're using words like *should* and *likely* because it's obvious that not every podcaster is paying very close attention to these data — and that's a little frustrating. If you happen to be one of those people who never use ID3 tags, hear our plea: You'll help us — and every one of your listeners — if you make a commitment to getting a good ID3 tagging system in place.

What they do

ID3 tags are *metadata,* which is extra data that describes — and is stored with — the primary data in your mp3 file. (Don't you just love it when portions of the word are used in the definition? How handy.) Let's try and break that down.

An mp3 file is a digital audio file. At the base level, digital audio is a whole bunch of ones and zeros, just like everything else in the digital world — in other words, data. Run it through the right translator (an mp3 player), and that data comes out as understandable information — in this case, audio. But while it's inside the machine, it's data nonetheless.

Beyond the ones and zeros that make up the audio portion of an mp3 file are additional data that describe the contents, origin, and other aspects of the audio file. Although they are contained within the file, they don't have any impact on the audio portion of the file. They exist simply to report to other applications that are designed to read them. In effect, they practice a strict vow of speaking only when asked a direct question.

There are actually two versions of ID3 tags: ID3v1 and ID3v2. In fact, each of these versions has a variety of sub-versions (okay, variants — they're not all that subversive), but that's only important if you're developing applications that make use of ID3 tags. Figure 25-1 shows you a representation of where the two versions of ID3 tags are placed inside the audio file. If that fascinates you and you want a deeper dive, visit `www.id3.org` and geek out to your heart's content.

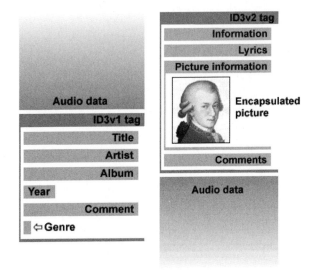

• **Figure 25-1: Placement and layout of ID3v1 and ID3v2 tags inside of audio files.**

Why they matter

Applications call upon ID3 tags to display descriptive information to the end user — presumably a human being listening to a file on an mp3 player such as an iPod. ID3 tags are, by and large, what causes the name of the audio file, podcast episode, date, and image to appear on the screen as the show is playing. And it's not just iPods; almost all mp3 players utilize ID3 data to display information as the file is playing.

Beyond serving the immediate needs of the listener, ID3 tags are also used by applications in a variety of ways. iTunes, the most widely used application to receive podcast episodes, makes extensive use of ID3 tags to help group things together and to sort them for later play. Music databases, such as CDDB (`www.cddb.com`) and FreeDB (`www.freedb.org`), rely heavily on ID3 tags. Though not often used, ID3 tags can also be used to automatically link audio files to various Web sites.

All these applications, from user interaction to program function, require that you — the creator of the mp3 file — properly fill out the ID3 tags on your file *every time*. When you get right down to it, ID3 tags make it easy for others to figure out where the file came from when they get curious. Besides, don't you want more traffic to your site? Don't you want more feedback from listeners? Don't you want more subscribers? Fill out your ID3 tags. It'll help.

Tagging the Files and Editing the Tags

The process of properly tagging your mp3 files is quite simple. In fact, the application you're using to create or manage your mp3 files probably provides you with the option to complete many of the tags.

 While almost all audio-editing applications provide an interface to your mp3 file, they don't always allow maximum flexibility for your tags. You may need to use a different application to get the most out of your tagging.

iTunes remains the largest tool for managing podcasts — for listeners and podcasters alike. It's also among the easier applications to edit ID3 tags with. Figure 25-2 shows the editing screen for ID3 tags found in one of two ways:

- **On a Mac:** Press the ⌘ + I keyboard shortcut.

- **On a PC:** Select an mp3 file and then choose File⇨Get Info.

If you're looking for the most flexibility possible, you'll probably want to invest in a dedicated ID3 editing application. The price tag is usually around $20 to $30 — and many podcasters will happily fork over this small outlay for some added convenience. ID3X (www.three-2-one.com/id3x) for the Macintosh system is one of those tools; its editing interface is displayed in Figure 25-3.

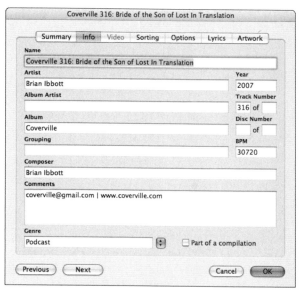

• **Figure 25-2: iTunes allows you to edit some, but not all, of the ID3 tags quickly and easily.**

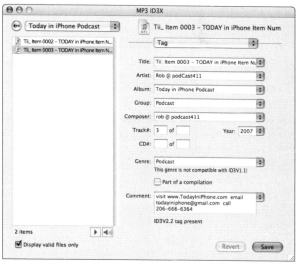

• **Figure 25-3: ID3X is a full-featured ID3 tag-editing application.**

The Essential Tags

All of this is great stuff, and you need to do it. But please DO NOT skip the last part of this practice where we discuss the monkey wrench that using iTunes as a podcatcher will introduce to your well-thought-out plans. And no reading ahead!

There are quite a few ID3 tags available, though most podcasters (and most applications, for that matter) use only a handful of them. (Your mileage may vary.) The next few sections form a list, in alphabetical order, of the essential tags you should use to describe and identify your mp3 files — every time.

ID3 tags were designed for describing music files, so some of them may not make obvious sense when you're adding them to your file. Bear with us; the podcast listening devices make use of the tags we're suggesting you use.

Album

This piece of information is the primary anchor of your show. It appears on most mp3 players' screens — and should be relatively consistent from episode to episode. Ideally, it never changes unless the title of your show changes. If your show is called *Today in iPhone,* then that's what you put in the Album field of the file. Keep in mind that some players, like the hugely popular iPod, will use the Album tag to group episodes together in the player. If you change the name of your Album from episode to episode, your files become harder for your listeners to find.

You can use as many characters as you like in the Album field, but anything longer than 30 characters (including spaces) may get truncated on the display screens of portable mp3 players.

Resist the temptation to use special characters (such as an * or ~) at the front of your show name. Yes, these tricks may cause your show to have a higher alphabetical listing than it would normally, but they also make it very hard for your listeners to find your content. They are already subscribed, so you don't need to find ways to trick them into listening to you first.

Artist

The Artist field displays the name of the host or podcast crew responsible for the episode. Much like the Album field, this tag should remain constant throughout your show's lifetime. Apple's iTunes system uses the Artist tag for grouping files together in the directory structure. Changing the contents of the Artist field will (again) cause your content to be scattered around a listener's system.

The contents of this field need not be the full and legal names of your hosts. If Fred Flintstone and Barney Rubble are the hosts, the phrase `Fred & Barney` may be simpler to use and easier on everyone. However, you should use this method of truncation only if the same diminutives are used on the show. Why hide from your audience?

In addition, don't feel obligated to list the entire crew in this field, or to add in special guests. (The Comment field may be more appropriate for that information.) Bottom line: Keeping this field short and consistent saves you from scattering your content around.

Comment

This field is accessible by many mp3 players and is best used to provide portable extra information about the show. Where other fields are designed to be short and sweet, you can get rather lengthy in this field without issues. Some podcasters choose to insert their entire show notes for a particular episode in this field.

At a minimum, the Comments field should contain the URL of your podcast. We highly recommend including your copyright statement — Creative Commons or otherwise — as well. This reduces the chance of anyone misinterpreting the rights you've assigned to the file.

Genre

The Genre field was designed to allow applications to group types of music files together — keeping all the Jazz tracks together, for example. As you look through your mp3 player or editing software, you'll find legions of possible genres to use. You may be tempted to look for a genre choice that's appropriate to the content of your show — but we recommend that you take a different route:

> *Unless you have a well-thought-out reason to do otherwise, always set the genre to Podcast.*

Yes, we realize that your show may consist of in-depth interviews with the masters of jazz. But that doesn't mean your audience wants to hear you talk between tracks of Miles Davis and The Scat Man. And no, your listeners really don't want to have your program show up in their Trance mix.

For now, podcasts are podcasts, and the listening experience is — by and large — much different from that of listening to spoken word, audio books, and the like. Someday we may find a better way to classify the types of podcasts we're producing. For now, Conventional Wisdom dictates that we all identify the genre of our files as `Podcast`.

 Using the term `Podcast` in your genre assumes you're working with ID3v2 tags, and not the older (and more restrictive) ID3v1 tags. There aren't any incompatibility issues, but you may find that some applications — like Audacity — continue to use the strict list of genres allowed in ID3v1. If you use a dedicated ID3-tagging application (or even iTunes), you can easily get around this little obstacle.

Name

This is the spot for the title of your specific episode. It can and in fact should be different each and every time you put up a new show file. The contents of that field are up to you, though you should come up with a formula or convention for naming your files.

In fact, it's probably more important to stick with a consistent Name convention than it is to concern yourself with any other ID3 tag. While the pod-catcher or mp3 player of choice for your listeners will attempt to arrange content in a predefined fashion, many listeners create their own playlists and rely on the Name field almost exclusively to figure out who you are and what you're talking about.

Consider also that your listeners may grab many of your previous shows all at once and add them to their players. If your shows follow any sort of sequence (for example, referencing things in past or future shows), make sure your naming convention allows your listeners to figure out (easily!) in what order they should listen to your shows.

Many podcasters have come up with many different conventions to use. And while we're not so bold as to assume we know the One True Way, we did write the book around the assumption that you wouldn't mind having us tell you what to do if it works. We're all too happy to oblige. With that, we recommend that your Name tags follow this convention:

```
Show ID > Sequential ID > Episode
    Title > Stuff
```

Allow us to explain . . .

Show ID

As discussed earlier, you'll be including the name of your show in the Album field, so it may seem strange to include it again. First, the Show ID need not be the complete name of your program; that works best in the Album field. Instead, the Show ID is an abbreviated version of your show name, usually done with initials. If your title is *Today in Sports Marketing*, you could simply use `TiSM` as your identifier.

Earlier we spoke of many listeners who manage their own podcast playlists, bypassing their device's efforts to categorize for them. Having a Show ID gives them a way to find your show quickly in a list of others — or to know what they're about to hear prior to the track changing.

Sequential ID

This is a sequential number of your show. It enables a podcatcher or listening device to stack your shows up in the order in which they should be played. But before you run with 1, 2, 3 . . . , remember that computers think the number 11 is really "one-one," which would appear *before* 2. Crazy, we know. To combat this, consider using three-digit numbers such as 001, 002, and so on. Of course, this approach causes issues again when you reach Episode 1000, which would be placed in-between 199 and 200.

The best numbering system — at least for the Name ID3 tag — is to use the date. Don't use May 4, 2008, but *do* use something like 080504 or 2008-05-04. Keeping with this Year-Month-Day format ensures that your files will always stack up in order. And it doesn't really matter if you use the recording date, editing date, or release date as your number system, so long as you stick with that *same* milestone going forward.

Episode title

What is this episode about? If you do an interview show, perhaps the name of the guest is sufficient. Or maybe there is a specific topic that you cover in depth? If so, add it here. It's free-form; you can make it as long as you wish. But remember that this is just the title of the episode; it should capture the spirit of the episode in total.

Yes, you can make it five sentences if you want, but three to five words will probably be sufficient. And please use spaces and proper capitalization. It just makes you and your program look that much more professional.

Stuff

Stuff is a sort of catch-all for the extra metadata you want to share with your audience by tucking it into the Name field. This is a relatively new approach, and not yet widely in use. One example of how it's used presently is a feature of the newer iPods (those that play video): The Name tag can scroll across the screen as the show is playing.

The pioneer in the use of Stuff is Rob Walch from the *Today in iPhone* and *Podcast 411* podcasts. He uses the end of his Name field to add his voicemail number — and actively encourages folks to get the number right from their iPods during the show. This is a great idea; many folks listen while driving, and the last thing you want to do is send them digging for a pen when they should be paying attention to the road.

Of course, there are other things you can place here besides a phone number. If your podcast is promotion (or contains a promotion specific to your podcast), you may want to include discount or coupon codes in the Name field for your listeners to use later. It's also a neat way to pass along a secret message, where the meaning is derived after several episodes. Let your imagination run wild!

When you're finished, you'll run all these elements together, and your final episode Name ID3 tag will look something like this:

```
TiSM 080504: Stadium Advertising -
    206.339.8765 Code: Baseball
```

Image

Tags can contain more than simply text. Of particular use to podcasters is the capability to embed an image associated with a podcast or individual episode. While we understand and accept that not all mp3 players display embedded images, the iPod certainly does, as shown in Figure 25-4. And as the most popular mp3 player on the market today, it's an excellent branding tool.

• **Figure 25-4: Showing the logo or image associated with your show leaves your listeners with a great impression.**

The obvious choice for your image is the logo of your show. If you don't have one — get one. A consistent branding message is important and helps remind your listeners of what they are listening to and what your show is all about. At a minimum, open up your graphics editor and create a JPG with the name of your show. While the nuances of graphic production are beyond the scope of this book, you should be able to create a 300 × 300 JPG image without too much difficulty.

Additional Important Tags

While the tags we just described are non-negotiable and truly should be included with each and every episode, there are a few other tags that you can use to help your listeners experience your show to the max. While not required, they can be very helpful to the listening audience — and might set your show apart from the rest.

Compilation

This check box can be very helpful if your artist changes from episode to episode, yet you still want some grouping inside iTunes. By default, iTunes

stores the files on your listener's computer system first by Artist and then by Album. However, if the Compilation ID3 tag is checked, that behavior changes: All the Artists in the compilation are grouped together by the Album itself. iTunes goes one step farther, isolating all Compilations together in one place. Figure 25-5 shows how the directory structure changes for Compilations.

• **Figure 25-5: Where Artists normally dictate the directory structure, Compilations behave differently.**

What's the point? In some cases, the Artist will be different on each file. Take the case of *Pseudopod,* a horror magazine in podcast form that distributes short stories each week. Up until the summer of 2007, they were setting the Artist ID3 tag to the name of the original author of the story. By default, iTunes was scattering these episodes through the folder structure, giving each author (that is, each of the Artists) its own folder. While finding the file to play within the iTunes application isn't difficult, tracking down the actual file within the directory structure is quite difficult; nothing was grouped by the name *Pseudopod.*

Upon learning of the power of the Compilation tag, the editors of this podcast simply checked this box, causing all future episodes of the podcast to be easily found on a listener's hard drive by simply navigating to the iTunes Music⇨Compilations⇨Pseudopod folder. (Yes, your authors are using their powers for good!)

Again, we stress that it isn't difficult for the average user to find these episodes within the iTunes application — or any other listening application, for that matter. But for the user with something more complex in mind — who wants to create a CD archive of past shows or perhaps share the mp3 file with a friend — having all the files grouped together is much easier.

Grouping

With the sheer number of podcast groups, networks, and loose associations cropping up all the time, it's a shame that more podcasters — or the administrators of these groups — aren't making full use of the powerful Grouping tag.

This little-used tag could allow all affiliated podcasts to fly under the same banner with minimum hassle. It doesn't require them to change their file names, titles, or anything else with their file. Just putting the name of their group (say, `Podshow`, `FarPoint Media`, `Friends in Tech`, or `Blubrry`) in this field would allow those who want to sort affiliated podcasts and group them together. Ground-shaking? No, not really. But there should be a reason that these podcasts affiliate themselves with each other, so why not take this designed-for opportunity and do it in your ID3 tags?

Track Number

The Track Number is traditionally used to designate the proper order in which audio files should play. In fact, some applications that you or your listeners may still use this as the "default sort" if contained in the ID3 tagging. But you have taken charge of ordering on your own with your cleverly implemented Name convention. However, `080504` doesn't really tell anyone how many previous shows have been released. Adding in a Track Number can do this

without calling out the episode number in the show itself. Plus, some applications may ignore your careful planning. It's always good to have fallbacks.

Year

Similar to the Track Number, the Year tag allows you to identify *when* your file was created. For most podcasts, this is taken care of inside the naming convention — if it is deemed important at all. While the immediate needs may not be apparent, it may be useful for future historians who are piecing together the timeline of your groundbreaking program. (Hey . . . it could happen!)

The Best Laid Plans . . .

Having built an airtight case for paying close attention to your ID3 tags, we feel obligated to tell you that all your efforts and attentions may be for naught. iTunes, the podcatching device with the largest audience share, has a nasty habit of overwriting ID3 tags with information found in the show's RSS feed.

Yeah. That can ruin everything you've put in place. And as of this writing, there is no way to tell iTunes to leave your ID3 tags alone. For now, just know that the following will happen to your ID3 tags before they can go to anyone who subscribes to your show through iTunes. (You can find out more about this in Practice 27.)

- **Name:** Overwritten by the contents of the `<title>` RSS tag
- **Artist:** Overwritten by the contents of the `<itunes:artist>` RSS tag
- **Image:** Overwritten by the contents of the `<itunes:image>` RSS tag

Your only defense is to implement an equally robust — as in "consistent with the tagging we've just talked about" — naming convention *in your RSS development* as well. Again, see Practice 27 for more information.

Adding a Blog to Your Podcast

Blogging and podcasting go hand in hand. In fact, we'll go so far as to say that podcasting probably could not have happened without blogs blazing the trail. A specialized form of blogging — audioblogging — predates the first podcast by several years. Though many would claim that audioblogging and podcasting are one and the same, we think that takes things a bit to far and completely ignores the value of an enclosed media file. But we are willing to recognize the important role that blogs played in shaping what we know today as podcasting.

You should know that it's entirely possible to produce a podcast without the use of blogging software. Some of the most popular podcasts, such as *Skepticality* (`http://skepticality.com`), were completely conceived and made popular by their fans on their own. If you have the technical chops to host your own pages, change your home page, archive your old content, and update your RSS 2.0 file without the use of a blog — go for it! However, if you don't posses those skills — or find yourself too busy to do that much maintenance to keep your show current — blogging software can take much of the burden off your shoulders.

Why Use a Blog to Host Your Podcast?

Blogging software makes it easier to podcast. Listen, you've got plenty of things to worry about while you're creating your podcast: Writing, recording, editing, hosting, posting, feedback . . . there are lots of moving parts to keep track of. Why not automate as many of the repetitive tasks as you possibly can?

Incorporating a blog to maintain nearly all of your Web presence takes a lot of the burden off your shoulders so you can focus on the ever-changing aspects of your show. A blog can benefit you in the following ways:

- ✔ **Provides a consistent layout and design:** The software ensures that all your pages — even old show notes — have a consistent look and feel. And if you want to change things, it takes only a few minutes to change every page to the new design.

✔ **Automatically archives content:** Blogs are content-management systems and keep track of their own directory structure. By assigning categories and tags to posts, you increase the chances of someone finding your older content.

✔ **Enables you to write text, not code:** Maybe your HTML skills aren't as up to date as they once were. With a blog, creating show notes and other pages is often as simple as typing in text. WYSI-WYG editors make creating links and adding bulleted lists a breeze — without ever having to write a line of code.

✔ **Provides automatic RSS updates:** If you needed a single reason why, this is it. While editing XML isn't hard, it's also very easy to mess up. A properly-set-up blog creates a perfect RSS file every time you create a new show. That helps a podcaster sleep better at night.

Blogging Solutions for Podcasters

Podcasters have a lot of choices when it comes to selecting blogging software. While all of these programs do basically the same thing, they each have unique characteristics that make them a preferred tool among podcasters. Rather than trying to cover the legions of applications available, we'll stick with the applications we have personal experience with, winding up with an explanation of why we decided on a single recommendation. Remember, however, that the blog host you choose should be the best fit for you and your needs.

Blogger

Now owned by Google, *Blogger* (www.blogger.com) was one of the first sites to offer blogging software. Blogger offers many templates, created by both users and the Blogger support team, that can be customized to fit your needs (provided you're fluent in the XML that creates the layout). Blogger's greatest asset is its simple interface. You can either use a GUI (Graphic User Interface) or an HTML Editor to compose your blog posts.

One setback with Blogger is the lack of expandability. Beyond what Blogger offers through its interface, there is no way to build on the basics. Unlike with WordPress (explained later in this practice) — which offers plug-ins such as Akismet (a spam filter) and PodPress (the must-have tool for podcasters that provides an embedded player in the blogpost) — you're restricted to what Blogger wants you to use. Blogger is a good starting place for beginning podcasters, but the limitations of it will come to light after your production's first season.

Blogger is free of charge, a low-cost investment when you're looking to start a podcast. So yes, it may be limited in expandability, but it's still a reliable blog host.

MySpace

There is no doubt that MySpace (www.myspace.com) has taken the world of social media by storm. In fact, many heavy users of MySpace rarely do anything but consume content found on MySpace.

Part of the MySpace experience, for registered members, is posting and maintaining their own blogs within their profiles. Much of the power and appeal of MySpace is the reported ease of use, and the included blog is no exception. With the click of a link, you can post show notes and add a media file (hosted somewhere else) to the RSS feed.

However, MySpace users have very little control over the look and feel of their blogs. Without question, the start of the relationship is the profile page, and the blog gets relegated to sidekick status. Because of this, MySpace blogs tend to get read — and subscribed to — by other MySpace users.

We give MySpace full marks for making it easy to create a podcast feed, but we don't recommend this option for anyone looking to move into the *expert* realm of podcasting. MySpace could be helpful to your cause, but probably more of a place to promote your show or interact with your fans. Social media work fine for that.

Movable Type

The Movable Type application (www.movable type.com) is a very popular and powerful blogging tool. Used by many large corporations, it features easy-to-modify templates, a broad developer community, and a host of plug-ins to make the whole experience of blogging and podcasting quite simple.

While a shared-hosting version is available (www.typepad.com), the software gives you the most flexibility if you install it on your own server. Many of the popular hosting providers — including Yahoo! Small Business hosting (http://smallbusiness.yahoo.com) — allow you to install Movable Type on your server with a few simple steps.

Movable Type is available for personal use free of charge, though the support package (if necessary) will set you back a few bucks for the year. You'll want to pay close attention to the language of the licensing to make sure your podcast qualifies for this personal license. If not, you'll need to shell out $149.95 to purchase a license if your podcast is of a commercial nature or has multiple authors contributing. More information (and current pricing) can be found at www.movabletype.com/pricing.html.

But as powerful as Movable Type may be, it doesn't come with built-in native podcasting support. Fortunately, this is easily remedied — just install a freely available plug-in called (oddly enough) MT-Enclosures. With this add-on, MT is a very robust and powerful podcasting solution.

WordPress

We saved the best for last. After trying the previously mentioned applications and a few home-grown solutions, the results are in: We highly recommend WordPress (www.wordpress.org) for podcasters. In fact, the rest of this practice is dedicated to the various options and settings to make WordPress into a great podcasting tool. Even if you opt not to use WordPress as your solution, you may find valuable insight in our discussions.

Podcasting with WordPress

One handy way to demonstrate the effectiveness of WordPress (www.wordpress.org) to podcasters is by looking at the actual level of use in the podosphere. While there isn't an accurate way to determine how many podcasters use WordPress, it doesn't take much browsing of podcasts to start noticing how many of them use the application. Keep your eyes open for the *powered by WordPress* note at the bottom of the page. Chances are, many of your favorite podcasts are using WordPress to power their sites.

There are a variety of reasons that we recommend WordPress as a blogging/podcasting tool. We've highlighted a few key characteristics that we feel set this program apart from the rest:

- ✔ **It's PHP-based.** Unlike other applications that make use of proprietary code, WordPress is written entirely in PHP. This widely used scripting language is easy to learn and has a vast developer community, should you get in over your head.

- ✔ **You can drag and drop plug-ins.** Find the plug-in you need, drop it into a folder, and activate it. That's usually all it takes to get your plug-in working and your blog's functionality extended. No need to add special code to your template pages!

- ✔ **It's free.** WordPress is distributed under an open source license. So regardless of whether you're using this to host your personal site or one for your company or organization, the code is free to use and edit. (Note: As always, have your lawyer read the Terms and Conditions.)

We'll save the deep-dive on how to install WordPress for the authors of *WordPress For Dummies*. This practice focuses on showing you how to configure WordPress for effective podcasting. Additionally, we'll cover a few must-have plug-ins — PodPress, FeedBurner, and WP-Cache — that we think every podcaster should use. As with most blogging tools, the full power of WordPress comes into play after it's been *extended* — usually through the use of previously developed plug-ins. They are, like WordPress itself, free to use.

All WordPress plug-ins come with different installation instructions. For most, it's a simple matter of dropping the files into the `plugins` directory and activating the plug-in from the WordPress interface. But not always. Please read the documentation to make sure your installation goes smoothly. It usually does.

Installing and Configuring the PodPress Plug-in

While WordPress can handle podcasting out of the box (just paste a link to a media file), it doesn't give you a lot of flexibility. Various ways around this are available, but PodPress is by far the easiest to use and the most robust among the lot. As creator Dan Kuykendall says:

> "The PodPress plug-in gives you everything you need in one easy plug-in to use WordPress for Podcasting."

He's not kidding. Get the latest version from `www.mightyseek.com/podpress` and follow the installation instructions. Be sure your Web server and version of WordPress meet the requirements, and read the comments-and-support forum if you run into trouble.

After you have the plug-in installed and activated, look for the addition of PodPress to your main menu bar of WordPress. (Yes, it's special enough to warrant its own primary menu. Figure 26-1 shows you the location.)

After the PodPress plug-in is activated and you've reached the configuration screen, you'll see four submenu options (detailed in upcoming sections):

- Stats
- Feed/iTunes Settings
- General Settings
- Player Settings

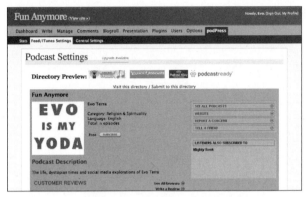

• **Figure 26-1:** PodPress is so powerful it needs its own menu bar inside WordPress.

Stats tab

There aren't any configuration settings for the Stats menu, but you may find yourself obsessing over the information you find here. Try not to, okay? Read Practice 35 for some insight on realistic expectations for audience size.

Feed/iTunes Settings tab

If you click the Feed/iTunes Settings tab, you'll first see some directory preview options for iTunes and other large directories (refer to Figure 26-1). Keep in mind that these are just approximations of how your podcast will appear on these directories. If this is your first time setting up PodPress, you won't notice much on there. Scroll down a bit.

Below the preview section are a whole host of options that allow you to customize your podcast's RSS feed, as shown in Figure 26-2. We'll run through the list, down the left column and then back to the right, giving you some tips on what information goes in each.

 Many of these settings override the standard behavior of those you get with the basic WordPress installation. That's the whole idea!

• Figure 26-2: Use these settings to customize your podcast's RSS feed.

iTunes:FeedID

After you've submitted your podcast to iTunes and its directory has accepted your podcast (see Practice 28), you're issued an iTunes Music Store ID, which is e-mailed to you. After you receive this ID, enter it into the iTunes:Feed ID field.

If you're already in the iTMS and don't know what your ID is, follow these steps to find it:

1. **Search for your podcast in the podcast directory of iTunes; when you find it, right-click your listing.**

2. **In the resulting pop-up window, choose Copy iTunes Store URL.**

3. **Lots of other information besides your ID is in this URL, so paste it somewhere else first.**

The URL should look something like this:

```
http://phobos.apple.com/WebObjects/
    MZStore.woa/wa/viewPodcast?id=25
    5781463
```

You remove the extra stuff from the URL in the next step.

4. **You only want the numbers after** `id=`. **Paste those into the PodPress iTunes Feed:ID field.**

In the example, that would be `255781463`.

To the right of the Feed ID, you'll see a button labeled *Ping iTunes Update*. This is a failsafe mechanism to let iTunes know that your feed has been updated. You shouldn't need to click this button every time you update a new episode of your podcast. But if you notice that your newest episodes are not appearing on iTunes, click away!

iTunes:New-Feed-Url

Here's where PodPress starts to get ahead of itself a bit; this option won't make a lot of sense until we get to the "Podcast Feed URL" section in a moment. Unless you have a good reason for doing otherwise, leave this set to Disable.

You'll notice that this section comes with its own warning. Pay attention to the caution, but don't be afraid of it. PodPress is good at giving you lots of flexibility, but it does require that you type things correctly.

During your career as a podcaster, you may decide to pack up your show and move from one location to another. This sometimes requires getting a whole new RSS feed address. iTunes makes it fairly simple to keep your current subscribers listening to your episodes without their having to subscribe to your new feed address. This is the tag.

If you are going to use this feature, Apple suggests also configuring your old feed to redirect to your new feed location. But in reality, you may not have this kind of control over the old feed. In practice, this isn't an issue — for your iTunes subscribers. But your subscribers who don't use iTunes as their pod-catching client will have to manually update their podcatchers with your new feed.

iTunes:Summary

This is the text that iTunes uses when displaying your podcast inside iTunes. You can say whatever you want, but we recommend being descriptive and brief. iTunes gives some very good advice on taking full advantage of this field:

> "Describe your subject matter, media format, episode schedule, and other relevant info so that they know what they'll be getting when they subscribe. In addition, make a list of the most relevant search terms that you want your podcast to match, then build them into your description. Note that iTunes removes podcasts that include lists of irrelevant words in the iTunes:Summary, Description, or iTunes:Keywords tags."

Great advice and an excellent warning. iTunes lets you use up to 4,000 characters, though you probably won't need to use that many.

iTunes:Image (300*300 pixels)

Here's the place to really make your podcast shine. If you've been podcasting for a while, you already have a logo. Make sure it's in JPG format and that its size is 300 pixels square. If that's gibberish to you, find someone to do it so that it looks great. Having an outstanding graphic for your podcast won't ensure you a spotlight by iTunes on their home page, but having a poor-quality one can keep you out of the running. See Practice 29 for more about why.

iTunes:Author/Owner

Enter your name or the name of your podcasting group. iTunes will use this to complete the Artist section of your listing.

iTunes:Subtitle

Keep this one short and sweet. iTunes uses it as your default description for each episode, but it will likely be overwritten by your episode descriptions.

iTunes:Keywords

You can add up to 12 keywords (spaces are okay). Make sure you separate them by following each one with a comma. It's also a good idea to repeat any keywords you used in the Summary field.

iTunes:Categories

Select the most appropriate listing(s) for your podcast based on the information in these drop-down menus. Try to get as specific as you can, but don't feel obligated to use all three of the entry areas. Many podcasts get by with just one or two.

iTunes:Explicit

If you are talking about adult situations or using profanity in your cast, be safe and mark it as Explicit, even though you may not find it offensive. iTunes tends to take a very conservative approach to listing shows. Err on the side of caution here.

iTunes:TTL (time-to-live)

This tag seems to have been deprecated (abandoned and no longer used) in iTunes 7.0. If you fill it out, iTunes will just ignore it.

iTunes:Block

We can't overstress the importance of being very, very careful with this option. It merits a warning of its own:

Once a podcast has been blocked by iTunes with this setting, it's nearly impossible to get it back and listed on iTunes without some major hurdles, like changing the URL of the RSS feed. It's really really hard. Take it from our experience. If you decide to podfade (as described in Part VIII) and choose to use this setting, understand that it's about as permanent as you can make it. So choose wisely.

And that brings us to the end of the current iTunes tags. Whew! But we're not finished yet. Now scroll back up and let's deal with the items on the *right* side of the screen, to get your RSS feed in tip-top shape.

Podcast Feed URL

This is the counterpart to that cryptic iTunes:New-Feed-URL tag from the previous section. Simply type in the full URL to your podcast. This could be your FeedBurner address (described later in this practice) or your default WordPress feed at `http://www.yourpodcast.com/feed`.

Blog/Podcast title

This one is pretty self-explanatory. How do you want your podcast to be listed? By what name should it be known? Enter it here.

Blog Description

The standard description for your feed goes here. Chances are, it will be exactly the same as the one you entered in the iTunes:Summary field.

Blog/RSS Image (144*144 pixels)

Similar to the iTunes:Image tag mentioned earlier, this tag determines the image that will display on many applications in association with your podcast. Follow the same rules as given for the iTunes:image tag, as it's always a good idea to make a great visual impression.

Okay, the size restrictions just given are misleading. The actual RSS specs place a width restriction of 144 pixels on these images. However, the maximum height of an image is 400 pixels. As long as your JPG, GIF, or PNG file is no wider than 144 and no taller than 400 pixels, it'll be fine.

Owner E-mail address

Time for another warning:

If you don't have enough spam in your life, you can get tons more if you put your *real* e-mail address here. Sad to say, it's easily harvested and fed to spambots. But it's also necessary to list a proper e-mail address so that people who find your feed might get in touch with you. We recommend adding the text *nospam* to your real e-mail address. For example: evo@nospam.podiobooks.com is what Evo uses; this format helps block most spam yet makes it pretty obvious what to take out for the humans who are trying to reach you.

Language

Select the appropriate value. Notice the various regional dialects.

Show Download Links in RSS Encoded Content

Sometimes the tech-talk gets in the way of the English; we apologize for the momentary lapse. All that it means is that PodPress will create a visual link for people to see on your site (or wherever your information is syndicated) so folks can easily download the enclosed media files without having to use a podcatcher. To make it even simpler, you no longer have to create your own Download This File link in your show notes. Get it?

RSS Category

Anything you like. There are currently no standards on RSS categorization, so it's up to you to decide how to list it. For example, Evo lists the Podiobooker Podcast category as *audio books*.

RSS Copyright

This is simply a date range. Unfortunately, you'll have to remember to return to this screen every year to update it. In future releases, we're all hoping for a perpetual feature here so the RSS copyright data changes right along with the Web-server date as it changes.

Show the Most Recent

You may be tempted to change this from the default 10 to something like 100. That's okay, more or less, but remember that RSS feeds are meant to contain *recent* information about your podcast and blog as opposed to containing *every* post and podcast you ever created. In fact, some useful applications — for example, FeedBurner — cease reading your file if it gets to be too large. 256K is the accepted norm for file size. So if you want to try 30 or 40 posts to display in your RSS feed, go for it — but make 'em short! You'll want to check the file size to make sure it isn't too large. Here's how:

1. **Change the value to 40.**

2. **Click the Update Options button.**

3. **Reload your Web page and click your Subscribe link to see your RSS feed.**

    If you are using FeedBurner or other RSS rewriting tools, you'll need to use your original or base RSS feed.

4. **Save the file to your desktop.**

    In Firefox, choose File⇨Save Page As and set your desktop as the destination.

5. **Check the size of the file you saved by right-clicking (or Ctrl-clicking) the file.**

    If the file is over 256K, you'll need to reduce the number of posts to display in the RSS 2.0 feed.

 Don't push it, because the size of each of your posts is probably flexible. We suggest trying to keep it under 200K; that way you have some wiggle room to accommodate lengthy show notes on a couple of episodes.

Encoding for Pages and Feeds

Unless you have a good reason not to, keep this as UTF-8. It will make sure that your feed is as accessible as possible.

Aggressively Protect the Feed

We're torn on this one. On one hand, strange characters (usually introduced when cutting and pasting from word-processing applications) can wreak havoc on RSS 2.0 feeds. On the other hand, links and images are just fine inside the feed — especially when using PodPress. If straight text is all you ever include in your posts, go ahead and use this setting. But if you think images inside your posts are important and should be used in the feed as well, leave it set to No.

And so ends the plethora of PodPress iTunes/Feed settings. (What? You thought we were done? Not quite.)

General Settings tab

You need to set some General Settings next, as shown in Figure 26-3. Luckily, there aren't nearly as many.

General Options

Media File Locations

URI of media files directory (?): http://media.libsyn.com/media/podiobooks

Local path to media files directory
(optional) (?): /home/.pappy/sliceofs/podiobooks.com/blog//wp

Directory Not Valid or Not Accessible
Suggested:
/var/www/podiobooks/trunk/blog/http://media.libsyn.com/media/podiobooks
(Auto Detection Failed.)

Download Statistics

Enable podPress Statistics: ☐   This will use the included stats support in podPress.

Enable PodTrac Statistics: ☐   This will use the new PodTrac service. More info...

Note: The two stats services can be used together

Post Editing

Max Number of Media Files: 20

The higher the number, the bigger the performance impact when editing Posts.

Premium Content (?)

• **Figure 26-3: The General Settings tab.**

Media File Locations

Chances are, you put your media files in the same directory each and every time you put up a new episode. If you do, you're in luck: PodPress anticipates this and offers to save you all that typing. All you have to do is type in the full path to the directory where you keep your audio files.

If you host with Libsyn, for example, this entry will look something like this:

```
http://media.libsyn.com/media/
   mypodcast
```

If you host your media files on the same server that holds WordPress and PodPress, it gets a little more complicated — and can look like this:

```
/usr/local/psa/home/vhosts/mypod-
   cast.com/httpdocs//wp-content/
   uploads
```

 Don't put the trailing slash at the end of your directories. PodPress will do that for you when you enter in the file name of your most recent episode.

Download Statistics

You get to choose whether to use the stats package that comes with PodPress. Personally, we use them but don't pay a whole lot of attention to them.

(We much prefer to count subscriber activity rather than individual downloads of episodes. But your mileage may vary.) Also, PodPress gives you the capability to integrate it with PodTrac's own tracking system. (We talk more about PodTrac and other advertising-driven networks in Practice 47.)

The rest of the options on this page are your preference. Try them out and see how they work for you.

The golden rule: If you don't know what it is, don't mess with it.

And that's it! You are now set to podcast with WordPress and PodPress.

Player Settings tab

Feel free to explore the Player Settings tab to change the look and feel of the player at your convenience.

Adding a Media File with PodPress

With all of those settings . . . *set*, it's now time to show you how to actually use PodPress to add an enclosed media file to your show notes.

Adding the media file

Follow these steps to add a media file:

1. **Choose Write⇨Write Post from the main toolbar of WordPress.**

2. **Complete the title and body fields.**

   Like nearly all blogging solutions, WordPress allows you to create a title and body for each of your posts. Complete these fields as you normally would — but don't put a link to your media file in either field. PodPress creates a new field to take care of that function.

3. Scroll down the screen to the Podcasting section (shown in Figure 26-4). Click the Add Media File button to reveal the input selections.

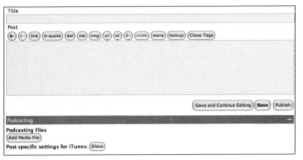

• Figure 26-4: PodPress adds a new section to WordPress for easily adding media files to your posts.

4. Assuming you've correctly completed the URL for your Media File Directory in the previous section, all you'll need to do is type the file name of your media file in the input field called Location.

5. Give the media file a description.

Keep it short — something as quick as `Episode 87` is descriptive enough. Don't forget that you have all the show notes to describe the file.

6. If your file is something other than a standard mp3 file, select the appropriate file type.

If you don't see your file type listed, select the (final) Other option.

7. Your next options are Size and Duration. Rather than getting your computer to tell you this information, simply click the Auto Detect buttons to the right of each.

PodPress will, in a few moments (depending on your connection speed), return the appropriate values.

 The Auto Detect feature doesn't always work, depending on the sever configurations of where your media files are housed. If it's not working for you, you can enter in the values manually.

8. Unless you have a very good reason not to (and we can't think of any), keep the boxes checked to include this media file in your RSS 2.0 and Atom feeds.

9. You may also opt to disable the automatic PodPress player if your site has trouble displaying the Flash player properly.

10. PodPress also allows you to display some of the detected ID3 tags of your media file.

See Practice 26 for specifics on how to take full advantage of these important tags.

11. Before you hit Add Media File, we highly recommend you take a look at the post settings for iTunes. Click the Show button, which is shown in Figure 26-4.

You'll note that by default the Post excerpt (the first 25 characters of your show notes) is used for both the Subtitle and the Summary. We're not big fans of that, and would prefer that you change it, as described next.

12. Change the following fields:

▶ **Subtitle:** A very brief description of this episode. Do not repeat the information in the title of the post.

▶ **Summary:** Copy the entire body of your show notes and put the copy right here.

The other values are likely okay as is, but feel free to change them as necessary.

13. Click the Add Media File button as shown on Figure 26-4.

That's it! You've just added your first enclosed media file to your WordPress blog and are now podcasting!

Testing

The price of freedom (and a smoothly running podcast) is eternal vigilance. Here are a few things to test:

✔ **Visit your blog and check to make sure that the Download button that PodPress created for you works — and that your episode plays.** If it doesn't, you may have entered the file name or the path to your media files incorrectly. Examining the link and make sure an extra / character isn't showing up and that you've correctly entered the path.

✔ **Check your RSS 2.0 feed visually.** To do so, click the link to your feed in your browser. We suggest viewing the source of the file and searching for the term *enclosure*. Your episode's media file should be listed.

✔ **Validate your feed.** Copy the URL of your feed (not of your podcast episode) and paste it in the field at `http://feedvalidator.org`. Doing so checks for any special character additions (often from those pesky word processors) and other errors. Correct any issues with your feed as necessary.

Now that we have PodPress wrapped up and you're podcasting with the big kids, let's talk about two more plug-ins we find invaluable. Don't worry — we won't take quite as deep a dive here!

FeedBurner Feed Replacement Plug-in

FeedBurner is a free service that does quite a few great things for podcasters — for instance, giving you the best set of stats (in our opinion) on how people are subscribing to and using your feed. Although plenty of folks don't use FeedBurner in their podcasting endeavors, many (and probably most) podcasters do. We use the service and can easily recommend it. For more information, check out `http://feedburner.com` for case studies and a thorough FAQ section.

If you decide to use FeedBurner, we highly recommend installing the FeedBurner Feedsmith plug-in. It ensures that all your subscribers are routed through FeedBurner — resulting in the most relevant stats possible. We detail how to set up FeedBurner in Practice 26. For now, download and install the plug-in from `www.feedburner.com/fb/a/help/wordpress_quickstart`.

 Don't activate the plug-in until you've created your feed with FeedBurner. Again, see Practice 28 for more about this simple process.

WP-Cache Plug-in

When your podcast gets popular and more people are checking you out from day to day, your Web site will get slow. Worse, as you get more subscribers, you may start to blow through your monthly bandwidth allotment. That won't be the fault of your media files, provided you host them on a dedicated media-hosting site. We're talking about the bandwidth hit your Web server takes when you start serving out *thousands and thousands* of RSS feeds and requests every day.

If you've noticed your site slowing down or are concerned about bandwidth, check out the WP-Cache plug-in at `http://mnm.uib.es/gallir/wp-cache-2/`. Here's how the creator of the plug-in describes it:

> "WP-Cache is an extremely efficient WordPress page-caching system to make your site much faster and responsive. It works by caching WordPress pages and storing them in a static file for serving future requests directly from the file rather than loading and compiling the whole PHP code and then building the page from the database. WP-Cache allows you to serve hundred of times more pages per second, and to reduce the response time from several tenths of a second to less than a millisecond."

If that got confusing, just read the first sentence again. It makes your site faster. 'Nuff said. Oh, except for this:

 Installing WP-Cache does require some effort. Some plug-ins can be installed in simple drag-and-drop format — but this isn't one of them. Because this plug-in requires some editing of your PHP files, don't attempt it if you shy away from editing code. *Yes, you can break things if you do this wrong.* However, if you get Dugg or BoingBoinged without it, you may be in trouble. Get a techie friend to help you out if necessary.

One final thought on caching: Some information, ranging from newly published episodes to PodPress statistics, won't be updated on each page refresh. Instead, it may take a few minutes to see changes to these items. That's what caching is all about — putting less of a stress on the database that powers your Web site. Our advice? Be patient. Then check again.

Practice 27

Validating Your RSS Feed

If you've come this far down the road to becoming an expert podcaster, you should have an understanding of what an RSS feed is and what it does for you. Should you be looking at those three letters for the first time and wonder, "What have I gotten myself into?" — well, we need to talk. Podcasting is not podcasting without an RSS feed. Recording an audio or video file and posting it on a Web site is not the same thing as podcasting. It's the "casting" part that's important to this conversation.

When you watch your DVD set of *The Sopranos,* you aren't watching a television broadcast. When you listen to the CD collection "I Heard It on NPR" in your car or at home, you aren't listening to a radio broadcast. Granted, the material — or content — in both might be the same as was available in a previous broadcast form, but you've skipped the "casting" part and are using a different medium to consume the content.

Why is this distinction important? Because *The Sopranos* would not have become the popular show that it is without the audience that the show reached from its *broadcast.* DVD sales are just icing on the cake. Incredibly profitable and expensive icing, but icing nonetheless. The same holds true for NPR. In order to make a collection titled "I Heard It on NPR," someone had to hear the content first as a *broadcast.*

Posting audio and/or video files to a Web site and allowing folks to download them at their convenience should also be considered the icing on a podcaster's cake. It's easy to do — and many folks choose this method of consuming the content — but it's not the primary intended distribution method. Where radio and TV requires either a transmitting tower or some sort of digital encoding system to deliver content, what you need is a very small, lightweight, and 100%-compatible text file to accomplish the same goal in the podcasting world.

That text file is called an *RSS feed.* In this practice, we show you how to take full advantage of your RSS feed — and how to avoid some common pitfalls that can (and all too often do) gum up the works. If you're interested in a deeper discussion on creating RSS feeds from scratch, check out *Syndicating Web Sites with RSS Feeds For Dummies* or take a hard look at Chapter 9 of *Podcasting For Dummies* (Wiley), an excellent resource for those just starting out in their podcasting careers.

RSS Deconstructed

RSS is nothing scary. It's just text in a specialized format known as XML. That's an acronym for eXtensible Markup Language — and it is, for the most part, pretty easy to read, understand, and edit. The good news is that you, as a podcaster, probably don't need to worry about it too much; most tools you use to create your podcast (see Practice 24) take care of most of the heavy lifting for you. But it's a good idea to have at least an understanding and working knowledge of this process — it's your main tool for distributing your content to listeners.

An RSS file consists of three main sections:

- ✔ A *Header* section that describes the technical aspects of the file.

- ✔ A *Channel* section that describes various aspects of the content of the file — and where it came from.

- ✔ One or more *Items*, each providing information and attributes about a particular . . . item (in our case, a single episode of a podcast).

These three sections work in concert with one another to make sure that your audience's podcast aggregators (or news readers, feed readers, pod-catchers, whatever) can translate the RSS feed and allocate the content in human-readable format. To illustrate this, let's look at the similarities between on off-the-shelf music CD and the RSS feed of a podcast. Oddly enough, the analogy holds — but it's best illustrated in reverse:

- ✔ **For purposes of this illustration, consider that the individual song tracks on the CD are the same as the various Items in an RSS feed.** Arguably, the individual song tracks on the CD are the most important or crucial parts of the music CD itself. Each track contains the content that the listener is trying to access. If there are any errors on the track itself, the song won't

play. Or maybe it skips. The same holds true for the Items in a podcast's RSS file. Missing or incomplete data results in an error or (more likely) prevents the episode from being delivered to subscribers. Both the CD track and the Item require the complete assembly of all necessary data to work properly.

- ✔ **The packaging of a music CD is analogous to the Channel section of an RSS feed.** The CD contains cover art, liner notes, the image stamped on the CD, copyright notices, and a few other data elements. This packaging is consistent for all the individual song tracks. In data terms, it's the equivalent of a larger *parent* directory that holds the Items. That's the exact purpose that the Channel element serves: It tells the listener who was responsible for the content, delivers images and information about the content's maker, and carries other data points to describe all the subsequent content (in this case, the various Items).

- ✔ **The CD and player communicate with one another to determine what to access and what to ignore; that's the very same role the header portion of an RSS file plays.** Because not all CDs are created equal, when you drop a new music CD into the CD drive for your computer, you may get a very different experience than if you used your home stereo. Music videos may play. Links to additional content on the band's Web site might become available. Your home stereo probably can't handle these functions, so the CD and the player communicate with one another to determine what should be accessed and what should be ignored. In a similar way, the header portion of an RSS file communicates with the feed reader, helping the reader determine which of the included data elements to access, and which ones to ignore.

Okay, so much for the high-level analogy. Next up is a look at some specific elements of RSS that you'll need to concern yourself with.

RSS Reconstructed

The enclosed DVD with this book contains a file called the *Perfect Annotated RSS File.* You may want to refer to that from time to time as you read this section. (If we could manage to shove the RSS feed into the format of this printed book, the result would be difficult to read at best.) Alternatively, you could just use that file (without the annotations) as your base file and skip the rest of this section altogether. We're nothing if not accommodating!

Header information

We mentioned earlier that RSS is simply a version of XML. True enough, but we need to get a lot more specific about describing the file inside the header. It should start with the following piece of text, in this exact form:

```
<?xml version="1.0" encoding="UTF-8"?>
```

This declaration requires that any reader application that attempts to process this file be able to understand version 1.0 XML and that it be able to handle the most commonly used character set, UTF-8. If the reader can't accommodate these requirements (and all feed readers must be able to), then it ignores the contents of the file. Bottom line: Always use the declarative statement shown here to start off your XML file. Always. Seriously.

If the reader application can get past that initial declarative statement, the RSS feed has to prep the application for the various sorts of data elements it can expect — and it needs your help.

- **First, you have to declare the version of RSS required — in this case, 2.0.** While there are many versions of RSS, only 2.0 includes the necessary `<enclosure>` tag that is used to automatically retrieve and store attached media files. (You know . . . podcasting!)

- **Additionally, you have to declare what other sorts of non-standard RSS data elements will be encountered in the later portions of the file.**

Think of this as like telling a visiting delegate what sorts of foreign languages she might encounter on her visit to another country, so she can arrange to have translators travel with her. In the world of RSS, these languages are called *namespaces,* and there are lots of them.

In fact, you could create your own namespace and make your own data elements — as long as you're willing to create the translation documents and convince the makers of the podcatchers and feed aggregators to include support for your elements.

For the purposes of this section, we'll concern ourselves with only two additional declarations:

- One to allow you to pass in images, HTML, and other non-standard elements

- One to allow you to pass the values necessary to take full advantage of iTunes, the most popular podcatcher as of this writing

To accomplish this, the next line of text in your RSS feed should look just like this:

```
<rss version="2.0"
   xmlns:content="http://purl.org/rss/
   1.0/modules/content/"
   xmlns:itunes="http://www.itunes.com
   /dtds/podcast-1.0.dtd" >
```

Note the URL passed after each namespace declaration. Although this Web site has no code that your newsreader can execute immediately, it does help ensure that the newsreader uses the right set of namespace variables. It's a complicated process; just make sure you type it in exactly as shown here.

Channel information

Remember that the Channel section of your feed describes your podcast show, not the individual episodes. Keep the music CD case and packaging metaphor in mind as you look through Table 27-1 for a list of the important tags. And refer to the Perfect Annotated RSS File on the DVD.

TABLE 27-1: IMPORTANT CHANNEL ELEMENTS

Tag	Description	Example
title	The name of your podcast.	`<title>The Perfect Podcast</title>`
link	URL to your podcast's Web site.	`<link>http://www.theperfectpodcast.com</link>`
description	A general description of your show's standard content. Use plenty of keywords that are relevant to your show.	`<description>The perfect place to learn everything about podcasting. From creating the perfect RSS feed to recording and editing using GarageBand and Adobe Audition, we have everything you need to get started and build a successful career in podcasting.</description>`
webmaster	E-mail of the person responsible maintaining your Web presence. This can be harvested by spambots, so be careful.	`<webmaster>webmaster@nospam.perfectpodcasting.com</webmaster>`
managingEditor	E-mail and name of the person generally responsible for the content of your podcast. Could be a show host or a producer.	`<managingEditor>producer@nospam.perfectpodcasting.com (Jane Doe)</managingEditor>`
pubDate	The last date your podcast was published. In effect, the last time you made an episode available. Note that it *must* follow the Date and Time Specification of RFC 822 (`http://asg.web.cmu.edu/rfc/rfc822.html`).	`<pubDate>Sun, 04 Feb 2007 15:33:00 -0500</pubDate>`
lastBuildDate	The last date the file was changed or modified. In many cases, it will be the same as the pubDate.	`<lastBuildDate> Sun, 04 Feb 2007 15:33:00 -0500</lastBuildDate>`
language	The code for the language used in the podcast. A complete list is available at `http://cyber.law.harvard.edu/rss/languages.html`.	`<language>en-us</language>`
docs	A URL that points to the documentation for the format used in the RSS file.	`<docs>http://blogs.law.harvard.edu/tech/rss</docs>`
copyright	Your copyright declaration.	`<copyright>CreativeCommons 3.0 - Some rights reserved</copyright>`

The image tag

The image tag should also be included, but it's complicated enough that it wouldn't fit well in the table we just showed you. It takes the following format:

```
<image>
  <url>http://www.perfectpodcasting/
  images/ cover.jpg</url>
  <width>144</width>
  <height>144</height>
  <link>http://www.theperfectpodcast.
  com</link>
  <title>The Best Laid Plans by Terry
  Fallis</title>
</image>
```

iTunes elements

iTunes elements are critical to the success of a podcast. We're not making a political statement here, but rather are acknowledging that over 50% of listeners to public podcasts do so with the help of iTunes. While there are many other directories and organizations — each with their own XML namespaces and special elements — none has the heft of iTunes. When that changes, we'll write another book and tell you how to take advantage of those as well.

 We cover much of this in Practice 26 (it's relevant to setting up WordPress). Even if you aren't using WordPress, you may want to read that section for additional information on how iTunes uses this information.

Table 27-2 shows you the required iTunes tags. Unlike the standard RSS tags we just showed you, these are all the current iTunes elements. Keep an eye on `http://www.apple.com/itunes/store/podcaststechspecs.html` in the event that any new elements are added. Which will probably happen.

iTunes categories

iTunes uses its own category system — which often trips up podcasters who are creating their own feeds. Start by selecting the right categories for your show from the list provided by iTunes. They have been known to change, but the most current list (as of this writing) can be found at

> `www.apple.com/itunes/store/podcasts techspecs.html#_Toc526931698`

TABLE 27-2: iTUNES TAGS

Name	Description	Example
subtitle	A brief description of your show.	`<itunes:subtitle>By podcasters, for podcasters </itunes:subtitle>`
summary	The same thing you have in your `<description>` tag. Duplicated? Yeah, we know . . .	`<itunes:summary>The perfect place to learn everything about podcasting. From creating the perfect RSS feed to recording and editing using GarageBand and Adobe Audition, we have everything you need to get started and build a successful career in podcasting. </itunes:summary>`
owner	The same e-mail address as `<webmaster>`, though iTunes would also like a name. Again, be careful of spam.	`<itunes:owner>` `<itunes:email> Webmaster@nospam.perfect podcasting.com</itunes:email>` `<itunes:name>John Doe</itunes:name>` `</itunes:owner>`
author	Probably the person in your `<managingEditor>` element above, though iTunes only wants their name.	`<itunes:author>Jane Doe</itunes:author>`
image	An image ripe for iTunes. The perfect size is 300 × 300, and it must be in .JPG or .PNG form, though iTunes prefers the former. Note the slight difference in tag form.	`<itunes:image href="http://www.perfect podcasting/images/iTunescover.jpg"/>`

(continued)

TABLE 27-2 (continued)

Name	Description	Example
explicit	Three possible values: yes, no and clean. If it has explicit material in it, set it to yes so iTunes can display a parental-warning icon. If it's squeaky clean so iTunes can show a "Clean" icon by your content, mark it as such. If it's neither, then set it to no.	`<itunes:explicit>no</itunes:explicit>`

You can select up to three categories on iTunes. When you make your selection, pay close attention to any category/subcategory relationship. For example, you cannot select the entire Technology category, because it has four subcategories beneath it. However, you *can* select the TV & Film category, because no subcategories are listed under the main category. (Yes, it's a little confusing.)

When listing iTunes categories to your file, consider that subcategories need to be *wrapped* by their parent category; categories that have no subcategories are listed with a trailing slash character (/) to signify the end. That's confusing to explain in text, so an example is in order. Here's exactly how you would add iTunes category statements to your file if you wanted to associate your show with the following categories:

- Comedy
- Games & Hobbies ⇨ Hobbies
- Music

Here's the corresponding code:

```
<itunes:category text="Comedy" />
<itunes:category text="Games &amp;
    Hobbies">
        <itunes:category text="Hobbies" />
</itunes:category>
<itunes:category text="Music" />
```

The Comedy and Music categories have no subcategories, so they are listed on their own, but with the trailing / to signify the end of the tag. Because the Hobbies category is a subcategory of the larger Games & Hobbies category, Hobbies has the trailing / character to end the tag, but the wrapped *parent* category has the more standard start-and-ending-tag sequence you're used to seeing in element tags.

 Notice that we didn't use a standard & symbol in our example for Games & Hobbies? That's because the ampersand is a special character — and can cause all kinds of headaches. We cover that in the "Avoiding Pitfalls" section directly ahead.

Item Information

Now that you have properly identified what sorts of readers can accept your information and provided the basic *packaging* information about your podcast in general, it's time to describe the actual content itself in a series of `<item>` declarations.

As stated earlier, the Items of your file are analogous to individual song tracks on a CD. They each have their own names, descriptions, and many more attributes. And our analogy goes further than you might think: Each Item will also need to have an associated — or *enclosed* — media file to go along with it.

The various attributes of the Item section look quite similar to the attributes we just discussed in the prior section. Let's start with Table 27-3, a list of the same elements — but with different content from that used in the Channel section. Instead of providing an example of how to format the tag (it's exactly the same formatting), we give you some pointers on what sort of information to include.

TABLE 27-3: ITEM ELEMENTS

Name	Description	Suggestions
`title`	Title of this individual episode.	Be a little more descriptive than `Episode #19`, but keep it brief.
`description`	A long form description of the contents of your episode.	Make sure this is text only.
`link`	URL to the page of the episode.	This assumes you're using blogging software or are creating an individual page where your show notes and other information about a particular episode are contained. If not, a link back to your Web site will have to suffice.
`pubDate`	The date the episode was released.	Make sure you follow the correct date format. See the "Avoiding Pitfalls" section.
`itunes:subtitle`	A brief description of this episode.	More words than you used in your `<title>` tag, but less than you'd find the `<description>` tag. iTunes uses this to display in the iTMS, so be brief but clear.
`itunes:summary`	A longer description of the episode.	Probably the same as your `<description>` tag, and again make sure this only contains text.
`itunes:explicit`	See Table 27-2.	If your content is normally not explicit, but a single episode is, be sure to mark it accordingly. Setting a single episode as explicit should not cause your entire podcast to be flagged as such. The same holds true for `clean`.
`itunes:author`	Enter the person responsible for this episode.	Most useful if you have multiple hosts or content contributors. In most cases, this will be the same person entered in your Channel section.

As promised, the Items section has a few new tags that are specific to this area only, as they don't have any application in the larger Channel context.

Setting keywords with the <itunes:keywords> tag

You can use up to a maximum of 12 keywords, separated by spaces. It's not well known exactly how iTunes uses these keywords when it returns search results, so we suggest entering them in the search box exactly the way you think others might enter them.

Keeping each episode unique with the <guid> tag

GUID stands for Global Unique IDentifier, though there's nothing global about it. Rather, it has to be a unique string of characters found within your podcast feed. The easiest way to accommodate this need is by setting your GUID to the same value as your Item's `<link>` value — provided you use a different URL for each of your episodes "pages" on your site. If not, you may have to use some sort of episodic-numbering system combined with the `<pubDate>` tag. It can be anything you like, as long as it's unique to your feed.

Attaching media files with an <enclosure> tag

This is it — finally — the part that makes a podcast a podcast: the enclosure file. This file requires three components to work:

✔ **The URL where the media file is located:** The easiest way to find this is to access the media file in your browser. When it starts to play, copy the URL. That's your path.

✔ **The size (length) of the file in bytes:** Most FTP clients tell you the size of the file in bytes. If not, find the file on your hard drive (you *do* keep a backup, right?) and use the File⇨Get Info option to display this information on a Mac. For Windows users, it's File⇨Properties. Don't enter the commas and don't try to enter the MB value. If all else fails, multiply the displayed MB size by 1024.

✔ **A standard MIME type for the file:** Table 27-4 lists common mime types for most media files.

TABLE 27-4: COMMON MIME TYPES

Filename Extension	MIME Type
.mp3	audio/mpeg
.m4a	audio/x-m4a
.mp4	video/mp4
.m4v	video/x-m4v
.mov	video/quicktime
.pdf	application/pdf

A properly enclosed media file for an item takes the following form:

```
<enclosure
  url="http://media.libsyn.com/media/
  superpodcaster/BBC-2006-06-05.mp3"
  length="36512373" type="audio/
  mpeg" />
```

Adding rich content

So far we've been content to add standard text and a few links to some images. You may recall that in the "Reconstruction" section of this practice, we asked you to add a namespace called simply content. That namespace allows for many new elements to extend the RSS format, but we're really only interested in one: <content:encoded>.

This new element allows us to embed HTML code inside the <description> element of our Items. This capability is becoming more important as newsreaders become more sophisticated and would-be Web visitors consume more and more of their content via RSS — without ever visiting the Web site where the content originated. If you've spent a lot of time adding the appropriate images and formatting to your show-notes post, the <content:encoded> tag lets you wrap up that hard work in a package and distribute it to the newsreaders that will accept it.

 Not all readers can display HTML, CSS, and other code inside posts. In fact, iTunes doesn't display the text at all unless someone goes looking for it. But this situation won't cause you a problem because you've made your declaration statement earlier. Any reader that cannot accommodate this section will ignore it — and default to the plain text found inside the <description> field.

The usage of the content:encoded tag takes the following form:

```
<content:encoded><![CDATA[DYAMIC_CODE
  _HERE]]></content:encoded>
```

and an example of its use might look like this:

```
<content:encoded><![CDATA[<p>What a
  <em>beautiful</em>day!</p>]]>
  </content:encoded>
```

Of course, you can do a lot more with this code as well. Here's a real-world example from one of Evo's feeds. We've put the dynamic stuff in bold to make it easier to see:

```
<content:encoded><![CDATA[<div
  style="float: right; margin-left:
  10px; margin-bottom: 10px;">
<a href="http://www.flickr.com/
  photos/evo_terra/536681453/"
  title="Photo Sharing"><img
  src="http://farm2.static.flickr.com/
  1354/536681453_ddefdde5ac_m.jpg"
  width="240" height="180" alt="Five
  O'Clock Shadow 37" style="border:
```

```
solid 2px #000000;" /></a><br />
<br />
<span style="font-size: 0.9em;
margin-top: 0px;"><br />
<a href="http://www.flickr.com/
photos/evo_terra/536681453/">Five
O&#8217;Clock Shadow 37</a><br />
<br />
Originally uploaded by <a href=
"http://www.flickr.com/people/
evo_terra/">evo_terra</a>.<br />
</span>
</div>
<p>There are some days when I love
having more than one job. I get to
bounce not only from project from
project from project, but also wear
very different hats and have
totally different responsibilities.
It's very liberating.</p>
<p>Then there are days when I wish
there was only one job, as it would
make life so much simpler for
me.</p>
<p>And then there are days like
today, when I wish I had none at
all.</p>
<p>Behind me is a clipping my
maternal grandmother sent me. Her
and my grandpa are being crowned
King and Queen of Valentine's Day.
They just celebrated 61 years
together. At least that makes me
happy. Kickboxing might help,
too.</p>]]></content:encoded>
```

So — as you can see — you can put a whole lot of content inside this tag.

Avoiding Pitfalls

Okay, we know all that was a lot to take in. And chances are good that your podcast's Web site or blogging platform already kicks out this data (and probably a lot more) on its own, and in fine form. However, there are a few pitfalls that you need to be aware of so you can make sure you don't fall prey.

Special characters

Remember that your RSS file is, at its most basic, a text file. Not a file kicked out by a word-processing application, but a plain text file. The distinction is important enough for us to stress a couple of times.

Word processes do not, by default, create text files. Instead they create stylized, formatted documents. What we call a *word processor* is really a layout-and-formatting application for text. During the stylizing process, the word processor takes your standard keyboard input and makes some subtle changes. When you end a sentence with three dots (an ellipsis) — as one of your authors does all too often — your word processor converts those three periods into a special character. It still consists of three dots, but it's much tighter and looks better. When you type in a colon followed by an ending parenthesis mark, your word processor probably converts that input to a happy-face icon on-screen. The same happens for quotes, double-dashes, and many other characters.

While that may actually make for a better-looking document, it can — and will — wreak havoc on your RSS feed if you leave these special characters in place when creating your feed. When you copy the body of your document, you're copying the special characters and *not* the true text you initially entered. And since these special characters are *not* UTF-8 characters (see "Header information" earlier in this practice), your RSS feed will be invalid — and many (or most) newsreaders will be unable to read the feed. In other words, your audience won't be able to get your show.

The best way to ensure that special characters do not wind up in your feed is to use something other than a word-processing application to create your show notes and other entries. Most operating systems come with a default plain-text application. It's called Notepad on the PC and TextEdit on a Mac. If you create and copy your text from here, you should have no special character issues.

But what if you're a terrible speller? Well, we certainly didn't write this book in TextEdit. You can do a few things to your word-processing application to make it friendlier to RSS creation.

Open Microsoft Word and follow these instructions to remove the special formatting:

1. **Choose Tools⇨AutoCorrect.**

This opens the AutoCorrect dialog box shown in Figure 27-1.

 These instructions were written for Word 2004 for Mac and Word 2003 for Windows. Your particular installation of Word may be slightly different.

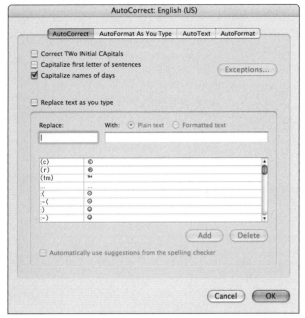

• **Figure 27-1: Turning off AutoFormatting in Word can reduce errors on your RSS feed later.**

2. **Uncheck the Replace as You Type box.**

This selection ensures that ellipses and other characters aren't replaced with special characters. However, this also means that Word will no longer auto-correct your common spelling

mistakes. If you want that option enabled, keep the box checked and delete the non-words at the top of the list.

3. **Click the AutoFormat as You Type tab and uncheck all of the boxes.**

This prevents the curly quote issue and double-dash problems.

4. **Click the AutoFormat tab and uncheck all boxes.**

They really want you to use curly quotes. You really don't want to.

5. **Click OK when you're finished.**

Just so you know: This procedure changes the way your word-processing application behaves from now on — or at least until you go back and change it again. If you really like the way that Word automatically did things for you previously, well, sorry, it won't do those things any longer. Consider whether you can live with those changes for all your documents, or whether you should use a text-only editor to handle anything you're inserting into your podcast feed.

 Special characters are a big problem when text from word-processing programs gets dropped into the text fields of blogging platforms. So even if you aren't editing your feed by hand, special characters can still cause issues. Text editors are your friends . . .

Duplicate <guid>s

If you're using a blogging solution such as WordPress to create your feed, duplicate <guid> tags should not be a problem. But everyone else should remember that the *U* in <guid> stands for *unique* — it cannot be repeated in your feed or it will cause errors on some (or all) podcatching clients. Be sure you use something that will always be different.

File size

Issues arise when your RSS feed gets too big for its britches. The feed readers have to *parse* (read: *read*) the entire file and they tend to get a little cranky when the file gets too large. Even worse, FeedBurner will not process RSS feeds that exceed 256K, and iTunes has been known to break when trying to read files above that size as well. Keep your file size down to less than 256K and you should have no issues. Remember that this refers only to the size of the text file itself. Your attached media files and images won't bulk up your text file.

Dates and times

The fields `<pubDate>` and `<lastBuildDate>` require that you pass in the date and time in a properly formatted fashion, following the RFC2822 standard. We'll save you the tech-speak and stress that the dates all follow one of the two following formats:

```
<pubDate>Wed, 6 Jul 2005 13:00:00
    PDT</pubDate>
```

or

```
<pubDate>Wed, 6 Jul 2005 13:00:00 -
    0700</pubDate>
```

Table 27-5 shows the acceptable abbreviations for days and months.

TABLE 27-5: PROPER ABBREVIATIONS

Day of week	Month
Mon	Jan
Tue	Feb
Wed	Mar
Thu	Apr
Fri	May
Sat	Jun
Sun	Jul
	Aug
	Sep
	Oct
	Nov
	Dec

The day of the month can be expressed in either single- or double-digit form; the year should always be expressed in four digits. Be sure to remember the comma after the day of the week.

The time stamp should be expressed in 24-hour or military time and always have all positions filled. In other words, 2:15 AM should be expressed as 02:15:00. Don't forget your initial zero, if necessary, and to include the seconds.

No media files in the feed

Many podcasters use their blogging platform to blog between episodes. That means the podcast feed might actually have non-podcast elements (that is, Items without enclosed media files) inside. This isn't a problem; most available feed readers can handle enclosures and non-enclosed items with ease. Even iTunes, the most popular podcatching client, is fine with Items without enclosed media files — it just ignores them.

But iTunes — and perhaps other directories — *will* have a problem with your feed if they don't detect *any* enclosure files in the feed at all. This is really only a problem for the serial blogger who also puts out the occasional podcast. If you post ten non-podcast blog entries and you're only including the last ten posts in your RSS feed, then iTunes (and possibly other directories) won't have a whole lot to show for you in the iTunes Music Store. Someone may search and find your podcast, but it will look like you haven't released any episodes — only because iTunes couldn't find any in your most recent feed.

To combat this potential misunderstanding, make sure you have enough posts inside your feed to always contain your last podcast. Don't forget the file-size restriction we mentioned earlier. If that doesn't do the trick, maybe you need to podcast a bit more!

Stop Worrying: Validate Your Feed Often

We finish this rather longish practice with a way you can seriously reduce your worrying about keeping a valid feed — and get back to worrying about making a great podcast.

You can stare at your podcast's RSS feed all day long and never see problems. That's because you aren't a feed-reader application, and aren't tuned to pick up on those problems. Luckily for you (and us), some smart folks have put together a free service that every podcaster should be using on a regular basis. The simple and elegant interface to this online tool is shown in Figure 27-2.

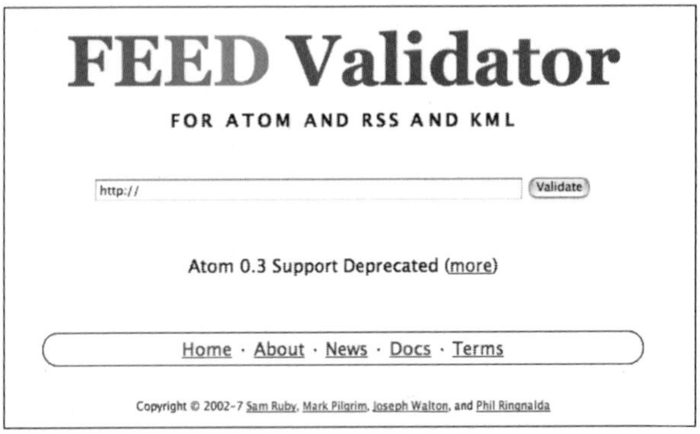

• **Figure 27-3: A properly formatted feed gets you kudos from the site. To be safe, check it each time you publish a new file.**

• **Figure 27-2: Using the free Feed Validator early and often can help identify problems in your feed.**

Copy your feed address and visit `http://feed validator.org/` in your browser. Paste the URL to your feed in the box and hit Validate. That's it.

If your feed is valid, you get a nice message telling you so — as well as a small graphic you can add to your Web site if you choose. Figure 27-3 shows a successful page, and Figure 27-4 shows when things don't go so well.

• **Figure 27-4: Errors may happen, but at least they tell you where the problems are.**

If your test returns something other than `Valid`, then scroll down the page to identify where the problem occurred. The Feed Validator will highlight problems in yellow, giving you an easy way to find the culprit. After making the necessary corrections, return to this page and try again. Keep this process going until you get a perfectly validated file. Then be sure to return to the page and repeat the process each time you update your RSS feed.

Practice

Submitting to Podcast Directories

Google and other search engines — it's nearly impossible to navigate without their assistance. However, tossing the word *podcast* into a larger search engine and then trying to sift through the results is the data equivalent of getting trapped in an avalanche. Even tossing in some more accurate search terms will probably get you way more than you bargained for. All you wanted was a podcast on (say) *Battlestar Galactica*, and you're snowed under by fan sites, pictures, and all sorts of other information you weren't looking for.

So nobody is ever going to lack for work in the vast job of trying to organize information on the Internet. Luckily, some intrepid souls have braved the wilds and tried to bring some order to the world of podcasting. These are the services that index and catalog podcasts — their goal is to bring you the podcast titles you're looking for without a lot of extra information. You may have used them to find podcasts for your own personal listing (as described in Practice 2), but in this practice, you're going to join their ranks and get listed yourself. It's a simple process, and you'll be surprised by how many people can find your program through these guides.

Submitting Your Application

As with joining a club or getting a job, you have to apply to have your podcast listed on a directory. Luckily, you don't have to go through a background check or submit a blood sample to make it happen. Podcast directories want to have more podcasts listed in their ranks — it makes them larger and more reliable, attracting more users to their sites (and probably selling more advertisements). So they've made it as easy as possible to get such things done. There's a little information you'll want to have pulled together before you get started, but it's a simple process.

RSS feed

More precisely, you'll need the URL (online address) of your RSS feed to continue from here. (If you need to refresh yourself on what an RSS feed is before moving on, check out Practice 27.) By this point, you should already have your feed up on your Web site or hosting service and validated. It's the lifeline between you and the directory, the only form of communication between your podcast and the service.

When you list a new episode on your feed, the directory picks it up from your feed and lists it on its service. It also takes information from your feed, such as the title and description of your podcast. Some services may even have you insert *metadata* — descriptive data that isn't listed in the feed but read only by the directory — in your feed to confirm your ownership of the podcast or handle other administrative business.

 iTunes contains tags that only its directory will recognize. It's a major directory, though, so you'll probably want to include some duplicate information in your feed with different tags to make sure you utilize all available services. Check the instructions for iTunes when adding information to your RSS feed to make sure you're using every possible advantage in distributing your podcast.

E-mail and Web site

Most directories want to know the home base of the show — but this doesn't necessarily have to be the exact location of your podcast's host folder. Instead, you'll want to use your podcast's Web site (your podcast *does* have its own Web site, right?) so podcast listeners can find you and communicate with you. An e-mail address will help the directory keep you up to date on what's happening with their site and provide current podcasting news.

 If you don't want this information to pop up in your personal account, or if you want a separate e-mail account to handle podcast business, consider setting up a Webmail account with a reputable online host such as Gmail or Yahoo! Mail. That way you'll still get the messages, but you can control when and how you receive them.

Show information

In this case, the directory is looking for the general background information on your show (such as its title and general focus), along with *keywords* (descriptive terms about the program). The directory uses keywords to help categorize your show and to help others use the search-engine functions to find your podcast. For example, if you were doing a podcast about the Fountain Square neighborhood of Indianapolis (it's a small but loyal listener base), you'd want to include tags about the subject's location:

- ✔ Fountain Square
- ✔ Indianapolis
- ✔ Indiana

You'd also want to include some keywords about the features of the neighborhood:

- ✔ Coffee shops
- ✔ Live music
- ✔ Restaurants
- ✔ Hair salons
- ✔ Art galleries
- ✔ Wine bar
- ✔ Real estate
- ✔ Swing dancing

With the keywords in place, anyone using these terms to search for podcasts is likely to run across your podcast and give it shot.

 You want to include as many descriptive keywords as possible without lying or stretching the truth. For example, even though *gambling* and *Paris Hilton* are popular keywords on the Internet, it wouldn't be right to insert them into your list of keywords just to lure in unwary listeners. Directories can — and will — eliminate directory listings for this kind of misleading descriptions.

The legitimate keywords you use should look familiar — because, as a savvy podcaster, no doubt you've already included them in your RSS feed. Although some directories pull this information straight from that feed, it's a good idea to enter your keyword info wherever requested, just to be sure.

Getting Listed in the Virtual Yellow Pages

Your proverbial ducks are in a row, and you're ready to submit your podcast to the masses waiting at each directory service. Let's just take a quick trip through each service and see what you'll need to do to get your podcast listed.

iTunes

Due to the overwhelming popularity of iTunes and the millions of people it has the potential to reach, it's extremely important to get listed on this service if you want to reach a big audience. Luckily, it's quite easy to make iTunes aware of your podcast. The iTunes folks will take a look at it and make sure it's up to their standards (that is, no technical difficulties with the feed, no extreme pornographic content, no other such extreme stuff to cause trouble), and they'll list it if they're satisfied.

It can't hurt to check the iTunes specifications for podcasters at www.apple.com/itunes/store/podcaststechspecs.

You'll have to download and install iTunes (www.apple.com/itunes) and sign up for an iTunes account before submitting your podcast.

Follow these steps to get listed with iTunes:

1. **Open iTunes and connect to the iTunes Music Store.**

2. **Click the Podcasts link in the store, as shown in Figure 28-1.**

• **Figure 28-1: The podcast link.**

3. **Scroll down to the bottom of the store and click the Submit a Podcast link in the bottom-left corner, as shown in Figure 28-2.**

• **Figure 28-2: Submitting a podcast.**

The Submit Podcasts to the iTunes Directory page appears (see Figure 28-3).

• **Figure 28-3: Enter your podcast's URL here.**

4. **Enter your feed URL and other information.**

 The more information you can put in, the better. It will help others find your podcast easily.

If the podcast is approved, it should appear in the iTunes podcast directory within a day or two.

Podcast Alley

iTunes has podcasting features added to its normal modes of operation, but podcasting obviously isn't iTunes' main business. It's like finding the music section in a larger store as opposed to visiting a smaller music-only retailer. In this case, Podcast Alley is that small music store, dedicated to help you find what you need — that's all it does. By getting your podcast listed on this directory, you're targeting listeners who want to find podcasts that may not be listed in the mainstream directories — and they're willing to search to find them.

Follow these steps to submit your podcast to Podcast Alley:

1. **Navigate to** `http://podcastalley.com`.

2. **Sign up for your free membership — only Podcast Alley members can submit podcasts.**

3. **Click Add A Podcast.**

4. **Add the URL for your feed, as shown in Figure 28-4.**

Add a Podcast to Podcast Alley

Welcome sweatyb! Submitting your podcast to Podcast Alley™ is a 3 Step Process:

1. Submit your RSS URL
2. Verify the details and fill in additional details
3. Comit Results
4. Verify that you are the podcast owner

What is the URL for your Podcast Feed:

`http://`

(Go To Step 2 : Feed Validation)

• **Figure 28-4: Adding your podcast's URL to Podcast Alley.**

---

5. Podcast Alley validates the feed and gives you some code to add to your URL feed, as shown in Figure 28-5.

6. **Copy and paste the code into your RSS feed and publish it to your site.**

Figure 28-5 shows the on-screen instructions for claiming a podcast.

How To Claim a Podcast

If you are on this page you are indicating that the podcast you clicked on is yours and that you would like to edit the details (show name, description, url, etc) on the podcast alley site. Good for you! This is the best way for you to maintain control of your podcast information and update it at any time.

Whats the Point?

There are lots of reasons to claim your podcast here at Podcast Alley. For example, you will be able to edit all the details about your show, link to album art, provide promos for people to listen to, create an itunes ready podcast feed and much more.

Instructions:

1. Copy all of the text in the box below.
2. Make a post to your blog or feed and paste all of that text into the main posting area.
3. Publish your post.
4. Thats It! The next time Podcast Alley checks your site for updates your podcast will be attached to your account and you can edit it at any time.

`<a href="http://www.podcastalley.com/"> My Podcast Alley feed!</a> { pca-90df8a67f6e44e327e4912d4188f259c}`

We couldn't find your claim hash inside your feed. Please follow the instructions above and use the button below to re-check your feed for your claim hash.

(Retry to Claim)

HELP!

Have questions or need help? Check out the Podcast Alley Forums or email Chris at info@podcastalley.com for more information.

• **Figure 28-5: Adding code to claim your feed.**

7. **Click Retry Claim to attach the podcast to your membership.**

You'll be able to edit information about your podcast once this process is completed.

This claiming process may seem a little tricky, but it's important to do. When you're done, you'll be the only one who can change your directory listing. (If you need more information about editing RSS feeds, refer to Practice 27.)

Podcast Pickle

Podcast Pickle is another podcast-centric service, so you'll be reaching dedicated podcast listeners here as well. Why did they choose "pickle?" Don't know, but it works. Follow these steps to submit your cast:

1. **Navigate to** `http://podcastpickle.com`.

2. **Click Add Cast.**

The Add Cast page appears, as shown in Figure 28-6.

3. **Enter your feed URL, an overall genre, tags, and a content rating for your podcast.**

Choices for the last category range from All Audiences to Adult.

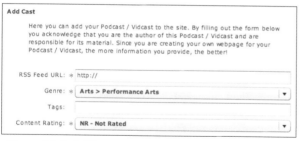

• **Figure 28-6: Adding a podcast to Podcast Pickle.**

Checking Directory Sites Regularly

Check your feed sites often and make sure that they're keeping up with your service. Broken feeds or mislabeled tags can keep others from finding your show. Some of these sites also have forums, comments, and other community-based services that help you network with other users and publicize your podcasts. In any case, it's a portal that represents your podcast to potential listeners — and you need to keep on top of how it looks and behaves. Check back early and often.

We've mentioned some of the larger podcast directories here, but there are about a hundred more to examine. Keep your ears (and your Google searches and your networking efforts) open to find more places to list your podcast and get more listeners.

 Some directories require you to put information in your RSS feed to claim it; Podcast Alley is one of those. Others have different authentication methods. Whatever the method in use, remember to take advantage of that function. It'll make managing your podcast's public image easier.

 Be sure to set your hosting and RSS feed in stone (so to speak) before submitting to podcast directories. You'll have a great deal of difficulty changing the directory listings later if you have to change the location of your host or feed.

Part V

Building Your Audience

Creating a Promotional Plan

In previous practices in this book, we go deep into the final details of creating your introductory episode, checking your feed to make certain it is working, and acquiring hardware and software that raises the bar for your podcast. This practice, though, provides you with a blueprint for letting people know about your podcast. Now comes the time to map out a strategy for tooting your horn.

Publicity.

The podosphere is not the place to be humble. You have to talk yourself up and let people know that a podcast is coming that is a *must have*. Even if you are with a podcasting network such as FarPoint Media or Podshow, people are not going to know where to find you or what your podcast is all about unless you tell them.

You need to put together your teasers and promos — and then begin planning a strategy for how to promote your podcast. Think first about whom you want to reach; from there you can get the hype machine underway. Get people talking — it's a terrific way to have an audience anxiously waiting for that introductory episode — and a solid motivation to keep producing content.

Deciding When to Begin Promoting Your Podcast

Hype is a beautiful thing. It builds anticipation. It gets people talking. It draws an audience.

The hardest thing about hype, though, is timing. You have to know when to start it; otherwise, it goes on for too long, and people lose interest — or are disappointed in the end result — or potential listeners are caught off guard by the sudden release of a new podcast and don't know of its existence.

A good example of a gamble in hype is *The Lord of the Rings* franchise. Director Peter Jackson and New Line Cinema went out on a limb and began promoting the first film of the trilogy, *The Fellowship of the Ring*, a year before its 2001 release. In the original trailer, they also announced the subsequent releases of *The Two Towers* in 2002 and *The Return of the King* in 2003. This was an unprecedented move on the filmmakers' part because no one really knew how the first film, coming from a relatively unknown cast and an unfamiliar director, was going to do at the box office — and they were advertising both sequels alongside it!

Then *The Fellowship of the Ring* was released, and raised the bar for filmmaking. Okay, that's a large-scale example. But it does illustrate that hype can be an art form in its own right.

As much as you might love to be Peter Jackson (living in New Zealand, hosting Sir Ian McKellen when he's in town, hanging out with Viggo and Orlando at the pub . . .), you probably won't spend a whole year generating hype for your podcast launch. Instead, consider promoting your upcoming podcast between one to three months prior to release. This window of time gets people talking and builds anticipation.

Building excitement prior to launch

To generate hype for your podcast, sure, you can rely on word of mouth, but there needs to be more to it than just friends talking up your desire to do a podcast and a few random posts popping up on your podcast's blog.

How about giving 'em an actual taste of your podcast? When those first five episodes are in the can, ready to post, you can take some time out and cut two more episodes: a *teaser* and a *promotional spot* (or *promo*). After you have those two spots — preferably close to one minute in duration, with neither spot exceeding two minutes — look at your calendar. Give yourself two months to promote before launching your podcast.

Two months? Is that some magic window of time, or a standard in the podosphere? But what if you're an unknown? Two months, while feeling like a long time, is an excellent and easily manageable cushion of time. We recommend two months because — between your promotional spots and sending out press releases — you can generate a lot of chatter in that time. As far as name recognition goes, podcasters all start somewhere. Two personalities in the podcasting arena, Christiana Ellis and Tony Mast, both started promoting their podcasts (*Nina Kimberly the Merciless* and *Tony's Losing It,* respectively) months ahead of their release dates. The end results were strong subscription numbers (well above the 500 and 1,000 listeners marks) that continued to grow after their premieres.

Examining two real-life promotional campaigns

Throughout this practice, we refer to Tee's own *Billibub Baddings and The Case of The Singing Sword* podcast as a benchmark. Along the way, we spotlight other successful hype campaigns for podcasters (such as the podcast novel *Crescent*) and review how their makers used time and hype to gather an audience for the launch date.

Billibub Baddings

In December 2006, Tee released a teaser spot for *Billibub Baddings* to some friends in podcasting. They were taken aback that he was advertising a podcast slated for mid-February (two whole months away — yikes), but he assured them it would be here before they knew it. Here was the two-month game plan:

- ✔ In December, Tee's request to podcasters he approached was simple: Play the teaser — and feel free to circulate this spot to other podcasters — throughout the month.

- ✔ In mid-January, provided the podcasters he initially approached were okay with it, he would release a second promo and have them play that spot up to the launch date (February 14, 2007).

With two months of advance notice, Tee could now have four weeks for each promotional spot to make the rounds amongst friends (and throughout the podcasting community). The two-month promotional window gave weekly and bimonthly podcasts a chance to promote the new podcast — and now monthly podcasts could pick up the teaser and promo to help in the hype.

Crescent

Another podcast that took advantage of a two-month time frame to promote itself is Phil Rossi's science fiction/horror podcast novel, *Crescent* (http://crescentstation.net), shown in Figure 29-1.

• **Figure 29-1: Phil Rossi's science fiction thriller, *Crescent*, used short stories to build an audience for its podcast launch.**

Here's how Phil's campaign unfolded:

- Phil's blog launched in late January 2007 with a simple graphic and a vague release date of Spring 2007.

- His first promo was released February 6, followed a week later by the first promotional episode he entitled *Crescent Vignettes*.

- Over the following six weeks, Phil released a short story related to the novel he was planning to premiere (a podcast within a podcast).

- Finally, on March 30, Phil announced the release date of *Crescent*'s first episode: May 3, 2007.

By mid-April, Phil had already garnered three reviews on iTunes and well over a thousand subscribed listeners, and the first chapter had not even gone live.

Why Promoting Before Episode #0 Is Beneficial

Just on Podcast Pickle (http://podcastpickle.com), over 12,000 podcasts are registered. On Podcast Alley (http://podcastalley.com), over 31,000 podcasts are registered. No matter how you look at it, no matter what directory you visit, the podosphere is saturated with podcasts. There are so many to choose from at present, and you are gearing up to add *just one more* show to the roster.

There's only so much time in the day, and so much room on your mp3 player. It's tough when a new podcast comes out and the hype on the podosphere is *"You have to listen to it!"*

Our practical answer is usually that we'd love to listen to it, but we need to know *why* we should listen to it; and then we ask ourselves, do we have the time?

Giving an audience a reason — a *really good* reason — to listen is the most important aspect of promoting a podcast before Episode #0. By having five shows ready to go, you know exactly how much work goes into creating your podcast. By promoting the podcast several months before its launch date, you can gauge the audience size and make accommodations at your host site, be it Liberated Syndication (http://libsyn.com), Dreamhost (http://dreamhost.net), or another service geared for podcasting. The initial numbers may not be a dead-on accurate idea of how many people will be listening, but you can estimate the growth potential of the show.

Trailers, teasers, and talkbacks

Filmmaker Earl Newton understood the attention-demanding nature of video and knew he had to come up with a plan for his own video podcast, *Stranger Things* (http://strangerthings.tv). He premiered his podcast on February 1, 2007, with a one-minute movie-style trailer and a simple three-minute episode with Earl reporting on the status of his first film. Both episodes were shot in high-definition video, and the status report announced that the first *Stranger Things* episodes would be an adaptation of Scott Sigler's short story "Sacred Cow."

With these two offerings, Earl not only gave potential audiences a look at things in the works, but also announced his first project would be an adaptation of a work from one of podcasting's most popular names. *Stranger Things* now had between February 1 and the release date of March 2 to get people talking — and in those few weeks, people on the Net and in the real world did just that. After two months, *Stranger Things* episodes had been downloaded over 30,000 times, an impressive number for a video podcast only a few months old.

Another benefit in getting the word out about your podcast is that it gives the podcasting audience time to consider whether your show appeals to them. Does your podcast fit with their interests and their schedules?

 This kind of promotion is key when you're video podcasting, because video tends to demand undivided time and attention. It's a bit harder to multitask with a podcast on because . . . well, when it's video, you might miss something. You have to watch.

Give yourself at least two promotional spots to circulate and two months to promote. If you decide that you want more time to generate hype, have content ready to submit to your feed. Whatever plan you choose to follow, make sure you give yourself a pocket of time. If your strategy plays out right, you will already have a dedicated audience in place before the first episode launches.

Would You Play My Promo if I Asked Nicely?

The podosphere, as Rob Suarez mentions in his *Ink 'n Doodles Creative Workshop* podcast (http://inkndoodles.com), is all about community. We are a community of audio enthusiasts, storytellers, musicians, and imaginative individuals all coming together to help one another get the word out about each other's podcasts.

At least that's the theory.

In the early days of podcasting, you wouldn't think twice about accepting promos and playing them on your podcast. With the number of podcasts steadily growing, and audiences focusing their time, attention, and aggregators on specific show categories, the need for a strategy has grown as well. These days you have to send that first promo or distribute the teaser in a way that connects with some pretty specific parts of the podosphere. The following sections give you some tips for getting the word out.

Target podcasts that reach your target audience

In your research on what other podcasts are out there, which ones would make good references beyond your podcast, or even which hosts are talking about the same subject matter, you should have collected a few podcasts that reach the same audience you're targeting. Find out where they're located on the Web and then drop these podcast hosts a query. Ask if they welcome teasers and promos for other podcasts? Build a contact list and make these podcasts your first wave of promotion; they're where you find the bulk of your audience.

Send promos only to podcasts that welcome promos

This idea may sound like common sense, but you do want to practice a bit of tact and decorum when it comes to asking people to promote your podcast. For free. In the *Billibub Baddings* podcast, Tee offers up an open-door policy to promos; but with the *Podcasting For Dummies Companion Podcast,* he can't accept or play promos. There is nothing personal about that; the show just doesn't lend itself to featuring promos because its running time is short, and it is being produced for another entity other than himself. (Yes, that is Tee's voice you hear on *Podcasting For Dummies,* but the podcast itself doesn't belong to him personally. It's a business arrangement with the publisher.)

 Not all podcasts are open to teasers and promos. It's considered good etiquette to query shows before sending them promo links or mp3 files. Always ask before sending.

If you're approached with a promo for another podcast, find out whether this podcast is one you'd feel comfortable promoting. If your podcast is focused on family-friendly content, for example, running teasers and promos for shows that feature adult-oriented programming may not work for you.

 When you run a promo, you are *advocating* that podcast. You reserve the final word on whether you run any promo. If you find that a promo is too edgy for your tastes, ask the podcast's representative whether there's a "clean" or "general audiences" version of the promo. There's nothing personally offensive about asking for an edited spot or even choosing not to play a promo — it's a question of what works and what doesn't. This is your podcast, and you should concern yourself with exactly what you are suggesting to your listening audience.

Pay it forward

When you approach other shows with your teasers and promos, make sure you return the favor by offering to play their shows' promos. It only reflect positively on you as part of the podcasting community when — after other podcasters show you the courtesy and kindness to feature your promos — you feature their promos in your episodes. After all, it amounts to two-way free advertising.

It's a good trade-off, and if the podcast is a favorite of yours, you can offer to play the promo repeatedly. Regardless of what you do, however, always return the favor in kind.

Invite other podcasters to help with your promos

If you invite other podcasters to help you promote your podcast, make sure that you work around their schedules. Do not demand too much of their time; work with them to make the promotion suit their needs. (For example, in a rough draft of a third promo, one author asked for a rewrite, and we happily obliged.) And be sure to thank them — either on your podcast or in promos featured in your episodes.

Strictly business

For the *Billibub Baddings* podcast, Tee always features other podcasts' promos at the end of each episode. A space is also reserved for paid promos in the middle of the show. A few podcasters were taken aback by this standard, and voiced puzzlement: "Well, I've been promoting Billibub quite liberally in my podcast. Why can't I be featured there?"

This is another situation where business concerns call for a delicate balance. No question that Tee appreciates the mention in other podcasts and responds in kind. But a standard has to be met here: When a podcast becomes a business, putting free ads alongside paid ads would be *bad* business — unfair to the paying clientele — so keeping the two separate is a good idea. For that matter, never take the placement of your promo personally. Regardless of where it is in a podcast, it's being played. That's what matters in the end.

Cast your promos out to wider audiences

Now that you have your target audience covered, you can now consider other podcasts and *demographics* (you know — what we used to call "groups of people with similarities") beyond your first wave of promotion. Here are a few ways to reach a wider audience:

- ✔ Register your promos with Podcast Promos (`http://podcastpromos.com`), a directory specifically geared for podcast teasers and promos.

- ✔ Begin submitting your feed to directories and then make your first offerings teasers and promos for your show — and offer them in your feed to your subscribers. Many of your subscribers will either be hosting their own podcasts or know people who host podcasts, and will gladly feature your promotional spots in their shows.

Tell Me About It: Recording Promos and Quickcasts

"If you podcast it, they will come."

Maybe that was true back in 2005, but since the great iTunes rush of September 2005, the podosphere has become rife with podcasters, all with their eyes on the iTunes Top 25 or an article in *The New York Times*. There have been dynamic personalities — Scott Sigler, Ronald D. Moore, Mur Lafferty, Steve Eley, Michael Geoghegan, Dan Klass, and Rob Walch — blazing trails for future podcasters, inspiring them to get their names and voices into the podosphere. With the competition for attracting listeners (and *keeping* them) as fierce as it is, many current and would-be podcasters go back to the trailblazers to try and figure out how they achieved success.

The common link is quite simple with all these podcasters: They told people about their podcasts.

What Is a Promo?

When podcasts are in the early stages of production (as discussed in Practice 29), a promo is one of the first things planned out, along with the first few episodes of the podcast itself. The reason a promo should be thought out beforehand is that many podcasts start out of the box strong with episodes, but they find themselves at a loss for words when other podcasters contact them and ask, "Do you have a promo? I would love to feature it on my show."

A *promo* is exactly what it sounds like: a promotional spot (okay, a commercial) for your podcast. It can be serious. It can be funny. It can be self-deprecating. It can be whatever you want, but what it needs to be is short.

The 30-second promo: Short and sweet

Thirty seconds may seem like a long time in front of a microphone, but it's over before it begins when you record copy about your podcast and then add bed music for atmosphere (as described in Practice 20). Go on and sit in front of your microphone for 30 seconds without saying anything. Now, start recording yourself reading an introduction for your show. You might be surprised how quickly the time passes.

In a 30-second promo, you have time to mention only the basics of a podcast: the who, what, and where. Once that's covered, you have a promo with a running time that podcasters love — short, sweet, and to the point. Promos also serve as quick and easy drop-ins for breaks in a podcast. So if you haven't the time and space on someone else's show (either through a guest segment or interview) to build up a joke or play extended clips from your show, a 30-second creation is welcome because you kept things short and quick.

The one-minute promo: Fun and informative

Some podcasters regard a promo lasting one minute as a bit long, but on average, a one-minute ad for a show is not out of the ordinary. One minute gives a promo latitude for a more relaxed pace: You can slow down when reading the copy, the music can play a few seconds longer, and you can feature a quick clip (or two) from previous shows.

When putting together *copy* (a script for your promo that includes all the necessary information concerning your podcast) for a longer promo, you need to practice an economy of words. It's all too easy to wander off on tangents; keep the message of your promo focused.

For example, Table 30-1 gives a breakdown of the copy created for the podcast *Give Us a Minute* (`http://joemurphymemorialfund.org`).

TABLE 30-1: COPY BREAKDOWN

Intent	Copy
What	With the passing of podcaster Joe Murphy, people have been asking lot of questions — what is leiomyosarcoma? Is there treatment for this? A friend of mine just got diagnosed with cancer — now what do I do?
Who	That's where *Give Us a Minute* comes in. *Give Us a Minute* is a podcast of hope. We invite you to share on this podcast your own trials and tests with cancer, to share memories of Joe and other loved ones, and to join a community that — with the help of Mason Rocket — will work together to combat this disease and find a cure.
Why	All proceeds raised by this podcast will go to benefit the Joe Murphy Memorial Fund in its ongoing battle against leiomyosarcoma.
Where	Subscribe at `www.joemurphymemorial fund.org` and tell everyone you know. *Give Us a Minute.* For Joe. For All of Us. For a Cure.

You want to make sure people know who you are, what you are podcasting, and where they can find your podcast.

The 1-minute-30-second promo: Are you sure you want to say that much?

A promo extending beyond the one-minute ceiling is usually frowned upon by other podcasters; breaks between show segments usually last one to two minutes, and now this promo has (regardless if this was the intent) monopolized a break segment, shutting out any other potential podcasts.

When your promo breaks the one-minute ceiling, you are going to want to step back from it and ask yourself, "Is it too much?" That said, sometimes a promo can dare the one-minute ceiling when the content incorporates some special features:

- Additional voices joining the main voiceover talent

✔ A "plot" where the voice talent in the promo deals with a situation or setting

✔ Multiple clips from previous episodes of the podcast

✔ Review quotes from other podcasters and from authorities on the show's subject

Provided your ad copy is engaging, doesn't wander off on too many tangents, and serves its purpose — letting people know the who, what, why, and where as detailed in the example in Table 30-1 — podcasters will play the spot. But if you can cut the promo down closer to the one-minute mark, it can earn more airplay.

Why *two* minutes is *too* long

When promos reach two minutes of running time, they are no longer promos but mini-podcasts in themselves — or what some podcasters call *quickcasts* (covered later in this practice). Instead of serving as promotional spots for show breaks, the promotion becomes a segment of the show itself. And if the podcast hosting your promo is attempting to keep its own running time under 20 minutes, this epic promo size probably won't be featured in a show break. If you're fortunate, it may appear at the end of a show.

 When it comes to promoting your show, brevity is the soul of wit. Keep it short, be concise, and let people know you're out there.

My Name Is Tee, and This Is My Podcast . . .

So what exactly do you say in a promo? Plenty of podcasters have a lot to say about their topic of discussion, but they're not sure where to begin when cutting a promo for their show.

It can be a little daunting to let the world know that you're out there, podcasting your heart and soul. It's tough enough to ask yourself, "Is anyone listening?" whenever you hit Record — and even tougher to tell others, "Here's *why* you want to listen. . . . "

Who you are

Yes, podcasters fail to mention in the podcast who they are, and that's very important to know. *Who* is the captain of this ship, the man with the plan, the femme fatale — who is the host of this podcast? This is also your informal introduction of yourself to the podosphere and a nice way to establish a connection between you and your potential listeners.

What the podcast is about

If you decide to just stick with promos, the *what* should be what your podcast is all about — for example, you discussing the subject matter of your podcast, or two people talking about the topic of your podcast. An example of letting people know the *what* can be heard in a promo for the Typical Mac User (www.typicalmacuser.com) podcast:

> " . . . check out the Typical Mac User podcast. It's got advice for switchers, reviews of different Mac accessories, and all sorts of cool tips for beginners and experts."

Where listeners can find this podcast

Apart from the *who* in a promo, the *where* is essential in a good promo because it communicates your podcast's location on the Web. Whether it's a Web site specifically for the podcast or a central Web site that links people to the podcast's location, you want to make sure a URL of some kind is in the promo so that people can find out more about the host (or hosts), the show's content, or its posting schedule.

Nina is such a tease!

In a promo, you let people know the details (within reason — remember, it's supposed to be short . . .), but if you simply give a *who* and a *where* (a Web site for the podcast), then your promo becomes a *teaser*. A teaser hooks the listeners just enough to get them to the Web site, and from there, the hype begins to build.

With dramatic music swelling in the background, voiceover talent Scott Fletcher boldly proclaimed:

> "She's on a mission . . . To kill the man who loves her . . . Why? Because he's an idiot. *Nina Kimberly the Merciless.* Coming soon."

Podcaster Christiana Ellis managed — in 15 seconds — not only to get people talking but also to increase traffic to her Web site. Her podiobook *Nina Kimberly the Merciless* (www.ninakimberly.com) went on to top the charts at Podiobooks.com and was a finalist for the 2006 Parsec Awards and 2006 Podcast Peer Awards.

And sometimes, why . . .

You have another option with your promo if you think the time and the podcast warrants it: State in brief *why* you are doing this particular subject matter. In the cancer-awareness podcast *Give Us a Minute* (detailed in Table 30-1), the promo copy reads

"All proceeds raised by this podcast will go to benefit the Joe Murphy Memorial Fund in its ongoing battle against leiomyosarcoma."

While this is not commonly heard in promos, you can mention the inspiration or drive behind your podcast. It's just a different way to promote your production.

When promos become podcasts

In the same vein as the Geico "So Easy a Caveman Can Do It" campaign, one of this title's authors — Tee Morris — got an idea while listening to two friends and popular podcasters — Scott Sigler (*The Rookie, Ancestor*) and J.C. Hutchins (*The 7th Son Trilogy*) — begin a light-hearted "turf war" on their respective podcasts.

After listening to the two authors rib one another, Tee decided it was time the creator of the podiobook showed them who's boss. He wrote a teaser and a promo depicting the two in a café, taken down by the mob; and then later bound and gagged in a remote location with the mob interrogating them.

The two spots were long in their running time, but they grew so much in their popularity that the spots spawned two more promos and earned Tee a glowing review from SFFAudio.com.

So don't be surprised if a promo suddenly gets a life of its own. It might even earn you a five-star review! Just as long as it gets people talking (in a good way) and helps you promote your podcast.

What Is a Quickcast?

The *quickcast* is a new trend popping up in podcasts everywhere. Quickcasts come in two sizes: a stand-alone episode in the middle of a podcast's season or a podcast *within* a podcast. These quick-and-dirty episodes usually run between five and ten minutes, have very little editing or post-production, and simply make the announcement they need to make (no tangents, no additional show segments, no opening or closing credits).

Quickcasts are terrific sound bites for podcasts that are on longer posting schedules (as opposed to frequent ones). In the case of special developments in the podcast's direction, honors bestowed to the host, or changes in the posting schedule, quickcasts are a terrific device for getting the word out to subscribers, assuring them that more is to come and *podfading* (disappearance from the podosphere, as discussed in Part VIII) is not an option.

The most common instances of quickcasts are segments of a podcast produced by a listener rather than the host. This kind of listener-generated content makes production of an individual podcast episode very easy, depending on the audio quality of the quickcast recorded.

For example, after hearing a serialized short story on *Jack Mangan's Deadpan Podcast* (shown in Figure 30-1), Paul Maki contacted the show and asked if there was any interest in serializing his novella, *Really Big Things*. For the next four months, *Deadpan* featured five-to-ten minute episodes featuring the surreal adventures of two friends as they photographed oddities and road attractions across the Midwest. Here the quickcast benefited both parties; Paul could give both his novella *and* podcasting a test drive, while Jack Mangan now had five to ten minutes covered for his 30-40-minute show. The quickcast, properly implemented, should be a true synergy between the show and the content producer.

• **Figure 30-1: Part irreverent comedy, part open-mic for podcasting talent, *Jack Mangan's Deadpan* features podcasts within its own podcast.**

 The quickcast you produce should be the right "fit" for a podcast. If you are reviewing anime, for example, maybe a podcast on cooking healthy would not be the ideal host for your segment. But if you're producing quick

segments on how to cook outdoors, then food podcasts or shows about the hiker's lifestyle may be interested in what you have to offer. Before submitting a quickcast to a show, always consider what you're offering them.

Two-to-three-minute quickcast: Welcome, friends!

The key to a good quickcast is keeping it short — much like a promo. The other good news about a quickcast in the two-to-three minute range is that the playing field is wide open for other quickcasts.

Say you want to record a quickcast for the MacCast, which will include a review of the iLap, a laptop desk designed for the various incarnations of the PowerBooks and MacBooks. Your basic quickcast should follow this plan:

- **Introduction.** "Hi, (*name of showhost*), this is (*your name*) of (*your podcast or your location in the world*), and I'm here to review the iLap."

- **The content:** Because this is a review, give a brief description of the product and then go into your opinions and final verdict.

- **Exit, Stage Left:** "Thanks, (*name of showhost*), for letting me contribute to (*the host podcast*)."

- **The optional plug:** "If you would like to find out more about what I do at (*your podcast*), check out my show at (*podcast's URL*)."

This plan assuredly yields a quickcast in the two-to-three minute range.

Before sending in your segment, contact the show's host and let him or her know you have produced a segment and would like to *submit it for consideration*. Never make the assumption that simply because you've produced the segment, it will get played right away. Always query a podcast's host before sending in the segment.

Five-to-ten-minute quickcast: Proceed with permission

Many podcasts prefer to keep the content and the delivery of the content short — that is, under fifteen minutes total, ten minutes preferred. A quick-cast of five to ten minutes may not be welcome because it may take up a majority of the show's latest episode. Longer podcasts, however — such as *Jack Mangan's Deadpan Podcast, Speaking of Beer,* and *The ScapeCast* — wouldn't mind the content running in this range, provided the parameters of that content are clear and within the recommended guidelines.

If you think the segment would be something you could do on a monthly (or more frequent) basis, ask the show host in your query if that is something that would interest him or her. You may get a "Well, let's wait and see . . . " response, or you might get the open invitation to contribute. Whatever the outcome, it's a good idea to coordinate with the podcast's host and provide as much detail as possible about what you're planning to do.

A five-to-ten-minute quickcast may not seem as big a deal as we're making it out to be, but a lot of work can go into it. Here's the anatomy of a "regular segment" quickcast:

- ✔ **Introduction:** In this kind of quickcast, bumper music (described in Practice 6) is a nice touch to let listeners know your segment is coming up. "Hey, everyone, welcome to (*name for your show's segment*), and this is (*your name*)."

- ✔ **The content:** Here is where you deliver the segment's main content. If it's an interview, an on-the-scene report, or simply a soundseeing tour, give yourself five to seven minutes of content so you have room to edit it if necessary.

- ✔ **The even-more-than-optional plug:** Because your time is limited and the quickcast is possibly becoming a regular segment, a plug may seem a bit much. If you do want to drop in the plug, do it here *before* your segment bids farewell.

- ✔ **Exit, Stage Left:** "And that will do for this month's (*name of segment*). Take it easy, everybody!" and then head out with your bumper music.

More planning tends to go into a five-to-ten-minute podcast, but that stands to reason. You now have more audio material to play with — and this segment is running the same length, if not longer, than podcasts such as *Aliens You Will Meet, The Myth Minute,* and even *Podcasting For Dummies: The Companion Podcast.*

Be careful what you wish for

Halfway through the 2006 Season of *Michael and Evo's Wingin' It,* show host Michael R. Mennega was complaining far too much about how hard it was to produce episodes because he found so little content and guest submissions left in his e-mail "In" box. "Please, people," he begged, "if you have an idea or want to produce content, send it to me! Please!"

Within a week, Mike received enough content to last him for the remainder of the season . . . but the quickcasts continued to arrive!

The lesson learned here is that not only are your audience members supporters of your podcast, but deep down inside, they're also curious about podcasting themselves. Listeners are simply waiting for an invitation. What's terrific about these contributions is that they can become regular segments for your podcast ("Uninvited Guest Editorials" with Indiana Jim, "MicroBrewed," "The MacCast Mac Minute Tip") or podcasts themselves (*SciFi Smackdown, A Different Point of View,* or *The One-Minute Tech Tip.*)

If you are invited to produce regular segments for a podcast, another good idea for your production planning is to record several episodes ahead. Get as many segments recorded as possible and then submit them to the podcast host. That way you've met a "content quota" for the show. Make sure you coordinate with the show's host to see what kind of schedule you'd like your segment to follow — twice a month? Monthly? Find a schedule that works for both of you.

By producing this quickcast, you've also created a means for promoting your own podcast (or for giving it a try before committing fully to your own show). For the host, it's instant "drop-and-play" content for his or her host podcast. It's a terrific relationship for all parties involved.

Quickcast over ten minutes: Whose podcast is it, anyway?

When you cross the ten-minute barrier, nothing is "quick" about your quickcast. Your segment is waltzing into the proverbial podcast's home, double-dipping the broccoli and pita bread across the various dressings, and propping its now-bare feet up on the coffee table, and changing the channel of your television . . . after it unbuttons its pants and sighs with contentment à la Al Bundy.

Any quickcast above ten minutes warrants an e-mail to the show's host. Perhaps it's an opportunistic interview with someone, an extended review of a product or a series of products that would appeal to the podcast's listeners, or a dynamic soundseeing tour of an event the podcast host is unable to attend. In this situation, contact the podcast host first — let him or her know the abnormal length of the segment and ask what you can do that would best fit the show's needs. You have several options:

- ✔ **Edit the segment.** The show host may ask you to edit the segment to under ten minutes. This

doesn't mean to edit it to 09:59.99. Technically, yes, that does make the running time under ten minutes, but doesn't it bother you when something is advertised as *under $100* and the price tag reads *$99.99?* Same deal. Edit the segment so it's comfortably under *nine* minutes (and if possible, under eight). If the show host has made this request to you, it's a gesture of good faith.

- ✔ **Offer it as a "Special Edition" podcast.** All podcasters need a break now and then. If you produce the segment well enough, and you feel that you and the host have a good working relationship, offer this extended quickcast as a full-out episode, or a "Special Edition" that can run either in place of a regular show or in an available slot later in the week after a normal show drops. This opportunity is great for both segment producer and podcast host; it gives the segment producer a chance to fly solo and the podcast host a breather.

- ✔ **Serialize the segment.** The host may offer to take control and serialize the segment into a two- or three-part segment across episodes. This compromise is good for both the show and the segment producer, requiring only a little bit of editing on your part.

- ✔ **Launch your own podcast.** If you notice your segments are getting longer and longer, harder and harder to edit under the ten-minute mark, it may be high time for you to consider launching your own podcast. You are more than ready to set up your own blog, get the RSS up to podcasting par, and tag your episodes under your own name. Even better, you have another podcast host to help you along and even promote your podcast. What a fantastic start!

Regardless of whether you choose to promote yourself or your podcast through a quickcast, a promo, or a series of promos, what's important is to remember that these segments should be short, concise, and focused. While the promo is all about you and your podcast, it should not monopolize a break spot — nor should it ramble aimlessly for a minute (or longer). If the quickcast is your promotional venue, remember that it's *not* all about you; it's about working with the host podcast to create a polished, professional segment that will continue the momentum of the episode, not bring it to a screeching halt.

With a promo or a quickcast strategy planned, you can begin to put together a promotional plan for your podcast.

Advertising to Attract Listeners

P opular programs don't just spring up fully formed on whatever media they exist on, whether it's television, radio, or the Internet. You have to let people know when and where the program can be found. Practices 32 and 33 look at networking and word-of-mouth routes to publicizing your program. This practice, however, takes a look at the old-fashioned method of advertising. Whether you buy space or trade it out for other services, ads can be an effective way to let people know about your podcast.

A Banner Day

By far, the most common form of advertisement on the Internet is the *banner ad,* shown in Figure 31-1. This shorthand term encompasses all forms of leased space on a site — from static images with links to their advertised service to "rich" media involving Flash animation, sound, or video.

• **Figure 31-1: Two sample banner ads.**

Web sites sell space on their pages for these advertisements so visitors to that site see the ads. The hope is that people see the ads, click them, and zoom to a page where they can see whatever is being advertised. Each Web site has its own rules on what kind of ads it hosts, but most of the cost is determined by the characteristics of the ad.

Size

The size of a banner ad plays a big part in how much it costs. Banner ads are usually measured in pixels, and they can appear anywhere on the page. Obviously, the bigger the ad, the more you pay.

Type of media

It takes a lot more bandwidth to transmit a rich media ad such as a Flash animation or a video insert. A simple image or animated GIF takes less room, making it easier to pass along. As your ad becomes more complicated and involved, expect to pay more (for both developing and hosting the ad). You should also be aware that loud, obnoxious ads tend to turn off many users of the Internet, so it might be best to go for a simple, clean ad that communicates your message effectively.

Page views

Just like buying an ad for the Super Bowl costs more than a 2:00 a.m. spot on the local cable outlet, buying an ad on pages that get thousands of page views a day costs more than getting some space on your cousin's family home page. Depending on the number of people you're trying to reach, be prepared to spend more to buy more *eyes* (views of your ad). Be sure that the site's owners can back up their information, though; there's no use spending money on empty promises. You also need to match the type of page on which you're advertising to your podcast. Investing in some space on (say) an auto-parts site is great for your racing podcast, but your podcast on knitting probably won't be helped much by advertising on Dave's Comic . . . er, Graphic Novel Web site.

You can see money in a couple of ways from these ads:

- ✔ **CPC (cost-per-click):** This method bases payment on the number or percentage of clicks — that is, the action of actually choosing to click a banner ad for more information.

- ✔ **CPM (cost-per-thousand impressions):** This method bases payment on how many thousand times the banner ad is displayed on a page.

Money in Stereo: Audio Ads

You're already producing an audio program, so the prospect of putting together an audio commercial for that program shouldn't be too much of a hassle. In effect, you're creating a short podcast to tell people why they should listen to your show. Broadcast commercials are usually either 30 or 60 seconds long, although you don't have to feel as restricted to that time if you're selling to other podcasts.

The commercial should include the following elements:

- ✔ A quick introduction to you and your show
- ✔ The online location of the show
- ✔ How often you update it
- ✔ Any other information that might be helpful

You can dress up the ad with appropriate music and sound effects, but make sure they don't overwhelm its message. From there, the only limit is your imagination. Think of the commercial as a business card for your podcast.

Keep in mind that other podcasters are usually willing to trade promo spots — "I'll play your commercial if you play mine." There's no money involved, so the price is right. You have to make sure, however, that the commercial you're trading for fits into your show — and that there's room for it. If you do end up paying for time, make sure you get exactly what you pay for. You should know how often the spot is played and where it's featured in the program.

 What you're doing is real business at this point — so get this information in writing and make sure the other party lives up to its end of the bargain.

Advertising in News Publications

Podcasting is the newest of the "new" media found on the Internet (at least, it is this week), but that doesn't mean you should ignore "old" media like newspapers and weekly publications — especially if a publication shares the same views and values you do. A weekly music paper (for instance) would be a great place to advertise your show on indie rock, and a community newsletter is a great medium for telling others about your community-affairs podcast.

Check with each publication about ad rates (usually sold in sections of pages, from quarter page to a full page). This option might not be as pricey as radio or television advertising, but it's still going to cost you. You have to weigh the cost versus the benefits of the ad.

It might also be a good idea to get an experienced designer (on the publication's staff or an independent designer) to make the ad for you. Graphics and layout expertise can really benefit your ad, even if it does cost a little extra. Again, remember to check your budget and balance the cost of the ad versus what you get out of it.

Hitting the Streets

All the methods we've discussed so far involve buying space. You can advertise in places for free, but you're going to have to pound some pavement to get there. Many businesses, such as coffee shops or music stores, allow people to post flyers for free. Of course, you still have to pay to have the flyers made (and that designer could come in handy here, too), but you won't have to pay to get them out there. Be sure to follow each establishment's rules for posting (no holes in the wall, no tape that could peel paint, and so forth), and don't ever cover up another flyer with your own. That's just bad form.

Finally, you can always pass around flyers and business cards, or even something like a bookmark or other token, by hand. Checking out events that might hold a great number of potential fans (say, standing outside Heinz Field to advertise your stellar Pittsburgh Steelers podcast) is a good idea. Be prepared to stand outside for a while — and to get rejected several times. Still, this approach has worked for lots of folks; the fans you could pick up from this activity can add up quickly.

Practice 32

Networking with Other Podcasters and Bloggers

In This Practice

✔ Using podcasting and blogging forums

✔ Contacting the authors directly

✔ Using comments and trackbacks correctly

When you've published a podcast, you've joined a legion of millions who are publishing their content on the Internet. Okay, we have no doubt that yours is a wonderful program — but your show still joins a vast wave of other content coming from people who are in much the same place you are: part of a larger collective. The problem is that your show stands alone without contact with others, and the Internet is based on links. You'll be able to learn so much more about creating and distributing podcasts by communicating with others who do the same thing — just like any other activity — and the more people you communicate with, the more new and different ways you find to make your podcast better. You'll also set up more ways for people to find and download your show, as well.

Communicating with Others in a Forum

One of the most ubiquitous features of the Internet is the *forum*, also known as the *messageboard*. It may look different in every instance you see, but the common feature is that it allows people with similar interests to communicate across great distances, different times, and sometimes without any respect to decency or civility. Once you've gotten past those jokers, though, you'll find that you can make some excellent connections through these services. The vast majority of them are free, too.

Start in a place you're probably already familiar with — the forums on many podcasting networks. (In this case, we take a look at the messageboards located on Podcast Pickle.) You usually have to have an account to post on the forums.

 Podcasting forums are a good place to start networking and learning, but don't limit yourself to just those forums. It's a good (nay, a stellar) idea to talk to people interested in the podcast's subject matter and let them know about your show. You'll find a lot more listeners and ideas for shows that way. Some forums may allow anonymous posting, but remember that you're trying to network here. How are you going to make connections if nobody knows who you are?

After you sign up for an account with Podcast Pickle, click the Forums link up at the top (as shown in Figure 32-1) to get to the messageboards. Most sites have their Forums links on the front page for easy access.

• **Figure 32-1: The Forums link on Podcast Pickle.**

On these forums (see Figure 32-2), you can read what others have posted, post something yourself, or reply to any comments people may have made. It's helpful if you think about this as a conversation — albeit one left like a series of notes on a wall somewhere. Each person leaves a note for the next, the previous posters come back and add to the discussion, and pretty soon you've got some communication going.

Topic Title	Replies	Starter	Views	Last Action
Book Hobby, Show #6 Vermont Eccentrics and a J.K. Rowling Anecdote!	0	NeilShapiro	1	19 minutes ago In: Show Off Your Show By: NeilShapiro
For What Its Worth - #80	0	Steve and dawn	1	An hour ago In: Show Off Your Show By: Steve and dawn
Everyday Danny	146	Danny	5389	14 hours ago In: Show Off Your Show By: samuel_whyte
Amateur Traveler - Episode 98 - The Netherlands And Belgium	0	Chris2x - Amateur Traveler	9	18 hours ago In: Show Off Your Show By: Chris2x - Amateur Traveler
Scapecast 34: Claudia Black Interview, Stolen Life And More!	0	Kurt_eh	7	20 hours ago In: Show Off Your Show By: Kurt_eh
Two Years!	1	Eclectic Mix	12	21 hours ago In: Podcast Discussion By: Stuart J
Podcasters Needed To Read Articles Blogger and Podcaster Magazine	0	Adam Raimer Madtown Audio	19	22 hours ago In: Voicework By: Adam Raimer Madtown Audio
New Front Page And Genre Listings Active	12	jifu	104	23 hours ago In: News By: tvindy
Hockey Podcaster Needed	0	switchpod	10	23 hours ago In: Podcast Discussion By: switchpod
Seminar: An Original Anthology Show		Pendant		A day ago

• **Figure 32-2: The Podcast Pickle Forums.**

The rules here are kind of like any other conversation you might have. It's impossible to interrupt somebody when they're typing, so don't worry about that. You do still want to be respectful and open in your discussion, however. Nothing derails communication like inappropriate or out-of-place language.

Listen (or read) up!

Whenever you take a look at a forum for the first time, it's a good idea to read some posts to get a feel for how the current participants post and interact. You'll find out how the community acts around each others' posts, and you'll also get an idea of what topics people are currently talking about. Although you'll be able to see how each conversation started, you might not be able to see all the history between the posters. You may notice some recurrent conflicts or partnerships, and it might be a good idea to make a note of those as you jump in. Get all the information you can before you start — it's always a good idea, really.

Search for a common topic before posting

If a forum has been around for a good deal of time, it's probable that a slew of the normal beginners' questions have been answered. Furthermore, most of these forums have their own personal search engines (like mini-Googles) to look for topics or subjects that have already been covered. Before you ask about what might be an oft-covered topic, run a quick search — see whether what you want to know ("What's your favorite podcast mic?") might already be waiting for you among the FAQs. You'll save yourself a lot of time (and retain some goodwill from messageboard denizens) with that one step.

Offer a quick introduction

The first time you post, you're basically anonymous. Unless you've met the participants somewhere else before (on- or offline), you're basically striking up a conversation with a bunch of strangers. Use the same amount of care you would with that instance here on the messageboards. It might also be a good idea to give a little bit of background with your first post (like your name, your location, your podcast title, and how long you've been doing this) so people know where you're coming from. Some forums also have newbie forums where you can introduce yourself in your own first post and get it out of the way.

Respect yourself and others

If everybody could express themselves completely and utterly through text, everybody would be Hemingway. As it is, it's sometimes difficult to properly communicate subtleties like sarcasm through the written word. Until you've gotten the hang of writing on forums, it might be a good idea to avoid extreme levels of snark. It's easier to establish a good reputation by being helpful, friendly and knowledgeable than it is to repair a damaged image on the forum.

Spam isn't just for dinner

First it was junk mail and inconveniently timed phone calls from telemarketers. Today's most annoying communications take the form of spam e-mail and posts. It's bad form to cover the forums with notices about your podcast and your podcast only. People come to forums to meet people with similar interests and exchange knowledge and information (and, yeah, sometimes write scathing reviews of whatever springs to mind). That dialogue isn't helped by anybody virtually shouting "HEAR MY PODCAST! HEAR MY PODCAST NOW!" It's acceptable to mention your experiences with your podcast and discuss ways to handle possible problems. It's *not* okay to spam the boards and clog the lines of communication.

 Avoid the spam and you'll be okay. That advice works on so many levels, really.

Taking it from there

Now that you know what to avoid, jump in and start talking. Most posters to podcasting forums have information about their podcasts in their profiles, so you'll be able to find people pretty quickly who are addressing topics you want to know about. Don't be afraid to talk to podcasters with different interests, though. The subject might be different, but the medium is the same.

Contacting the Authors Directly

You've already discovered how to search out other podcasts through directories in Practice 2, and there's always the magic of Google and other search engines (how DO they find all those pages?). It's amazingly easy to find other podcasts and podcasters (as well as bloggers) who share your interests. Because they all have pages, they're almost guaranteed to have ways for you to contact them, from direct e-mail addresses to automated message forms. Those conveniences are free to use, and they wouldn't be there if the author didn't want you to use them.

It's always a good idea to lead with some praise ("Hey, I saw your blog and really like it. Nice work!"), and questions are usually welcome as well ("Where did you find that Gamera keychain mentioned in last week's post?"). If you want to try a more businesslike approach, you might propose an exchange of links so readers and listeners of one site might find the other, and vice versa. It's a good idea to make sure that they have a list of links or a *blogroll* (a list of favorite or often-read sites) before recommending such a transaction (see Figure 32-3). Links can be like currency, though, so most authors are willing to share.

More than anything, remember that you're trying to build a network and make connections with fellow podcasters. It's always good to have a link, but a trusted contact can be even more valuable.

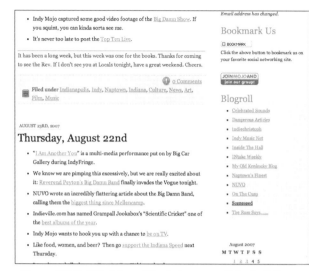

- Indy Mojo captured some good video footage of the Big Damn Show. If you squint, you can kinda sorta see me.
- It's never too late to post the Top Ten Live.

It has been a long week, but this week was one for the books. Thanks for coming to see the Rev. If I don't see you at Locals tonight, have a great weekend. Cheers.

Filed under Indianapolis, Indy, Naptown, Indiana, Culture, News, Art, Film, Music

AUGUST 23RD, 2007

Thursday, August 22nd

- "I Am Another You" is a multi-media performance put on by Big Car Gallery during IndyFringe.
- We know we are pimping this excessively, but we are really excited about it: Reverend Peyton's Big Damn Band finally invades the Vogue tonight.
- NUVO wrote an incredibly flattering article about the Big Damn Band, calling them the biggest thing since Mellencamp.
- Indieville.com has named Grampall Jookabox's "Scientific Cricket" one of the best albums of the year.
- Indy Mojo wants to hook you up with a chance to be on TV.
- Like food, women, and beer? Then go support the Indiana Speed next Thursday.

Email address has changed.

Bookmark Us

Click the above button to bookmark us on your favorite social networking site.

JOIN MOJO AND join our group!

Blogroll

- Celebrated Sounds
- Dangerous Articles
- indiechristzsh
- Indy Music Net
- Inside The Hall
- INtake Weekly
- My Old Kentucky Blog
- Naptown's Finest
- NUVO
- On The Cusp
- Sceneseed
- The Russ Says...

August 2007
M T W T F S S
1 2 3 4 5

• **Figure 32-3:** This blogroll includes some links to fellow podcasts.

Questions and Comments

When you first listen to a podcast or read a blog, you may get a full listing of all available episodes or stories. If you click a specific story or episode title, though, you might see a place where fans can leave comments or questions about each entry. Go ahead and communicate with the author through these sections — they make it possible to carry on a decent conversation and learn a lot about the podcaster's craft. You can also link to these stories in your own podcast or blog. It's all about establishing links.

You might also hear about *trackbacks* or *linkbacks,* an automated form of communication between two online sites. If both Web sites support this feature, you can use it to provide automatic summaries of stories and comments exchanged between the sites. This feature only works between blogs that *both* support it, however, so don't count on it being a common feature in all your discussions.

 The same rules about messageboard posts apply here as well: Make sure you're courteous and clear in your communication, and don't use another person's comment section to advertise your own show. Go in and show your good intentions, and you'll get more out of it.

Practice 33

Spreading the Word with Social Media

In This Practice

✔ Using social networks to publicize your podcast

✔ Bookmarking your way to more listeners

✔ Using a virtual world to promote the real one

Traditional radio uses (well, yeah) radio and television ads, billboards, and the like to get you to listen to their shows. And sure, ads can help (that picture sure shows how wacky that morning zoo is, doesn't it?). But even more effective is getting friends to tell their friends and get them to listen to the show themselves. A billboard is, at best, just an impersonal plea to listen — and at worst, a blight on an otherwise-impressive landscape. By contrast, a friendly word from someone you like or respect (or two hours in a locked car being forced to listen to a show) is much more influential.

In the brave new world of the Internet, it's possible to get a note from anywhere in the world about a show from anywhere in the world. There's just too much information — and programs available — to go through all of it yourself, so the recommendation of a friend becomes even more valuable. That word is likely to come through popular social Web sites, where people come to meet and exchange information. These are sites you can use to your advantage and make your podcast spread to a wider audience.

Getting the Word Out through Social Networks

The biggest advantage of using most social-networking resources is that they're free. You can set up a site on just about every network at no cost to you. From there, you start sending out the notices and forging the connections that will get your site recognized. From there, hopefully you'll see a chain reaction that spreads the word about your podcast to the far-flung reaches of the Internet.

Bulletins, blogs, and comments

Take a look at the functions on MySpace — most social networking sites have similar features, but MySpace sees the most traffic, so it's definitely the best place to start. You may even already have an account on the site. If you don't, it's free, so there's no excuse. Hop to it.

 For more information on using MySpace, check out *MySpace For Dummies,* published by Wiley Publishing.

Bulletins

There are a few ways to notify people about your podcast through MySpace (http://myspace.com). The first is by *bulletin*. This feature sends out an immediate notice to everybody on your friends list. On your profile's main home page, look for the link under the My Mail section to post a bulletin, as shown in Figure 33-1.

Post Bulletin link

• **Figure 33-1: The Post Bulletin link.**

From here, you just type your message in the Post Bulletin page, shown in Figure 33-2, and click the Post button. Be sure your bulletin carries all the pertinent information about your podcast, including the location of the files and feeds, the main Web site, how often you post updates (you DO post regular updates, correct?), and a little about the podcast's subject matter.

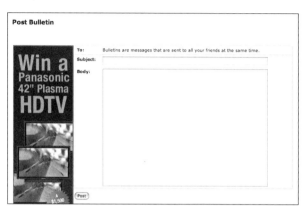

• **Figure 33-2: Writing your podcast bulletin.**

 Bulletins on MySpace tend to move quickly, especially if you have a lot of friends. Be prepared to post bulletins early and often.

Blogs

MySpace pages also carry their own blogs with RSS feed capabilities. (See Practice 27 for more on RSS feeds; blogging is covered in detail in Practice 26.) If you're already familiar with blogging and RSS feeds, then you're ready to start using these simple controls:

1. Click the Blog link at the top of your home MySpace page.

2. Click the Post New Blog link in the My Controls section of the page, as shown in Figure 33-3.

• **Figure 33-3: Posting a new blog with the supplied control.**

The form shown in Figure 33-4 appears.

3. Enter the subject of your blog and change the Category drop-down menu to whatever is appropriate for your entry.

• Figure 33-4: Tell them what your blog is about.

4. Enter the information about the podcast in the body of the blog (it'll be similar to what you put in the bulletin), and include optional information below the body section, if it seems relevant.

5. Include a link to the specific podcast episode (*not* to the RSS feed) in the Podcast Enclosure section of the blog entry.

The link to the episode is added to the MySpace RSS feed.

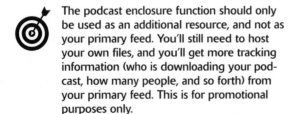

The podcast enclosure function should only be used as an additional resource, and not as your primary feed. You'll still need to host your own files, and you'll get more tracking information (who is downloading your podcast, how many people, and so forth) from your primary feed. This is for promotional purposes only.

6. When you're finished click the Preview & Post button to save your changes.

Comments

Another way to publicize your podcast is by leaving comments on people's pages. Not only does this let the recipient know about your podcast, but it also tells anybody who happens to visit that person's page as well. That said, it's *extremely* rude to leave multiple comments about the same thing in the comment section — that's called *comment spam,* and it's frowned upon; it amounts to cluttering up somebody else's profile with your own mess. It's better to tailor an individual comment to that person and not to include all the promotional material you'd normally put in a blog or bulletin.

To add a comment, just look for the Comments section on a profile and click the Add Comment button. In the form shown in Figure 33-5, for example, you enter your text and link and click Post a Comment.

• Figure 33-5: Adding a comment.

Your comment's recipient may have enabled the option to approve comments before they're posted, so try not to be too self-serving with your post. It's entirely possible that your "OMG! GO LISTEN TO MY PODCAST NOW!!!" calling card will never see the light of day if it's phrased pretty much like that.

A MySpace site for your podcast

So far, we've looked at using your own site to promote your podcast. Why not give your podcast its own MySpace site, though? As mentioned before, it's free. Using a MySpace site for your podcast allows people to search directly for the podcast in the MySpace search directory, instead of looking for you and getting it the roundabout way.

It does mean you're going to have to maintain two different sites, so it will be a little extra effort. Still, it does provide a more precise focus for promoting your podcast, and you can restrict your bulletins and blog entries to the podcast. That also means that you can save your own profile for leaving funny cat pictures in comments for your friends and avoid besmirching the podcast's reputation. (Hey, it deserves better — right?)

Video sites

If you've got a video podcast (and don't mind sharing it on free video services), consider tossing it up on YouTube (`http://youtube.com`) or another free hosting service. The advantages of taking this step include putting your video in a searchable database (like a podcast directory) and taking a little strain off of your bandwidth. People will also be able to copy code directly from the site and embed it in their MySpace or personal Web pages, further exposing your work to the world.

To upload video to YouTube, follow these steps:

1. **Sign up for an account.**

2. **Click Upload Video and verify your e-mail account.**

3. **On the Video Upload page, shown in Figure 33-6, fill out the information about your video, including the all-important tags.**

Tag early, tag often.

4. **Choose the video to upload.**

It must be less than 100MB in size and 10 minutes in length.

Be sure to include mention of your main site and feed in your video podcast for promotional purposes. Remember, you're posting it on YouTube to attract more people to your RSS feed and site.

You should also consider other similar social networking sites such as Facebook (`www.facebook.com`) and Virb (`http://virb.com`). They're all possible additional sources of audience members.

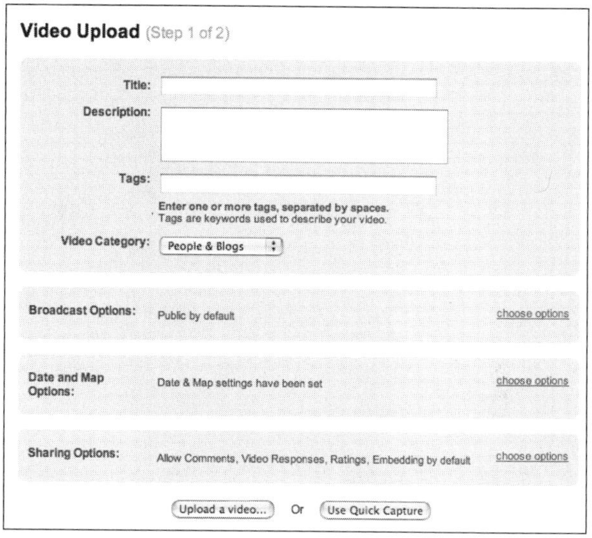

• **Figure 33-6: YouTube video options.**

Using Bookmarking to Promote Your Podcast

Think of social bookmarking sites like Internet-acceptable graffiti. You're tagging your favorite sites with your endorsement, and other people can see you've been there (and that you like the site). It also allows you to store your bookmarks online, so you can see them from any computer you use. In this case, though, it's more interesting to show how to use these bookmarks to promote your own podcast.

Two popular services are StumbleUpon and Del.icio.us. Both sites require log-ins, but this profile is what allows you to centrally locate your bookmarks and make them available to others. All you need is an e-mail address and some basic information.

Follow these steps to bookmark your podcast:

1. **Navigate to** `http://stumbleupon.com` **and click Join StumbleUpon.**

The sign-up page appears, as shown in Figure 33-7.

• **Figure 33-7: StumbleUpon sign-up screen.**

2. **Enter your information and download the tool-bar, shown in Figure 33-8.**

You're required to download a toolbar for either Internet Explorer or Firefox.

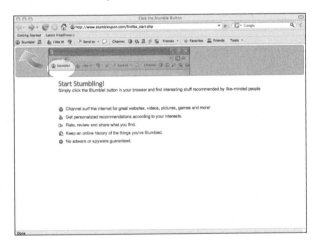

• **Figure 33-8: StumbleUpon installation.**

3. **After you finish the installation, navigate to your podcast's site and click the thumbs-up button on the toolbar there.**

The podcast is marked in your account.

Not only does this mean your friends will be able to see the podcast link in your bookmarks, but also that those searching for podcasts or sites with the same tags as yours (using the random Stumble button in the toolbar) will have a chance to find your podcast.

Del.icio.us (`http://del.icio.us`) also functions as a way to tag Web sites for others to examine. The sign-up screen, shown in Figure 33-9, is similar to StumbleUpon, and this site only puts two links into your regular browser toolbar (although there is a separate Firefox extension if you choose to use it).

• **Figure 33-9: Del.icio.us installation.**

One of your new bookmarks allows you to tag your interesting sites (such as your podcast), and the other allows you to review your bookmarks and use the Del.icio.us search engine to find similar tags (as described in Practice 2). You can also set up links to your friends and start networking. After you post a link to Del.icio.us, as shown in Figure 33-10, you'll be able to add tags and descriptors, and you'll have the option of informing your network about these links.

Once your podcast had been bookmarked, friends of the friends you've linked to can examine that list and hear it for themselves. It gets added to other lists, more people see it, and the process continues. It's an example of *viral marketing* — the name may sound negative, but it's just a description of the way the word gets spread (and that's okay when you're the virus).

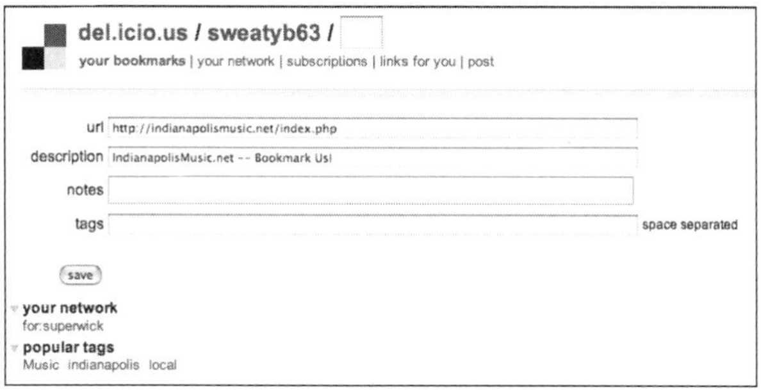

• **Figure 33-10: Del.icio.us bookmarking.**

Virtually Promoting Your Podcast

Here's a wild new wrinkle on social networking: What if the word-of-mouth you're spreading belongs to a pixilated avatar you created in Second Life? Hey, it could happen. Just because the podcasts take place in the real world, separated from your online avatars and characters, doesn't mean you can't tell people about them. Of course, this approach can be an expensive proposition — it involves maintaining a premium account and virtual land in Second Life or in online games — but simple conversations and posted ads can help people find your site. Talk it up, no matter what land you're in.

34
Practice

Soliciting and Incorporating Listener Feedback

Why do you podcast? Is it for money? Fame? Accolades from your peers? To give back to the world and help shift the balance toward the greater good? If you're like many podcasters, the answer to all of those is, "No, none of that, just doing this to communicate." That means the currency we trade in is called FEEDBACK. In this practice, we discuss the various forms of feedback listeners can provide you — and how to make the most of their comments to enhance your show.

But a word of caution before we show you this particular peek behind the closed doors of the sausage factory: Everyone is entitled to his or her opinion, but you're not obliged to go along with it; you can take it or leave it at your own discretion. Remember that only a very small subsection of your audience will ever provide you with feedback — the vast majority of your listeners just listen passively, in varying degrees of happiness. Are the comments you receive indicative of the opinions of your audience at large? Or do they represent the lunatic fringe? You'll need to think about those two questions long and hard before making any lasting changes to your show based on the sparse and sporadic comments that come in from out there. Let's get started.

Is Your Show "Feedbackable?"

(Hey, if that isn't a word, it ought to be — it means a show that attracts feedback easily.) What if you made a podcast and nobody cared? That's a pretty big issue for many podcasters — and has caused more than one show host to contemplate premature podfading (disappearing from the podosphere). You can hear them from time to time, lamenting the lack of audience response, nearly begging for someone — anyone — to send them something — anything — to let them know someone is out there listening. But the hard reality is that all shows are not created equal in the eyes of the listening audience — and that there is no direct correlation between audience size and volume of feedback.

Think about all the times during your day you have the chance to provide feedback to others. How often do you do so? And when was the last time you filled out a comment card for a service that was 100% acceptable? If it was more recent than we're giving you credit for, did you fill out anything beyond the required "circle this" rating system? As a culture, we expect things to be okay. Barring the extremes of service, we accept that we're going to have a pleasant experience and, at the most, may offer a polite "everything was fine" if we're asked how everything was. (See if you don't catch yourself doing that very thing the next time you go out to dinner and the server asks how your meal was.)

The same holds true in podcasting. People need a reason to provide feedback. If the content of your show does not cater to one of those reasons, you shouldn't expect to get a lot of feedback. Here are a few reasons people will provide feedback:

- To praise
- To criticize
- To debate
- To correct
- To ask questions of
- To provide answers to

Now consider the last podcast you produced. Unless it was a monumental improvement or a horrible failure compared to your other episodes, you probably shouldn't expect a lot of praise and criticism. (If you aren't putting forth controversial topics, by and large don't count on praise.) If you've done your homework, the fourth reason — to correct — shouldn't happen very often. The last two — asking questions and providing answers — are more common, though they vary from show to show depending on format and the style of the hosts.

 Even the most feedbackable shows see only a small fraction — around 1–2 percent — of their audience providing feedback. This is especially

true as the size of your audience grows. Remember that listening and watching remain for many a passive medium. Podcasting is changing that, but not to the point where half (or even a quarter) of your audience will call in to your show each week.

Remember that where feedback is concerned, there is no magic bullet; some shows simply don't entice listeners to provide feedback. This isn't necessarily a bad thing. Take a hard, objective look at your show — and set your feedback expectations accordingly. If you think you should get more or would like to get more, read on.

Encouraging Your Listeners to Provide Feedback

Let's look at this as a simple cost/benefit analysis situation. Your listeners will expend a certain amount of effort (cost) to provide you with feedback. Even the most altruistic of your listeners do so because they get some sort of reward (benefit) for their trouble — even if that reward is simply the feeling they get from a selfless (?) act. Unless you're giving away money or prizes, there isn't a lot you can do to increase the benefit side of the equation. Instead, your power to encourage feedback lies in lowering the barrier to entry. The following sections discuss how to encourage listener input via e-mail, voicemail, comments, and forum posts.

E-mail

E-mail is arguably the most ubiquitous application made possible in the information age. It remains the killer app and is, for many, the main and preferred method of communication. With such a high rate of adoption (who *doesn't* use e-mail?), e-mail should be the #1 way people communicate with the podcasts they listen to. But it rarely is — usually because of shortcomings on the side of the podcaster.

Getting your listeners to send you e-mail relies on a single factor: making your e-mail easily accessible to them *when they need it*. Here are a couple ways you can do that:

✔ **Display a Send Me Comments on This Episode link on your Web site.** People enjoy most podcast episodes when they are sitting at their computer. You probably have enabled some sort of Flash player on your Web site to allow for that. Place a Send Me Comments on This Episode link right next to that Flash player. Don't bury your e-mail address on a Contact Us page or hide it behind a form that they have to go digging for.

✔ **Say your e-mail address out loud during your podcast.** And for the listeners who are taking advantage of the *portable* nature of podcasting — how are you helping them to send you e-mail? Kudos to you if you're saying your e-mail address out loud in your show. Extra bonus points if you say it more than once. But how many times are *you* waiting with pen and paper while you listen to podcasts? True, there's nothing stopping someone from hitting Pause and tracking down the items you mention — nothing, that is, except for the 37 other podcast episodes in the player waiting to be listened to.

Of course you should repeat your e-mail address in your show. Of course you should spell it out and speak very slowly. But you are probably better served by encouraging your listeners to visit your Web site for contact information — and by making sure that contacting you is as easy as possible.

Voicemail

Ah, voicemail — the application that makes so many listeners wonder why all these podcasters have phone numbers in area code 206 (Seattle, WA). Voicemail works well with podcasting for a couple of reasons:

✔ Much of the podcast listening audience has a phone strapped to a hip most of the time.

✔ Talk radio has trained us all to pick up the phone and call rather than wait until we get home to pen a letter.

 So why do so many podcasters have 206 numbers for their voicemail? Because many of them use the free voicemail service from K7.net. There are many providers, but K7.net got the jump on the competition when some big-name podcasters started using its service. Plus, K7.net used to provide free vanity numbers. It doesn't any longer, but many podcasters have stuck with them.

One word of caution: K7 numbers expire if you don't get a call for 30 days, and you can't get the number back. So be smart: Set up a reminder every 20 days or so to give yourself a call.

Voicemail numbers also have the advantage of vanity numbers, providing a catchy mnemonic device to help listeners remember the number in case they can't hit the Pause button fast enough. If your voicemail provider doesn't offer this service and you aren't getting many (if any) calls, consider researching other services.

As with e-mail, it's important to put your voicemail number in front of your listeners at the right time. Because calls can be initiated by most listeners as they are listening to the show, go ahead and place it somewhere obvious — say, adding it to the NAME tag in your media file. This causes the number to scroll across the track display of most media players — whether portable or on-site.

Comments on your blog

If you use a blog to power your podcast, the blogging software you use probably gives listeners a very easy way to attach comments to the show notes of your podcast episodes. And if your blogging software doesn't do that, dump it and read Practice 26 for a great replacement suggestion.

Listeners tend to be more comfortable leaving comments about an episode rather than sending e-mail or leaving a voicemail. This isn't all that surprising; the listener loses a bit of privacy when e-mailing or leaving a voice message. Both are easy to reply to, and folks are concerned about their privacy. But a comment on a post on a Web site? That allows for true anonymity.

Or does it? If you have a feedbackable show but aren't getting many comments on your posts, it could be because your listeners perceive a privacy issue where there doesn't have to be one: Most comment systems ask for, but do not require, an e-mail address and a Web site URL. How inviting is that? (Hint: not very.) Many smart podcasters have hacked their sites' comment templates to add "not displayed on site" or remove the fields altogether. Decide what's right for you.

Barring that little hassle, site-side comments are usually quite prominent and rarely need extra positioning. But you can encourage comments on your site just by asking. And when you ask for visitors to leave comments, tell them all the other things they can find on your site, like an archive of past shows, links to additional content, or perhaps your upcoming schedule of appearances. More reasons to visit means more benefit to them.

Forum posts

Okay, people do like to carry on conversations inside forums — but those conversations tend to be the least-effective way of gathering comments about a specific podcast episode. With e-mail and voice-mail, the experience is one-on-one between the listener and the podcaster. With Web-site comments, the activity is a bit more social — but comments can (and do) live alone, isolated from others of their kind. All that is out the window in a forum post.

Forums are places where conversations develop and change significantly after the initial thread is posted. They are notoriously difficult to control and many are dominated by powerful figures, sometimes to the detriment of others.

None of this is necessarily a bad thing, you understand. It just depends on your audience and your show's ability to nurture compelling conversations beyond the relative merits of a single episode.

Because forums allow your listeners to respond more easily to one another than with blog comments, forums can foster a much greater sense of community.

 There is, however, one bad thing about forums: They present nearly irresistible targets for script-kiddies and vandals. Many exploits for the most common and widely used applications exist; some of these, after they establish themselves, allow a hacker access to the entire Web server. This can bring everything to a screeching halt very quickly and make it nearly impossible to recover deleted assets. Sometimes those assets may be your entire database of posts and threads. You have been warned.

One podcast of note, Escape Pod (`http://escape pod.org`), has found great success using forums and has suffered none of the bad juju we've discussed here. Steve Eley uses Simple Machines Forum (`http://simplemachines.org`) and hasn't had a single spam post or exploit since rolling out the application.

If you intend to use a forum, it's a good idea to

- ✔ **Keep tabs on the conversation.** Not necessarily to make sure everyone plays nice, but to let your listeners know that an entirely new facet of your program exists. Everyone probably gets the concept of "leave us a voicemail." But a forum offers many more opportunities for a conversation to develop. Make sure you are fostering that conversation — and a sense of community.

- ✔ **Use your show to talk about the conversations that are developing on your forum.** Also, mention your most prolific posters and work some comments about their contributions into your podcast.

- ✔ **Try to funnel as much traffic to the forum as possible.** As with all forms of feedback, if people don't know about it, they can't use it to participate.

Adding Feedback as a Show Element

Collecting feedback is one thing, but figuring out what to do with those e-mails, comments, and audio files is another matter altogether. Sure, you can use it to help improve your show, but also consider making feedback a portion of your show's content.

When you expose feedback to your listening audience, you can start a positive cycle that generates more feedback — more content, which sparks more feedback, and so on. If you can get past the Catch-22 of *acquiring* the feedback in the first place, judicious use of it in your show will help get your audience actively involved. It seems to appeal to our hive mind that we should want to do as others are doing — and leaving feedback for a podcast is no exception.

Responding to feedback during your show

Here are a few ways you can incorporate feedback into your show:

- ✔ **The most common way to incorporate feedback is *on the backside*.** This means reserving the reading of e-mail or playing of audio comments for the tail end of the show, after the substance of the program has concluded. For the standard "I love your show" comments, this is a perfectly acceptable — and perhaps even preferred — location. But understand that many of your listeners won't stick around to hear these comments.

- ✔ **If the feedback is more substantive, or is of a nature that lends itself to further discussion on your show, play the voicemail as an element within the show.** You can decide whether to play the file clean or provide voiceover comments while it's playing. You decide. Practice 13 helps you reduce any noise that may be a part of the audio file; Practice 18 provides some ways to make sure the audio level matches the rest of your program.

 Why add discussion about the feedback at all? It's true that some podcasts will simply string voicemails and audio comments one after another without adding any reciprocal feedback from the show hosts. At the risk of generalization, this seems a bit narcissistic. The idea behind feedback is to respond to the feedback, even if it's a simple thank you — if you don't see the value in adding your two cents about the feedback, then your audience probably doesn't care to hear that either.

- ✔ **Read an e-mail or a pertinent forum post on your show.** If possible, see if you can track down a friend or co-worker to voice the feedback text for you. While this isn't required, the new voice on the program will help provide a clear distinction between the feedback and your comments.

Managing feedback overload

But what do you do when the amount of feedback turns from a trickle to a deluge? Chances are that your audience is choosing to listen to your podcast to hear your main content, not the comments from other listeners *about* your content. You have to keep good control over how much feedback you add to your show, lest you change the nature of your program.

The best way to achieve this balance is by selective addition of feedback:

- ✔ Receiving a voicemail comment does not obligate you to play the comment. (Remember, however, the previous suggestion about the positive feedback loop.)

- ✔ You may wind up with several comments on a topic that by and large offer up the same viewpoint. Select *one* of these to play on your show, but mention that many more just like this came in if you feel it necessary.

You may get a few "why didn't you air my comment?" questions from your listeners, but if they respect your show, they should respect your decisions of final show content.

Ultimately, you may find yourself with more comments than you have content for your show. While that may sound far-fetched, it is not. One of your authors faced this very dilemma and came up with an innovative solution — create a separate-but-related episode that features only feedback and the responses from the hosts. Not only did this allow substantially more feedback and comments to be aired, but the listening audience can skip the entire episode if they aren't interested in the listener feedback.

Keeping Track of Conversations Off Your Site

So far this practice has covered ways of encouraging and dealing with the feedback your listeners provide directly to you. But the decentralized nature of the Internet and the advent of social online media are giving your listeners the power to create their own conversations on their own terms.

Some sites, like BoingBoing (`http://boingboing.net`), embrace this idea fully — and have gone so far as to completely remove the capability to comment on their blogs. Instead, they encourage their readers (and listeners to their infrequent podcasts) to create their own blog posts — and then they use the Trackback system to link the two together. It's beyond the scope of this book to cover the intricacies of how trackbacks operate, but the functionality is built in to most blogging applications and is nearly automatic.

Responding to these off-site comments, be they on personal Web sites, on social-networking sites, or inside forums, can give you some immediately obvious benefits: Your response shows you care enough to pay attention to what's being said about your show that you take the time to find it.

Luckily for you, the process of finding it is fairly simple. In Practice 2, we demonstrate how you can use Google, Technorati, and other online tools to do automated searches for the content you're interested in. With some slight tweaks to those directions, you can set up a few "ego filters" to send you an alert when new comments about you or your podcast are introduced to the Web.

 At a minimum, set up a Google Alert and a Technorati Watchlist (both covered extensively in Practice 2) for your name, your podcast, and the URL of your Web site.

Getting Featured on Podcast Directories

There's more to podcast directories than just being listed in the rolls. After all, there's a huge difference between being in the paper and having the headline all to yourself. People have to put less effort into discovering you if you've already been thrust to the top of the heap, and more people will be interested in finding out about you because you've gotten that notice. These front-page notices are almost invariably good news, as well. Sites don't waste the home page's space discussing terrible podcasts.

Making Your Numbers Count

Podcast directories don't have access to the tracking numbers for your podcast host, so they're not going to know whether you have hundreds or *thousands* of listeners unless you run those numbers through them. Most directory services have links to assist listeners in subscribing to their listed podcasts, even if it's just a request for subscription information.

So how do you boost your subscription numbers? You make it as easy as possible for your listeners to know where and how they need to subscribe. You also use every method of communication available to you.

Your podcast

Designate a part of your podcast to talk about the specific directory you want to target and explain to your listeners what you're trying to do. Subscribing to a podcast doesn't cost any money, so listeners who haven't subscribed (for instance, if they've been downloading specific episodes from your site and not your feed) can be directed to the site of your choice and boost your subscription numbers.

Your Web site and blog

There are quite a few ways to use your Web site or blog to get some attention from podcasting directories. And it's much easier than telling your listeners what to do. In this case, you can set up links directly to the directory and its subscription page, leading prospective listeners directly to where you need them to subscribe. Furthermore, you can include links to multiple directories, so you can take advantage of all the possible services without wasting time in your podcast.

Some blog services also provide a *pinging* service, which automatically sends a notice to podcast directories when new material is available on your feed. Instead of allowing them to find out on their own schedule, this gives them the heads-up immediately. Directories really like podcasts that provide new content on a regular basis — they're not going to waste their time promoting material that's going to go stale or fade out. Keep the episodes coming, and let everybody know when they do.

Each Web service or software package has a different way to set up a ping, but let's take a look at the popular WordPress system. To set up a ping each time your podcast and blog are updated, follow these steps:

1. **Log in to your WordPress site.**

2. **Select the Options tab from the top WordPress menu.**

3. **Select the Writing tab from the menu that comes up.**

4. **Enter the diectory's ping server in the Update Services field.**

The ping server address will be available from the directory itself.

For more information about integrating a blog into your podcast service, take a look at Practice 26.

Social networks and bookmarks

Sites such as MySpace (www.myspace.com) and Facebook (www.facebook.com) are more than just places for teens to throw hundreds of self-portraits on the Internet and leave comments for their friends and favorite bands. These Web sites are established portals for linking together people from all over the globe — and everybody on those sites should be considered a potential listener. You're looking at two main ways to show off your podcast on these sites:

✔ **Tell your friends — send out bulletins and messages to those on your friends list, and talk about the podcast in your blog.** Try to go beyond crass self-promotion, though. People will respond more to an actual message about the podcast than they will just an update that says "Hey, my new podcast is up!" Tell them about the show, make it easy for them to subscribe, and you'll notice the difference in the numbers.

✔ **Get your friends to tell others — that's what makes social networks so important and vital.** Word of mouth is one of your most valuable marketing tools. Once you get your friends talking about your podcast, the word will spread through their friends, through their friends' friends, and so on. It sounds cheesy, but it works. Make sure your friends know you want them to subscribe — and that they have all of the details to make it possible.

Beyond social networks are social bookmarking sites, like StumbleUpon (www.stumbleupon.com) and Del.icio.us (http://del.icio.us), shown in Figure 35-1. These sites take the bookmarks you normally store on your browser and put them on a common Internet server. From there, your friends and acquaintances can see what you're looking at on the Web and take it from there. Not only that, but they can share those bookmarks from there, starting the same sort of chain reaction we looked at with social networks.

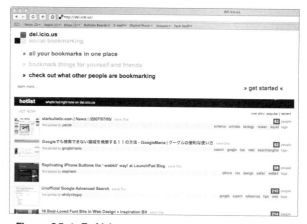

• **Figure 35-1: Del.icio.us.**

In the case of StumbleUpon, shown in Figure 35-2, you can even have others *stumble* on to your link and check it out, if they are so inclined. It might be a random discovery, but you should never underestimate the power of a bored office worker surfing the Web. The more people tag your site, the more times your site will be referenced and passed on to other users. It's still word-of-mouth advertising. People are just putting their bookmarks where their virtual mouth is (so to speak).

• **Figure 35-2: StumbleUpon.**

For more information on using social networking to advertise your blog, check out Practice 33.

Two Thumbs Up!

Podcast directories (and just about every other site on the Internet, for that matter) have sections where you can rate and comment on various podcasts. For example, Figure 35-3 shows comments and ratings for a podcast listed in the iTunes Music Store. You want people to leave good ratings and comments in order to help spread the word about your show, and consequently get you more notice on the directory. After all (and despite the better judgment of many), folks still believe what they read on the Internet.

The strategy here is the same as the one you were using with social media. Ask your listeners to leave

comments and good ratings, ask your friends to leave comments and good ratings, have your friends tell their friends to leave comments and good ratings, and so on. You can even leave a comment yourself, but constantly inventing new "people" to give your podcast five stars and stellar comments (talk about cheesy) can backfire. It's best to rely on real and honest feedback. It's okay to ask for it, but don't fake it.

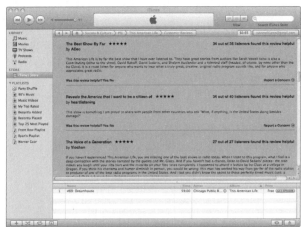

• **Figure 35-3: iTunes comments and ratings.**

Building Bridges

There's a reason they call those connections you click on to find Web sites *links* — they create a network of connections between sites, referring one site to another in a never-ending string of paths to new sites. Links are prized for their ability to drive traffic from one site to another, increasing the popularity of sites amongst both users and search engines. The more links you have between sites, the more traffic gets driven from one site to another.

If you're driving a significant amount of traffic to a podcast directory, the site will take notice. Therefore it's a good idea to feature a list of the directories you use on your podcast's Web site. Here are a few ways you can do that:

✔ **Make a separate section for the listings on your site.** A static collection of links that point to these directories, placed on your site's home page, is an excellent way to point traffic in their direction.

✔ **Text links are fine, but graphics or banners can attract more attention.** If the directories provide these goodies, consider using banner ads (as in Figure 35-4) with links to drive traffic to their sites.

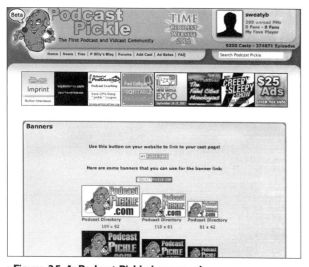

• Figure 35-4: Podcast Pickle banner ads.

✔ **Make sure the directories know you've added the link.** They'll notice increased traffic primarily, but a quick e-mail or comment wouldn't hurt, to let them know where it's coming from!

The podcast directories have already set up their reciprocal link to you — that happens when they host your profile in their directory. This is just a good way to spread the word that your podcast is part of their directory, and that people can subscribe at their site. You're happy, they're happy, everybody's happy. It's like a virtual campfire, minus the singing and burnt marshmallows.

Practice 36

Joining a Podcast Network

In This Practice

- ✔ Understanding what makes a podcast network
- ✔ Using the advantages of the network
- ✔ Knowing what you'll be giving up
- ✔ Deciding whether a network is for you

A podcast *network* goes far beyond what a podcast directory (discussed in Practice 28) can do for you. A podcast directory makes sure you're listed and available. You still have to do all the legwork of putting together your show, making sure it gets onto your server, and selling any advertising you may want to include. Think of the podcast network as the equivalent of a record label offering a contract for your CD — or having NBC pick up your pilot — they take some of the work off of your plate and make it easier to concentrate on your show. They may even put some money in your pocket through the use of advertising or sponsorships. It may not be a multimillion-dollar deal signed in the Capitol building, but it could be a big boost to your show.

Finding the Right Network for Your Podcast

Because so many podcasts are available these days, having a network to help distribute your show can really help get you some recognition. It also means the networks have a lot of competition for spots; you have to stand out from the others. The first thing to do is find the network that could benefit both you and your show. While your podcast on financial affairs could fit on a more general-interest network, you might find a money-specific outlet that could bring you more listeners — and maybe more money as well.

Begin your search where most things on the Internet begin — the search engine. Just entering *podcast network* on Google pulls up millions of references; some might be a little vague (although it does pull up some very popular entries and podcast networks). Just a few more keywords and you can narrow those choices down to some more-manageable choices. From there, most of the work is looking at specific sites and seeing what podcasts they host (you may even recognize some of the names) and assessing whether you think your show might fit in. Some examples include these (of which Figure 36-1 is a sample):

- ✔ **The Podshow Network** (http://podshow.com): This network represents a huge audience, and it's headed up by one of the founding figures of podcasting, Adam Curry.

- ✔ **BackBeat Media Group** (http://backbeatmedia.com): Home of the extremely popular (legal) music podcast *Coverville*, this network maintains some boutique networks that group like-minded podcasts together.

- ✔ **Indiefeed** (http://indiefeed.com): This network distributes several music podcasts based on genre, and it's also featured in the giant instrument-retail chain Guitar Center.

- ✔ **MySportsRadio.com** (http://mysportsradio.com): Looking for news about your favorite sports team? This is where you go. The site is concerned with mainly teams from the mainland United States, but there's quite a bit to choose from here.

• **Figure 36-1: The BackBeat Media Group.**

It's also a good idea to refer to Practice 32 and talk to other podcasters and bloggers about what they think of these networks — and get their opinions on which ones might be a good choice for you. Talk to those involved with specific networks; find out what they think about being involved with those organizations. You should also check out messageboards and forums to see what (if anything) is being said about the networks you're interested in. And be sure to give every comment the same treatment you should give all information on the Internet — it may be interesting, but remember the source and use that in evaluating your response to it. Good news can be self-serving babbling, bad news can be spite, and no news could mean the network isn't doing its job in getting the word out.

What Your Network Can Do for You

Different networks provide different levels of services, depending on their podcast-circulation and revenue numbers. Some provide hosting services, production assistance, and advertising sales. They also group your show together with others that could share audiences. That way you get exposure to audiences who should be interested in your subject matter but might not have wandered across it before. This kind of help can be huge in exposing your show to thousands more potential listeners or viewers.

Those services might well be necessary if your podcast does get a larger audience. You'll need the added bandwidth and advertising support if there's more demand for your show.

What You Can (And Must) Do for Your Network

Most networks require you to bring an already sizable (for podcasting, anyway) audience with you. Some may require 500 listeners, some may require more. You can be sure, though, that most require far *more* subscribers than just your friends and family. You have to have an audience for your show already, and you have to be able to show that this audience exists — specifically, through tracking numbers. Each Internet service provider has different tools for tracking downloads from your site, but you're going to have to get the numbers.

Yep, we're way beyond the level of podcasting as a hobby here, and well into the realm of business. No surprise that the networks expect you to go along with their business plans. The podcast networks have likely put together a business plan (with the help of lawyers and other expensive business types), and you're going to have to get with their program if you want to be part of it. Bottom line: When you enter into a podcasting network agreement, that network is going to have a say in how your show gets publicized and distributed.

 Before you sign anything, make sure you're comfortable with what the network is trying to accomplish — and get your own legal expert to review the agreement before you sign anything. Podcasting can be a fiercely independent medium, and you might not want anybody telling you *how* you can talk about (say) the intricate plot maneuverings of the various *Star Trek* series.

Finally, you have to be consistent. Early on, your podcast may have been a labor of love, something you put together just because you wanted to. Others picked up on that passion, and you have a sizable listenership. Now that you're on a network, though, there are other considerations. In exchange for its services, the network is going to want a regular network show — likely with involvement from you that goes above and beyond the podcast recording (such as sharing ad revenue, producing advertisements for use on other podcasts, and promoting your podcast in other forums like blogs, interviews, or real-world events).

Making the Decision

You might want to take out the notepad and start your pro/con list right now. You have to balance what you want to do with your podcast versus what responsibilities you'll have to the network. You probably already have a decent audience if you're considering this move. Here are some points to ponder when making your decision:

- ✔ Do you want more listeners, or are you okay with what you have?

- ✔ Are you looking to make some money off your efforts, or is this just something you do for fun?

- ✔ Are you open to working with others to produce your show, or is it something personal that you want to keep under your own control?

After you evaluate all the factors and made your decision, have fun with it! No matter what happens, you've considered all the factors that affect the immediate future of your podcast — and you're doing what you want with your show. It's important not to lose sight of what drove you to make this show in the first place. That will be with you whether you're sticking with your original plan or making the leap to a bigger pond.

37 Practice

Connecting with the Media

In This Practice

- Preparing press releases
- Making cold calls
- Creating a press kit for you and your podcast
- Following up with media contacts

While podcasting is gaining momentum and notoriety with every episode that finds a place in the iTunes directory, getting the word out that you *have* a podcast worthy of attention remains reliant on the traditional media. Print. Radio. Television. The big three. Contacting the media isn't difficult; the challenge lies in getting the media to contact *you*. Podcasting is still new to the world and a growing movement in media, marketing, and promotion — and now the big three are beginning to take notice.

There is a science in reaching the media. You need a certain amount of patience and thick skin as you go about trying to convince the media that this isn't a run-of-the-mill podcast you're recording in your basement (even if that's where you did it), but a podcast that they *need* to listen to.

Getting the media's attention is not an easy task, but it's not impossible either.

Writing Press Releases

Press releases are the tried-and-true devices used for connecting with the media. The typical press release can be easily broken up into several sections: who, what, where, and when. Sounds like a promo (as described in Practice 29)? No surprise there. Much like the minute-long audio commercial, a press release needs to be a short, efficient statement about your podcast.

Title

The title of your press release can sometimes be the hardest thing to write because it has to capture the entire newsworthiness of your article *in just one line of attention-grabbing text!*

When writing the title, ask yourself what this press release is all about. The answer, boiled down to one sentence, will be your title:

New Podcast Novel from
Award-Nominated Author Officially Launched

Introductory paragraph

The introductory paragraph provides a lead-in to the story you are presenting to the media. It can begin with the *who* and provide some background about the podcast host or the inspiration behind the podcast. By the end of the introductory paragraph, you should reach the intent of the press release. Here's an example:

Tee Morris challenged both publishing and audiobook conventions in January 2005 by giving away his fantasy novel, *MOREVI: The Chronicles of Rafe and Askana,* as a podcast. Done as a serial, each chapter of the novel was made available to mp3 players every-where. The co-author of *Podcasting For Dummies* officially returns to the podcast fiction arena with *Billibub Baddings and the Case of the Singing Sword,* now playing at TeeMorris.com and Podiobooks.com.

The body paragraph

The body is the portion of the press release where you cover the basic facts about what your podcast is all about. You can include more detailed behind-the-podcast background, as well as any feedback you may receive — in advance or after the initial episodes are released.

Another option with the body of a press release is to include quotes from either cast members or yourself concerning the podcast. It may seem a little odd holding a mock interview with yourself, but it can give the media a jumping point for questions they may ask in a future interview. Here's an example:

"If *MOREVI* is described as *Crouching Tiger, Hidden Dragon meets Pirates of the Caribbean,* then *Billibub Baddings* is *The Lord of the Rings* written by Mickey Spillane. Instead of the pirates, swordfights, and swashbuckling adventure of my first podcast, I'm offering an axe-wielding dwarf standing toe-to-toe with the mob in 1929 Chicago." No one in either the hard-boiled detective or high-fantasy genre is safe in *Billibub Baddings,* and in this produc-tion Morris is bringing a few friends along for the ride. "*Billibub Baddings* will showcase an international cast, contributing their voices to my novel."

His cast includes podcasters Leann Mabry of *Tag in the Seam,* Paul S. Jenkins of the U.K. podcast *Rev Up Review,* and Chuck Tomasi of *Technorama.* Morris' voice talents also include award-nominated authors Scott Sigler (*EarthCore, Ancestor*), J.C. Hutchins (7th Son), and New Zealand author Pip Ballantine (*Chasing the Bard*); award-winning author Paul Levinson (*The Silk Code*) and *New York Times* Bestseller Tracy Hickman (The *Dragonlance* novels). "Podcasting *MOREVI* was a lot of hard work, but it was also a lot of fun. Bringing friends into this production has just stepped everything up a level, and I could not be hap-pier with the end results."

The closing paragraph

End your press release with the *where* of your pod-cast. *Where* will they find it? *Where* will people be able to listen to it? By now the who, what, and why have all been covered. By concluding your press release with the *where,* which should also include where you can be contacted for an interview, you leave the media with all the essential information needed for a follow-up call.

Here's an example of a closing paragraph:

> Tee Morris launched the *Billibub Baddings* podcast on St. Valentine's Day, February 14 and is now available on Podiobooks.com, iTunes, Podcast Pickle, and other podcast directories. If you can't wait to hear the end, the print version is also available at leading retailers, online in digital formats, or directly from the publisher. Tee Morris can be contacted at (*phone number here*) or tee@teemorris.com for interviews. For more information on the author and the *Billibub Baddings* Mysteries, visit www.teemorris.com or www.dragonmoonpress.com.

Making Cold Calls

Cold calls are an early-morning or late-afternoon process: running down a list of press contacts you have collected, giving each one a call, and repeating the same salutation and message to the press contact on the other end of the phone, one by one.

This type of contact is by far the most aggressive, the most self-testing, and the most demoralizing of approaches you can take when calling media contacts. A thick skin and a strong stomach are basic equipment when you take on the task of cold-calling media contacts.

Why are cold calls so difficult? Well (for openers), the sheer number of people doing them. Media contacts, from the local newspaper with a staff of five all the way up to the staff of *NBC Nightly News* in New York, receive hundreds of calls — all concerning an event or an individual — that must be covered for their publication or news show. Morning wake-up radio shows, afternoon variety newsmagazines, and the late-evening news are bombarded with leads. So if the contacts seem curt with you on the follow-up call, consider that they are on deadlines, are still polishing up stories from previous days, and are following up from yesterday's cold calls — all at the same time.

When you're engaging in the martial art of cold-calling, be sure you've done some prep work beforehand — and then be ready to pitch your podcast when you dial the phone.

Do your homework

Do a little homework to find out whom you'll be contacting. Calling a newspaper or a radio station is merely the first step. For the typical media affiliate, the first person to answer a call is usually a receptionist or switchboard operator who asks you where to direct your call.

To find out where you're headed (before you even get to that encounter), surf over to your media affiliate's online resource. You can find Web sites and direct e-mail contacts at the end of articles, at the bottom of the front page, or inside the first page of a standard newspaper — and in directories of staff contacts on Web sites for radio stations and television affiliates. Departments that you have the best chance of scoring a hit with include these:

- Local News
- Style
- Tech

Script out and rehearse what you are going to say

This mantra can also be applied to approaching people with an on-the-street interview, but you should know — before dialing the phone — exactly what you're going to say. The only thing *cold* about the call should be the fact that it is coming unannounced and unexpectedly. Speak up, be clear, and be *confident*. That will really ring true and help sell you as a potential feature.

A good script to follow for talking to media contacts looks like this:

> "Good (*morning/ afternoon/evening*). My name is (*your name*), and I am calling to talk to you about an upcoming podcast concerning (*quick one-sentence sum up of your podcast*). Do you have a few minutes?"

This will get you one of three things: a follow-up date in the future when you can talk, a polite "No, thank you," or an abrupt dial tone. But read on.

Don't get discouraged

If you get the dial tone as a reply, forge ahead. Don't allow this action to demoralize you; *there is nothing personal in the hang-up*. These folks get a lot of calls like this, and if you can't grab them in the first minute, they have another lead to pursue, another fact to double-check, or another deadline to attend to. There are people who cold-call media contacts for a living, and they deal with this sort of thing all the time; so if you get dial tone as a response, remember: *It's not you*. Just cross off that contact and start again with the next contact on your list.

Be ready to talk

What's the worst thing that could happen when you do a cold call to the media? The hang-up? No. The opposite — a "yes" that catches you flat-footed: "Oh, you want to talk to me *now*?! Um, okay (papers shuffle), just, ah, let me take care of some things over here. . . ." If the cold call is a hit, then you need to be ready to talk *immediately*. Have any notes you want to get across about your podcast, about your approach to the project, and about your future plans for the podcast, at the ready.

 You should prep for the best reaction possible, and the best reaction you can have to a cold call is an interview. The possibilities are slim that this might happen, but it's best to be ready in case it does.

Remember whose time you are taking up

You may hear this bit of advice again and again. Yes, your time is very valuable; but time's value is relative to the current deadline you face. At media affiliates, every day is a deadline. Remain polite, remain professional, and never get snippy or curt with the media contacts you make. That will be a hard bridge to rebuild after you burn it.

Don't take rejection personally

If you get turned down for an interview, remember Tee's two-word mantra: "Their loss." An interview — a really, really good interview — can make the rounds on the Internet, getting you a good amount of press outside your region *and* earning the reporter you talk with a memorable byline.

If you're turned down for an interview after a cold call, take a breath and say out loud, "Their loss." Okay, you're done. Move on to the next contact.

 When you're doing your prep work on what department or section of a media affiliate would be a good fit for your podcast, consider the topic of your podcast. If you do a sound-seeing tour of Ireland or a show on how to pack for vacations across the country or overseas, then Travel would be a good contact to make. If you are hosting a podcast on NASCAR or your favorite NFL or NHL franchise, give the Sports section a call. Along with the broad appeal of podcasting as a medium, look at the topic of your podcast and find a good niche for it.

Creating an Effective Press Kit

Another great way of grabbing the media's attention is to provide them with background research on you and your podcast. You don't want to send them a truckload of material that will overwhelm them, but just enough information to get the questions rolling. To accomplish this, you need a *press kit* to put online, send in via mail, or drop off in person.

A press kit also travels under other monikers — *press package, media kit*, and *press materials* — but whatever the name, it's a collection of descriptive and promotional materials, usually organized in a snappy portfolio to accompany a press release. Consider the press kit a jumbo-size combo press release with curly fries and the Hoover Dam–size soda. The DVD that comes with this book includes three excellent real-life press kits that you should be sure to check out.

The essentials

Putting together a press kit is only one more variation on the same themes involved with writing a press release. You need to include the "who, what, and when," but along with that, you can include "look, listen, and enjoy" options.

Here are the essentials of a podcast's press kit:

- Cover letter introducing yourself, your podcast, and your desire for an interview
- Current press release
- Cast photos or press photos of podcast's host/hosts either in studio or recording
- Cast biographies
- Contact information
- CD (preferably with uncompressed files on it, otherwise include with the CD instructions on how to play the mp3s) of the first five (or five favorite) episodes

 You may think a CD doesn't need a set of instructions; but not all CDs are the same: On seeing a CD, recipients make two assumptions: (1) "It's an audio CD that will play in my computer's CD/DVD drive or music player, or on my car CD," or (2) "It's a data CD and should be treated as such." Audio CDs, depending on the length of your show, may hold only an episode or two. They can play on more than just computer CD drives, but you won't be able to feature as much of your podcast as you might like. mp3 CDs easily hold five episodes, but they can make some press contacts scratch their heads if the CD doesn't play in their car player. If you decide to include a CD for this press kit, make sure you include a set of instructions for playback.

Extras you may want to include

With the essentials taken care of, a podcaster's press kit may appear a little thin at first, but you can add a few more items to grab the media's attention.

Here are some additional options to consider for your press kit:

- Printed articles or copies of other news and media articles (no more than three)
- A list of accomplishments and accolades for the podcast (featuring pull quotes from celebrities, subject authorities, and other podcasters)
- A business card with your immediate contact information
- Additional CD or (data) DVD of previous live appearances or interviews (and with data DVDs, it's even more important to include an instruction sheet that explains how to read and retrieve the data)

 Never send originals. The information you include in a press kit is considered disposable. Rarely will you get a press kit back, even if you express in a cover letter that you wish to have the press kit returned to you. If you include a self-addressed stamped envelope big enough to hold the press kit, it may be returned to you without fail, but the condition of the press kit may be a different matter. When you're sending press kits, always send high-quality copies of originals and expect that you will not receive the materials back. If you need to get a press kit in the mail quickly, remember, there is *always* a FedEx/Kinko's open somewhere where you can make sharp photocopies and build up a press kit in no time.

As with promos, less is more with both press releases and press kits. You don't want to overwhelm media contacts with clippings, CDs, DVDs, and photographs. You want to keep your facts clear, your information organized, and your resources easy to process.

The Follow-Up

As busy as media outlets get, it's all too easy to fall between the cracks or to have the press kit arrive, only to be buried under a mountain of other press releases and press kits. All that traffic is a definite pitfall in your pursuit of press coverage.

This is why it is not a bad idea, after the press release or the press kit is delivered, to do a follow-up call. And that's all about timing.

 Timing is also key when you write your press release. Writing a press release the night before a podcast's launch, for example, is not the best strategy; you don't have any time to build anticipation or hype. If you know when your podcast will be launching, write your press release *two to three weeks before the launch.* That way you have time for the press release or kit to circulate, and for following up as recommended here. If your press release is announcing the conclusion of the podcast's season, release it a few weeks before the finale. You want to make certain that the press release's content, timing, and circulation all work well together.

The same-day follow-up: Proceed with caution

If the fax machine you're using is on the blink, or if you just came home from hand-delivering a press kit to local media affiliates, the same-day follow-up is not out of the ordinary. When you make the follow-up call, you're simply practicing good form and looking for confirmation that the package was received.

But watch out for assumptions: If you're doing a same-day follow up with media affiliates and you expect them to have reviewed your materials *already,* the same-day follow-up comes across as a little pushy. It is also a bad idea to assume the media has considered your press release and decided whether or not to interview you. Remember that the media contacts are working on yesterday's leads and today's deadlines, so your press kit may not have been reviewed yet. A same-day follow-up won't kill your chances for an interview unless you're expecting an interview or a decision concerning your press release *at that moment.* Such an overly aggressive approach can sour a reporter's opinion of how newsworthy your story is.

When doing a same-day follow-up, keep it simple:

> "Hello, my name is (*your name*) and I'm just calling to confirm that you received my press (release/kit)."

On the acknowledgment that the package arrived, thank the contacts for their time. If they have not received the press release or package, simply state, "That's fine. I left the press kit at the front desk, so it should be there. Thanks for your time . . ." or "Do you have an e-mail address that I can send the press release to?" Remember, you're not looking for an immediate interview, just confirmation that the contents of the kit have arrived.

Same-week follow-up: A happy medium

When sending press kits, the U.S. Postal Service's Delivery Confirmation is a terrific investment. You can track your package from mailing date to arrival date. After you get the confirmation, give your press release or kit two to three days to be looked at. Then make the follow-up call to the recipient.

It starts much like the same-day confirmation call:

> "Hello, my name is (*your name*) and I'm just calling to confirm that you received my press (release/kit)."

Wait for a reply. If the media contact has the kit or release, you can ask, "Have you found a moment to review it yet?" That is a genuine, honest question, and it may yield you an equally genuine, honest answer. It may not be the answer you want to hear; but regardless, you will want to say, "Thank you so much for your consideration . . . ," ending on a favorable and professional tone.

 You're competing against other leads, other features, other news bites — and there will be times when you will grab someone's attention and times when other items (such as how a home featured in a Woody Allen film sold for a cool sum) take priority over your audio creation. (No lie, it happened to Tee!) Hope for the best; but if the worst befalls on you, handle it like a pro.

The week-after follow-up: You are who again?

In all things concerning news, timeliness is everything. What is the hottest story early Monday morning is old news a week later. And even for features that don't date themselves by their content, newsworthy information has a shelf life. And with the kudzu-like growth of information distribution via RSS feeds, that shelf life is fleeting.

Waiting a week to follow up after sending in a press release is far too long. In that time, many more press releases have stacked up on the desk of your potential contact, and you can bet that interns are currently sorting through faxes arriving during the weekend that will add to this poor reporter's pile. All this is happening before the reporter checks his or her e-mail. A lot of news can happen in a week's time, so it is something to consider when waiting a week to follow up on your press releases.

Of course, waiting a week to follow up a press kit may actually work in your favor. The press kit's contents are more robust than a press release's, so you may want to allot plenty of time for the contact to review the contents. (Just remember that it's no guarantee that the press kit has been reviewed.)

When you reach the contact, introduce yourself again with, "Hello, my name is (*your name*) . . .," " but this time ask, "I'm just calling to see if you have reviewed my press kit concerning (*your podcast*)?" Wait for the reply.

The media contact could still be considering it or may answer with "Yes, and I don't think there's any news there." The other possibility is that the contact will want to talk to you and arrange a formal interview or conduct one there and then. (Again, *be prepared* for the best as well as the worst.)

No matter the outcome, you'll want to maintain a positive, professional demeanor: "Thank you for your consideration." That's always a nice way to end a conversation with the media.

The frequency of the follow-ups

In the age of voice mailboxes, trying to talk to a flesh-and-blood voice can be as challenging as finding the courage to make the follow-up call. Here are some suggestions for the timing of your follow-ups:

- **First follow-up:** Two to three days after sending the press release or kit
- **Second follow-up:** Four days after first follow-up
- **Third follow-up:** Four days after second follow-up

Is there a magic formula here? No, not really, but each call here is less than a week after the previous one, so not too much time elapses between calls. Usually by the second follow-up, the press contact will attempt to reach you. If no response comes after the third follow-up, it's best to cross off that contact and move on to the next press contact or follow-up.

The process of establishing media contacts makes editing and post-production of the podcast itself a joy. This contact process isn't easy, not by a long shot. But with some perseverance, the end result — media coverage — can be an addition to your (now growing) press package and perhaps even win you some new listeners in the process.

38

Practice

Talk to Me: Interviews

If you do a search on Amazon.com or hit your local bookstore of choice, you find a lot of books about interviewing. It might surprise you how many people have written books on how to sit down with someone and carry on a conversation with them because, after all, that's all an interview is, right?

Actually, an interview is a lot more than just asking the other person on the opposite end of the table, "So tell me, what do you do for a living?"

Body language, appropriate questions, and delivery of said appropriate questions are just a few things that are important and essential in making an interview a pleasant and positive experience for both the podcast host and the guest. An interview goes well beyond the questions asked; it's all about the experience shared. In this practice, you find out what is waiting for you under the thin candy shell surrounding a really good interview.

The Interview Query

You have two ways of asking people for an interview, and both require an outgoing personality to pull them off, and pull them off seamlessly. The "asking part" is perhaps one of the toughest hurdles for people to clear when asking for an interview. Yes, you may hear people like the GeekLabel Crew, Victor Caijao, and Leann Mabry say, "Just go up to them and ask . . ., " but on *meeting* the GeekLabel guys, Victor, and Leann, you know they have the personalities to pull off this approach.

On the street: Guerrilla journalism

From your local news affiliates to irreverent mavericks like Tom Green, Howard Stern, and Don & Mike, "on the street" interviews are some of the toughest interviews to make happen and happen well. Interview subjects — be they celebrities, authorities, or just people-on-the-street — are completely caught off guard and unprepared. If you're fortunate, the people you stop can think fast on their feet and provide lengthy answers that can be included in your episode with no editing or chopped up to provide quick sound bites for segments of the topic you're discussing. This aggressive approach to journalism, where the interviewer comes at the interview subject on the spot, usually flying by the seat of his or her pants, is *guerrilla journalism*.

This style of interview may *seem* totally spontaneous, but there is an art to it. Here are some tips to keep in mind when doing your own "on the street" interviews:

✔ **Be clear and concise when asking the interview subject to stop and talk.** True, in a crowded setting of paparazzi, people are screaming for the attention of celebrities, but most on-the-street settings don't require such an aggressive tactic. You want to keep it quick: "Hey, would you like to be interviewed today about *(subject matter)*?" may be all you need. Where it gets tricky is when you have to say it over and over again until finally someone stops and says, "Sure, I'll talk to you."

Attempt to make eye contact with passers-by and remember to speak up, be clear, and be *confident*.

✔ **Have a release on hand for people to sign.** It's a good idea to have a *legal release* on hand for your interview subjects to sign before the interview begins. A release is a permission slip that grants you the right to use the interview subject's voice and likeness in your podcast. This means you owe the subject no money or compensation (although notification of the podcast's posting is extremely polite) for the interview, and the subject is granting you permission to use his or her voice and likeness in advertising and promotion. (For more on legal releases, see the later section "Legal Releases: Podcasting Paperwork.")

For downloadable examples of legal releases, take a look at Current TV (www.current.tv/make/resources), which offers PDFs of basic releases.

✔ **Keep it to four questions or ten minutes, whichever comes first.** These are fast and furious interviews you're conducting, and while it is a nice idea and good practice to have more questions ready than you need, consider the setting and the subjects. You don't know if the interview subject will deliver, or if the interview will be gold, but limit the time. Have four questions at the ready. If you manage to hit ten minutes before you've asked all your prepared questions, then end the interview, thank the subject, and move on to the next interview.

✔ **Try to hold interviews with a backup, that is, somebody to cover your back.** Whether you have a friend standing a few sidewalk tiles away, watching from the diner in front of you, or physically present, remember you're dealing with the general public — complete strangers. Personal safety should always come first.

✔ **Remember whose time you're taking.** The interview is happening in real time with no preparation on either side. If your interview subjects need to leave, thank them for their time and let them leave. The gesture of thanks ends the interview on a positive note.

Scheduled interviews: "Do you have 30 minutes?"

You can schedule some interviews ahead of time, on location. This type of interview falls between the on-the-street interview and the formal query (described next). Here, you happen to run across the interview subject and simply ask, "Hey, we are recording between the hours of 1:00 and 3:00. Come on by!" In this situation, the subject may have time to mentally prepare for the interview. The interviewee may need to leave after a pre-scheduled amount of time, but whatever time the subject can give you is quality time; don't waste it with introduction banter. Simply ask, "Are you all set?" and then begin the interview.

A variation on this theme is at a formal event (convention, expo, and so on) featuring authorities and celebrities in certain fields, where media organizers formally arrange time slots for interviews. In certain situations, the *handlers* (personal assistants that sometimes double as bodyguards, PR agents, and so on) of the interview subjects may want to see the questions you wish to ask beforehand. Other times, you may simply go up to the individual — or the individual comes to you — and the clock starts running when the subject takes his or her seat.

Regardless of the setting for this kind of interview, the practice and approach are the same:

- **Prepare more questions than needed.** It's your 30 minutes (or more or less) with this guest. You want to make it count. Therefore, prepare as many questions as you like. A good formula for interview questions is to figure two-minute answers for every question, and then five-minute answers for every question. For example, if you have five questions for a fair interview subject (two-minute answers), your interview covers ten minutes. If the subject gives you an exceptional interview (five-minute answers), you have almost 30 minutes of material to pull from. With this in mind, come up with twice as many questions as you think you need.

- **Have a release on hand for people to sign.** As mentioned earlier, the release form is good to have on hand so you and the subject are clear as to what the recorded material will be used for. The handler and subject may wish to review the release before starting. (In this case, it's best to have them look at the release beforehand so it doesn't cut into the interview time. If it does, adjust. Don't pressure anyone to sign anything. Ever.) Be sure to have a pen on hand, too.

- **Be gracious about the interview.** If your subject or your subject's handler wishes to review the questions being asked, it is a good idea to let him or her know upfront that you may not get to all these questions. (As fun as it is to watch an interview subject's eyes bug out when he or she sees all the questions you wish to ask, it's better to have a relaxed subject.) Go one step further and ask, "If you have any specific questions you'd like to address, please let me know." While this is a scheduled interview time, the subject may wish to talk about something specific based on one of your questions or something you did not have noted as a topic of discussion.

- **When time is up, time is up.** No matter how well the interview is going, keep an eye on the time, particularly if the subject needs to leave your interview to go to another event or, most likely, another interview. If your interview subject needs to leave, thank that person for his or her time. As with the on-the-street interview, end the interview on a positive note.

The six-million-dollar interview

Paul Fischer and Martha Holloway, hosts of *The Balticon Podcast,* scheduled an interview with science fiction luminary Harve Bennett. Bennett, while not known for his time on camera, is one of the major players of science fiction television, having produced *The Six Million Dollar Man, The Bionic Woman,* and the blockbuster films *Star Trek II, III, IV,* and *V.* (Chances are good that if you've watched science fiction on TV, you've probably seen something that Harve Bennett has produced.) Paul sat down and wrote five questions for a 30-minute interview.

Paul asked his first question, and it was the only one he needed: "How did you find yourself involved in producing the *Star Trek* film series?" Bennett's answer, never rambling but a passionate and engaging perspective on his own journey — beginning with *The Wrath of Khan* and concluding with *The Final Frontier* — clocked in at just under 25 minutes.

At the end of the answer, Paul smiled and said, "Thank you very much, Mr. Bennett." Truly, everything Paul could have asked for in an interview happened with one question.

Formal interview queries: Marking your calendar

Some interviews come with plenty of notice and allow ample time for preparation. These interviews usually begin with a formal query, either through media channels or directly (via e-mail, voicemail, a phone call, or face-to-face), where introductions are made and goals for the interview are set.

Here's a suggested format for a formal interview query via e-mail:

> "Hi, my name is (*your name here*) of (*your podcast title*), a podcast that takes a look at (*what your podcast is all about*). I would love to talk to you for my podcast about (*the reason why you want to have this person on your show as a guest*). At your earliest convenience, please contact me at this e-mail address or at (*best phone number*) with your availability for an interview. Thank you for your time."

If you're conducting a formal interview query via phone, try this format:

> "Hi, my name is (*your name here*), and I am host of (*your podcast title*), a podcast that talks about (*what your podcast is all about*). I would love to schedule an interview with you at your earliest convenience concerning (*the reason why you want to have this person as a guest on your show*). Please contact me at either (*mobile number*) or (*home number or work number*) if you would care to schedule an interview. Thank you for your time."

That's all there is to it! While both queries differ slightly in approach and delivery, the following suggestions work well for contacting potential subjects for both types of interviews:

- ✔ Open with a friendly greeting telling the potential contact who you are and with whom you're affiliated with.

- ✔ Give a *one-sentence summary* of what your podcast is all about. (The query is not a pitch for your show or for podcasting, so keep your show summary to one sentence.)

- ✔ Explain why the interview subject is being invited to appear on the show.

- ✔ Provide the contact information for the subject to reach you.

 You may be asked to share the questions you want to ask in the interview. Just as discussed in the scheduled interviews, be upfront about the questions you want to ask. In some situations, you may have an extended discussion with a handler or some sort of media contact, and it is good practice to be as forthcoming with your intent and direction for the interview.

Legal Releases: Podcasting Paperwork

As defined earlier, a *release* is a permission slip from the interview subject allowing you to use his or her voice and likeness in your podcast. Releases are usually worded this way:

> I consent to the use by (*your podcast or your studio name*), or their agents or assignees, of my name and/or portrait, picture, photograph, video recording, audio recording, or any other visual or audio likeness of me for use worldwide in the podcast, (*your podcast*), and its promotion. This consent applies to use in any medium now known or to be developed in the future.

I expressly release (*your podcast or your studio name*), and their agents or assignees from any privacy, defamation, or other claims I may otherwise have arising out of podcast, broadcast, exhibition, cablecast, Webcast, publication, promotion, or other use of my portrait, picture, photograph, audio recording, or any other visual or audio likeness of me.

This release sounds very formal, almost too formal, for podcasting, doesn't it? Well, it is, and podcasters (at present) do not fall under all the restrictions the FCC and other communication organizations impose on radio, television, and film. However, with the RIAA stepping in and restricting playback of copyrighted material (discussed in Practice 20), this may change.

Some forward-thinking podcasters have adopted a legal release for their podcasts, just to get into this practice in case things change. Even if the FCC and lawmakers decide that podcasting is best self-policed rather than government regulated, having your interview subjects sign a legal release puts you in a good position should any future regulations befall podcasting.

Finding Good Interview Subjects

Depending on the subject matter of your podcast, landing interviews can be difficult. For example, say you have a sports podcast and you want to interview Sammy Sosa about the art of hitting home runs. Unless you work for ESPN, it's not like you can call Sammy's staff or even the Texas Rangers' office and schedule an interview. You may be able to make it happen with a few repeat follow-ups, patience, and some (but not too much) persistence; but finding good interviews may not be as hard as this.

Establishing contacts

The best way to go about securing an interview is to ask questions. If you want to interview a museum curator, call the museum's administrative offices and ask for the media contact. If the museum or other organization doesn't have a media relations department, then ask, "With whom can I arrange an interview with (*name of the desired interview subject*)?" The person on the phone may reply curtly before hanging up on you, or politely ask you to submit questions and even a one-page proposal explaining why you want to conduct this interview and how this interview will go. Your results may vary.

The contacts you make when searching for interviews may produce for you right away or provide subjects for you to interview later on. This is why you need to keep a professional attitude and a pleasant disposition when making the initial queries.

Attending special events and conventions

Do a quick search on the Web or in your local or regional paper to find out about upcoming special events in your area. Many of the following events feature guest speakers with whom you may want to seek interviews:

- Conventions
- Expos and trade shows
- Book signings and speaking events

It's a good idea to bring your portable recorder with you to these events, just in case you have the opportunity to schedule an interview on the spot with the featured special guest of one of these events. However, the main reason for attending these events is to establish contacts for future interviews. Have on hand a business card, preferably with your name, your show's name, and your contact information so interview subjects can either follow up with you personally or pass along your contact information to their media staffs.

When querying celebrities and authorities for an interview at these events, consider the timing of the query. If the subject invites audience members for questions at the end of a lecture, that is not the right time to ask for an interview. However, if the subject is signing autographs, stand in line and wait your turn. Then step up, present your business card, and simply ask, "I was wondering if you are granting interviews this afternoon and how I could schedule an interview. If today is not an option, are you available sometime later in the month?" This way, you can make contact with the subject but not take up too much of his or her time or hold up the line of autograph seekers.

 At many of these events, a media relations representative is present. Contact that person first to inquire about the availability of a celebrity or authority you want to interview. The subject may be in the company of a handler who has the final say on if and when the interview will happen.

Making direct contact via the Internet

Sometimes, an interview can happen simply by sending someone an e-mail. Look for Web sites, online forums, and blogs that focus on the chosen topic of your podcast. Here, you can follow leads, click e-mail addresses, and find yourself arranging interviews with award-winning authors, local politicians and newsmakers, medical professionals, and a wide array of authorities who are more than willing to sit down with you for an interview.

Again, the same rules apply — have a legal release ready, offer the questions up front, and make sure you're respectful of the interview subject's time. This time, however, the connection can be arranged over time and taken at a much slower pace than the on-the-street or scheduled interview. You can take time to prep questions, test audio recording equipment, and make sure you're ready.

When you're ready for the interview, it's in your best interest and in your interview subject's interest to run down a final checklist:

- ✔ **Test your recording equipment over Skype, the telephone, or whatever device you're using to record the interview.** Make sure the audio equipment is working properly before the interview; don't wait until the interview for testing.

- ✔ **Prepare for the interview as thoroughly as you can.** Find out a few facts about your subject prior to the interview so that you don't struggle with questions and get your facts jumbled over the course of the interview.

- ✔ **Have your questions at the ready.** However, don't concern yourself with hitting all the questions or remaining steadfast to just the questions before you. Allow yourself to go into another direction if the conversation takes an unexpected turn; the exchange may be even more engaging and entertaining.

- ✔ **Prior to the interview, ask the subject how long he or she is available for the interview.** Some subjects can interview for well over an hour, but your target time should depend on your show's average running time, in particular your time allotted for interviews. During the interview, keep an eye on the time.

- ✔ **Thank your interview subject at the beginning and end of your conversation.** If possible let the subject know when you're planning to post this interview. If you don't know, tell the subject you will send him or her an e-mail when you know the date the interview will be available.

Interviewing Unconventional Experts

When searching for guests to feature on your podcast, nothing is wrong with having guests that people wouldn't normally consider "experts" on the topic at hand.

For example, suppose that your podcast's topic of discussion is applied technology in the corporate world. Who would make a great interview for advancements in the work environment? How about an award-winning science fiction author? Robert J. Sawyer, when he is not writing award-winning books, lectures in Canada and the United States about this very topic.

Or say you have a podcast about writing, and you want to talk about the process of writing a graphic novel from the ground up. How is the process of writing graphic novels different from writing novels? How do you avoid losing key elements in transitioning from an idea on paper to a visual one? You know who would be a good guest to have on your podcast about this? Richard Hatch (shown in Figure 38-1). Yes, as in the Classic Captain Apollo and Tom Zarek from *Battlestar Galactica*. Richard Hatch is also an accomplished writer, currently working on *The Great War Magellan*, a project that is in the works to be released as a graphic novel.

How you find these potential interview subjects? Check out Web sites, printed biographies, and blogs. Accomplished authors, noted celebrities, and authorities of all kinds often mention in their biographies their interests outside of what established them as experts in their fields. Along with authors who serve as keynote speakers for universities and corporate functions and actors who are branching out into writing, you have doctors who are martial-arts black belts, school teachers who are rock'n'roll musicians . . . all kinds of fascinating folks are out there waiting for you.

 You can discover quite a bit about potential interview subjects by surfing Web sites and tracking certain blogs; and from there, an interview that may take your audience (and you) by surprise can occur.

• **Figure 38-1:** In the casual atmosphere of Farpoint 2007, Tee interviewed actor Richard Hatch about his experiences as a writer for both novels and the gaming industry.

Part VI

Creating a Video Podcast

The 5th Wave   By Rich Tennant

Oh come on –
how fatal
can it be?

FATAL
ERROR

Video Podcasting

Video production in the late 1990s was just beginning to break into the home consumer and amateur filmmaker market, but getting your computer and your home (or office) equipped with Hollywood-grade hardware usually involved bank loans and a hope that you might break even with what you'd just invested. These days, cinematic special effects, professional-grade cameras, and the capability to produce broadcast-quality video have all become commonplace. Digital video technology is affordable, and creative minds are exploring the possibilities of podcasting their videos to content-hungry audiences around the world.

So, in a nutshell, yes, video podcasting poses many more challenges and many more demands. The end results, though, are worth it all!

Understanding the Demands of a Video Podcast

Video demands a lot of time and attention not only from its audience but also from its creators. Similar to enhanced podcasting (described in Practice 24), video podcasting is a step up in production and more challenging than producing standard audio podcasts.

There's no denying that enhanced podcasting is very, very cool. Unlike enhanced podcasts put together in GarageBand 3 or Podcast Factory, video podcasts are *not* easy to do. Impossible, no. But easy? Hardly, especially when working with various camera angles, lighting, ambient noise, and so on. The advantages of the video podcast are similar to the enhanced podcast in that you have a captive audience and you are appealing to the visual senses. The video you are providing is content found nowhere else, and unlike *webisodes* (exclusive mini-episodes of television shows like *Monk* and *The Office*) viewable only online or television episodes purchased via iTunes, video podcasts are free and reside in your iTunes library or on your iPod until you decide otherwise.

In the same vein as enhanced podcasts, most video podcasts will play only on iTunes (for the desktop computer) and iPods (portable players), depending on the compression format you decide on. Video podcasting doesn't rely on any particular platform, but it is reliant on the playback device. Do you want it playing back on iTunes, by default? QuickTime? Or Windows Media Player? Your choice of format limits how audiences can subscribe to and (in this case) *watch* your podcasts.

Video podcasts, unlike enhanced podcasts however, can be created using a variety of applications running on Windows or Mac OS X. You can use Apple iMovie, Windows Movie Maker, Apple Final Cut Pro (shown in Figure 39-1), or Adobe Premiere Pro to create your episode. (See Chapters 40 and 41 for more on Premiere and Final Cut Pro.) With Final Cut and iMovie, you can export your video podcast directly to a format optimized for the iPod. With a Windows application (as described in Practice 40), there will be an extra step involving QuickTime Pro (a $30 USD upgrade available from www.quicktime. com) that can do the same export that Final Cut Pro and iMovie can. (Yes, you could do the compression by hand, but we're big believers in letting the software do the heavy lifting for you!)

• **Figure 39-1: Final Cut Pro from Apple is a fantastic tool for video podcasters and makes exporting the episode to an iPod format a breeze!**

As mentioned with enhanced podcasting, your audience must commit to *watching* your video podcast.

In effect, no multitasking is allowed if users want to get the most out of the podcast. Besides, because it's video, it demands attention — audiences have to pay close attention to their iPods (or iPhones) or iTunes. Potential subscribers may reconsider subscribing to your podcast as the difference between watching your podcast and a new television show premiering on Showtime, The Discovery Channel, or NBC.

Playback devices, audience commitment level, and accessibility are only the beginning of what you'll be facing in your list of demands in video podcasting. In this section, we take a closer look at some additional considerations for your new video venture.

Lighting

Unlike audio — recorded just about anywhere, at any time in the comfortable, swanky settings of a dimly lit studio — video needs light of some kind so you can see what you're shooting. Even nighttime video needs some kind of "lighting" (be it digital, infrared, or some other means), so now you have lighting issues to contend with. For your video podcast, here are a few issues to consider to light your way to good lighting:

✔ **Where are your principal light sources?** Fluorescent light easily fills a room but plays havoc with actors' skin tones, fabric colors, and the general warmth of a room. Natural lighting may produce vibrant colors and realistic looks for on-screen talent, but that means placing your show's lighting in the chancy hands of Mother Nature. Lighting, whether natural or otherwise, directly affects how your talent looks.

Take a look at the lighting of an episode of *24* (studio lighting, accent on shadow, and so on) and then compare it to the film *Sleepy Hollow,* where only natural light was used to light the talent. Then think about how to use light in your own podcast. Are your light sources true to the look and feel you want? Also, consider how your principal light sources affect the look of the show hosts or talent. Which leads us to the next point . . .

✔ **How's the weather from one day to the next?** Simply put, lighting on a cloudy day differs greatly from the lighting on a clear day. If you can't shoot everything in one day, will the weather conditions be the same the next day?

✔ **Are you filming (or are you able to film) at consistent times of the day?** The position of the sun is very different between 10 a.m., 1 p.m., and 5 p.m. Sure, that point may seem obvious, but when you're filming, you may think in passing, "Yeah, we still have light." You do, but how are the shadows being cast? Do you have the same intensity of light as you did in earlier shots? You have a few more considerations when using nature as your light designer.

✔ **If you are investing in lighting, what kind of lighting is it?** Make sure you have enough of this lighting to give your podcast the right amount of warmth and depth. (See "Lighting fixtures," later in this practice.)

Set and wardrobe

Audio creates a theatre of the mind. With the right amount of Foley and effects (described in Practice 19), you can create any kind of setting — museum corridor, waterfront warehouse, deck of a pirate ship — but with video, if you don't have direct access to a desired setting, you have to build it or find the closest likeness to what you picture for the scene.

After finding the right setting, you need to decide whether you need props for your video podcast. If so, what is appropriate for your production? Will the host or screen talent get an opportunity to work with them beforehand or not?

Finally, you need to think about wardrobe. What will your on-screen talent be wearing? Audio gives podcasters the luxury of podcasting in whatever they are most comfortable in wearing. Khaki shorts? Pajamas? Au naturel? Whatever you want to do, you can do because it's audio — all the visuals are in your listeners' heads. With video, keep the following wardrobe considerations in mind:

✔ Stark whites can cause problems such as overexposure and ghosting of video. They can also be extremely difficult to light on account of glare, and even harder to watch.

✔ Stripes and plaids are horrific choices, especially when you are attempting to set a visual balance between the subject's wardrobe and the setting.

✔ When more than one host or actor is introduced into the podcast, the participants' clothing needs to work well together. You don't want it to clash, making for distracting colors (for example, a formal party setting where everyone is in black tuxedos, but one guy shows up in a pastel-colored tux).

✔ If you are working with blue- or green-screen mattes for special effects, this will dictate what your talent will be wearing in the production. *Blue-* or *green-screen* is where talent is placed in front of a backdrop of brilliant blue or lime-green, and a different backdrop or setting is placed behind them. Films such as *Sky Captain and The World of Tomorrow* and *300* were able to create "virtual sets" this way, but this also meant that the actors were prohibited from wearing shades of blue or green, which might destroy the illusion of the new setting.

On-screen persona and appearance

You might hear people jokingly say, "I have a face for podcasting . . . ," which is simply a variation on an old radio-industry joke.

Cruel but true: When you're video-podcasting, you have to evaluate the podcast's on-screen talent with visual impressions in mind:

✔ **How does your talent look?** This doesn't mean that your video podcast should be a "pretty people" parade, but the talent being filmed should accurately portray your podcast's image.

✔ **How relaxed and natural are they on camera?** You want your show host or company of actors to be relaxed, focused, and natural when on-camera, not tense and wooden. If your subjects appear uncomfortable, your audience may also feel uncomfortable watching your podcast.

✔ **What kind of makeup do you need?** Yes, even for the guys — *makeup*. Studio lights can catch glares off a person's skin, throwing off the white balance of your video equipment. Also, particularly as high-definition video grows in prominence, you have to watch for slight skin imperfections that stage makeup can correct temporarily.

Makeup brings its own questions and decisions: Do you have a makeup artist on your staff, or will you rely on the actors to provide their own makeup? If they do their own makeup, are the actors consistent in how they look? Is one host's makeup heavy and the other's nonexistent? Along with a balance in the wardrobe, there should be a balance in the makeup as well.

Podcast file size

Now we address the file itself. A standard audio podcast of roughly 28MB will cover around 30 minutes (so if you round up, 1MB = 1 minute). For many listeners, 30 minutes of audio is a lot to take in, particularly when compared to other podcasts that are far more economical in their running times.

With video, 28MB might buy you *three minutes,* depending on the compression settings. If you have a 30-minute podcast and are expecting to get your file down to the same size (or thereabouts), well . . . that just won't happen.

Keep in mind that video demands a lot more in playback because it's playing audio and moving images (29.97 images in one second of video, to be exact), and the audio data and video data also need to say in sync with one another. All these factors will cost you in data size and storage.

Keeping it simple is the Ninja way

One fantastic way of avoiding the problems of set, makeup, appearance, and (to some extent) lighting, is to dress your host in a ninja costume, shoot him or her from the waist up, and change the camera angles and tightness of close-ups in post-production.

Sound a little crazy? Who would watch such a podcast? Quite a few — as one ninja and his crew at Beatbox Giant discovered.

Ask a Ninja (shown in the following figure) is a five- to ten-minute video podcast hosted by . . . well, a ninja. In these five to ten minutes, the mysterious, masked host gives his take on television, politics, film, and just about anything people are asking him about. The end result is a hysterical monologue delivered with a katana-sharp wit and fall-over-dead-with-laughter timing.

Part of *Ask a Ninja*'s success can be attributed to the show's simplicity of concept: a host in a ninja costume, a static backdrop, basic lighting, one camera . . . and that's it. Where *Ask a Ninja* becomes a challenge is in its host. Without props, makeup, sets, or any other visuals, all the attention is on him. So, before following the way of the ninja, be certain you have the confidence, the talent, and the timing to pull off that kind of simplicity in your podcast.

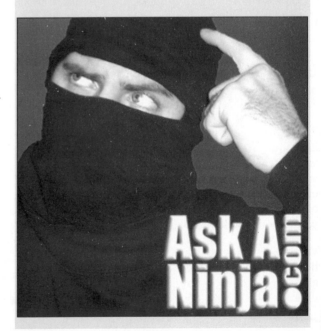

Bandwidth demands

As discussed elsewhere in this book, bandwidth can be costly, especially if your podcast is 50MB or higher per download. If you garner over 1,000 listeners, for example, you've gone through 5GB simply for that file transfer. If these 1,000 listeners are going through your archives, the bandwidth your podcast is burning through increases exponentially.

Now, suppose you decide to go for the longer running times for your podcast — and even dare to explore the possibilities of high-definition video podcasting. What happens? Your first episode is 100MB — a very hefty download.

It's even heftier if your podcast is a runaway success and you have 2,000 subscribers. In one week, you have used 200GB — and that's your first week. What about the weeks — and the listeners — to come? Depending on the kind of podcast you want to produce and the audience you want to win over, you'll want to plan for the bandwidth demands.

Particularly with long video podcasts, bandwidth is the sharpest of double-edged swords. You want the podcast to be a success, but that success means you have to work more bandwidth into your operations budget.

Giving Yourself Enough Time to Produce

Producing even a weekly audio podcast — especially if it requires a lot of editing and post-production — is a grueling schedule to keep. This is why, before launching your first podcast, you should have five episodes already completed and prepared for online distribution. By the time you have five in the can, you'll know the demands of your podcast up front.

Video podcasting, no matter how simple the production, can also be a chore — especially because video gives you much more to contend with than audio does. The reality of video podcasting is that podcasts like *Ask A Ninja, Tiki Bar TV,* and *Stranger Things* make this kind of podcasting look easier than it is.

Many of the video podcasts in production that dominate the iTunes top rankings have a crew involved or are simply television segments repackaged and distributed as video podcasts. If you are launching a video podcast independent of a studio, production house, or network, you may find the weekly schedule tough to follow; even with a support crew involved, a weekly schedule is nothing less than intense for everyone involved. By the time one episode is done, another one is already submitted for logging and rough cuts. Video podcasts may even shoot two episodes in one session, doubling the workload for crews as well as cast.

While nonlinear video applications such as Adobe Premiere Pro and Apple Final Cut have dramatically improved the productivity needed for video podcasting, it's still far from a pushbutton technology. Even with simple applications such as iMovie, you need lots of time to render the video and then output it in the desired format — be it podcasting, full-screen video, or DVD. Video created overnight or at the eleventh hour can be riddled with mistakes, continuity errors, sloppy edits, and small trips and tumbles that can affect the impression of the video.

The bottom line is that when you're making the decision to go video, make sure you give yourself time to shoot, time to edit, time to render, and time to review. Log in the time dedicated to those first five episodes of your video podcast — and from there, make the judgment call on what you want your podcast's posting schedule to be.

Exploring Studio Accessories for Video Podcasting

Suppose that your video podcast is a go, but you want to make sure your set is ready for filming. Along with prepping the set, you'll want to have your notes organized and ready for your day of shooting. As there can be more to an audio podcast than just a microphone and a recording application, a video podcast can be more than just a miniDV camera and a video editor.

Lighting fixtures

If you're planning to shoot indoors, the natural lighting coming in from outside may not be enough to illuminate your set and talent. This is when you need to go shopping for different lighting fixtures.

On-camera lighting can remedy a lot of indoor lighting issues, but it can also produce hard shadows on set pieces and background. You can invest in *directional lights* that stand on tripods (as in Figure 39-2) and then use *reflectors* to diffuse the light. (Reflectors are shiny umbrellas that soften the light being sent out by the directional units. This will effectively light your subject without creating harsh glares or shadows.) You can get many of these lights and accessories in kits, but the kits can be extremely costly, depending on what you need and what you want for your podcast.

Digital recorders

On-camera recording devices can be very good, but when your subjects are more than 2 feet away from the camera, their voices will sound hollow. This is why it is a good idea to record your sound on a different device than the video and then sync up the digitally recorded sound in post with your video.

Recording devices can be in plain view and part of the set, or you can use a mic attached to a *boom* (a horizontal support that suspends the mic over the on-screen talent, as shown in Figure 39-3). By capturing the sound independently, you can create a clear reproduction of the audio instead of having to rely on built-in camera microphones (which tend to pick up additional room ambience).

• **Figure 39-2: Directional lighting units, like the one pictured here, can cut down on unwanted shadows or add light to a setting.**

• **Figure 39-3: Boom mics give the sound crew (like Jeff Traywick of Stranger Things, pictured here) the ability to stay out of the video while extending mics closer to the talent.**

When using boom mics, it can be difficult to determine how low can you position the microphone before it is visible on-screen. On many miniDV and HD-DV cameras, the view screen has two sets of boxes visible. The outside box is known as an *Action-Safe Margin,* and the inside box is the *Title Safe Margin,* as shown in Figure 39-4. If your boom mic is outside of the Action-Safe Margins, the microphone will not be seen because anything beyond that margin is cropped out. Using the Title Safe margins during your shoots gives you an idea where captions and IDs will be placed in post-production. In both Premiere and Final Cut, you can view Action and Title Safe Margins — and place text accordingly — or enlarge the video in order to crop out any unexpected "mic in picture" moments.

attributed to the unsteadiness of the hand-held camera, which became an effective way to heighten the scary realism of the movie. However, if you'd rather not take the "reality TV" approach to your video podcasting, tripods are a terrific investment for your camera equipment.

When shopping for tripods, you will probably notice $10 tripods propped next to a $100 tripod *stand.* Videographers will tell you, "Your video will look like it was shot on a $10 tripod."

The higher-grade tripods are more stable, you can more easily pan the camera while filming, and their meters allow you to achieve more level angles for a camera on uneven ground (see Figure 39-5 for an example). Look at all the functions offered — and then consider what kind of tripod will work best for your video podcast.

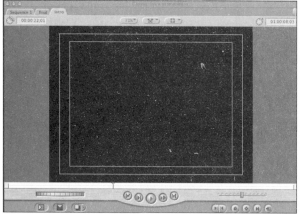

• Figure 39-4: Action Safe and Title Margins appear in both Final Cut (pictured here) and Premiere in order to give you an idea of what televisions will display and what will be cropped out.

Tripods

While *The Blair Witch Project* has been picked on, parodied, and poked fun at, it was an innovative film because it was primarily shot with hand-held cameras. Coupled with the incredible hype of the film, its accomplishments were impressive: An independent film *shot and produced on a podcaster's budget* earned millions at the box office. Some of its success can be

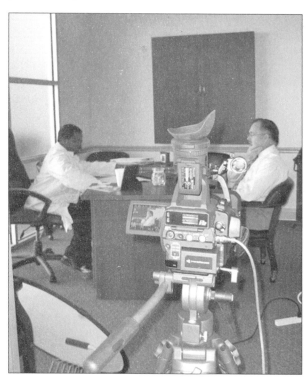

• Figure 39-5: On the set of Stranger Things (www. strangerthings.tv), tripods like the one pictured here ensure still, stationary shots.

Shooting schedules

A daily shooting schedule is important not only for you but for your cast and crew as well. Will you be shooting the podcast in a linear fashion, or will you be shooting (for example) specific interviews or scenes based on the availability of the subjects or cast members involved?

Shooting schedules are a real benefit to your video podcast. They make clear to you and your company (or, if you're a one-stop shop for a podcast, just you) what the agenda is for the day and what you're going to accomplish with the available time, light, and resources. They also serve as hard-copy progress reports for you on what you'll be shooting, what you accomplish, and what you need to reschedule if something isn't quite right. Shooting schedules are your road map for the day. Implement them.

Putting together a shooting schedule "just for a video podcast" may seem a bit excessive, but if you want to take your video podcast up a notch from Public Access television or the often-mentioned *Wayne's World,* the effort is worth it. The podcast you create is as professional as you make it, and by applying some of the Hollywood approaches to things (lighting, makeup, shooting schedules), you can make the video-podcasting experience a positive and productive one. To find out more about working in video on a shoestring budget (Wow, you got it in your budget for new shoestrings?!), check out Stephanie Cottrell Bryant's *Videoblogging For Dummies* (Wiley).

When to Say, "That's a Wrap!"

Whether you are using Adobe Premiere Pro or Apple Final Cut Pro (covered in Practices 40 and 41), you'll have a good idea of the planning and production demands of a video podcast after editing 20 seconds (okay, 20 and some change) of video. Video production may seem like a lot of hard work, but it might surprise you when you edit your first video and then note the episode's running time. Time flies not only when you edit video but also when you review your work. You think, "I'm halfway through my first episode . . .," and suddenly notice that your podcast is nearing the 20-minute mark.

As with any podcast (video or otherwise), brevity is the soul of wit. As discussed earlier in this practice, video demands more production time and — after posting — more storage and bandwidth. So, before launching your video podcast, it may be a good idea to look at your *first* episode (not the first five episodes, but the *very first* episode you complete in your choice video editor) and consider the production schedule you're creating as well as the commitment you're asking from an audience.

Many independently produced video podcasts rarely break the ten-minute ceiling for their running times. These quick, down-and-dirty podcasts are the most popular video podcasts. Shows like the earlier mentioned *Tiki Bar TV* (http://tikibartv.com), *Ask a Ninja* (http://askaninja.com), and *The Onion News Network* (http://theonion.com) are easy (and yes, we're using "easy" as a relative term here) to produce on a regular basis, can require very little in terms of production demands, and are fast downloads for subscribers.

The short-and-sweet video podcasts demand less of a commitment from the viewing audience. A subscriber can watch a few video podcasts on a work break or maybe sneak in a "viewing block" when stuck in rush hour traffic. A video podcast's short running time is one aspect of a show's popularity, be it an audio or a video podcast. If you can keep the running time of your podcast to ten minutes or less, your listenership can be dramatically larger than that of a podcast that sports episodes running 45 minutes to an hour on average.

The Doctor is in!

Tiki Bar TV (shown in the following figure) was one of the early adopters of podcasting with video, and with every episode, this company of wayward actors has taken an unlikely ten minutes to incredible heights of slapstick humor and special effects.

Perhaps *Tiki Bar*'s finest moment concerning what you can do with video podcasting on a writing, performance, and post-production level was "Episode 20: The Son of the Internet." In just seven minutes, this episode managed to parody the overnight development of technology, soap operas, the Internet, Internet-speak, and the Disney film, *Tron*.

Oh, and the episode teaches you how to make the "Short Fuse" cocktail. All this, in seven minutes.

With the improv, blooper-esque chuckles, and creative mixology at the bar, Dr. Tiki, Johnny Johnny, and La La produced an impressive (and extremely funny) installment of Tiki Bar TV — and proved just what you can accomplish in a short video podcast.

 Shorter running times always equate to larger audiences because audiences can quickly consume an episode or two and then return to the podcast later in the day, week, or month, and consume another few episodes.

The major downside of the short podcast is that you have little to no room to explore tangents, establish subplots in your episodes, or introduce a large number of characters, guests, or show hosts without taking the chance of cramming too much in a single episode. Podcasts that keep it quick and brief also keep it simple.

And when you see longer podcasts like *Stranger Things* (http://strangerthings.tv), *Missing Pages* (http://speaking-pictures.com/missingPages.html), and *Martial Arts Explorer* (http://martialartsexplorer.thepodcast network.com), the advantages (and the rewards) of longer running times and intense video production become clear. After you find the desired effect of your video podcast, commit to it; but make certain you are putting in the right amount of time and effort for your video podcast. The end result, whether brief or epic in its presentation, will be worth the investment.

Editing Your Video Podcast with Adobe Premiere

In This Practice

✔ Editing video with Adobe Premiere Pro

✔ Adding titles to your video

✔ Exporting video for podcasting

Adobe Premiere Pro is one of the first applications to affordably bring the art of video editing to the home computer. Some high-end video-editing software programs (and their accompanying systems) cost tens of thousands of dollars, but Adobe Premiere costs less than $800. Its nonlinear editing capabilities are used widely for creating video in-house for broadcast, podcast, and other means of distribution. (*In-house* means that instead of farming out the video for editing elsewhere, the video is produced and output at your place of work, in your home, or by you personally wherever you work on it.) For in-house Windows users, Adobe Premiere Pro is the editing tool of choice.

The curtain is up, the stage is ready, and now you're ready to create a diamond from the rough footage you've amassed. In this chapter, we cover what you need to get started editing in Adobe Premiere Pro.

Editing Video in Adobe Premiere Pro

Adobe Premiere Pro (shown in Figure 40-1) is the must-have video editor for Windows users, offering sharp transitions between scenes, an array of effects, and various output formats for broadcast, podcasting, and other forms of playback. Adobe Premiere Pro even lets you color-correct oddly lit video footage.

Keep in mind, this practice will not make you fluent in Premiere. This practice assumes that you have the footage already shot, captured, and imported into your computer. Premiere Pro has many excellent features, but for this title, we are covering the basics of editing.

The DVD accompanying this book includes a directory for Practice 40. The clips and titles found here are for the introduction to Man Vs. Child (a parody of The Discovery Channel's Man Vs. Wild), filmed by Dancing Cat Studios and Tee Morris. With these clips, you can use Adobe Premiere to re-create an introduction for this mockumentary.

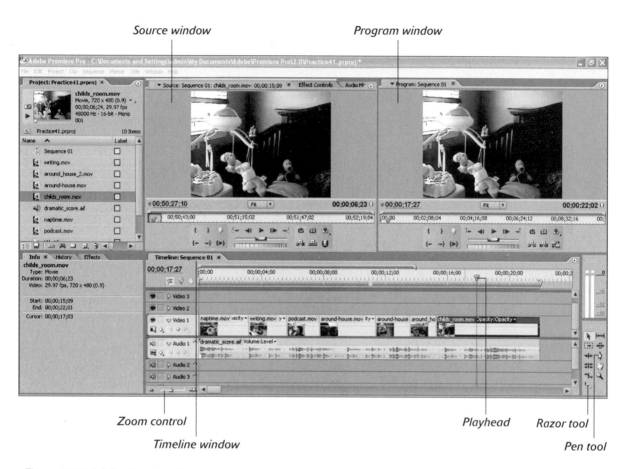

Source window   Program window

Zoom control   Playhead   Razor tool

Timeline window   Pen tool

• **Figure 40-1: Adobe Premiere Pro.**

Getting the files for the video podcast

Because the sample video has already been shot
and captured in a digital format that your PC can
understand, you can now import the files into your
project:

1. **Copy the Practice 40 folder from this book's
   DVD onto your PC.**

2. **Launch Premiere Pro.**

3. **From the introduction window, click New
   Project.**

   By default, your selected preset is Standard 48
   kHz, which is what you need for this project.

4. **Select a location for the project and name it**
   Practice 40**.**

5. **Choose File⇨Import and import the Practice 40
   folder.**

   To import an entire folder, browse for it on your
   PC, click it, and then click the Import Folder button on the lower-right side of your screen.

6. **Expand the Practice 40 *bin* (the editing term
   for a folder) so you can review its contents:**

   ▶ around-house.avi

   ▶ around-house_2.avi

   ▶ childs_room.avi

▶ dramatic_score.wav

▶ naptime.avi

▶ podcast.avi

▶ title.tif

▶ voiceover.wav

▶ writing.avi

7. **In the Practice 40 bin, find the** MvC-intro_ final.avi **file. Review it in either QuickTime or Premiere so you know what your final should look like.**

Video History 101

The term *linear editing* refers to video editing done between two playback decks and a third central deck that compiles the material into one master tape. In linear editing studios, you can perform basic transitions (fades, wipes, and iris transitions) from one video source to another and (with upgrades, of course) create inset video. The downside of linear editing is that because the edits follow a linear progression, you have to edit the video in the exact order of the clips you want to compile — from beginning to end. If you want to add any new footage, you must find that point in the video, add in the new footage, and then re-edit the whole film from that point on. By contrast, Premiere and Final Cut (covered in Practice 41) are *nonlinear* editors: You can edit the video footage in any order you prefer. You can add more footage (or new footage) by simply cutting, dragging, and replacing — no re-edits required. Simply drag, drop, and replace.

With your files in the Project window, you're ready to edit your footage.

 If you're working in video- or audio-editing applications with only one monitor, you tend to lose screen real estate inside that monitor very quickly as all the panels, tool boxes, and project files proliferate. An inexpensive alternative to pricey 30-inch flat-screen monitors is to invest in a second monitor and a *video accelerator card* (such as the NVIDIA GeForce7300GT or the Radeon X1600 Pro). Accelerators add monitor ports to your computer so you can connect additional monitors.

Using two monitors, you dedicate one to panels and the other to the project's Timeline and preview. Accelerator cards are inexpensive, easy to install, and only a fraction of the investment you'd have to make if you brought home a cinema-style display. The two-monitor approach also puts to good use any extra monitors you may have tucked away.

Taking the first steps with Premiere Pro

Now that you have your resources in place, you're ready to edit. These steps lay the foundation for your introduction:

1. **In the Project window, find** dramatic_ score.wav **and double-click it.**

The audio appears in the Source window.

2. **Click the Source window, and then press the spacebar or click the Play button to review the audio.**

The Source window is where you perform simple edits (such as designate In and Out points) and place markers in your video for specific cues. In this window, you are going to designate an Out point in the audio to indicate where the theme music ends.

3. **Click the Go to In Point button or press the Home key on your keyboard to return to the beginning of the audio.**

If you look just under the timecode indicators of the Source window, you should see the *Zoom Control* bar.

4. **Click and drag the right end of the Zoom Control to the left to zoom in on your audio.**

Figure 40-1 shows the Zoom Control in the Timeline window.

5. **Press the right-arrow key once to hear the opening drum strike. At the moment of the first drum strike, place a marker by clicking the Set Unnumbered Marker tool (see Figure 40-2).**

With your arrow keys, you can *scrub* through audio and video. Scrubbing is the process of listening and viewing audio at a user-designated speed. You scan through segments, find what you're looking for, and make edits.

6. **If you need to, zoom out from your audio and then press the spacebar to review the audio again.**

As the audio begins to play, watch for `00:00:22;00`.

In the timecode, you'll notice semicolons in between the numbers. The semicolons indicate Premiere is working in Drop-Frame Timecode, a certain kind of timing standard that keeps audio and video in sync. The timecode breaks down this way — hours; minutes; seconds; frames. Use the timecode to keep track of where you are in the Timeline.

7. **Just after** `00:00:22;00`, **when you hear a guitarlike instrument begin playing, stop playback.**

8. **Use the arrow keys to scrub backward in your audio to exactly** `00:00:22;00`.

You can see where you are in the timecode by using the *Current Timecode Indicator* (the numbers in blue) found on the left side of the Source window.

9. **At** `00:00:22;00`, **click the Set Out Point button (see Figure 40-2) in the Source window or press O on your keyboard.**

You have now designated a new Out (or end) point for your audio.

10. **In the Source window, click the Overlay Edit button (see Figure 40-2) to place your audio in the A1 Audio 1 Track in your Timeline.**

Notice that the audio you've marked — and to which you've given a new Out point — now reflects those changes. This process of making simple edits and changes before placing the file in the timeline is called *trimming*.

Additionally, you will be performing *Overlay* edits, where you place one track of video over audio without changing the running time. Performing Overlay edits is a bit like layering images in Photoshop, only you're doing it with video.

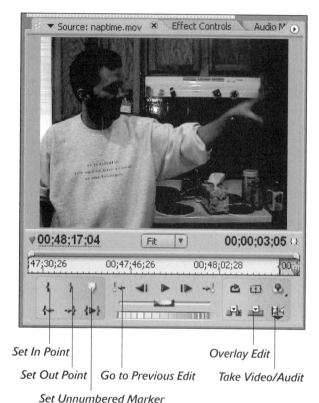

Set In Point
Set Out Point | Go to Previous Edit
Set Unnumbered Marker
Overlay Edit
Take Video/Audit

• **Figure 40-2: New In and Out points show up in the Timeline ruler.**

Your score is in place. You can now begin placing video in the timeline.

11. **In the Project window, double-click** `naptime.avi` **and review the clip in the Source window by clicking the Play button or pressing the spacebar.**

For this opening clip, you need only the final few seconds.

12. **When you've reached the end of the clip, use the arrow keys to scrub back to** `00:00:45;20`. **Make this the new In point of your video by clicking the Set In Point button (see Figure 40-2) or pressing I on your keyboard.**

When you designate new In and Out points in your video, Premiere indicates the change in the clip's Timeline ruler.

13. **Scrub forward to** `00:00:48;17` **and click the Set Out Point button or press the O key.**

Next, you need to tell Premiere that you need only the video from this clip.

14. **Click the Toggle Take Video/Audio icon once to get the filmstrip icon (Take Video).**

In the lower-right corner of the Source window, you see an icon of a filmstrip and an audio speaker. This is the Toggle Take Video/Audio option (refer to Figure 40-2).

If you click the icon again, you get the speaker icon (Take Audio). Click it a third time if you want both Video and Audio.

15. **Press the Home key on your keyboard to return to the beginning of the timeline and then use the Zoom slider to zoom in.**

You'll want to view it in two-second increments. You can tell this by looking at the timeline ruler extending across the top of the Timeline window.

 You're viewing in two-second increments when the numbers read `00:00:02;00`, `00:00:04;00`, `00:00:06;00`, and so on across the Timeline window.

16. **In the Timeline window, click and drag the playhead (the small blue object connected to the edit line, located in the Timeline ruler; refer to Figure 40-1) to the right until it reaches the marker in the audio.**

This is one way to perform an *Overlay* edit.

17. **Click and drag the clip from the Source window into the Program window, as shown in Figure 40-3.**

When you release the mouse button, this clip appears in the Timeline.

18. **Save your project by either choosing File⇨Save Project or pressing Ctrl+S.**

Now that you've completed these steps, you have the basics under your belt. In the next section, you complete the video portion of this *Man vs. Child* introduction.

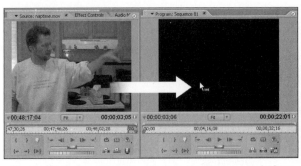

• **Figure 40-3: Dragging the clip into the Program window.**

Finishing the video portion of the introduction

You have successfully taken your first steps toward putting together this introduction. Now continue to build on this project by completing the video portion:

1. **In the Project window, click the name of Sequence 1 and change it to read** Intro.

It's a good idea to change the name so that you can see at a glance what this sequence is.

2. **Still in the Project window, double-click the** `writing.avi` **clip.**

The clip appears in the Source window.

3. **Click Play or press the spacebar to review the clip.**

 This may seem to be some of the driest, dullest video footage ever captured by a camera on a tripod, but what you're looking for are some moments to use as *b-roll* — footage you've already shot that can serve as background video for titles, establishing shots, or montage clips (as in this opening). B-roll is good to have on hand; if you don't have any, you can always find stock video footage online, some offered for free (`www.free stockfootage.com`) and some available for purchase (`www.digitaljuice.com`).

In these next steps, you will trim the clips by setting various In and Out points, taking only what you need from the footage.

4. Find the point in this clip's Timeline of `00:00:47;06`; make this the clip's new In point by clicking the Set In Point tool or by pressing I on your keyboard.

5. Progress forward to `00:00:49;08` and mark this clip as your new Out point by clicking the Set Out Point tool or by pressing O on your keyboard.

6. Toggle the Take Video/Audio icon to take video only, and then press the period (.) key on your keyboard to perform an Overlay edit.

7. Return to the Project window and double-click the `podcast.avi` clip. Play this clip to review it.

8. Progress to `00:00:09;07` in the clip and make this your new In point by clicking the Set In Point tool or by pressing I on your keyboard.

9. Progress to `00:00:11;15` in the clip and make this your new Out point, using one of the two methods mentioned in Step 5.

10. Toggle the Take Video/Audio to take only video, and then press the period (.) key on your keyboard or the Overlay Edit button to perform an Overlay edit.

Note that because you've left the source and destination tracks disconnected, you're importing only video (which is what you need).

11. In the Project window, double-click the `around-house.avi` clip and review the clip.

From this segment, you will extract two clips. This method is used in nonlinear editing to allow you to grab multiple clips from one long shot.

12. Progress to `00:00:42;24` in the clip and make this your new In point, using one of the two methods illustrated in Step 4.

13. Go to `00:00:45;20` in the clip and make this your new Out point, using one of the two methods illustrated in Step 5.

14. Toggle the Take Video/Audio to take only video and then perform an Overlay edit.

15. Return to the Source window and progress to `00:01:35;03` in the clip and make this your

new In point, using one of the two methods illustrated in Step 4.

16. Progress to `00:01:37;15` in the clip and make this your new Out point, using one of the two methods illustrated in Step 5.

 When you established the new In point in this clip — beyond the previous In and Out points you set back in Steps 11 through 12 — the points were removed, and a new In point was established. If you make new In points after previously established Out points, Premiere resets the clip and allows you to work outside of an earlier-designated range. The same is true if you set new Out points earlier in a clip than previously established In points.

17. Perform an Overlay edit, using one of the two methods featured in this practice.

Note that the clip in your timeline is unaffected. When you bring a clip from a source of video and incorporate it into a timeline, the clip becomes independent of the original source material. Therefore you can make new edit points in the original source material without affecting what is already in play in the Timeline. The only time clips set in the Timeline are affected is if the original source clip's location in the computer changes, or if the original source clip is deleted or replaced. Provided your source material remains where it is logged and captured, you can pull multiple clips from that single source.

18. In the Project window, double-click the `around-house_2.avi` clip and review the clip.

19. Progress to `00:00:02;07` in the clip and make this your new In point, using one of the two methods illustrated in Step 4.

20. Progress to `00:00:03;09` in the clip and make this your new Out point, using one of the two methods illustrated in Step 5.

21. Perform an Overlay edit, using one of the two methods featured in Step 10.

22. In the Project window, double-click the `childs_room.avi` clip and review the clip.

Because you're using this footage as b-roll, start from the beginning of the clip so you already have your In point.

23. Progress to `00:00:06;05` **in the clip and make this your new Out point, using one of the two methods illustrated in Step 5.**

24. **Perform an Overlay edit using one of the methods featured in Step 10.**

25. **Save your project. After saving your work, click your Timeline window, press the Home key on your keyboard, and press the spacebar to review your work up to this point.**

And you're done! Well, with the video part anyway. You have completed the basic video edits needed for the *Man Vs. Child* introduction. The next order of business is to go through the video and set opening titles, adjust audio levels, and incorporate voice-overs by using a powerful recording tool built into Premiere.

Adding titles

Opening titles are your opening credits. You can feature the production companies involved, talent, and the title of the podcast, or just open with the title of the podcast as you will do here. Titles can simply appear and disappear on the screen, or they can fly in and out of view.

In the following steps, you not only incorporate an opening graphic for the podcast, but also alter the accompanying video (providing background for the title) for extra drama:

1. **In the Timeline window, double-click the last clip of the child's room with the mobile in the foreground.**

By double-clicking the clip in the Timeline, you're now making changes to the clip in play. Any changes you now make to the clip in the Source window will be reflected in the Timeline.

You can determine whether you're working on an original source clip or a clip from the Timeline by looking at the source's tab. If you

see the sequence's name and timecode in the tab, you're working with a clip from the Timeline (as shown in Figure 40-4), not the original source. A clip from the original source is identified only by its name.

2. **Select the Effects tab to view possible options for this clip.**

3. **In the Effects window, choose Video Effects⇨Blur & Sharpen⇨Gaussian Blur. Click and drag this filter into the Timeline, onto the** `childs_room.avi` **clip. Then click the Effects Controls tab nested within the Source window.**

4. **Expand the filter's options and click and drag the slider for Radius to 15.**

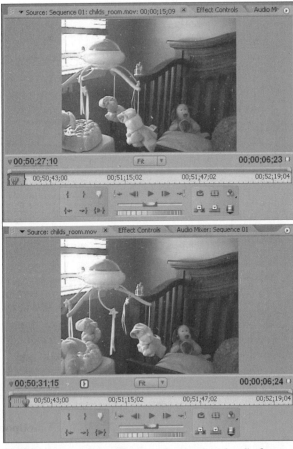

• **Figure 40-4: A clip in the Timeline (top) and a clip from the original source (bottom).**

What you get is a blur effect, 15 pixels wide, across the whole video clip. When you put the playhead in the clip that you're applying the filter to, you can apply changes to the filter in the Source window and watch the changes occur in the Program window — in real time.

5. **In the Program window, click the Go to Previous Edit button (refer to Figure 40-2) to go to the start of this clip.**

6. **Expand the Motion option in the Effects Controls window.**

To simulate a slight camera pan and a zoom in, you're going to apply *keyframes* to the clip and make adjustments. Keyframes are moments you designate in the Timeline when something is changing. By using keyframes, you will simulate a zoom-out of the background.

You see a button (a grayed-out stopwatch) next to certain motion parameters (Scale, Position, Rotation, and so on). These are your *Toggle Animation* buttons, as shown in Figure 40-5.

7. **Click the Toggle Animation button for the Scale and Position options.**

8. **In the lower-left corner of the Effects Controls window, click the Current Timecode field to select the timecode, type in +300, and then press Enter.**

Doing so advances you three seconds ahead in your clip.

Active columns of diamond-shaped buttons appear in this interface. These are the *Add/Remove Keyframe* tools (see Figure 40-5); you use them to designate keyframes in a clip or on the Timeline.

9. **With the Motion options, establish two new keyframes at this point by clicking the Add/ Remove Keyframes tools for Scale and Position.**

Using the Motion options to add keyframes and adjust parameters are handy ways to change size, rotation, and opacity in a clip, as shown in Figure 40-5.

Next to the Add/Remove Keyframes tool (the diamond icon), you should see two triangles, one pointing left and the other pointing right. These are the Go to Previous Keyframe and Go to Next Keyframe tools (see Figure 40-5).

10. **Click the (now active) Go to Previous Keyframe tool to go back to the first keyframes you created.**

You can pick any of the attributes to which you gave keyframes, and click the Go to Previous Keyframe tool to go back to an earlier keyframe.

11. **In the Scale section of the Motion options, move the slider to the right until it reads** 165 **in the Scale field.**

Or simply type **165** in the field.

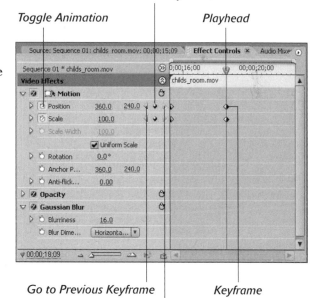

• Figure 40-5: Using keyframes to change size, rotation, and opacity in a clip.

12. Move your mouse to the Program window. Click and drag the mouse pointer up and to the left until the out-of-focus image of the stuffed dog appears just off-center on your screen.

You can also type **197.6** and **96.2** into the Position fields to reposition the video.

13. Save your project. Then change the size of your windows (if necessary) in order to view the Video 2 track above the main video you've been working with.

14. From the Project window, click and drag the `title.tif` file into the Video 2 track, placing it to the right of the playhead.

If needed, trim the clip to end with the video. You can do this by placing your cursor on the end of the title clip in the Timeline and clicking and dragging its end point back to where the footage of the child's room ends.

15. If needed, click and drag the playhead back to the ending video clip of the child's room.

The title — *Man vs. Child* — is now superimposed over the soft-focus b-roll of the child's room.

Animating the title

You now have a title for the podcast; but for even more punch, animate it. Follow these steps to fly in the title from off-screen:

1. Click the Go to Previous Edit button in the Program window to go back to the beginning of this clip with the out-of-focus child's room and title.

2. Double-click the new title clip you just incorporated into the Timeline and then establish keyframes (as you did in the previous section) for the following:

▶ Scale

▶ Rotation

▶ Position

3. In the Current Timecode field (in the lower-left corner of the Effects Controls window), type +100 to advance one second into the title clip. Add keyframes here as well.

4. Click Go to Previous Keyframe in the Motion options.

You're now at the beginning keyframes of the title clip.

5. In the Rotation section of the Motion options, type –21 in the field and press Enter.

6. In the Scale section of the Motion options, move the slider to the right until it reads 525 in the Scale field.

Or simply type in **525** in the field.

7. In the Position section of the Motion options, type –254.1 and 614.3 into the fields to reposition the title.

The Motion interface shows a graphic representation of the changes you make — and where they happen in the Timeline — as shown in Figure 40-6.

8. Click the Go to Next Keyframe tool in the Motion options.

9. Go to Scale and type 95 in the Scale field.

10. Save your project. Then press Enter to render the video and its animation.

Fantastic! Your video is almost done. You have compiled the clips and completed the animation for the title, and everything is looking good. All that remains are the final touches with the audio. As soon as you complete this task, the video will be ready for exporting into a solid video-podcasting format.

Adding the final touches

"Final touches? What? I'm not done?"

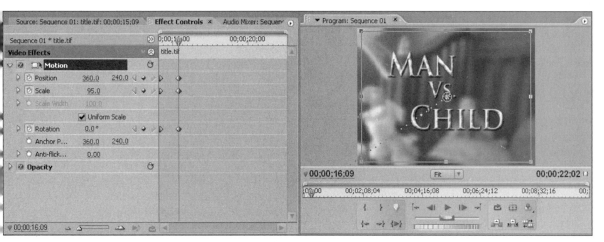

• Figure : The Motion interface helps you keep track of your simple animations.

It's all about the details. You have a voiceover track and an abrupt ending of the video. With only a few quick edits and the application of an audio effect, your video will be ready for the exporting and compression to a video podcast format:

1. **Your playhead should be at the end of the audio. If it is not, click and drag the playhead to the end of the video.**

2. **In the Effects window, close the open folders and then choose Audio Transitions⤳Crossfade⤳ Constant Power. Click and drag this transition to the end of the audio clip.**

   The end of the audio now has a transition in place that will fade out your music on cue when you review it, as illustrated in Figure 40-7.

3. **In the Timeline window, place your cursor at the end of the title clip and extend it to match with the end of the audio. Repeat this step for the video of the child's room.**

4. **In the Effects window, close the open Audio Transition folder and then choose Video Transitions⤳Dissolve⤳Cross Dissolve. Click and drag this transition to the end of both the video and title clips.**

The transitions should appear to extend *beyond* the video and audio, deeper into the Timeline. Because there is no video here to transition to, Premiere will render this as a Fade to Black.

5. **Save your project. Then press Enter to render the video and its animation.**

   The video will play automatically, and you can review the changes you have made.

6. **Press the Home key on your keyboard to return to the beginning, and then click and drag the** `voiceover.wav` **file into Audio 2.**

   The voiceover will be the following:

   My name is Tee Morris. I am a science fiction/fantasy author and podcaster. My wife has left me alone with my two-year-old. I will show you the skills on how to survive.

With the voiceover for this introduction in place, the next step is to break this one long audio segment into smaller segments — allowing precise timing for when the voiceover comes in with the video's action. Here's what those steps look like:

1. **From the Tool Palette, click the Razor Blade tool (refer to Figure 40-1).**

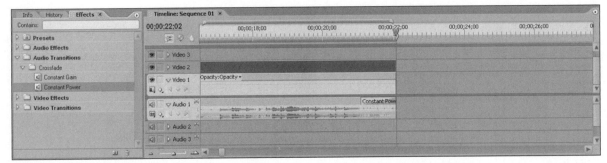

• Figure 40-7: The audio transition Constant Power creates fade-outs to other audio or silence.

2. Look in the Timeline window and expand the audio track, if necessary. Review the voiceover's *waveform* (the graphic representation of sound) and note the flatline gaps within your voiceover.

These gaps of silence are where you want to apply the Razor Blade tool. Find the first gap between "My name is Tee Morris" and "I am a science fiction . . . " and click anywhere in the pause between these two points.

3. Repeat Step 2 throughout the voiceover clip. When you're finished, you should have six clips (as shown in Figure 40-8).

4. Choose the Selection tool from the Tool Palette.

5. Click the last audio clip, which should be silence after " . . . on how to survive." Then delete the clip by pressing Delete or Backspace.

6. Place your Selection tool at the beginning of your first segment of the voiceover. Shorten this segment in two stages:

  a. *Click and drag its In point closer to the beginning of the audio.*

  b. *Click and drag its Out point closer to the end of the audio segment.*

7. Repeat these steps for the other voiceover segments so that your voiceover recording looks like Figure 40-9.

8. In the Timeline window's Current Timecode (in the upper-left corner of the Timeline window), click to select the Timecode and type 100 to place your playhead at 00:00:01;00. Position the beginning of audible voiceover (where you see something in the waveform) at this point.

9. Click the Page Down key to advance to the next edit point in your Timeline. Advance in your project until you reach the In point of the writing.avi clip.

10. Position the In Point of the audio segment for "I am a science fiction/fantasy author . . . " at the edit point.

11. Using the Page Down key, advance in the Timeline to the In point to the clip of Tee and his daughter mugging for the camera. Move the "My wife has left me alone . . . " audio to begin at this point.

12. Using the Page Down key, advance in the Timeline to the In point to the clip of Tee shot at the angle of a "follow camera." Move the "I'm going to show you the skills . . . " audio to begin at this point.

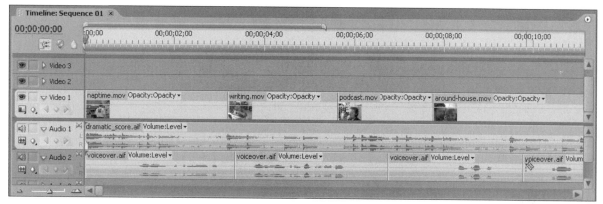

• Figure 40-8: Use the Razor Blade tool to divide the long voiceover file into clips.

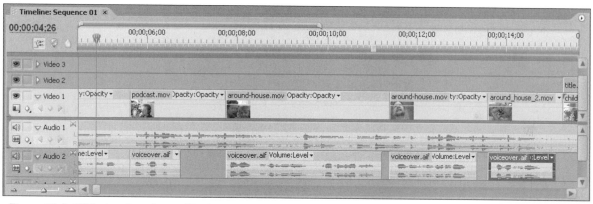

• Figure 40-9: With the clips trimmed in the Timeline, you can easily place the audio at precise moments in the video.

13. Using the Page Down key, advance in the Timeline to the In point to the clip of Tee's daughter. Move the "On how to survive" audio to begin at this point.

14. Press the Home key to return to the beginning of the Timeline.

15. Go to the Tool Palette and select the Pen tool (refer to Figure 40-1).

This is the tool used for placing control points in the audio.

16. With the Pen Tool, click at the beginning of the audio to establish your first control point.

 You can always zoom in using the Zoom slider and do more detailed work in tighter time increments without severe eye/neck/back strain. Take advantage of that Zoom slider when you can!

17. In the Timeline's Current Timecode field, type 100. Using the Pen Tool, click here to establish your next control point.

18. Place your Pen Tool on top of this new control point.

You'll notice that the Pen Tool icon becomes a large plus sign (+). Now you can adjust the point to a new volume.

19. **Click and drag this control point to –16 dB.**

Using the audio editors and the control points, you have adjusted the volume to be softer when the voiceover begins.

20. **Save your project. Then press Enter on your keyboard to render a preview of the video.**

The video plays automatically.

Congratulations! You're done! Your video is edited, complete with fade-outs, titles, and now voiceovers. All that's left to do is export the video for podcasting purposes.

Exporting Your Video for Podcasting

Here we're assuming you're exporting to iTunes. Before you do, remember that iTunes accepts video for playback the following formats:

- ✔ `.mp4`
- ✔ `.m4v`
- ✔ `.mov`

 Just because iTunes can play a video doesn't mean that your iPod can follow suit. To play on an iPod, the video must be compressed in a certain way. So far you've gotten a good start on preparing your Premiere files for podcasting.

Here are the tech specs that your video has to meet before you can export it from Premiere:

- ✔ A screen resolution not to exceed 640 × 480 (4:3 standard ratio) or 640 × 360 (16:9 widescreen ratio)
- ✔ 30 fps (frames per second)
- ✔ H.264 codec (either 1.5 Mbps or 768 kbps)

  A *codec* is compression for video. Many video codecs are available. For video podcasting, you will be using H.264.

- ✔ 48 Khz, stereo audio

The end result is a file with the `.m4v` extension — and that means you have a video that's ready for video podcasting.

To export that file from Premiere, here's what you need to do:

1. **Click anywhere in your Timeline window and choose File⇨Export⇨Adobe Media Encoder to access the Adobe Media Encoder.**

2. **Choose Format⇨QuickTime.**

The Adobe Media Encoder (shown in Figure 40-10) is a built-in video compressor that gives you myriad options for exporting your video for DVD, podcasting, or online downloads.

3. **In the Video Codec section, select the codec H.264.**

4. **In the Basic Video Settings section, change the Frame Width to 320 and the Frame Height to 240. Scroll down to just underneath the Basic Video Settings to see Bitrate Settings. Set Bitrate Settings to 128.**

5. **In the Export Settings section, click the disc icon to save this new preset. In the Choose Name window that appears (see Figure 40-11), label these settings Video Podcasting.**

6. **Click OK to accept the new preset you've created and then click OK to begin encoding.**

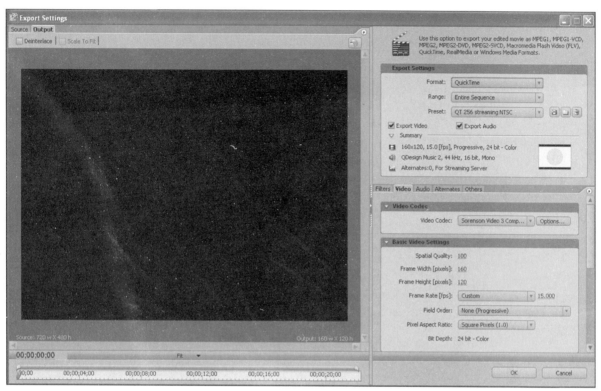

• **Figure 40-10: The Adobe Media Encoder.**

7. Import the `.mov` file you just created into iTunes. iTunes will list it under Movies. Right-click it and select Convert Selection for iPod.

8. Right-click the new video that iTunes just created and then choose Get Info⟳Info to edit and complete ID3 tags.

And that's it. You're done creating your first video podcast episode in Adobe Premiere Pro. The steps may seem numerous, but nonlinear editing quickly becomes second nature as you do it. From here, you can now shoot, edit, and produce your podcast at will. Good luck!

Apple's QuickTime (www.quicktime.com) is regarded as a Mac thing — but a Windows version of the popular media player is available. Also, for an upgrade of $30 USD, the QT Player can be upgraded to a QT *Pro* version. The Pro version offers extra features, not the least of which is exporting video and audio to various formats (including Export to iPod). Instead of the multistep process we outlined previously, you can prepare a file for podcasting in a matter of a few clicks. For more on this nifty procedure, look at Practice 41.

• **Figure 40-11: You can save your settings in the Adobe Media Encoder for future episodes.**

Editing Your Video Podcast with Apple Final Cut Pro

In This Practice

✔ Editing video with Apple Final Cut Pro

✔ Compressing video from Final Cut Pro

In 2000, Apple entered the nonlinear editing market with Final Cut Pro to stand toe-to-toe with the major players of video editing. Today, Final Cut Pro continues to gain ground; it's a contender for becoming a new standard in video editing. With tons of drag-and-drop capabilities for video editing, an easy-to-follow export process, and the functions of Final Cut Studio 2's supporting cast members (Soundtrack Pro, Motion, and so on) bundled with it, this application is ready to deliver video podcasting in a matter of a few mouse clicks. At $1,300 USD, the Final Cut Studio may give you sticker shock, but we're talking pro-level tools here. When you consider the other applications bundled with it, you get a lot in that beautiful black box for that price. If it's still too pricey for your taste, you can pony up $299 USD for Final Cut Express HD, which offers the basics for video podcasters at an affordable price.

Welcome to nonlinear editing, Apple style!

Editing Video with Final Cut Pro

Final Cut Pro from Apple, part of the Final Cut Studio 2 suite, offers an elegant and efficient interface (as shown in Figure 41-1). The exporting options for video editors make the editing process easy.

On the companion DVD, you will find a directory for Practice 41. The clips and titles are for the introduction to *Man vs. Child*, a parody of The Discovery Channel's *Man vs. Wild* (filmed by Tee Morris and Dancing Cat Studios). With these clips, you will re-create the opening of this spoof with Final Cut.

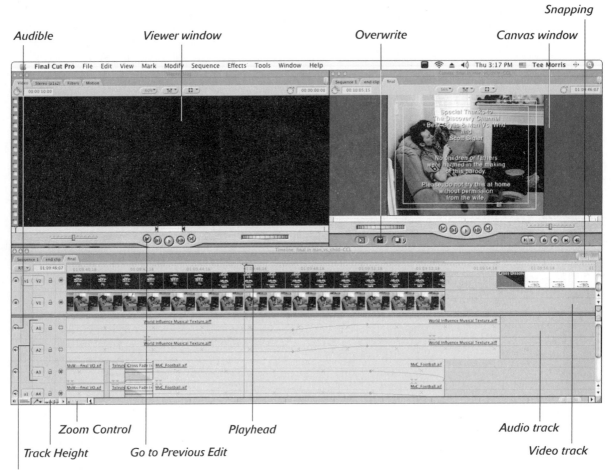

Snapping

Audible

Viewer window

Overwrite

Canvas window

Zoom Control

Playhead

Audio track

Track Height

Go to Previous Edit

Video track

Source Destination (audio)

• **Figure 41-1: The Final Cut Pro interface.**

Getting ready to edit the video podcast

The following steps help you set up your computer for video editing and audio recording with Final Cut. You will be importing clips and even confirming that Final Cut sees your audio recording hardware so that you can record live into the project. So just take a few preliminary steps here before editing:

1. If you have audio recording equipment set up for your computer, confirm that your setup is your source of audio input. To do so, choose System Preferences➪Sound➪Input and select your mixer board.

    Figure 41-2 shows what this process looks like. With the mixer set as your default audio input source, you can record live voiceovers directly into your Final Cut project with ease.

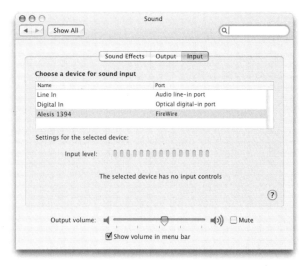

• **Figure 41-2: Making your mixer the default source for audio input.**

2. Copy the `Practice 41` **folder from the companion DVD onto your Macintosh.**

3. **Launch Final Cut Pro.**

4. **Choose File⇨Import⇨Folder and import the** `Practice 41` **folder.**

The folder appears in the Browser window of Final Cut Pro. The *Browser* window is where you can organize all the resources that make up your editing project. You can create bins, access video and audio clips, and manage sequences from here.

5. **Expand the** `Practice 41` ***bin* (the editing term for a *folder*) so you can review its contents:**

- ▶ `around-house.mov`
- ▶ `around-house_2.mov`
- ▶ `childs_room.mov`
- ▶ `dramatic_score.aif`
- ▶ `naptime.mov`
- ▶ `podcast.mov`
- ▶ `title.tif`
- ▶ `writing.mov`

6. **In the** `Practice 41` **bin, find the** `MvC-intro_final.m4v` **file. Either in QuickTime or in Final Cut, review the file so you know what your final file should look like.**

With your files in the Browser window, you're ready to edit your footage.

 If you're working in video- or audio-editing applications with only one monitor, you tend to lose screen real estate inside that monitor very quickly because all the panels, tool boxes, and project files proliferate. An inexpensive alternative to pricey 30-inch flat-screen monitors is to invest in a second monitor and a *video accelerator card* (such as the NVIDIA GeForce7300GT or the Radeon X1600 Pro). Accelerators add monitor ports to your computer so you can connect additional monitors. Using two monitors, you dedicate one to panels and the other to the project's timeline and preview. Accelerator cards are inexpensive, easy to install, and are only a fraction of the investment you'd have to make if you brought home a cinema-style display. The two-monitor approach also puts to good use any extra monitors you may have tucked away.

Laying the foundation of your video with Final Cut Pro

All the resources needed for this video (with the exception of the voiceover that you will record later) are now waiting for you in the Browser window. In the following steps, you bring in the theme music and perform the first edit for this project:

1. **Find** `dramatic_score.aif` **in the Browser window and double-click it. When the audio appears in the Viewer window, click the Viewer window and then press your spacebar or click the Play button to review the audio.**

You will place a marker and designate an Out point in this audio to indicate where the video begins and where the theme ends.

2. In the Viewer window, click Go to Previous Edit (see Figure 41-1) or press the Home key on your keyboard to return to the beginning of the audio.

3. Click and drag the Zoom Control to the left to zoom in on your audio.

The Zoom Control (identical to the Timeline Zoom Control) is located in the lower-left corner of the waveform, as shown in Figure 41-1.

4. Press your right-arrow key once to hear the opening drum strike. At the moment of the first drum strike, place a marker by either clicking the Add Marker tool or pressing the M key.

 With your arrow keys, you can *scrub* through audio and video. Scrubbing is the process of listening and viewing audio at a user-designated speed. You scan through segments, find what you're looking for, and make edits. This capability makes zooming in especially useful for syncing specific moments of audio to video (as shown in Figure 41-3).

5. Zoom out on your audio and then press the spacebar to review your audio again. Just after 00:00:22;00, you will hear a guitarlike instrument begin playing. Stop playback there.

6. Using the arrow keys, scrub back in your audio to exactly 00:00:22;00.

You can see where you are in the timecode by checking the Current Timecode Field in the upper-right corner of the Viewer window.

 You may notice that Final Cut Pro has a strange way of measuring time with a number separated by colons (like a normal clock) and the last two numbers separated from the others by a semi-colon (not so normal). This Timecode is a variation of *Drop-Frame Timecode,* a method of timing that keeps audio and video in sync. Keeping it simple, the timecode breaks down this way — hours; minutes; seconds; frames. And your video is moving at **29.97 frames per second (fps)**. This is what keeps audio and video running together in your project.

7. At 00:00:22;00, click the Mark Out Point button in the Viewer window's interface (as shown in Figure 41-4) or press O on your keyboard.

You've designated a new Out (or end) point for your audio.

8. In the Viewer window, click and drag the Take Audio icon (a small speaker with a hand on top) into the A1 Audio Track in your Timeline.

Note that the audio you've marked up and given a new Out point to reflects your changes. The process of making simple edits and changes to the media file before placing it in the Timeline is called *trimming.*

Your score is in place. You can now begin placing video in the Timeline.

9. In the Browser window, double-click naptime. mov and review the clip in the Viewer window by clicking the Play button or pressing the spacebar.

For this opening clip, you need only the final few seconds.

• Figure 41-3: Zooming in to audio for easier editing and marking of clips.

10. When you've reached the end of the clip, use the arrow keys and scrub back to 00:00:45;06. Make this the new In point of your video by clicking the Mark In Point button (see Figure 41-4) or pressing I on your keyboard.

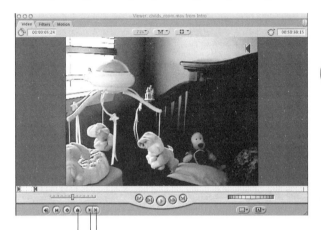

Add a Marker | Mark Out Point

Mark In Point

• Figure 41-4: Final Cut indicates the new In and Out points in your video with icons in the top right and left corners of your Viewer's preview. In this instance, the new Out point is indicated with an icon in the upper-right corner.

11. Scrub forward to 00:00:48;07 and click the Mark Out Point button or press the O key.

This process of making simple edits and changes before placing the file in the Timeline is called *trimming*. Simply put, you're taking only the video you need from a longer clip and applying it to your Timeline.

You want only the video; the next step lets Final Cut know that.

12. In the Timeline window, find the two interlocking icons in the audio tracks: a1 (the *Source*) connecting to A1 (the *Destination*), and a2 connecting with A2. (Refer to Figure 41-1.) Click each of these icons so they disconnect from each other, which tells Final Cut you don't want anything sent from the Viewer into the Timeline. Leave v1 and V1 connected.

13. Press the Home key on your keyboard to return to the beginning of the Timeline, and then zoom in to your audio with the Zoom Control.

You will want to view your audio in 2-second increments. You can determine this by looking at the Timeline Ruler extending across the top of the Timeline window.

 You're viewing audio in 2-second increments when the numbers read 01:00:02;00, 01:00:04;00, 01:00:06;00, and so on.

14. To the left of the Zoom Control is the Toggle Timeline Track Height feature (refer to Figure 41-1). Select the viewing option that's second from the right.

The Track Height viewing options for your clips are similar to those found in Soundtrack Pro. They make editing audio and video easier.

15. Click the playhead in the Timeline window (the small yellow triangle in the Timeline Ruler; refer to Figure 41-1) and drag it to the right until it snaps to the marker in the audio.

16. Click the Viewer window and then click and drag the clip from the Viewer into the Canvas window.

An interface appears that gives you options you can use to incorporate the clip.

17. Drag the clip into the Overwrite option and then release the mouse button (as shown in Figure 41-5).

The clip is now in your Timeline. Throughout this practice, you will be performing what are known as *Overwrite* edits, where you place one track of video over audio without affecting the running time. Performing Overwrite edits is a bit like layering images in Adobe Photoshop, only you're doing it with video.

18. Save your project either by choosing File⇨Save Project or by pressing ⌘+S.

• Figure 41-5: One way of incorporating clips into your Timeline is to click and drag them from the Viewer into the Canvas.

Finishing the video portion of the introduction

Now that you have an idea of how you bring clips into the Timeline, you will now incorporate the other clips into the project. We show you several ways to perform simple edits with Final Cut.

Follow these steps to get rolling:

1. **In your Browser window, click the name of Sequence 1 and change it to read** Intro **so you know what this sequence is at a glance.**

2. **Still in the Browser window, double-click the** writing.mov **clip to bring it up in the Viewer window. Click Play or press the spacebar to review the clip.**

 This may seem like some of the driest, dullest video footage ever captured by a camera on a tripod, but what you're looking for are some moments to use as *b-roll* — footage you've already shot that can serve as background

video for titles, establishing shots, or montage clips (as in this opening). B-roll is good to have on hand; if you don't have any, you can always find stock video footage online, some offered for free (www.freestockfootage.com) and some available for purchase (www.digital juice.com).

3. **Find the** 00:00:47;15 **point in this clip's Timeline and mark this as the clip's new In point by clicking the Mark In Point tool or by pressing I on your keyboard.**

4. **Progress forward to** 00:00:49;14 **and mark this clip as your new Out point by clicking the Mark Out Point tool or by pressing O on your keyboard.**

5. **Press ⌘+F10 on your keyboard to perform an Overwrite edit.**

   Note that because you've left the Source and Destination tracks disconnected, you're importing only video (which is all you need).

Normally the Final Cut Pro Help Tags identify the keyboard shortcut for performing an Overwrite edit as F10. If (however) your operating system is Mac OS X and you're running a system program called Exposé, you've got a slight conflict: Its default settings already use F10 as part of the F9–F12 range of keys. You have two ways to bypass the Exposé command: Hold down the key while you press F10 or (if you want to reassign the Exposé commands) choose ⌘⇨System Preferences⇨ Dashboard & Expose and adjust the Preferences there. If you reassign key commands or change Preferences, you can simply follow the Help Tags that Final Cut provides.

6. **Return to the Browser window and double-click the** `podcast.mov` **clip. Play this clip to review it.**

7. **Progress to** `00:00:08;20` **in the clip and make this your new In point, using one of the two methods mentioned in Step 3.**

8. **Progress to** `00:00:11;00` **in the clip and make this your new Out point, using one of the two methods mentioned in Step 4.**

9. **In the Canvas window, find the Overwrite button and click it to perform the edit.**

The Overwrite button is a red icon located between the Insert (yellow) button and Replace (blue) button. (Refer to Figure 41-1.)

10. **In the Browser window, double-click** `around-house.mov` **and review the clip.**

From this segment, you'll extract two clips from one. This method is used in nonlinear editing, and it enables you to grab multiple clips from one long shot.

11. **Progress to** `00:00:29;15` **in the clip and make this your new In point, using one of the two methods mentioned in Step 3.**

12. **Progress to** `00:00:31;25` **in the clip and make this your new Out point, using one of the two methods illustrated in Step 4.**

13. **Click and drag this clip over to the Canvas viewer; release the mouse button with the**

pointer over the Overwrite option to perform the edit.

14. **Return to the Viewer window, progress to** `00:01:03;05` **in the clip, and make this your new In point using one of the two methods mentioned in Step 3.**

15. **Progress to** `00:01:37;07` **in the clip and make this your new Out point, using one of the two methods mentioned in Step 4.**

Note that when you established the new In point in this clip beyond the previous In and Out points you set back in Steps 11 through 12, the points were removed, and a new In point was established. If you make new In points after previously established Out points, Final Cut resets the clip and allows you to work outside an earlier-designated range. The same is true if you set new Out points in a clip earlier than previously established In points.

16. **Perform an Overwrite edit, using one of the three methods featured in Steps 5, 9, or 13.**

Note that the clip in your Timeline is unaffected. When you bring a clip from a source of video and incorporate it into a Timeline, the clip becomes independent of the original source material. Therefore, you can make new edit points in the original source material without affecting what is already in play in the Timeline. Clips set in the Timeline are affected only if the original source clip's location in the computer changes, or if the original source clip is deleted or replaced. Provided your source material remains where it is logged and captured, you can pull multiple clips from one single source.

17. **In the Browser window, double-click** `around-house_2.mov` **and review the clip.**

18. **Progress to** `00:00:02;00` **in the clip and make this your new In point using one of the two methods illustrated in Step 3.**

19. **Progress to** `00:00:04;00` **in the clip and make this your new Out point using one of the two methods illustrated in Step 4.**

20. **Perform an Overwrite edit using one of the three methods featured in Steps 5, 9, or 13.**

21. In the Browser window, double-click `childs_room.mov` and review the clip.

Because you are using this footage as b-roll, you will start from the beginning of the clip so you already have your In point.

22. Progress to `00:00:06;15` in the clip and make this your new Out point using one of the two ways illustrated in Step 4.

23. Perform an Overwrite edit using one of the three methods featured in Steps 5, 9, or 13.

24. Save your project.

After saving your work, click your Timeline window, press the Home key on your keyboard, and press the spacebar to review your work up to this point.

Adding titles

You've got the basic video edits needed for your *Man Vs. Child* introduction. The next order of business is to set opening titles, adjust audio levels, and incorporate voiceovers by using a powerful recording tool built into Final Cut Pro:

1. In the Timeline window, double-click the last clip of the child's room with the mobile in the foreground.

Double-click the clip in the Timeline to make changes to the clip in play. Any changes you now make to the clip in the Viewer will be reflected in the Timeline.

You can tell whether you are working on an original source clip or a clip from the Timeline by looking at the Viewer's scrubber bar. If you see dots along the top and the bottom of the bar, you're working with a clip from the Timeline (as shown in Figure 41-6, top), not the original source (shown in Figure 41-6, bottom).

2. From the Viewer window, select the Filters tab to view your Filter options for this clip.

3. In the Effects window, choose Video Filters⇨ Blur⇨Gaussian Blur. Click and drag this filter into the Viewer's Filter window to apply it to

this clip. To view the changes to this clip as they happen, click and drag the Timeline's playhead back anywhere into this clip.

4. With the Gaussian Blur filter checked, click and drag the slider for Radius to 15.

You get a blur effect, 15 pixels wide, across the whole video clip. As shown in Figure 41-7, when you put the playhead in the clip that you're applying the filter to, you can apply changes to the filter in the Viewer and watch the changes occur in the Canvas window — in real time.

Scrubber bar

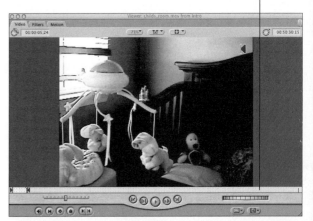

• **Figure 41-6:** A clip that comes from the Timeline (top) displays dots along its scrubber bar, and a clip from the original source (bottom) has a clean scrubber bar.

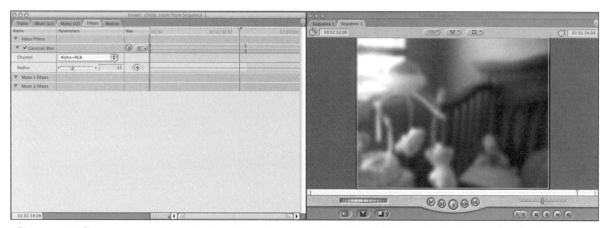

• Figure 41-7: Changes applied to a clip in the Timeline are rendered in real time with the playhead in the clip.

5. In the Canvas window, click the Go to Previous Edit button (refer to Figure 41-1) to go to the start of this clip.

6. Click the Motion tab in the Viewer window (shown in Figure 41-8).

To simulate a slight camera pan and a zoom in, you are going to apply *keyframes* to your clip and make adjustments. Keyframes are moments you designate in the clip's Timeline to signify something is changing. By using keyframes, you can simulate a zoom-out of the background.

7. In the Basic Motion interface, find a column of diamond-shaped buttons — your keyframe tools — and click the ones for the Scale and Center options.

With these tools, you can designate key moments in your clips where things change.

8. Click the Current Timecode field (in the lower-left corner of the Motion window, as shown in Figure 41-8) for the clip you're working on.

9. Type +300 and then press Enter or Return.

Doing so advances three seconds ahead in your clip.

10. In your Motion interface, establish two new keyframes for Scale and Center at this point.

Go to Next Keyframe   Clip duration

Go to Previous Keyframe | Playhead

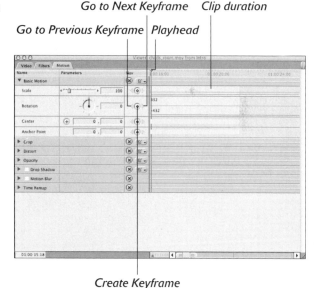

Create Keyframe

• Figure 41-8: The Motion interface allows you to change the clip's size, rotation, and opacity for the effect you want.

11. Next to the Create Keyframe tool (the diamond icon; refer to Figure 41-8), find the two triangles, one pointing to the left and the other pointing right.

These are the Go to Previous Keyframe tool and Go to Next Keyframe tool.

12. Click the (now active) Go to Previous Keyframe button (refer to Figure 41-8) to go back to the first keyframes you created.

You can pick any of the attributes you gave keyframes to and click the tool to do this.

13. In the Scale section of the Motion window, move the slider to the right until it reads 165 in the Scale field, or simply type 165 in the field.

14. In the Center section of the Motion window, click the plus-sign (+) icon to see the Center point of your image and move your mouse pointer to the Canvas window.

15. Click and drag the pointer up and to the left until the out-of-focus image of the stuffed dog appears in the lower-right corner of your screen.

Another way to reposition the video is to type **–112.8** and **–68.04** into the Center fields.

16. Save your project. Then change the size of the windows (if necessary) so you can view the Video 2 (V2) track above the main video you've been working with.

17. From the Browser window, click and drag the title.tif file into the V2 track, placing it to the right of the playhead.

If the clip needs trimming, you can trim it to end at the same time as the video. Place your cursor on the end of the title clip in the Timeline, and then click and drag its end point to where the footage of the child's room ends.

18. If needed, click and drag the playhead back to the ending video clip of the child's room.

The title — *Man vs. Child* — is now superimposed over the soft-focus b-roll of the child's room.

Animating your title

You now have a title for your podcast, but you still need to animate it so it flies into the frame. That's the next goal; here's how you do it:

1. Click the Go to Previous Edit button in the Canvas window; go back to the beginning of this clip, the out-of-focus child's room that (now) shows the title.

2. Double-click the new title clip you just incorporated into the Timeline and then establish keyframes (as you did in the previous steps) for the following:

▶ Scale

▶ Rotation

▶ Center

3. In the Current Timecode field in the lower-left of the Motion window, type +100 to advance 1 second into the title clip. Add keyframes here as well.

4. Click Go to Previous Keyframe in the Motion window.

You are now at the beginning keyframes of the title clip.

5. In the Rotation section of the Motion window, type –21 in the field and press Enter or Return.

6. In the Scale section of the Motion window, move the slider to the right until it reads 525 in the Scale field, or simply type 525 in the field.

7. In the Center section of the Motion window, type –513.89 and 338.97 into the Center fields to reposition the title. Then press Return.

The Motion interface shows a graphic representation of the changes you make — and where they happen in the Timeline — as shown in Figure 41-9.

8. Click the Go to Next Keyframe button (refer to Figure 41-8) in the Motion window.

9. Go to Scale and type 95 in the Scale field. Then go to the Center section, click the plus-sign (+) icon to see the Center point of your image, and click and drag the title to center it in your video.

You can also type **1.39** and **14.85** into the Center fields to reposition the title.

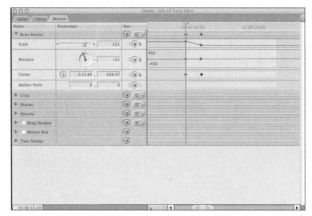

• **Figure 41-9: A graphic representation of the changes you've made appears in the Motion interface.**

10. Save your project. Then press Option+R or choose Sequence➪Render All➪Both to render the video and its animation.

11. Review your work: Click inside the Timeline window, press the Home key on your keyboard, and then press the spacebar (or click the Play button in your Canvas window).

Adding the final touches with Final Cut

You have compiled the clips and animated the title, and everything is looking good. All that remains are the final touches with the audio. As soon as you complete the following steps, the video will be ready for exporting into a solid video podcasting format:

1. With your playhead at the end of the audio, click and drag the playhead back to the end of the video.

2. In the Effects window, close the open folders and then choose Audio Transitions➪Cross Fade (0 dB). Click and drag this transition to the end of the audio clip.

The end of the audio now has a transition in place that will fade out your music on cue when you review it, as illustrated in Figure 41-10.

3. In the Timeline window, place your cursor at the end of the title clip and extend it to match the end of the audio. Repeat this step for the video of the child's room.

4. In the Effects window, close the open Audio Transition folder and then choose Video Transitions➪Dissolve➪Cross Dissolve. Click and drag this transition to the end of both the video and title clips.

The transitions should appear to extend beyond the video and audio, deeper into the Timeline. Because there is no video here to transition to, Final Cut renders this as a fade to black (as shown in Figure 41-11).

• **Figure 41-10: Transitions include cross-fades of audio sources or fade-outs to silence.**

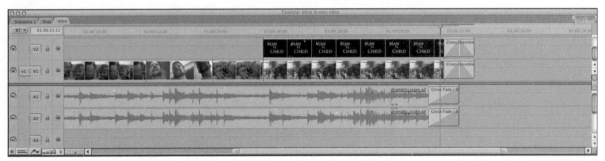

• **Figure 41-11:** When a Cross Dissolve Video Transition ends up in an area with no video material, you essentially create a fade to black.

5. Save your project. Then press Option+R or choose Sequence⊅Render All⊅Both to render the video, its animation, and the transitions. Click inside the Timeline window, press the Home key on your keyboard, and then press the spacebar or the Play button in the Canvas window to review your work.

6. Press the Home key on your keyboard to return to the beginning and then press Option+0 or choose Tools⊅Voice Over to activate the Voice Over recorder in Final Cut Pro.

Final Cut's *Voice Over* tool (shown in Figure 41-12) is a recorder built into the application itself. This tool is a terrific feature of Final Cut Pro. You can set it to see your mixer as an audio input device, and you can also label the recording as Voice Over - MvC or whatever name you wish to call it. Final Cut Pro's powerful built-in recorder allows you to review video without sound, enabling you to read scripts or voiceover segments in time with the playback of the video.

7. In the Voice Over tool, make sure the Source option sees your mixer or audio interface as the incoming audio source. Select it from the menu.

If your mixer or audio interface is not offered as an option, then save your work, quit Final Cut, and double-check your System Preferences (as suggested in Step 1 of the "Getting ready to edit the video podcast" section, earlier in the

chapter). After the audio source is confirmed, launch Final Cut Pro and pick up from this step. (Final Cut will remember the point where you left off in the project.)

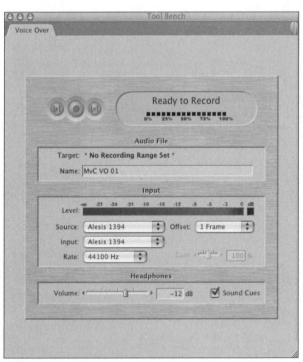

• **Figure 41-12:** Final Cut's Voice Over tool, a powerful, efficient option for creating voiceovers that accompany video.

8. Before proceeding, go to the Browser window and double-click `writing.mov` so that you have available in the Timeline the Source and Destination for *audio*. Click and drag a1 (Source) down to A3 (Destination) and click either icon to connect them. Repeat this step for a2 and A4.

When you have a destination for your Voice Over, it is time to record.

9. Check your levels in the Voice Over by speaking into your mic and watching the Level section.

10. Your script for this voiceover is as follows:

His name is Tee Morris. He is a science fiction/fantasy author and podcaster. His wife has left him alone with his two-year-old. Today, he will show you the skills on how to survive.

The delivery for this should be dramatic and tense. (Reading this in a British accent, like the host of the Discovery Channel's *Man vs. Wild*, is strictly your call!) You can either read it along with the video or take short one- to two-second pauses between complete thoughts.

11. In the Name section of the Voice Over window, name this voiceover file MvC VO 001.

The file is saved in this project's `Capture Scratch` folder, labeled by the project's name.

12. Mute the tracks of your video's music by clicking the Audible buttons (refer to Figure 41-1) for Audio Tracks 1 and 2.

13. When ready, click the Record button (the red button to the left of the display currently reading Ready to Record) and wait for the countdown to cue you in. When the `Recording` status shows on-screen, begin your voiceover.

As you are recording, Voice Over not only keeps track of how much you are recording but also counts down how much video remains, stopping the recording automatically when the video material concludes. Voice Over records your voiceover on one of the Destination tracks; after that's done, it creates a name for a *new* voiceover (in this case, MvC VO 002) and stands by for any new audio you want to add.

The Voice Over tool allows you to adjust the Gain (input signal) and Rate (44 kHz or 48 kHz), but you can also adjust the level from your mixer. When the Voice Over finishes recording, your playhead in the Timeline immediately returns to the beginning of your project. You can now edit the audio as you like.

With the voiceover in place, the next order of business is to break up this long audio segment into smaller ones, allowing precise timing when the voiceover comes in with the video's action:

1. From the Tool Palette, click the Razor Blade tool.

2. Look in the Timeline window and review the voiceover audio's *waveform* (the graphic representation of sound) and note the flatline gaps within your voiceover.

These gaps of silence are where you want to apply the Razor Blade tool. Find the first gap between "His name is Tee Morris . . ." and "He is a science fiction . . . " and click anywhere in the pause between these two points.

3. Repeat the previous step throughout the voiceover clip. When you're finished, you should have six clips (as shown in Figure 41-13). When your six clips are complete, choose the Selection tool from the Tool Palette.

4. Click the last audio clip, which should be silence after " . . . on how to survive." Delete the clip by pressing the Delete key.

5. Click the Snapping icon or press N on your keyboard to turn off the Snapping option.

You can find the Snapping icon in the top-right corner of the Timeline window (refer to Figure 41-1); it appears green when turned on.

6. Place your Selection tool at the beginning of the first segment of the voiceover. Shorten this segment by clicking and dragging its In point closer to the beginning of the audio, and by clicking and dragging its Out point closer to the end of the audio segment.

7. Repeat Steps 1–6 for all other voiceover segments so your voiceover recording looks like Figure 41-14.

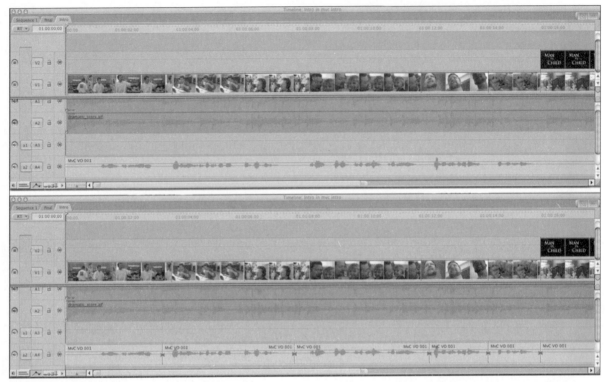

• Figure 41-13: Segmenting the long voiceover file (top) into clips with a few well-placed clicks of the Razor Tool (bottom).

• Figure 41-14: With the clips trimmed in the Timeline, you can easily place the audio at precise moments of the video.

8. In the Timeline window's Current Timecode (located in the upper-left corner of the Timeline window), click to select the Timecode and then type 100 to place the playhead at `00:00:01;00`.

9. Position the beginning of the audible voiceover (where you see something in the waveform) at `00:00:01;00`.

10. Press the down-arrow key on your keyboard to advance to the next edit point in your Timeline. Press the key repeatedly until you reach the In point of the `writer.mov` clip.

11. Position the In Point of the audio segment for "He is a Science Fiction/Fantasy author . . . " at the edit point.

12. Using the down-arrow key, advance in the Timeline to the In point to the clip of Tee and his daughter mugging for the camera. Move the "His wife has left him alone . . . " audio to begin at this point.

13. Using the down-arrow key, advance in the Timeline to the In point to the clip of Tee shot at the angle of a "follow camera." Move the "Today, he will show you the skills . . . " audio to begin at this point.

14. Using the down-arrow key, advance in the Timeline to the In point to the clip of Tee's daughter. Move the "On how to survive" audio to begin at this point.

15. Press the Home key on your keyboard to return to the beginning of the Timeline. Click the Audible buttons to make your soundtrack active.

16. Go to the Tool Palette and select the Pen tool (which has the image of a fountain pen on it).

The Pen tool enables you to place control points (similar to those found in GarageBand, and Soundtrack Pro, and Premiere) in the audio.

17. In the lower-left corner of the Timeline window, click the Toggle Clip Overlays option.

A Volume Level line extends across your audio.

18. With the Pen Tool, click at the beginning of the audio to establish your first control point.

You can always zoom in using the Zoom Control and do more-detailed work in tight time increments — all without a hint of eye/neck/back strain. Take advantage of that Zoom Control when you can.

19. In the Timeline's Current Timecode field, type 100. Then with the Pen Tool, click here to establish your next control point.

20. Place the Pen tool on top of this new control point, and you will notice that the Pen Tool icon becomes a large plus sign (+), which allows you to adjust the point to a new volume. Click and drag this control point to –16 dB.

21. Save your project. Then press Option+R or choose Sequence⇨Render All⇨Both to render the video.

22. Press the Home key on your keyboard and then press the spacebar (or click the Play button in the Canvas window) to review your final work.

Congratulations! You're done with the hard part. Your video is edited, complete with fade-outs, titles, and now voiceovers. All that's left to do is export the video for podcasting purposes.

Now that you've completed the video, take a look at how long it has taken you to create this 22½-second video. For a short video, you've invested a good chunk of time to make this introduction happen. Even after you get to a level of familiarity with the software, video editing is a time-consuming process. Be ready to make that kind of investment. (For more on the time demands of video podcasting, take a look at Practice 39.)

Exporting Your Video for Podcasting

As you've no doubt noticed, the process of video editing can be a long trek through many, many steps. But the beautiful thing about Final Cut Pro is how easy it makes the process of exporting a video specifically for podcasting.

It really doesn't get any easier than this:

1. **Click anywhere in the Timeline window and choose File⇨Export⇨Using QuickTime Conversion.**

You are now accessing the QuickTime Conversion tool built into the Export function of Final Cut Pro. Much like the Adobe Media Encoder covered in Practice 40, this is a handy collection of QuickTime presets that allows you to export your video to a format that you need.

2. **Choose Format⇨iPod.**

In the Format window, the QuickTime extensions installed with Final Cut Pro allow for a wide variety of formats — including iPod, iPhone, and AppleTV, as shown in Figure 41-15.

3. **In the Save As field, rename the file MvC-Intro.m4v and then click the Save button.**

Surprise! That's it. You're done. Three steps and you've created your first video for the podcasting community. From here, you can shoot, edit, and produce your own podcast. Final Cut's easy exporting makes it a real friend to podcasters.

Apple recommends that the original video be at least 640 pixels wide during the editing process; when exporting, use the built-in iPod converters in Compressor (H.264 for iPod), QuickTime Pro (Movie

to iPod), or iTunes (Convert Selection for iPod). These compression settings maintain the aspect ratio and yield podcast-ready .m4v files.

But we're still talking basics here. This practice just scratches the surface of this incredible video-editing program. If you are looking to find out more about the more-potent capabilities of Final Cut Pro, take a look at the many titles available at your local bookstore or online. You can move through the basics and then onward to the advanced techniques in video production, video editing, and video editing in Final Cut Pro.

• **Figure 41-15: The QuickTime extensions in the Format window.**

Practice 42

Posting and Distributing Your Video

After you've got your killer video podcast finished and ready to go, the question asked here is usually, "Okay, now what?" It's not a bad question to ask, really — there are a few options you can explore beyond the simple addition of the video to your RSS feed. You can (for example) either post your video content exclusively into your podcast or have another service shoulder the hosting and bandwidth issues that come with hosting a video podcast.

Beginning with the basics, this practice explores the options you have for releasing your video content out into the wild, including YouTube, Google Video, and Lulu TV.

Distribution through Your Feed

If you are working with your own feed, as discussed in Practices 25 and 27, you know that the most important line in your feed is the enclosure. As an example, here's the enclosure line for a video called *Man vs. Child:*

```
<enclosure url="http://mywebsite.net/podcast
   /ManVsChild.m4v" length="121774210" type="video/
   x-m4v"/>
```

Sure, all the other lines of your RSS feed play a part in making your podcast happen, but it's the enclosure that everyone wants — and that everyone plays on their media players of choice. Without the enclosure, no media file is exchanged between the host and the podcatching client, so you will want to be certain that the feed you're managing — whether you're doing it by hand, using PodPress, or having LibSyn take care of the feed for you — has the right enclosure tag in place.

With video podcasts, the enclosure needs to be the right format and right type in order for iTunes to recognize it and play it properly. Table 42-1 sums up the possible formats.

TABLE 42-1: ENCLOSURE TAG ATTRIBUTES

File Format	File Type
.mp4	video/mp4
.m4v	video/x-m4v
.mov	video/QuickTime

Although it does say on Apple's Web site that the .mov format (the uncompressed "movie" file usually created from Final Cut or Premiere files when you're exporting with QuickTime) is a supported file for video podcasting, this file format equates to extremely large files. That means extremely slow downloads. You are better off saving your files either as the compressed .mp4 or .m4v formats, provided the compression does not affect the video's appearance too much. For more on compressing your video for podcasting, refer to Practices 39, 40, and 41 in this book.

When you're writing or confirming the tag for your podcast episode in your RSS-generator, consider the following:

1. **Check the filename of your** .m4v **or** .mp4 **file to make sure you're matching cases, using underscores, and have the right extension.**

   The *Man vs. Child* video filename looks like this:

   ```
   ManVsChild.m4v
   ```

2. **Make certain the enclosure tag is pointing to the proper URL.**

   Here's an example:

   ```
   url="http://mywebsite.net/podcast
     /ManVsChild.m4v"
   ```

3. **Get the** length **value for your video podcast's episode.**

   How you do that depends on your operating system:

   ▶ **For a PC:** Right-click on the video file in Explorer and select Properties.

   ▶ **For a Mac:** Right-click on the video file in the Finder and select Get Info.

   After you've made the selection, look for Size. The number of bytes is your show length. Here's an example:

   ```
   length="121774210"
   ```

4. **Make sure the file type is the correct type.**

   For an m4v file, that line looks like this:

   ```
   type="video/x-m4v"
   ```

   Your enclosure tag should now look like this:

   ```
   <enclosure
     url="http://mywebsite.net/
     podcast /ManVsChild.m4v"
     length="121774210"
     type="video/x-m4v"/>
   ```

You are ready to finish up any other episode details in your RSS feed (including double- and triple-checking your feed's iTunes tags). Then you can upload your episode to begin video podcasting.

Posting on YouTube

Perhaps you'd prefer not to host the videos yourself because of the high bandwidth required — or maybe you want to see how well the video will perform before committing yourself to a host blog and a super-size server. That's where a service like YouTube (www.youtube.com) comes into play. YouTube is an online service that streams video and Flash animation content created by its members to anyone and everyone who wants to watch.

Videos appearing on YouTube must fit certain technical criteria. They must be

- Shorter than 10 minutes
- Smaller than 100MB
- In one of these formats: .avi, .mov, .mpg, or .wmv

Uploading your video to YouTube

If your video meets the previous three criteria, you can upload it to YouTube:

1. **If you haven't done so already, set up an account with YouTube. (No worries — it's free!)**

   Click the Sign Up link at www.youtube.com and follow the steps under Create Your YouTube Account.

2. **After you've registered, click the Upload link located in the upper-right corner of the YouTube home page.**

3. **Enter your video's identifying information into YouTube's Video Upload interface.**

   Make sure you enter a title, brief description, and meta-tags (for YouTube and other search engines), as shown in Figure 42-1.

4. **Choose a Category appropriate for your podcast.**

You Tube
Broadcast Yourself™

Hello, TeeMonster68 ☒ (0) |

Videos   Categories   Channels

Searc

Video Upload (Step 1 of 2)

Title: Man Vs. Child

Description: Tee Morris takes on his daughter in an afternoon at home.

Tags: vival documentary Discovery parenthood fatherhood

Enter one or more tags, separated by spaces.
Tags are keywords used to describe your video.

Video Category: Comedy ▾

Broadcast Options: Public by default   choose options

Date and Map Options: No date or location has been set   choose options

Sharing Options: Allow Comments, Video Responses, Ratings, Embedding by default   choose options

• **Figure 42-1: Adding in as much information as possible makes your video easier to find.**

5. **Click the Upload a Video button.**

   This takes you to the next step, where you find the video on your local computer.

6. **Click Browse to find your video podcast and click the video's filename to highlight it.**

7. **Click the Upload Video button.**

   Depending on the traffic to YouTube and the speed of your connection, your video begins the uploading process — and is online and running within minutes.

> The specifications covered in this practice cover the technical specifications of YouTube only. The *content* of your video is a different matter altogether. YouTube, in its Terms of Service agreement, states ". . . you will not submit material that is copyrighted, protected by trade secret or otherwise subject to third-party proprietary rights, including privacy and publicity rights, unless you are the owner of such rights or have permission from their rightful owner to post the material. . . ." That means *the rights to the content you submit must belong to you*. Additionally, if your content likes to "walk on the wild side," YouTube also reserves to right to terminate your account if it finds your content has " . . . pornography, obscene or defamatory material, or excessive length."

After the video is online, your content is offered up on a designated YouTube page, with the video embedded in the page until it's removed from the server (either you or YouTube may do that). There's even a subscription option that allows you to subscribe to a particular user's videos. Then, when a new video is posted, you're notified via e-mail.

Embedding your YouTube video on your blog

Many video podcasters embed their current season's videos on their host blogs with accompanying blogposts. YouTube makes this process easy.

The following steps use WordPress (www.word press.com) as a common example of a host blog; however, the steps should be similar with other hosted blog platforms:

1. **On the video's host page, look for the Embed field (located to the upper-right of the clip).**

2. **Select the code in the Embed field and copy it to your Clipboard.**

Press either Ctrl+C (Windows) or ⌘+C (Mac).

3. **Go to your WordPress dashboard and choose Users⇨Your Profile.**

Confirm that the option for using the visual editor when writing is *not* checked. If it is checked, click the option to turn it off and then click Update Profile.

4. **Choose Write⇨Post and compose your entry.**

5. **When your entry is finished, press Ctrl+V (Windows) or ⌘+V (Mac) to paste the code you copied from YouTube.**

When embedding your video, you have to use the Code editor, not the Visual editor. For best results when you're embedding video, make certain your blog defaults to a Code editor for your posts. To go from Visual Editor to Code, simply click the "Code" tab in the blog's posting interface.

6. **Save, edit, or publish the entry.**

Here are your options:

▶ Click Save to save the draft for later.

▶ Click Save and Continue Editing to preview the post or continue editing.

▶ Click Publish to make the post go live.

At this point, you have incorporated video with a blogpost, which keeps your audience in the know about what you're doing with your video podcast. But is this podcasting?

YouTube's subscription model does appear (at the outset) to be podcasting, but there's a distinction: Actual podcast content is brought to you automatically and waits on your computer; with the subscription service, YouTube simply notifies the subscriber that new content is online, and the subscriber has to go get it and review it online. And if a month or two goes by and the creator of the content decides to pull it, there are no guarantees it will still be there when the subscriber goes looking for it.

The upside of posting to YouTube is that its heavy traffic means lots of exposure for your video. YouTube is the most popular site for online video content; there's no denying that it has evolved into the proverbial 800-pound gorilla from its humble beginnings. So if you're looking for high numbers of potential viewers and pre-existing traffic that might find you in random searches, YouTube is the place for your videos.

Posting on Google Video

Not to be outdone, the 800-pound gorilla of search engines now offers Google Video (http://video.google.com) as friendly competition for YouTube. Google Video offers many of the same features as YouTube, only this time the power of the Google search engine is behind it, accessing videos on its own server and other video streaming services like YouTube. Featured on the home page is a range of offerings from music videos to AOL videos to movie trailers. Google Video also gives recommendations, special featured clips, and even a quick cross-section of popular videos.

Videos appearing on Google Video differ slightly from those on YouTube in their technical specifications:

✔ Frame rate per second (fps) should be 12 fps or higher.

✔ All screen resolutions up to 640×480 are acceptable.

✔ The recommended codecs (explained in Practices 40 and 41) are H.264, H.263, MPEG 1/2/4 or Motion JPEG.

✔ Use one of the following formats: `avi`, `.mov`, `.wmv`, `.mpg`, `.mpeg`, `.mp4`, `.asf`, `.ra`, `.ram`, or `.mod`.

If you decide to utilize Google Video, uploading videos to it is straightforward:

1. Go to www.googlevideo.com, **and in the upper-right corner, click Sign In to access Google Video uploading privileges.**

   If you do not have a Google account, click Create an Account Now and follow the steps.

2. **After you've registered and logged in, click the Upload Your Videos link, which is under the My Videos heading on the upper-right side of the Google Video home page.**

3. **Click the Browse button in the Video File field to find your video podcast.**

4. **Specify a title, brief description, and chosen category and language, as shown in Figure 42-2.**

![Google Video Upload and share your videos screen]

All fields are required.

Video file: /Volumes/Book Four/Man Vs. Child/man_vs_child.n Browse...
We accept AVI, MPEG, Quicktime, Real, and Windows Media Learn more
If your video file is over 100 MB, please use the desktop uploader.
No copyrighted or obscene material

Title: Man Vs. Child

Description: Science Fiction and Fantasy author Tee Morris faces off against his 2-yr old daughter in an afternoon alone at the house.

Include details such as location and story summary

Genre: Comedy
Language: English
Access: ○ Public - your video will be included in search results.
        ○ Unlisted^New^ - your video will not be included in search results. Learn more
        ☑ I agree to the Upload Terms and Conditions.
        Upload video

Depending on the file's size and connection speed, the upload may take several minutes.

• Figure 42-2: Google Video gets your video online in only a matter of moments.

5. **Designate whether you want this video to be Public or Private.**

6. **After reviewing the Upload Terms of Service, check the I Agree box.**

7. **Click the Upload Video button.**

As with YouTube, your upload time will vary depending on Google's traffic and your connection.

The same rules concerning copyright and ownership of the video content still apply here — but unlike YouTube, Google Video doesn't restrict running time. Whether it is one minute or one hour, you can post it on Google Video.

With Google Video, however, there's no subscription option; users have to check either the host blog or Google Video for any new content. Also, finding the code allowing you to embed the video into your host blog is not as easy to find as it is on YouTube. We cover that in the next section.

Embedding Your Google Video on Your Blog

You are now going to embed your Google video into a blogpost. Although the steps might vary from blog interface to blog interface, we're going to show you how to embed a video using WordPress as an example. Regardless of what blog software you are using, you will find that Google Video makes embedding video into your blogs very easy:

1. **On the video's host page, click the blue button labeled Email – Blog – Post to MySpace (at the upper-right of the clip's window).**

2. **Click the link for Embed HTML to reveal a field with code.**

3. **Select the code in the Embed field and copy it to your Clipboard by pressing either Ctrl+C (Windows) or ⌘+C (Mac).**

4. **Go to your WordPress dashboard and choose Users⇨Your Profile.**

Confirm that the option for using the visual editor when writing is *not* checked. If it is checked, click the option to turn it off and then click Update Profile.

5. Choose Write⇨Post and compose your entry.

6. When your entry is ready, press Crtl+V (PC) or ⌘+V (Mac) to paste in the code copied from Google Video.

7. Save, edit, or publish the entry.

Here are your options:

▶ Click Save to save the draft for later.

▶ Click Save and Continue Editing to preview the post or continue editing.

▶ Click Publish to make the post go live.

Another advantage of working with Google Video is a downloading option. Located just above the blue Email – Blog – Post to MySpace button is a Download button and a drop-down menu offering a download for the following formats:

✔ Windows/Mac

✔ Video iPod/Sony PSP

By selecting a format and clicking the Download button, the user gets additional instructions for downloading and transferring the video from the computer to a portable device.

 Only videos uploaded to Google Video offer the download feature. When you're surfing through Google Video's Web site, you may notice (in both the top frame and the main window) that some of the videos featured are actually hosted on YouTube; these are marked by a small YouTube icon. (The Google Video content is marked by the signature "G" of Google, as shown in Figure 42-3.) The YouTube videos hosted on Google are streaming videos only; they can't be downloaded through Google Video.

Google Video is definitely a step closer to podcasting than is YouTube — but again, is *this* really podcasting?

• Figure 42-3: Google Video not only shows search results from its own server but from YouTube as well.

Google Video doesn't notify users when new content is online. There are a couple of advantages, though, in allowing users to download video from Google:

✔ You can offer an iPod-friendly version of the content to users.

✔ Users can transfer the video from your server to their computer or iPod for viewing on their schedule.

Google Video still delivers video far less efficiently than a true video podcast. It relies on users to check for the video and doesn't inform users that new content is online.

Although YouTube and Google Video offer many perks for video podcasters, the do-it-yourself podcasting approach has a potent advantage: automatic delivery of content to a feed that offers the video media to your subscription list without requiring anybody to go looking for it.

Bottom line: YouTube and Google Video offer homes for video but lack the capability to use RSS to inform or deliver new content to their subscribers. Things stayed like that till Lulu TV went online and changed everything.

Posting on Lulu TV

Lulu TV (`http://lulu.tv`) has upped the ante for the YouTube and Google Video power players. At first glance, Lulu TV offers many of the same functions as its counterparts, but on closer inspection, you'll notice the easily recognized RSS-feed symbol to the right of the screen with the words "video podcast" right next to it.

Yes, Lulu TV is a *host* for video podcasts — a host that does not charge hosting fees and can potentially *pay* you for your content!

Lulu TV gives you the best of both YouTube and Google Video but with the added bonus of that all-important RSS feed that distributes the podcast for you.

We bet your mind is still lingering on the "getting paid" part. Isn't it?

Lulu TV (see Figure 42-4) offers two accounts (both of which are free to join) for their filmmakers — a Standard and a *Shareholder* account. The Shareholder account offers uploads up to 200MB but also makes you part of the Lulu TV machine. Lulu TV takes 80% of the site's ad revenue and sets it aside in a cash pool reserved for the shareholders. The video content that you create and upload earns revenue based on your share of traffic through your Lulu TV URL. The revenue might not be enough to quit your day job, but it's a nice little boost to your bank account, good for a night out or adding another gadget to your studio. Again, how much revenue you receive depends on how much traffic visits your Lulu page. (And no, subscriptions to the podcast don't count.)

Here are the tech specs for Lulu TV:

- ✔ File size can be up to 100MB for Standard accounts and up to 200MB for Shareholder accounts.

- ✔ Video should be at a 4 × 3 screen ratio at 480 × 360. (A 16 × 9 widescreen resolution at 352 × 288 is supported but not recommended.)

- ✔ Set the bit rate to 400kbs, use 20–25fps, and turn off "interlace" options.

- ✔ Audio should be at 44 mHz, 128 kbps, and compressed using either `mp3` or `aac` format.

- ✔ Export video using the codec H.264.

- ✔ Content should be in the format of `.avi`, `.mov`, `.wmv`, and `.mp4`, in order for Lulu TV to convert it to Flash video, iPod/iTunes/PSP-ready MP4, and cell-phone-ready 3GP.

• **Figure 42-4: Lulu TV brings to the table free hosting for podcasts and some extra cash on the side!**

When your podcast episodes are ready to go, you can click the Uploads link at the top of the home page to begin the process. It will involve setting up a free account — but that's typical of many podcast-service providers.

Uploading on Lulu TV is, again, similar to the other hosting services listed here:

1. **At the top of the Lulu TV home page, click Log In; then either log in if you have an account or follow the steps under Register to set up an account.**

2. **At the top of the home page for Lulu TV, click the Uploads link and select the Upload option.**

3. **Follow the three-step process outlined on the page that appears.**

   For more details on preparing your video for uploading, click the Conversion Assistance Guide link.

4. Click the Browse button and locate your video episode on your computer.

5. After reviewing the Upload Terms of Service, check the I Agree box.

6. Click the Upload Video button.

7. Provide a description of your video.

8. After the video is uploaded, go to your Profile, which you can access by clicking the My VLog link at the top of the Lulu TV home page.

9. Under the My Links section of your profile, you will find feeds for My Video Podcast that are iTunes and straight RSS. Register these feeds at FeedBurner (www.feedburner.com) and other external directories.

After you upload a new video to your account, Lulu TV automatically updates the feed.

 Lulu TV may appear to be a haven only for video podcasters, but audio podcasters are also starting to feel the love because Lulu TV now offers these services for audio and music podcasters. So if you are looking to make a little cash at this podcasting thing, take a look at what Lulu TV is offering to the audio creators and musicians of the podosphere.

A not-so-secret society of podcasters

Lulu TV is putting out a call to creative people everywhere — tired of the restrictions of DRM (digital rights management), distribution, and the status quo of entertainment — to bring their content to them. The Lulu folks want you to join their order — and they're so intent to bring you in, they're willing to pay you for it!

The Order of the Digital Trebuchet (ODT) is Lulu TV's creative community; its members are invited to join the new-media revolution on account of their professionalism, high production values, and creativity. Lulu TV is still working out the details of membership, but ODT members get a subscription to a private mailing list, Lulu TV swag, and (of course) money for commissioned work that's featured on the home page.

To join the ODT, you need to generate content that will catch the eye of Lulu TV. After the invitation is accepted, your responsibilities to the ODT will include these:

- **Creating commissioned work for Lulu TV.** If time does not allow for you to create commissioned work, that's fine. However, the more you create, the more cash you earn.

- **Following Lulu TV's Monthly Memes.** If you're invited to create a Monthly Meme (a video following a theme specified by Lulu TV), Lulu pays you $100 or more for making a video that fits the meme.

- **Helping to build Lulu TV's community of creators.** Members are asked to represent Lulu TV and recruit new talent. If you come across creative video podcasters with a pro's attitude and a creator's passion, tell them about the ODT.

What makes the ODT different from the rest of the Lulu TV community is that you are now part of the Lulu TV crew, giving back to the company that is allowing you to share (at no cost to you) your creative side with the world. The ODT is your way of "paying it forward" to Lulu TV.

Join Lulu.TV's Order of the Digital Trebuchet!

With your distribution options before you, the next step is to decide which method works best for your podcast. Will you stick exclusively with your feed, combine your own RSS with Google Video or YouTube to deliver your video content to the world, or turn to Lulu TV (for all of the above)? Review your options (as well as the Terms of Service) for each Web site and then finalize the plan that works best for you and your video podcast.

Part VII

Podcasting as a Business

The 5th Wave   By Rich Tennant

OUR TECHNOLOGY HISTORY:
Radio during the Silent Era

Practice 43

Deriving Revenue from Your Podcast

Tell someone that you're a podcaster, and you'll likely get two questions right away: *"What the heck is a podcast?"* and *"Are you making any money from this?"* Try it out on five acquaintances who don't already know about your podcast (or your plans for podcasting). We'll bet you that one or both of those questions come up at least three out of five times. Been there, done that.

The second question is a valid one: Exactly how *can* you make money from your podcast? The title of this book is *Expert Podcasting Practices For Dummies*, for crying out loud. Surely we'd be remiss if we didn't share with you the secrets of getting rich quick (uh-huh . . . well, okay, *possibly deriving at least some income from this activity*). At this point, you're investing (or are about to invest) a lot of time, energy and/or money into building your program — and surely there must be some ways to cover those costs and put a few bucks in your pocket, right?

The answer: Maybe. Without a doubt, several podcasters who consider themselves full-time podcasters actually do make plenty of money in their podcasting careers. An even larger number have kept their day jobs but have found ways to supplement their main income via podcasting. But before we go too far down the road to the riches some of you readers are desperately seeking, may we offer a dose of reality? The vast majority of podcasts — easily over 90 percent by sheer volume — never see a penny in revenue for their trouble. And for most of them, that is totally and completely okay.

In this practice, we'll briefly cover some of the approaches you might consider that could bring in revenue to your podcast. If you're part of the vast majority who is less interested in making income right now and more interested in making your podcast look and sound the best, feel free to skip this practice altogether or just skim it. Some of the best expert podcasts we know are income-free, and we're perfectly happy with them as-is. So with that disclaimer, let's get started!

Making Money "from" Your Podcast

There are quite a few ways of making money with — also called *monetizing* — your podcast. Individuals and companies found out long ago how to make money with audio and video content, so all of those time-tested models still have applications in the podcasting world. Yes, we can hear the new-media purists crying heresy and sacrilege, pontificating about how podcasting shouldn't follow the old ways. (Didn't we warn you people off in the intro-duction? This isn't the practice you're looking for; it's just a little practical entrepreneurial schmoozing.) Now, where were we? Oh yes, making money.

Advertising

You've worked hard on your show to improve the quality and content, and you've amassed a sizeable audience. Congratulations. You're doing something very similar — though likely on a smaller scale — to what the various TV and radio networks, producers, and stations have done: You're focusing the attention on a relatively large number of people who will share in an audio or video experience. There are advertis-ers out there who will pay you for the privilege of putting their message in front of your audience.

Paid advertisements often take the form of a pre-recorded clip, ranging in size from 15 to 60 seconds on average. These clips are then inserted into the podcast, sometimes at the front, sometimes at the end, and sometimes in the middle, before the pod-cast is released to the listener or viewer. As you can see, this arrangement isn't much different from what goes on when you're dialed into a commercial radio or TV program. The true *content* of the program is broken up by one or more (usually many more) commercial messages.

We cover advertising plans in detail in Practice 47, but it's probably a good idea to hand out some advice early on for those of you who are considering adding ads to your podcast. While the radio and TV audience has grown numb to getting as much as 20 minutes of commercial messaging in a single 60-minute program, podcast listeners have a much different experience — and, now, expectation.

 You can usually get away with a simple pre-roll or post-roll (these terms are defined in Practice 47) ad in your episode, but your audi-ence will likely not put up with three or four commercials in a 20-minute episode.

Podcasters who have decided to try running ads on their podcasts really have only two options when it comes to finding advertisers willing to spend money on their podcast:

- **Join an advertising network and let it act as your salesperson.** This is the simplest option. Many networks have active salespeople looking for large advertisers with significant sums of cash — these, for example:

  - ▶ Kiptronic (`http://kiptronic.com`)

  - ▶ PodShow (`http://podshow.com`)

  - ▶ BluBrry (`http://blubrry.com`)

  - ▶ PodTrac (`http://podtrac.com`)

  When they find advertisers, they then

  - ▶ Offer a price list to the companies or organi-zations to run their ads across one or many of the podcasts represented on the network.

  - ▶ Negotiate pricing, taking a significant chunk for themselves, and then (in most cases) allowing individual podcasters a chance to participate in the program.

  Checks are cut from the network to the pod-caster depending on how many ads were run in the various episodes during the campaign period, rinse and repeat. No fuss, no muss.

- **Act as your own sales force.** Pick up the phone and call companies whose products would be a good match with your listening audience. Podcasts such as Trader Interviews (`www.traderinterviews.com`) and Grape Radio (http://graperadio.com) have found lucrative ad deals by adopting this strategy.

This option requires a significant amount of work, a very good understanding of the size and makeup of your audience, and a specific set of skills in a variety of areas — including sales and marketing, tracking and reporting, and accounts receivable. We're not trying to push podcasters away from this option — far from it. In fact, podcasters who can *go it alone* will more than likely make a larger paycheck, if only because they cut out the commission and fees charged by the networks.

Both approaches are equally viable; each podcaster has to determine which works best for his or her situation.

 Prior to joining any network or engaging any sales force, read the contracts carefully. That's solid business advice and probably doesn't even need to be said. However, we understand that most podcasters got into this activity as a hobby and because it was fun. When money is involved, you have to put the fun on the back burner and become a fierce enough businessperson to protect your interests. That means getting rather ruthless in your examination of any legal agreements. In fact, it's worth spending the cash and getting an experienced intellectual-property attorney's opinion. Yes, we're quite serious.

Direct sales

Some podcasts are created with the express purpose of selling a product. The content is, for all points and purposes, one big sales pitch. For those of you pooh-poohing the thought of anyone subscribing to and listening to a weekly sales pitch, might we direct your attention to The Home Shopping Network? Lots of money is made in the direct-sales business, with HSN, QVC, Sunday morning infomercials, and pay-for-play talk radio raking in huge piles of cash.

But let's be realistic: The success of these networks and programs is largely predicated on reaching — or

on the potential of reaching — a massive audience. Most podcasts reach a niche market — usually a very small one in comparison to what passes for a "mass" audience. But while that might not be a true apples-to-apples comparison, there is no question that people will listen to or watch direct sales programming and purchase the items offered — enough people to keep the process going.

Companies already involved in direct-to-consumer sales will find the most benefit from this approach. Of course, if you just sell one type of widget, you're probably going to struggle to come up with compelling content for more than a couple of episodes. But if you have a full product line (say, in cosmetics or automotive tires), your marketing department probably is loaded down with compelling case studies, product specification sheets, and consumer surveys — all of which can help you sketch out the content for a dozen shows or more. Can you say, "Season One"?

So what do you say about these products to get people to buy? Why are you asking us? The pros don't have any hidden secrets — they put it all in their program! Tell your boss to give you tomorrow off so you can do some research. Sit on the couch, open the TV guide, and watch as many infomercials as you can for inspiration. Take those ideas back, figure out how you're going to get it done, and start making a plan.

You should realize that the part of the general public already listening to podcasts probably won't get overly excited about your new "podcast commercial" programming. That's okay — they aren't the ones you're appealing to. Rather, you're going after your prospective and repeat customers. Here are a few ways you can do that:

- Print the URL of your podcast on your promotional material.

- Promote the heck out of the show on your Web site.

- Make sure you've made it extremely easy for your customers to listen to or watch.

Affiliates

Affiliate marketing can be a great idea for a pod-caster who wants to run advertising but doesn't really want to hire a sales force or let a network do the selling for the show. Start by signing up with one of the following clearinghouses for affiliate relation-ships (shown in Figure 43-1):

✔ Commission Junction (`http://cj.com`)

✔ LinkShare (`http://linkshare.com`)

• **Figure 43-1:** Commission Junction and LinkShare, two premier affiliate marketing sites anyone can join.

It costs nothing to join, and you get to choose which companies you act as an affiliate for. This book isn't the place for us to go into the nuances of making a fortune with affiliate marketing (though some really smart people are doing that all the time). As a pod-caster, you can run affiliate links on your Web site, causing you to get paid when someone clicks and buys. Other podcasters have figured out that they can drive their listeners to a specific URL that links through the affiliate system — again allowing them to get paid if someone buys after using that link.

The process is a bit complicated, and you have to be able to redirect traffic from your Web site or domain name.

 Before you try this, check with your Web server or ISP to find out whether your site can handle redirects.

So far we've discussed ways of selling *inside* your show, but what if you've sold your show altogether? If your name is (say) Tony Robbins and you already have thousands of people dishing out hard cash to get your latest series of instructional content on CD, you should seriously consider using podcasting to help distribute your information — and bring in rev-enue. But if your name is Gern Blanstien and you think that people should pay to hear you play a few tunes and talk about why you left the gym early last night, you're probably going to find few folks willing to play along.

Candidly, few people have been able to crack the nut when it comes to getting paid for content in podcast form. Podcasting is very much a free medium by and large — so know that you're swimming against the stream if you decide to go this route. You should make sure that your content is worth the cash you'd be asking, and move forward with eyes wide open. To underscore this point, we remind you that Audible, a company that has sold audio content successfully for years, recently abandoned its paid-podcast division WorldCast after 18 months. It turns out that there just wasn't that much interest in self-produced paid podcasting content.

Interested parties should take a look at PrivaCast, a secure method of selling podcast content. It was created by Michael Geoghegan, a pioneer of podcasting since 2004.

 Podiobooks.com had success with both affiliation and listener donations early on.

Making Money "Because of" Your Podcast

As we said earlier, the podosphere is largely filled with free content produced by people who don't have primary goals of making money from their podcast. Radio is commercial. TV is commercial. Podcasting is still (and, with luck, always will be) dominated by the hobbyists who are more interested in having fun and exploring their art than collecting a paycheck. But a few of those intrepid "non-trepreneurs" have discovered something interesting: All those hours months and years spent perfecting their craft are paying off in profitable opportunities that they would not have had if not for their podcast.

The following sections give you examples of three podcasters (Scott Sigler, Amanda Congdon, and Rob Walch) who have made significantly more money *because of*, rather than directly from, their podcasts.

Promoting yourself

In our first book, *Podcasting For Dummies*, we mentioned Scott Sigler. At the time, he was a rookie to podcasting, using the method to release an audio version of his novel *EarthCore*. Since that time, Scott has gone on to release three more books in audio-podcast form — and has managed to infect more than 50,000 self-proclaimed junkies with his ancestral style of storytelling.

But these people do more than just listen to what Scott has to say — many of them follow his very specific instructions — to a clear advantage. On April 1, 2007, the print version of Scott's second book, *Ancestor,* was made available for purchase on Amazon.com. Prior to that date, Scott reached out to his fan base and the podosphere, asking people to purchase copies of *Ancestor* from Amazon at exactly 9:00 a.m. PST on April 1. They did — to the tune of around 6,000 purchases made — driving *Ancestor* to the No. 4 overall top-selling book for the day. In an interesting halo effect, *EarthCore* (previously published and still available on Amazon.com) had similar success.

It was a huge coup for Scott — and a huge win for the power of podcasting, with big media taking notice. Not long after, Scott was offered a three book deal from Crown Publishing, a division of Random House. He was able to prove his ability to draw an audience, something publishers are constantly on the lookout for.

Showcasing your skills

Amanda Congdon hosts ABC's (yes, as in the American Broadcasting Company) weekly video podcast called *Starring Amanda Congdon.* Prior to that, Amanda was one of the first video podcasters, hosting a show called *Rocketboom* back in October 2004. According to *BusinessWeek*, *Rocketboom* was the most popular podcast by September 2005, with over 50,000 daily downloads.

Someone took notice. Amanda left the show in June 2006 — with her audience approaching the half-million mark — to "pursue interests in Hollywood," according to *Rocketboom*'s co-founder Aaron Barron. Since that time, she has been interviewed on CNN, MSNBC, and a host of other media outlets. Her current show on ABC has been successful, and she is working on developing a comedy show with HBO.

Of course, Amanda's story is far from typical. But it does demonstrate the power of podcasting. There is little question that Amanda's personal approach to podcasting played a pivotal role in developing the huge following of *Rocketboom*. As the host of the show, she was able to demonstrate her ability not only to grow an audience, but also to show how she handled herself in front of the camera. That's important to traditional media.

 You don't have to be a compelling video presence to showcase — or refine — your skills. Maybe you're a great writer, have excellent editing skills, or are one heck of a camera operator. Use your podcast to let the world know. And don't be afraid to sing your own praises.

Becoming a consultant

Long ago in podcasting, all the way back in early 2006, it was somewhat fashionable to quit your day job and go make a living from podcasting. Rather than charging for the podcast or getting massive ad deals, many podcasters serious about this career path followed an obvious route — they went into the consulting business.

Take Rob Walch, for example. Rob was and is the host of *podCast411,* the definitive show that covers the movers and shakers of podcasting. Think of him as the Larry King of podcasting and you won't be too far off.

Rob spent a year in the consulting side, working with corporations and organizations that were trying to understand how they could use this new medium to get their message across. He parlayed his experience back into a full-time position, working at a public-relations firm that added Rob to the staff when more and more of its clients were curious about the medium. And just days ago (as of this writing), Rob accepted a job as Vice President of Podcaster Relations with Wizzard Media, the largest podcast hosting company.

And here's the good news: Rob and his compatriots who tried to get podcast consulting going back in the day probably were jumping the gun just a bit. Back then, independent podcasters made up the lion's share of all available content. Today, the scene is changing — more and more media properties and commercial entities are entering the space. For the last few months, it's been hard to find an independent podcaster represented in the iTunes Top 20 Podcast list. That's not likely to change anytime soon.

Think you've got what it takes to be a podcasting consultant? Well . . . you probably do. So update your résumé. Get a profile on LinkedIn (`http://linkedin.com`). And start checking Craig's List and other job boards. Those of you who have been podcasting for a while are about to be in a pretty position.

Corporate Podcasting

Bringing podcasting into the workplace can be a very tough sell. The majority of podcasters and podcasts available are being given away for nothing and produced independently from the basement of someone's home.

But enough about the *Podcasting For Dummies* podcast. Seriously . . .

If you look on iTunes, you will find big names entering the podosphere: *The Washington Post*, Apple, and *BusinessWeek* are voicing their opinions and overviews of the business world, reaching out to a truly global audience on improving business, financial tips, or reports concerning the status of the national or global economy. Both big and small businesses have a place in podcasting. And your company can carve out a niche of its own, provided you clearly communicate the aim and expectations of the podcast to the powers that be.

Great Expectations for Your Company's Podcast

When you approach your boss or higher-ups with the idea of hosting a podcast, you should put together a slick PowerPoint or Keynote presentation that explains exactly what you're doing. Chances are, the higher-ups don't even know how to launch iTunes on their own laptops, so you'll want to make certain you answer these questions:

✔ What a podcast is

✔ What the company will gain from having a podcast

✔ How much it will cost

It is up to you to clearly communicate in your presentation exactly *what* a podcast is. After you've explained the concept of podcasting, it's a natural progression to head into what the company will gain from hosting a podcast and how much it will cost to create one. Although it's tempting to ask for high-end podcast gear, don't; it may be more beneficial for you to work economically (but not *too* economically) at first and then upgrade later. You'll want to prove the podcast's worth before asking for the audio toys that carry the steep price tags.

Making your case to management

The hardest question for you to answer is: "What will the company gain from the podcast?" How does the company benefit from giving away quality content for free? What is the reward or advantage for all the time, effort, and investment you're asking the company to put into this podcast?

You will want to make perfectly clear to the interested parties — the managers, the executives, and those who make the final decisions concerning promotional vehicles such as podcasting — that this is *not* the new get-rich-quick vehicle. Businesses looking to podcasting as a revenue generator will be somewhat disappointed in the end result. Even with corporations such as ESPN and Disney throwing their talent and resources into it, and iTunes launching iTunesU (featuring college courses from prestigious universities and colleges from coast to coast), podcasting is still new media. The average person-on-the-street is more familiar with how a DVR works than with the simple, one-step process of subscribing to a podcast.

Therefore, before you sit down to record those first five episodes of the company podcast, be sure you've made clear the *intent* behind the podcast. Why do you want to launch this podcast? Here are a few examples of why some businesses choose to launch a podcast:

- Reach out to a larger audience
- Training for staff
- Generate public awareness of a specific issue that the company is related to or has a vested interest in

 Without focused intent, the podcast is adrift in the podosphere. Give it direction and purpose in your initial pitch — and keep that focus to carry your podcast through its first and following seasons.

Choosing the right equipment for your company's budget

Another good strategy for setting expectations is to have an inexpensive rig already priced out and ready to present to management. We've thrown out several recording options and ideas in this book that may work for you, but the easiest setup is perhaps the best one when you're beginning a corporate podcast.

The M-Audio Solution (starting at under $250 USD)

Using M-Audio's USB MobilePre as your audio interface (see Figure 44-1), you can easily build a starter studio for less than $250 USD. Along with this preamp, you can also purchase some basic goodies, such as the following:

- MXL990 condenser microphone
- Desktop microphone stand
- Male-to-female XLR cable

For software, opt for a free download of Audacity (http://audacity.sourceforge.net).

• **Figure 44-1: M-Audio's USB MobilePre is a cost-effective beginning for a clean, professional-sounding podcast.**

This starter package for your podcast is a minimal investment that will yield better-quality audio than some out-of-the-box solutions. Setup is simply a matter of plugging the USB-powered preamp into your computer or laptop and then plugging the microphone into the MobilePre. Audacity is a free download that gives you a good basic audio-editing capability with little investment. You can then record a few episodes and, after the podcast begins to take shape, look into upgrading the software (first) and (eventually) the hardware.

The Alesis Solution (starting at under $400 USD)

With the Alesis Multimix-8 FireWire mixer (shown in Figure 44-2) as your audio interface, you still retain the ease of setup (you just plug the mixer into an electric outlet and into a FireWire/IEEE-1394, and then plug the microphone into an available channel), but now you have more potential for expandability. At the time of this writing, both Alesis (www.alesis.com) and BSW (www.bswusa.com) offer a podcast package priced at $300 USD that includes these essentials:

- ✔ AKG Perception-100 condenser microphone
- ✔ Desktop microphone stand
- ✔ Male-to-female XLR cable
- ✔ Pyro 5 (Windows) or iLife, featuring GarageBand 3 (Macintosh)

This proposed package gives you the power of FireWire and accommodates additional equipment, such as more microphones, external devices such as compressors or noise gates, and extra headphones for co-hosts and guests. While still remaining under the budget of $400 USD, you can implement some more capable software such as Pyro or GarageBand. The investment is a step up from the M-Audio solution but still not too intimidating to start with.

• **Figure 44-2: For under $400 USD, the Alesis Multimix-8 offers ease of setup with terrific sound and expandability.**

This Alesis deal is just one of many package deals offered by vendors. Deals come and go, of course, so there is no way to guarantee that this Alesis package deal will be available when you get this book. Don't fret, however; Zzounds (www.zzounds.com), BSW (www.bswusa.com), and other online vendors offer great deals similar to the one described here. Ask other podcasters to point out which online vendors and brick-and-mortar stores have the best deals.

The H4 Zoom Solution (starting at under $500 USD)

The Samson H4 Zoom, shown in Figure 44-3, offers endless options as a starter podcast package — the device can be used as a portable recorder, an audio interface, and a four-channel mixer. The device also offers two additional XLR line inputs, a built-in compressor and limiter, and microphone emulators that can reproduce the audio results from several audio-industry favorites (including the Shure SM57). Add to all this the convenience of recording your audio onto a simple SD card and importing your recording sessions into your computer via clicking and dragging.

• **Figure 44-3: Enjoy the best of both worlds — portable and studio recording — with an investment in the Samson H4 Zoom.**

All this portability and versatility comes at you for $300 USD, but this is merely the foundation for this recording option. If you want to take advantage of its full potential, you can also invest in some of these add-ons:

- Two MXL990 condenser microphones (@$50 USD each)

- Two desktop microphone stands (@$9 USD each)

- Two 3-foot male-to-female XLR cables (@$6 USD each)

- Pyro 5 (Windows) or iLife, featuring GarageBand 3 (Macintosh)

For less than the $500 USD budget, you have just built a studio that not only yields a clean sound but is also portable — allowing you to do remote podcasts if necessary.

From these humble beginnings, you can begin to build your podcasting dream studio. You don't need to break the bank (yours or your company's) on your first outing as a podcaster — but once you prove your worth to the company's mission and time, upgrades are easy to come by.

Coloring within Corporate Lines

Corporate America, no matter how big or small the business is, tends to be gun-shy concerning new media. As mentioned earlier, you'll encounter a fear factor: nervous voices asking what podcasting is, how it works, what the price tag is, and what happens if it doesn't pan out.

And when it comes to the Internet, companies ask even more questions:

- Who will be receiving and reviewing this new media production, and are there security issues?

- Will this new medium reach our target audience?

- How do we get the word out to our target audience about this new medium?

- How will this new medium reflect back on the company?

As far as the art of podcasting goes, corporate podcasting may seem like a somewhat restrictive arena, with all these questions and considerations coming along for the ride. Compared to shows like *GeekLabel Radio* (which is a corporate podcast), *The GeoLogic Podcast,* and *TikiBar TV,* podcasting on a corporate level can be subject to some very rigid rules about what you can and can't do. Your guidelines for the audio or video you want to produce are already defined for you in your company's policies and procedures. Talking with your managers, too, is a good resource when you're defining the boundaries.

Sometimes, however, it's just a matter of common sense.

Corporate image

When Tee was producing the first season of *Podcasting For Dummies: The Companion Podcast,* he was breaking new ground. Wiley was doing something it had never done before: a podcast. Additionally, the podcast was hosted by a Wiley author — technically, part of the Wiley team but not armed with the company policies or the like.

While planning the launch of this podcast, Tee thought, "If I were a corporation, what would I be concerned about?" Here were his conclusions:

- ✔ Keep the podcast short. Stick to the facts and try to stay under 15 minutes.

- ✔ The *For Dummies* series is family-friendly. (Even the book Dr. Ruth wrote.) Keep the podcast along these same lines.

- ✔ Be respectful of the Wiley support crew, other *For Dummies* authors, or other Wiley imprints. You are all — what? — part of a team.

Remember that the podcast you're producing isn't your podcast, but the *company's* podcast. You are the podcast's host, but the company will have the final say.

Corporate policy

The podcast you create for your company should further the mission statement featured in orientation manuals and company Web sites. If you check these statements, you will notice that airing out dirty laundry is notably absent. This means that the podcast is not your platform to question or rebuke the policies and practices of the company. Here the concern gets back (as just mentioned) to the corporate image: Officially or unofficially, your podcast is now the voice of the corporation in the podosphere.

And yes, that's one reason why getting approval for a podcast may be a tough sell to the folks in charge.

Corporate policies will apply to a podcast in much the same way as they would apply to a booth at an expo, a promotional event, or some other appearance where the company is represented. The more you adhere to those policies, the easier it will be to define the parameters of your podcast. Sure, this may seem like common sense, but it may surprise you how often this is overlooked.

As also mentioned earlier, it never hurts to ask whether a certain topic is off-limits to discuss on the podcast (And yes, please refer to the "If you have to ask . . . " advice just given.), but the podcast is not the place to push the boundaries. Remember that the podcast is now giving a voice to the company, and you'll want to respect that, especially if it's on the company's dime.

The professional attitude

There is something to be said for being good sports in the professional sector. A podcast may appear to be a great place to slam the competition, but the podosphere is the last place you would want to do that. Word travels fast (at the speed of sound if you think about it), and when people hear you dishing on your business rivals, opinions and commentaries begin to take shape. When that happens, you may want to prepare for the backlash.

Sure, there's nothing unhealthy about healthy competition, but while you want to be part of the team among your own corporation, you should also remember that what you say and do reflects on your company. Do you really want to brag on how much better your product or service is over another, or blatantly thumb your metaphorical nose at the competition? How will a smear campaign like that reflect back on you and your company?

 As with politics, smear tactics are tempting but do very little to improve one's image in the public. Keep this in mind when you are putting together your podcasts.

Also take a listen to how your podcast sounds. Does the podcast sound like you're recording inside a broom closet? Have you planned out your podcast's format? Will you have guest segments, special features, or simply a presentation of the content with a simple sign-on and sign-off? An eye for detail will allow you to shape the podcast into a top-notch production and establish it as an essential part of your company's Web site and overall image.

Working with IT

When I refer to "IT," I'm not referring to Tim Curry as the clown from Hell. I'm referring to Information Technologies. Those frighteningly intelligent people in that department who are looking at you (the podcaster) as if you're the "stranger in town" . . .

. . . and you want to upload something on the company's Web server? Hmmm?

The IT department is not necessarily out to make your job — or your podcast — more difficult. These folks are simply trying to prevent any security issues that could arise if someone other than them uploads anything to the server. The best thing you can do is arrange a meeting with a member of the IT staff and explain *in person* (as in not via e-mail or over the phone, but a real-life talk) what you're planning to do. From there, you can get feedback about any potential problems in making this podcast happen.

To prepare for this face-to-face, you will need a crash course in IT-speak.

When you do sit down and speak with the IT representative about your podcast, you will want to have some essential data ready:

- ✔ The average file size and running time of your podcast

- ✔ An estimate of how much bandwidth an average episode will use when transferring to X listeners

- ✔ What kind of Web presence you'll be using (for example, will you be using a new blog, the company's blog, or a static Web page with XML that you update yourself?)

- ✔ What resources (if any) will be needed from the IT department

You will already have a grasp of most of this information when you record your first five episodes. As far as figuring out the amount of bandwidth needed for your podcast, refer to the handy sidebar "Bandwidth demystified," which provides a compact formula for figuring out bandwidth usage based on file size and subscribers.

Bandwidth demystified

Bandwidth refers to the online space needed to handle the amount of stuff you push out of your Web site every month. The bigger the files, the more bandwidth consumed. Compounding the problem, the more requests for the files, the more bandwidth consumed. This makes success in podcasting a double-edged sword.

Pretend that you produce a weekly show, and each episode requires 10MB of bandwidth. You publish the show on Monday, and your 100 subscribers receive your show that evening. You've just consumed 1000MB of bandwidth (100 × 10MB) for that week. In the next week, more people have found out about you, and now there are 200 subscribers. Next Monday, your bandwidth increases to 2000MB, which gets added to your previous week's total to bring you up to 3000MB.

But those extra 100 subscribers? They weren't satisfied with just the last show. They also download the previous week's show, tacking on an extra 1GB of bandwidth. Now you're at 4GB for the month.

Next week, your numbers spike again. Now you have 500 subscribers. Everyone gets the first file (which costs you 5 GB), and 300 of them are getting the previous two weeks' files (300 × 2 × 10 MB), which rings you up for and extra 6GB. You're now at (4 + 5 + 6) 15GB for the month. See how things stack up?

It's difficult to estimate how much bandwidth you'll need for your podcast because it's hard to guess how many people might be interested in your show. As a general rule, the longer your podcast episodes, the more bandwidth you need. If you plan on a five-minute biweekly podcast, you have less to worry about than someone contemplating a thrice-weekly hour-long show. The latter podcaster will be quite concerned with how to manage bandwidth because it will be an issue with even a small subscriber base.

Resource demands on the IT department will be based on how confident you feel about your abilities in updating the XML file, or how confident your IT crew feels about working third-party plug-ins like PodPress into their company's blog — or (say) allowing FeedBurner to amend the company's RSS feed to allow enclosures.

 The more self-sufficient you can be with your podcast, the happier IT will be.

To prepare for this discussion, you will also want to ask the right questions:

- What will I need to make the IT Department relax about uploading mp3 files onto the company's Web server?

- What cap, if any, is there on bandwidth usage?

- Would the IT Department prefer to handle the RSS feed, or would they prefer that I handle feed issues?

- How can the IT department and I work together to make the podcast run efficiently?

IT standards and practices vary from corporation to corporation. The more informed you are about how your IT department conducts business, the happier you, they, and your podcast will be.

And remember: As with many companies and corporations, the IT department is stretched thin; quite often, they have conversations that amount to sudden marching orders (one side just "wants it to work" with no planning or preparation). The more questions you have already answered for the IT Department along with your planning and research on the technical aspect of your podcast will win you some valuable respect points.

Working with Marketing and PR

Making a podcast on your own can be a very lonely gig. But that's not often the case when you're making a podcast for your corporation. So far you have involved the higher-ups in the company and you have just finished talking to the folks in IT. Now you turn your attention to the Marketing and Public Relations people.

Podcasting is a natural in this area: It's a new marketing, promotion, and public relations tool, seemingly built to handle all three simultaneously. That's why it's a good idea to get these people involved in what you intend to do with the company podcast. Marketing and PR people will help you in the best way possible: They will help you *promote* your podcast.

It's crucial that Marketing and Public Relations stay in touch with your plans for the podcast. Milestones such as the opening episode, the season's ending episode, interviews, and the 50th show are all newsworthy events. The Marketing and PR staff will cover these periods of your podcast for internal publications, trade magazines, local or national news services, or all of the above. If you keep them up to speed on what your podcast is doing, they may find venues to spread the word about your production.

The Marketing and Public Relations staff of your company can also assist in the planning of your podcast by suggesting or even making arrangements for guests to appear. Bringing in new voices and perspectives will keep the content fresh and lively, and open up your company's podcast to a wealth of new listeners.

 When you bring guests on the show for interviews, be sure to center the discussion around them. You are, in a manner of speaking, giving them the floor and the spotlight. Keep your show within the parameters of your company's policies but make certain to keep the focus on your guests. For more on interviews and interview tips, look at Practice 38 in this book.

The podcast will self-destruct in five seconds . . .

For a museum dedicated to the art of espionage and intelligence gathering, the International Spy Museum (www.spymuseum.org) has been attracting a lot of attention. First there was the black-tie affair that launched the Spy Museum in 2002. Then came the special exhibit on terrorism, The Enemy Within, now on tour; and the latest innovation is Operation Spy™, an intense, immersive exhibit that enables visitors to take on the mission of a spy.

Now there is *SpyCast*™, the official podcast of the International Spy Museum.

The museum is a for-profit endeavor owned by The Malrite Company, based in Cleveland, Ohio. Known for developing innovative museums and educational projects, The Malrite Company approved *SpyCast* — and for Peter Earnest, the museum's Founding Executive Director and host of *SpyCast*, it has been a success. "*SpyCast* is an extension of our mission to educate . . . another way for people, wherever they are, to meet people they would not normally meet and to hear what I hope is an intelligent conversation about intelligence and current affairs."

The podcast, Peter notes, is also a fantastic promotional vehicle for the museum. "More people are now aware of The Spy Museum and its role, which may capture their interest in wanting to visit or know more about it. [The podcast] helps extend the brand."

Knowing Your Audience

When you've touched base with everyone in the corporation who needs to bestow their approval on this podcast, there's only one thing left to do . . . and recording Episode #0 isn't it. You have a final question to ask: "Who is the audience?"

After all, the podcast that you create for stockholders may be very different from the podcast you would create for the general public.

Once again, you return to the pre-planning for your corporate podcast. You need to find out who your audience is — and from there, begin to develop the podcast to give that audience what it needs. And whether they know it or not, they just might need your podcast.

Stockholders and executives

For these podcasts, you stick with the facts, figures, and bottom lines. There's very little, if any, wiggle room for creativity, but you're hardly sentenced to a dry podcast. You can exercise a touch of professional creativity with an intro and outro that features a theme. A title — even one as straightforward as "Welcome to the Shareholders Podcast for Widget, Inc." — is a detail that your listeners will appreciate. For the outro, make certain you include the company's Web site, contact information, and even feedback specifically for the podcast itself. If the shareholders and board of executives really enjoy what they hear and want to build on it, they'll assuredly let you know.

Enhanced podcasts (described in Practice 24) are terrific podcasts for stock reports and other business issues because you can feature relevant images, charts, and links to what your audio is referring to. Your enhanced podcast becomes an interactive stockholders meeting in your iPod.

Company employees

This is a podcast for the co-workers, for the rest of the worker bees in the great corporate hive hosting the podcast. Unlike the podcast for the executives, you have (within company policies) a bit of creative latitude. Your podcast can cover a wide range of topics from training (a terrific application for enhanced podcasting), to welcoming new employees, bidding farewell to co-workers who are moving on to other opportunities, or offering an audio version of the company newsletter, broken up into segments, such as current headlines, upcoming events, and department heads' reports.

Podcasting can also bring special events such as a regional or national convention to employees who are unable to attend. Keynote speakers can have a seat with the podcast's host for an interview concerning the convention or expo, or convention attendees can sit behind the microphone for a man-on-the-street-style interview. Virtual conventions provide terrific content for podcasts, and with the portable options recommended in this practice, they're really easy to engineer.

The general public

You still answer to company policies when you're recording and editing your podcast; but depending on your target audience, you can exercise your creativity as much as you like.

In effect, you walk the line between an official podcast that represents the company and a promotional vehicle for the products, services, or merchandise your company produces. The creativity comes in when you're figuring out how to make your podcast an entertaining, informative, and professional production.

Over at Right Stuf (www.rightstuf.com), the business is anime and manga — an online warehouse of Japanese animation, posters, production cells, and more. Right Stuf also hosts *Anime Today,* a podcast

hosted and produced by various members of the online anime vendor (see Figure 44-4). The show is broken up into various segments that go into much more than what's on sale at Right Stuf. *Anime Today* includes interviews with animators, magazine editors, and voiceover talent, lessons in Japanese, and a glimpse of what's happening at RightStuf.com — both in its releases and behind the scenes. The format of the show considers what the audience wants, what would pique their interest, and (more important) what would hold their attention. Figure 44-4 gives you a look at what it's got going.

• **Figure 44-4: The Right Stuf hosts Anime Today, a podcast sponsored and produced by RightStuf.com.**

When your audience is the general public, the corporate podcast can do more than just discuss what's happening at the company. There is more artistic latitude granted to the podcaster, provided the podcast remains within those oft-mentioned company policies. Allow yourself opportunities to explore, but keep the podcast's purpose in mind. Consider what an audience would like to hear from a company, and then allow yourself a little bit of fun in reaching out to your clientele, pulling back the curtain, and showing them how everything happens.

Podcasting for Government and Not-for-Profit Agencies

Practice 45

In This Practice

✔ Examining the benefits of podcasting for government and not-for-profits

✔ Putting together your pitch

✔ Dealing with IT policies

The White House. The ACLU. The Pentagon. The Peace Corps. At first glance, you wouldn't think there was a common thread among these four, but there is: podcasting. With the success of the *One America* podcast, which launched in 2004, politicians, lobbyists, not-for-profit organizations, and government entities are discovering the power in podcasting. There is a real potential in reaching out to the public through podcasting, but also a hint of apprehension on account of the distribution method and how much access and information is granted to the general public.

In reality, it's quite easy to launch an informative and educational podcast for your agency or not-for-profit (NFP). It's also easy to follow security protocols, control distribution, and accomplish a quality podcast with minimal financial investment.

Why Government and NFP Agencies Should Podcast

The big question that begins the debate: *Why should our agency podcast?* That question launches the brainstorming and eventual direction of the podcast. Without the reason behind the podcast, your podcast goes nowhere.

And there are plenty of reasons why you want your agency to podcast:

✔ Training

✔ Current events and announcements

✔ Public relations

✔ Outreach programs

Training

On-the-job training to implement new software, new hardware, or new policies is always a continuous sinkhole of time. While trying to meet goals and deadlines for the fiscal year, something new is presented in the workplace, and time must be set aside for proper orientation and training to understand what it will bring to the office.

The problem with training is that it can (and in most cases, does) take employees away from the office for days. In the meantime, e-mail, responsibilities, and current to-do items begin to stack up — slowing productivity till it lags behind the current schedule.

With podcasts, employees can download training sessions to their computers and either transfer them to portable mp3 players or listen them to at their desks while meeting other goals of the day. Yes, this kind of efficiency will rely on how good you (and your co-workers) are at multitasking, but one great benefit is that this type of training does not take individuals away from their desks for days on end. Training delivered through this method can also be given a hint of flexibility. The sessions can be entertaining, informative, and — if enhanced podcasts are implemented — interactive.

Current events and announcements

Printed newsletters have long been the preferred way to get the message out to your staff concerning news, upcoming seminars, and events beneficial to your agency. The problem with printed newsletters is in their distribution, cost, and — more importantly — the time they take to produce and to read. Take a casual survey and find out exactly how many of your co-workers have *read* those newsletters. Compare those numbers to how many employees have set them aside for later reading. For some agencies, e-mail bulletins have attempted to replace the conventional print newsletters, but the temptation to "print for later" (or even set aside and mark for a later review) is no different from the impulse to set aside a hard-copy newsletter.

Podcasting provides a cost-effective solution to newsletters in that time, finances, and resources invested into print are replaced by the production time of recording and editing news articles. The audio medium can also provide a more direct means of delivering news to agencies, depending on how the news is delivered. It's one thing to read about a current event or a policy change, but *hearing* news and issues can carry more of an impact. Along with taking advantage of the impact of audio, delivery of the file can be confirmed easily with a check of the subscription list and download stats.

The content of your news podcast will also be more dynamic than its print counterpart. With audio, interviews and comments featured in printed material suddenly come alive with the actual voice of the person interviewed.

 Every section of your podcast can be voiced by a different department head or editor, and reports from seminars and events can be on-location interviews with convention attendees and keynote speakers. Through podcasting, a newsletter has more of an impact on its target audience.

Public relations

The best way to deal with misconceptions and misinterpretations of agencies' agendas and actions is to improve public relations between your organization and the outside world. One definition of *public relations* is "the state of the relationship between the public and a company or other organization or a famous person," and podcasting is quickly becoming a new means of strengthening this relationship.

A podcast allows you to give either a formal look at your agency (with a structured, organized show format) or a more casual view (with a free-form behind-the-scenes look). Whatever option you decide to pursue, your podcast becomes an audio connection to the outside world and a platform for the general public to hear your agency's perspective.

U.S. government organizations such as the USDA, Armed Forces (all branches), and National Park Service all use podcasting as a way to get their message (and their angle on what's happening) out to the world. Your podcast can be a window into *your* world, and that's what PR is all about.

Every week, the Pentagon Channel does just that with *Rucksacks & Rations,* a podcast featuring interviews with American soldiers stationed everywhere from Alabama to Afghanistan (see Figure 45-1). This podcast is less about the news and more about the people who are making the news. Alongside *Rucksacks & Rations,* the Pentagon Channel presents programming of all kinds for both active military and families and friends of the military, offering a different viewpoint on situations at home and around the world.

• **Figure 45-1:** *Rucksacks & Rations,* **a podcast from the Pentagon Channel, serves as part of public relations for the Armed Forces.**

Outreach programs

Many NFP agencies are geared for education and social awareness, but getting your agency's message out to the public can provide a challenge when you have a limited budget. Podcasting, though, offers up your NFP's mission to a worldwide audience and can attract new traffic to your Web site.

NFP organizations benefit the most by networking with other NFP groups. Podcasting can provide your subscribers (be they supporters, potential supporters, or other NFP representatives searching for solutions) with a weekly, biweekly, or monthly report on what your organization is doing to further the mission of your NFP.

Other applications of your podcast can include interviews with other NFP representatives, experts in the field your NFP focuses on, and individuals who are part of your agency and help make it run. Your podcast can also encourage community from your subscribers, giving them a way of becoming involved in your NFP's mission.

This podcast is your chance to inform your subscribers and even your own group. Some podcasts specifically educate NFP groups on how to keep things running efficiently or how to start up a NFP for a cause they believe in. *The 501c3Cast* (www. 501c3cast.com) is an independent podcast hosted and produced by people dedicated to helping NFP professionals and volunteers through a bi-weekly podcast. *The 501c3Cast* (shown in Figure 45-2) covers issues, concerns, and solutions from personal experiences and other NFP groups, nationwide and from around the world, creating a community dedicated to making things happen.

• **Figure 45-2: The 501c3Cast is a podcast for NFP groups by those who work with NFP groups.**

Working within Government Guidelines

Practice 44 offers some tips for opening discussions and keeping the IT staff happy when you approach them with plans to upload mp3s onto the company's Web server. If you think facing IT groups is difficult, try making the podcast pitch to the government.

The government can make the implementation of a podcast an act of Congress. (Literally.) Along with security issues, many government agencies have stringent policies on what can (and cannot) be downloaded to office computers and servers. Some of these prohibited applications include Skype and iTunes, two of the most important tools covered in this book. You also need to go through the approval process to download other applications essential to podcasting such as HotRecorder, Call Recorder, and other applications.

Doing your homework

Before planning a podcast, you will want to prepare for tackling paperwork and policy, and this will mean coming up with answers for your supervisors and IT representatives. Here are some of the questions you'll need to answer:

- ✔ **How secure will the downloading be?** If your agency's podcast is geared more to the internal employees of the agency, you can create secure RSS feeds that cannot be downloaded outside the agency's intranet. If you want to be listed on nonsecure directories, such as Podcast Pickle, Podcast Alley, and iTunes, then you will want to make clear that the RSS feed will be featured on your agency's public Web site. (Heck, even the CIA has a public Web site.) The RSS feed, be it private or public, is a one-way port of access. This isn't peer-to-peer, but rather a syndication of mp3, PDF, or video files going from the server to subscribers.

- ✔ **How safe are these downloads?** While Skype can be used as an instant messenger, the most basic of firewalls disables the ability to exchange files from user to user. Skype, HotRecorder, and Call Recorder are all safe, virus-free downloads. iTunes, developed by Apple, Inc., is also a completely safe download. Other well-known mp3 player software — such as Windows Media Player (developed by Microsoft), Real Media (developed by Real Media), and QuickTime (developed by Apple) — are also checked and verified as virus-free before they're offered for downloading.

- ✔ **Who will the audience be?** This will decide exactly how much work you will have when developing the RSS feed for the podcast. The advantages in developing a podcast for a government intranet is that you have control over what people will be using as their listening device. You can decide on either iTunes or Juice for everyone in the agency (using a player like Juice limits access to distractions at work, such as the iTunes Music Store). These standards can also be applied to recording software and other post-production applications.

If your podcast is for the general public, the RSS feed can be kept to the basics and even iTunes-friendly. Then you'll need to have a show format planned so your supervisors and superiors have an idea what your podcast is about.

Considering workarounds

There will be other discussions and issues beyond the three just mentioned — and you might face some opposition to the downloading of unapproved software. So while the podcast itself may be encouraged, applications such as Skype may not be allowed. If you run into software roadblocks, what are your options?

- ✔ **Download Skype at home.** Because Skype is a safe and free download, there is no risk on your end for downloading and using it for interviews on your home computer. It may be a challenge to be reimbursed for your download of HotRecorder or Call Recorder, but the investment is inexpensive at $16 USD. You can then record your own interviews at home and bring in the audio for post-production editing.

- ✔ **Record after hours, off-site.** You may be unable to record during work hours (or from your cubicle after hours) due to security clearances and the like. Still, the podcast needs to be produced. Take your production off-site. Record from your home or a comfortable social location like a quiet corner in a favorite restaurant. The podcast may sound more informal if placed in a social setting, but you can find a location elsewhere and bring the audio in for additional editing. The cost here is in the time and effort required to set up your podcast for recording on your time.

✔ **Limit early episodes' running times.** Who will your audience be? What are the expectations? How much bandwidth will your agency allow for your podcast? Your first few shows should be short and sweet, somewhere within the 10-to-20-minute range. From here, superiors can listen or review the early episodes, and either greenlight longer episodes or approve the current direction of the podcast. By keeping the running times of your starting five episodes to between 10 and 20 minutes each, you keep the investment in recording and post-production time to a minimum. There is still an investment, but hardly at the level of a podcast running close to the hour mark.

Keeping your eyes on the prize

It may sound like you have to jump through a lot of hoops before you get to Episode #0 of your agency's podcast, but remember: Keep your focus on the intent of your podcast. The road to the podcast's launch may not be as easy as launching your own podcast, but are you keeping in mind the goals that you've mapped out? This production is not necessarily for you but for the agency you work for, furthering its mission statement and finding a new audience that will support your organization in the future.

A legacy reaches a global audience

Part not-for-profit, part Presidential memorial, The Kennedy Center (www.kennedy-center.org) in Washington, D.C., is the continuing legacy of President John F. Kennedy, who wanted to offer the arts to everyone, everywhere. Had he lived long enough to see the advent of podcasting, he would have seen his dream realized.

ArtsEdge (http://artsedge.kennedy-center.org), the National Arts Education Network, is hosted by the Kennedy Center, dedicated to bringing the arts, art history, and art-related programming to the Internet. In January 2006, Director Nuit Hansgen and Instructional Media Developer Kristin Holodak launched the ArtsEdge Podcast with *The Sounds of China,* highlights from the 2006 China Festival. They observed, "We knew we wanted to podcast, but what would make great audio? What's going to make a great story?" Hansgen then turned to the upcoming China extravaganza: "We had an amazing opportunity with the China Festival, so we started taping as much as we could. Could we come up with a fantastic piece or a beautiful failure that we can learn from?"

Instead, ArtsEdge created a fantastic piece that *everyone* could learn from. More separate feeds followed, including one large master feed that features both audio and video podcasts, called (rather appropriately) *The Kitchen Sink* (http://artsedge.kennedy-center.org/podcasts/allArtsedge.xml).

The Kennedy Center's ArtsEdge figured podcasting would be a hit with their ArtsEdge users, but it was the global response that caught Hansgen off-guard. "A huge majority of our subscribers were in China. It wasn't just local community-Washington, D.C., folks who were coming out to the festival. It wasn't just ArtsEdge users. It was the power of being able to pull it up through the podcast catalogs and subscribing to it."

Holodak finds that what ArtsEdge is doing seems tailor-made for podcasting: "I'm generating content constantly. We are either shooting video or talking to [artists] on audio. Endless source material, and it becomes a matter of how do I get this out to my users? Podcasting fits that so well. They find us once, they subscribe, and then I arrive on their doorstep."

And what is the next podcasting idea from ArtsEdge?

"Ben Franklin's iPod." Hansgen reveals. "What would be on Ben Franklin's iPod, if he had one?"

So long as you keep an eye on the drive and the intent of your podcast, the application of your podcast is limitless. Government and NFP agencies now have the ability to reach out to the public and distribute content to branches and representatives on a national and international level — with minimal financial investment.

Further your mission and offer up your agency's agenda to the world. It may surprise you to discover whom you hear from in reply.

Practice 46

Promotional Podcasting

*P*odcasting will make you an overnight success! (Uh-huh.) Business entrepreneurs, aspiring writers, and ambitious politicians who've scaled that peak may lead you to believe that when it comes to big bucks, windfalls of critical acclaim, and runaway notoriety, podcasting is the Acela of gravy trains. That, sad to say, would be podcasting in the still-elusive perfect world we all long for.

But how essential is podcasting in the promotions arena? Can podcasting get the word out about your business, your book, your music, or whatever you wish to introduce to the consumer? And can podcasting get the word out to a captive audience without breaking your financial budget? The answer to these questions is yes, yes, and *ooohh yes*. For a fraction of the cost of conventional radio advertising, your message, product, or upcoming event can reach an audience that is local, regional, national, and international.

You may not become an overnight success on account of podcasting, but you can get your message around the world and back again overnight. As a promotions tool, podcasting is invaluable.

Examining What Goes into the Promotional Podcast

As much as we, the creative minds behind this book, would love to tell you differently, podcasting is *not* the get-rich-quick solution of the Internet, nor is it going to make you a superstar. Did it reinvent MTV veejay Adam Curry? Yes. Did podcasting introduce Scott Sigler to the publishing industry? That it did. Did two stay-at-home moms win over a major advertising budget for their podcast about being stay-at-home moms? Very true. All these people — Curry, Sigler, and The MommyCast — had to work their tails off in the beginning days of podcasting and *continue* to work their tails off to maintain the momentum. So, is podcasting a profitable venture? It can be, but rarely.

On a promotional front, podcasting helped these folks reach new audiences, audiences hungry for the content these podcasters were talking about:

- ✔ For Curry, *The Daily Source Code* (`www.daily sourcecode.com`) is the promotion of podcasting, a brand-new way of generating and delivering content to people everywhere. Indirectly, the podcast is also a promotional vehicle for Adam Curry, establishing him as an authority (otherwise known as The Podfather) in this new medium.

- ✔ For Scott Sigler (`www.scottsigler.net`), his podcast novels *EarthCore, Ancestor, Infection,* and *The Rookie* promoted his books. Ultimately, he scored book contracts with two publishers.

- ✔ *The MommyCast* promotes the art of being stay-at-home moms, shattering the myth that stay-at-home parenting is a cushy job. Dixie Cups, serving up the sponsorship paycheck, knew that these women would also promote its product because it was something they used around the house. Everyone listening to *The MommyCast* is, in fact, the target audience.

So, how did these folks make their shows a hit while promoting consciously or subliminally an idea, product, or concept? The secret to their success is in what makes a good podcast into a *really* good podcast: *content*. These podcasters had a clear idea of what they wanted their podcasts to offer — whether it was commentary on the world around them or worlds they dreamed up — and they delivered it with conviction, confidence, and clarity.

Podcasting has proven itself to be a fantastic way to reach new audiences. National Public Radio, by podcasting its popular offerings like *Car Talk, Fresh Air,* and *Studio 360,* opened up these shows to new audiences downloading content from iTunes. Via video podcasting, Pixar Studios generated hype for the film *Ratatouille,* with *The Ratatouille Video Podcast,* which went behind the scenes of this culinary comedy.

Then, in the political arena, Barack Obama has taken a page from Senator John Edwards' podcasting playbook with *The Official Barack Obama Video Podcast.* What all these podcasts focus on is not so much what they are promoting, but what their episode's *content* will be.

When planning a podcast that will be a promotion of something or someone, go back to the basics of planning the podcast itself:

- ✔ What will the podcast's direction be?

- ✔ Do you have content that can span five shows and still engage the audience?

- ✔ Where will the show be six months from now?

- ✔ What's the show's posting schedule?

- ✔ What's the show's running time?

When you have the content for the podcast planned, *then* focus on the promotional angle. How do you want to promote your agenda? In the opening? During the outro? You can also cite Web sites and organizations in your ID3 tags (See, *told* you those things would come in handy!) and even at key moments in enhanced podcasts.

 A successful promotional podcast plans for the promotion around its content. Without good content, the podcast fails.

Making Sure You Have a Plan for Your Promo

So suppose you decide that promotion should take precedence over planning a format or mapping out content for your podcast. Let the show just happen and evolve on its own. After all, isn't that what podcasting is all about? Spur-of-the-moment? Off the cuff? In the moment?

Well, in most cases, probably not. Shooting from the hip is a very dangerous path for your podcast to take. That's because it's emphasizing the promotion and not the *content* being delivered. Be advised: In such a case, the podcast is well on its way to becoming an infomercial. If that's what you want, check out Practice 44 for ways to make the show effective in that role. Otherwise, indulge your inner master planner a bit.

In some situations, companies and corporations want to launch a podcast "because it's a cool thing to do" and an even better way to promote their business. But if you ask the potential podcaster, "So what will your podcast be about?" you may want to prepare for the answer of "I don't know" because that is usually the inevitable one. It's also a clue: These are the potential podcasters needing to be talked *out* of podcasting because they care little about the podcast and are caught up in the high returns with minimal investments.

Well, let's be clear — minimal *financial* investments.

Podcasting to promote yourself, your business, or your agenda is a good *reason* to podcast, but it shouldn't *be* the podcast. When putting together your promotional podcast, ask yourself the following questions:

- ✔ What do you want to say?
- ✔ What is your message?
- ✔ Are you willing to invest your time, resources, and efforts into creating a good podcast?

Promotional podcasting, contrary to the message of self-made millionaires who work from home, is not a one-way ticket to overnight success; it's merely a tool. Anyone can buy a power drill and a nail gun, but the carpenter who has the plans to the summer home is the one who knows how to get the most out of them. The same thing is true with your podcast: Without a plan, your idea goes nowhere.

Sadly, we'll always have Paris

The textbook example of what *not* to do in a podcast occurred in April 2005 when the publicity crew behind a remake of the 3-D horror classic *House of Wax* decided it would be a good idea to launch *The Paris Hilton Podcast*, hosted by the heiress, supermodel, and the film's supporting actress herself. Paris would record podcasts running between 5 to 10 minutes that would generate hype for the upcoming thriller.

From the overly produced opening and the vapid, bored demeanor of the show's host, it was clear that Hilton was handed a recorder and told to talk about anything (apparently she could only do this in 10-minute increments) and to promote the movie at least once during the podcast. She did mention *House of Wax*, usually in the first minute. The remainder of the show's content consisted of contrived banter, shopping, and patronizing photographers and fans all screaming for her attention.

The podcast did little to help generate hype for *House of Wax*, a movie that lasted at the box office as long as the podcast lasted in production. The lesson learned is that there is more to a podcast than just hitting the red button on a digital recorder and flying by the seat of your pants. Particularly when it comes to promotion, a *plan* is needed. Otherwise, the end result is *The Paris Hilton Podcast*, one of the most ill-executed promotional podcasts due to its lack of direction and planning.

Show's Over — Nothing More to See Here

Podcasting for promotional purposes has a quality about it that many other podcasts do not have (and which we zero in on at the end of this book): an end. With a podcast that pushes your upcoming product, election, or appearance, you're generating hype and attention for yourself, and then the event happens. Provided you implement other means of getting the word out, you have a fantastic showing at your event. A day or two later, you begin to think a bit about the podcast and the listenership that you have cultivated. Depending on when you do your podcast — weekly, bi-monthly, or monthly — you note the date and think, "They're expecting more content."

But . . . you're done. Now what do you do?

Unlike podcasts that launch and plan for the future, promotional podcasts should actually do the opposite: Plan for the future before you launch. After your event, product release, or ultimate goal is reached, what will you do with the podcast audience you have amassed? Will the podcast end? Will you want to revisit it in the future? Will it sit in the Podcast Pickle directory, merely gathering dust until someone comes across it? The easiest thing to do when your podcast is done is simply to say, "We're done. Goodnight. Go home. It's over!" But there are also other options you can consider:

✔ **Scale back show postings to a monthly schedule and make it a "What's Happening Now" show.** When Scott Sigler's podcast novels hit their conclusions, he podcasts a monthly show called *The Bloodcast* where he podcasts other (but related) content: short stories, updates to upcoming appearances, and any developments on his upcoming titles. He maintains the connection with his listeners with the periodic updates.

 Scaling back your show to a monthly posting schedule is an excellent way to keep your audience engaged without cutting ties completely.

✔ **Announce a hiatus between this podcast and a new season.** Perhaps you will want to revisit this podcast in the future, either as a recap of what has happened since the event you are promoting or to announce upcoming appearances and developments of your podcast's original promotion. In this case, announce that your podcast will be taking a break. Encourage your listenership to stay subscribed to this podcast's feed for an upcoming second season and give an approximate date for the new season.

✔ **Record content from the event your podcast is promoting and offer it as future installments for the podcast.** Paul Fisher and Martha Holloway of DancingCat Studios produce and host *The Balticon Podcast* (http://balticon podcast.org), a bi-monthly and monthly podcast that promotes Baltimore's Memorial Day science-fiction-and-fantasy convention. Before the weekend that *TBC* is currently promoting, Paul and Martha play interviews from the previous Balticon, ending these episodes with, "If you like what you've heard, make plans for Balticon this year." After the current year's Balticon begins, Paul and Martha start collecting interviews and events for the next season of *TBP*. By following this pattern, promotion continues for Balticon, and new content is generated for the next season of the podcast.

✔ **Package the podcast episodes and either distribute them for pay or as part of another product.** For Tim Borouquin of The Podcast Brothers and Podcast and New Media Expo (both found at http://newmediaexpo.com), special events and speaker presentations are recorded and offered as both free and paid subscription podcasts. The free podcasts are his promotion for the upcoming expo, featuring status reports, acknowledgment of new sponsors, and selections from featured speakers of the previous expos. On the paid subscription feed, listeners can virtually attend the previous year's programming, hearing the panels and talks recorded live.

NBC/Universal and The SciFi Channel on their DVD release of *Battlestar Galactica* will package Ron Moore's podcast as an extra feature. And Wiley Publishing has included Season One of *Podcasting For Dummies: The Companion Podcast* on the DVD that comes with this book. Repackaging the podcast is a terrific solution for any possible issues with server space — and also provides your clientele with an invaluable audio resource.

A plan, a promotion, a successful podcast

Back in the summer of 2005, Wiley Publishing was kicking around some ideas for promoting *Podcasting For Dummies*. Tee Morris, suggested, "Why don't we do a companion podcast for the book?"

The phone went silent for a moment, and then came, "Why didn't we think of that?"

Podcasting For Dummies: The Companion Podcast went online in January 2006, posting twice a month with something new in podcasting or offering a more in-depth look at a topic from the book. Tee initially planned out 12 episodes, but the season eventually grew to 20 episodes as the podcast rocketed to the top of the iTunes Technology rankings, increased traffic to ForDummies.com, and (more importantly) sold books.

And yes, with this title, Tee returns with Season Two of *Podcasting for Dummies: The Companion Podcast*. He is also bringing to the podosphere *Podcasting For Dummies: Enhanced,* a special feed that offers enhanced and video episodes! New media in action, folks.

There is also the choice to simply end the podcast with a "Th-th-th-that's All Folks!" kind of episode, closing up shop and letting the podcast end on your terms, your way. What is important to keep in mind here is that you have many options for your podcast after the promotion is done. You can keep it simple with a farewell episode or *hard podfade* (covered in detail in Part VIII) or explore other options of distribution and production. The way you want to wrap it up is your call.

Adding Advertising to Your Podcast

In This Practice

✔ Why adding ads to a podcast doesn't make you evil

✔ Why adding ads to a podcast may make you commercial

✔ Getting ready for and executing successful advertising plans

In Practice 43, we give a brief overview of several ways in which you can derive revenue from your podcast. We also try to stress that podcasting and profiting don't necessarily go hand in hand — and that the road to podcast-driven riches is largely unexplored territory as of this writing. But we recognize that this won't always be the case, and that many enterprising people and organizations will figure out the secret sauce that enables them and others a clear path to the pot of gold at the end of the RSS feed. (How's that for a mixed metaphor?)

This practice focuses specifically on running advertisements inside of your podcast. As we have tried to repeatedly stress, you are not required to turn your podcast into a moneymaker in order to be considered *expert*. But we do recognize that many of our readers would like to see some income in exchange for their efforts. For those folks, advertising represents the low-hanging fruit of revenue generation. Okay, implementing advertising in your podcast may not actually be all that easy to do, but it's by far the easiest methodology to explain. There's more to it than you might think.

Measuring Audience Demographics

Before you start firing off the e-mails or calling up potential sponsors of your show, you'll want to get your ducks in a row. Many of the companies you'll be approaching have been spending money in traditional media (radio, print, TV) for a long time. They probably have sophisticated media property evaluation processes already in place and are likely to ask you for some hard facts about your show. "My show is really good" is not a hard fact.

It's going to be very difficult to convince someone to pay for the privilege of marketing to your audience if you don't know much *about* your audience. Figuring out how many people are listening is important, but so is understanding who these people are — and what sorts of behavior they are likely to engage in when they're not listening to your podcast.

Determining the size of your audience

A good place to start is audience size. You have a variety of tools at your disposal to help you gauge how many people are listening to your podcast:

- **Count your subscribers.** If you are already using FeedBurner (`http://feedburner.com`), this is a simple task. FeedBurner uses a sophisticated (though not perfect) methodology of analyzing all of the accesses to your podcast's RSS feed. You can read up about it on the FeedBurner Web site if you like. Or you could take our word for it — it's the most likely candidate for a standardized method of estimating subscribers.

- **Count your downloads.** Not all your listeners will bother to subscribe to your RSS feed. In fact, many podcasters find that subscribers make up less than half of their total downloads. If you are using PodPress (covered in Practice 26) and have enabled tracking, you are already covered. PodPress will give you a count of the number of times one of your episodes was downloaded — whether from a subscriber or someone listening to your show right from your Web site.

 A quick note on the accuracy of these — and all other — metrics discussed in this practice. They are, at best, imperfect. Eliminating duplicates and trying to get to the true meaning of unique downloads are puzzles that have yet to be solved. So take these — and all other — numbers with a grain of salt. In fact, make that a whole dash of salt.

This is all good and fine if you're using both FeedBurner and PodPress. But what if you aren't? Well, in that case you have to get into some fairly heavy Web-server-log analysis; the log is where all these statistics are tracked. But the brass tacks of parsing server log files is outside of the scope of this book. Try *Web Analytics For Dummies* (by Pedro Sostre and Jennifer LeClaire, from Wiley) if you find yourself in this situation. Or better yet, really consider using FeedBurner and PodPress. We know that quite a few technical-minded podcasters prefer to use

solutions other than these, and we applaud them for their efforts. But if you just want reliable and near-standardized numbers, try out these good tools.

Profiling your audience

Knowing how many people are listening is helpful, but potential advertisers are also going to want to know some information about these people:

- How old are they?
- How much income do they have?
- What products are they interested in?
- How much money do they have to spend?

This is the true meat of audience profiling, and you get that data by conducting surveys.

Choosing a service to create the survey

Plenty of survey-creation options exist, many of which are completely free to use. Try FreeOnlineSurveys.com or SurveyMethods.com to start. They'll allow you to create your own list of questions, but keep in mind that these tools don't give you many options beyond that. If you don't want your audience exposed to the advertising from these services, or want a lot more control on the look and feel of the survey, check out Survey Monkey (`http://surveymonkey.com`) and Zoomerang (`http://zoomerang.com`). You'll part with a few bucks, but you'll have a lot more say over the look and feel.

If you are with the advertising network Kiptronic (`kiptronic.com`), it has a built-in survey application that all of its affiliate podcasters can use. There are some basic questions, but the system is flexible enough to allow for some custom questions.

Deciding what questions to ask

Before you start driving your audience to your survey, you need to plan out your questions. Remember that the goal of the survey is to gather information that's important to potential advertisers, and not to satisfy your own curiosity. Advertisers probably don't care what other podcasts your audience is listening to and how folks discovered your program. In fact, their needs whittle down to three main pieces of information:

- ✔ Age
- ✔ Sex
- ✔ Income

Understanding these three data points about your audience will give you and your potential advertisers a good look at who is listening to your show. Once you know who is listening, you can start to make some assumptions as to what types of products and services your audience is likely to care about.

Not all advertisers will be satisfied with these three data points. Because podcast advertising is still new to many companies, gathering additional data, such as the following, is a good idea:

- ✔ Occupation
- ✔ Education
- ✔ Family size
- ✔ Marital status

Going a step further, try to anticipate what information an advertiser might be interested in. If you're going to approach companies that do the majority of their business directly with consumers via the Internet, you may wish to ask how much money your listeners have spent online in the last 12 months. If you are going after the automotive industry, find out what kinds of cars your listeners drive and how often they have their cars serviced. Going after a do-it-yourself home-improvement company? Find out about home ownership. Think about whom your company's target audience is likely to be — and then ask your listeners whether they fit the bill.

One company, PodTrac (`www.podtrac.com`), takes care of much of this heavy lifting for you. You don't

have much (read: *any*) control over the questions asked, but it asks a wide enough range of questions so that you can get a good handle on who is listening. Even better — it uses this data to build you a very nice media kit to give out to potential advertisers. (We cover media kits a bit later in this practice.)

Compelling your audience to take the survey

Once you have the questions planned out and have selected a company or service to collect the information for you, you need to get your audience to participate in the survey. Make this easy for them by providing a link to your survey in the show notes on each episode — that's where you talk about the survey and drive your audience to take it.

Don't think you can mention it just once and have most of your listeners rush to take the survey. For four to six episodes, plan on talking about the survey and asking more and more of your listeners to take it. After the first mention, be appreciative of those who have taken the survey on subsequent episodes. Feel free to plead for their compliance, but do it in an apologetic manner. Few people enjoy taking surveys, and your understanding of this can go a long way toward convincing reluctant people to help you out by taking part.

 And now for a dose of reality — you should expect only a small percentage (perhaps in the single digits) of your listeners to actually follow your request. But that's okay; you need not get a 50% compliance rate to generate relevant findings.

Keep in mind that most of the statistics you see on the news or in print are derived from extremely small sample sizes in comparison with the total population. We know we've never been called by someone to inquire about our opinions on the job the President is doing. But someone is comfortable enough with the science of statistics to extrapolate the feelings of the country based on a few thousand (or hundred) random samples. And if that's good enough for politics, it's good enough for podcasting!

Building a Media Kit

Once you understand enough about your podcast to sell it, you need to package that information in a *media kit*. The purpose of the media kit is simple — to get someone at an organization or company interested to the point of calling you back. It's not designed to sell your podcast. Sorry, but it won't. That's *your* job. (Or the job of some salesperson you hire.) But before you can do that, you need to get the company's attention with a rock-solid media kit.

In Chapter 37, we give you the lowdown on what types of materials you'll want to include in your media kit. Additionally, we also wanted to give you some excellent real-world examples of media kits. So take a look at the DVD that comes with this book. In it, you'll find media kits for

- Trader Interviews
- Grape Radio
- J.C. Hutchins

Examine them. Borrow from them. And make them your own. Remember: The idea is to get someone interested enough to listen to your pitch. A great media kit (yeah, you'll want to spend a few bucks on it) can be what gets your foot in the door.

Establishing a Fair Rate

You've received great survey data from your audience. You've developed an exceptional media kit that will strike fear into the hearts of those who dare not sponsor your show. You are ready to start the thrilling undertaking of making cold calls and knocking on doors. And you don't have the first idea of how much to charge.

Hey, welcome to the club. It's a brave new industry that you've found yourself in, and it's just different enough from anything else as to render years and years of historical advertising pricing completely worthless to you. Here's yet another place where podcasters have to strike out on their own.

While we don't have an easy answer about what to charge advertisers, we do have some advice:

- **Pick a price and stick with it.** You never want to pick up the phone or make a sales call without having preselected how much you're going to charge. So figure out how much you want, and then finesse that into some numbers that might help justify the amount. What does that break down to on a per-listener basis? How amazingly targeted is your show that the advertiser is getting no waste? Be confident, and be firm.

 Don't discount your rate right off the bat — and never discount it much more than 15%. If you deepen that discount, it implies that you've padded your original number. As Dave Slusher of the Evil Genius Chronicles says, "You can never sell out. You can only sell too cheap." Those are words to live by.

- **Don't sell yourself short.** Large companies like to write checks for large sums of money. We're not suggesting you should overcharge, but you should also know that companies are presented with fantastic opportunities every day. They have limited resources — they're forced to pick and choose the ones that can have the greatest impact on their business.

  Also, the larger the sum, the more likely someone with greater decision-making potential will get involved. If you ask for a few hundred dollars, no one important may take note. Change that to a few thousand? Now you're getting someone's attention.

✔ **Don't price-gouge.** Yes, we realize this dictum may seem to be in opposition to what we just said here. But in all honesty, you have to give them their money's worth. Since you need to charge a lot to get their attention, *give* them a lot. You could make the campaign longer (like several months instead of a few weeks), or you can sweeten the pot with additional ad units. (See the next section for ideas.) The takeaway: Make it worth their while.

✔ **Follow the market.** Advertising in podcasts, while still in the early stages, has been happening since 2005. That's given ample time for ideas to be tried and tested, and fair rates to be set.

Find a podcast similar to yours that is accepting ads, and see what it charges. You can just call the podcasters who run the show, or e-mail them to ask, if you like. If you feel a little strange about this, you can fall back to the same thing that traditional media sites do to keep up with the competition — price-shop them. Yes, it's rather dishonest to pretend to be someone you are not, looking for a service that you really won't buy. But it's how things work in business. If that makes you uncomfortable, so be it. But we'd be remiss if we didn't give you the option.

 The various ad networks discussed in Practice 43 are usually quite happy to discuss the pricing terms they think they can get for your podcast. Call or e-mail them to see what they have to say. Be prepared to discuss download numbers, show composition, and other pertinent details about your show — and to sit through a sales pitch on why you should join their network. (Which maybe you should. Your call.)

Creating an Advertising Plan

So . . . do you have all of that stuff figured out? Great. Time to figure out a plan for how you'll integrate advertising messages into your podcast as a whole — including your Web site. There isn't (and shouldn't be) a one-size-fits-all approach to designing a successful advertising plan for podcasts. Too many divergent factors come into play — and way too many podcasters are staunch independents who want to do their own thing. We embrace this philosophy and encourage lots of creative flexibility while you're coming up with a plan.

 Some of this flexibility may become more standardized in the near future. Recently, a group called The Association for Downloadable Media was formed, with the express purpose of developing some standards for podcasters who are seeking advertisers. It's still very early in the formative stages of this organization; we fully expect that other competing organizations will come on the scene. Keep your eyes on this space.

Pre-/post-rolls

As you might have guessed, a *pre-roll* ad is one that plays before your episode gets started. Conversely, a *post-roll* happens after the episode has finished playing. As of this writing, pre- and post-roll commercials are the mainstay of podcast advertising; networks like Podshow (`http://podshow.com`) and Kiptronic (`http://kiptronic.com`) have their own customized ad-insertion technologies that allow ads to be dropped into shows before they're downloaded by listeners.

That's the big plus of a pre-roll ad to podcasters — no extra work is required to add the audio to existing or future episodes. Of course, you can use pre- and post-roll ads without these inserting technologies. And it's not like the editing is that hard, anyhow. Inserting technologies also make it easy to remove or change ads after a campaign is over. Again, you can do this on your own, but now you're talking about re-editing old shows to update the ads. Not very fun.

But pre-roll and post-roll ads suffer from a bit of a character flaw: Many podcasters don't see them as effective. And some, like Rob Walch from *podCast411* (`http://podcast411.com`), see them as a downright hindrance. The main argument? You want the very first thing a potential subscriber of your show to hear is your voice — or at least the sights and sounds of your podcast. When you run a pre-roll, your show runs behind the ad. It's possible that the ad will turn some people off or confuse others who didn't have their expectations met immediately.

The issue with post-roll is a bit different. The question is raised: Who's hanging around to listen to an advertisement *after* the show has concluded? Unlike broadcast media, podcasting is vulnerable to easy fast-forwarding by the podcast audience. How big of a concern is this? That depends on whom you ask. There is little question that, as of this writing, pre-rolls dominate the industry, while post-roll ads only account for a small fraction of that size.

Our advice:

- ✔ **Keep pre-rolls short.** Fifteen seconds is a long time to a listener — plenty of time to get most promotional messages across. You can go longer than this if you wish, but then you run a serious chance of alienating your audience (which increases with the length of your commercial messages).

- ✔ **Pre-sell the post-roll.** Knowing that many listeners are quick with the FFW button when they near the end of your episode, give them a reason to keep listening. The chance to hear a wonderfully produced advertisement usually isn't much of an incentive, and you certainly don't want to trick anyone into listening. But special offers and other beneficial incentives are fine ways to pre-sell — perhaps in a pre-roll advertisement to use in conjunction with the post-roll.

Interstitial ads

The polar opposite of the pre-/post roll — in application and design — is the *interstitial*. Interstitial ads run between segments of your show, or when you change from one topic to another. If you've listened to U.S. commercial radio or watched any amount of U.S.-based television, you've been exposed to countless hours of this type of advertising.

Benefits? You are playing ads inside of the show, with plenty of show content before and after the advertisements. You don't have to worry about turning someone off before you start your program. Nor do you have to worry (too much) about them sticking around after the show is over to hear the ads. Interstitial ads can also (surprisingly enough) make your show sound more professional, as you are mirroring a format (broadcast media) that the audience is most familiar with.

 That last piece of advice can come back to haunt you. A large section of the current podcast listening audience enjoys this medium precisely because it does *not* sound like traditional media. So exercise caution before making your show sound too produced.

As you might have expected, interstitial ads do bring some challenges. First of all, it's very difficult to run any sort of automated ad insertions inside a show. Sure, many of the networks claim to be able to do this seamlessly, but we've yet to see a good solid execution of this premise. So for now, most podcasters are stuck dropping in the ads, either as they create or edit the show.

Also, it's easy to overload a show with interstitial ads. Pre- and post-roll ads are self-limiting, but there's nothing stopping a podcaster from stringing together two or three ads at a break, and making three or four breaks in the show. Nothing, that is, except two factors: (a) not having enough advertisers and (b) a good implementation of common sense. Keep the ads in your show infrequent and short. Please?

Host endorsements

Here's another trick borrowed from traditional media — have the host of your show talk about the product or service as he or she narrates the shows. As with the ad types mentioned before, keep these short and infrequent. And follow this advice: Don't shill. If you are going to have the host talk about how wonderful a product or service really is, it's a good idea to make sure that (s)he's actually a fan of the product. No one likes a liar. Have the advertiser send samples of the product to you before the endorsements run.

Here are some things to keep in mind as you plan for endorsements:

- **They are easy to add.** Since they're not pre-produced commercials, endorsements are simply read by the host. No muss. No fuss.

- **But they are hard to take out.** Once they are in a show, they are there for the life of that episode. Remember that people can (and do) download archived episodes, so anything your host says on an episode is there for posterity.

 You could probably get very creative and use some auto-insertion technology to combat this fact. As we said previously, we haven't seen this work well in practice, but radio has it down to a fine art. If you construct your show properly, you may be able to insert endorsements in such a way that they sound live. If you are able to get that working, let us know for future updates to the book.

- **Your listeners trust you.** Let them know when you are being compensated for singing a company's praises. Hopefully, it's a company that you're happy to endorse. But even so, your audience needs to know when you're fulfilling a financial obligation, versus just letting them know about something you're excited about.

Site takeovers

Here's where your podcast has (for the moment) an advantage over radio and television programs. For most podcasts and many podcast listeners or viewers, the accompanying Web site for the podcast is an integral part of the enjoyment of the show. People visit the Web site to access past shows, comment on an episode, or interact with other listeners.

 Mainstream media has figured this out. Most of the popular television programs and syndicated radio shows also have well-designed companion Web sites. However, podcasters still have the advantage here; we're actually *using* the Internet and a computer (in almost all cases) to distribute the files to our audience. In other words, we've already got them thinking Internet from the beginning.

Giving your advertiser(s) a visible presence on your Web site can be beneficial. In the strictest sense, a *takeover* means that all of the ad units on a Web page (or an entire Web site) are owned by a single advertiser. The large movie houses will run these sorts of ads on large portals like Yahoo! when launching an expected blockbuster. Podcasters can offer their advertisers something similar. Running visual ads on your Web site ties in and reinforces the ad message the audience heard, strengthening the value of the ad impression.

The nuances of designing a Web site that is ready to successfully run banner ads is too complex for discussion in this book. We suggest delving into *AdWords For Dummies* and *Web Marketing For Dummies,* or other relevant texts for the juicy details.

Creating an Insertion Order

Before anyone will write you a check for ads running on your podcast, they're going to want to know exactly how you plan on spending their money. While you may be able to get away with a handshake deal, most serious advertisers will expect an insertion order.

An *insertion order,* or IO, details when ads will run, where they will be visible or audible, and the size or length of the ads. The IO also spells out the terms of the agreement, such as when payment is to be expected and any sort of performance guarantees built into the agreement. Unless you are very comfortable with your metrics and your ability to deliver, we suggest you stay away from performance guarantees, at least for the initial ad run with a client.

Rather than blather on about the intricacies of IOs, it's probably simplest if we just show you one in Figure 47-1. (See? It looks nothing like a shoehorn.)

Your Podcast Logo Here!

Order Number 123
Date 10/31/2007
Page 1 of 2

Advertising Insertion Order
www.superpodcast.com

Order # 123
Campaign
Client Ref #
Date Created 10/31/2007

Sales Contact
Name Jack Horner
Phone 123
Fax 212.555.1212
email jack@superpodcast.com

Ad Rep
Name
Fax
email

Advertiser
Name Sandy Clause
Address 1 Snowshoe Way
North Pole, AK 90567

Agency
Name n/a
Address

Contact Information

Media Contact
Company Sandy Clause
Address Clause, Inc
1 Snowshoe Way
Phone North Pole, AK 90567
Fax 212.555.3333
email
sandy@clause.com

Billing Contact Same as
Company media contact
Address
Phone
Fax
email

Advertiser/Agency
Signature ____________
Name/Title ____________
Date ____________
email ____________

Super Podcast
Signature ____________
Name/Title ____________
Date ____________
email ____________

• Figure 47-1: The IO is what you use to insert advertising.

Note that this is just a sample. There may be additional points that your podcast can deliver upon — or changes you need to make to have this approach fit with your show's offerings. Make it happen!

Handling Listener Complaints

Not surprisingly, not everyone will be happy when you start running ads on your program. Even if you start a brand-new podcast and immediately run ads, you are going to get complaints. Hey, such is the nature of the beast. How you respond to those complaints determines their impact on your show.

Here are a few tips for dealing with complaints from listeners:

- **Don't respond.** You can't make everyone happy all the time. Some complaints — such as "I hate ads. You should stop." — don't really warrant a response. You aren't going to convince the complainer that ads are acceptable to you (after all, isn't that obvious?), and you aren't likely to be swayed to that person's side of the issue, either — not without some better arguments.
- **Don't knee-jerk.** A single complaint doesn't necessarily mean you should drop everything and implement the "suggestion" offered by the complainer. People are motivated by their own interests, and you must weigh their interests against what goals you have set for the show. If you thought long and hard about adding advertisements, you probably should put the same amount of thought into making any changes from a single negative comment.
- **Listen and adapt.** But if the feedback from the listener is more specific, or you are getting a significant amount of complaints, analyze what the issues are. Maybe the ads don't fit your the demographics of your audience. Maybe you've put in too many. Tweaking your plan as you move forward isn't a crime. In fact, it's a really good idea.

✔ **Always be honest and open.** Transparency, the act of keeping nothing hidden, is always a good idea. If you've made a mistake with an ad, or something has gone horribly wrong due to your running an ad in your show, 'fess up. We don't always make the best decisions in life, and mistakes in advertising are common. It's okay to run a special piece on your show that apologizes or explains what has happened. Trust us, your audience will love you for it.

Does This Make You "Commercial"?

In a word, probably. We'd give you a more solid answer if we could agree on one. So instead of fighting amongst ourselves, we'll cop out and run the standard WE ARE NOT LAWYERS disclaimer and ask that you seek counsel before making decisions that might impact your legality. These issues might include

✔ Invalidating your ability to run some Creative Commons material on your show

✔ Having an impact on a nonprofit designation

✔ Tax and revenue-reporting considerations

✔ Personal liability issues

And that's just a quick list from us non-lawyer types. We're betting that a good intellectual-property attorney can come up with all sorts of things we haven't thought of.

One final note, to those who read all the way through this practice and are seething at our suggestions for commercializing a podcast: Not every podcaster is interested in creating a viable commercial entity. We've said as much, and stand by that statement. But many are interested — and you were warned early on that this is the case. Hopefully other parts of this book work better for you. Bottom line: We figure you're in podcasting to enjoy it, so enjoy it your way!

Part VIII

Reengineering Your Podcast

The 5th Wave   By Rich Tennant

"I can be reached at home on my cell phone; I can be reached on the road with my pager and PDA. Soon I'll be reachable on a plane with e-mail. I'm beginning to think identity theft wouldn't be such a bad idea for a while."

Podfade Prevention

In This Practice

✔ Reaping the benefits of taking a break

✔ Reconnecting with your passion

✔ Saying "no" to one more podcast idea

*P*odcasting *For Dummies* gave co-author Tee Morris the closest experience ever to what it must be like to be the obsessive-compulsive TV detective Adrian Monk. As star Tony Shaloub says (with all the vulnerability he can muster), "It's a gift . . . and a curse."

What is? Well, for one thing, all that validation. Tee had been a writer of fiction for years, but while writing under the *For Dummies* brand, he wound up invited to all the right parties, hobnobbing with the stars, getting the "A-List" treatment. . . . That was the "gift."

The "curse" came when — less than a month after the book's initial release — the podcasts featured in the book started disappearing, one after another. What was going on? Because podcasting was still a new medium, no one really considered the possibilities of a podcast *ending*, for whatever reason. Perhaps it was the same assumption behind a blog — you never think about a show calling it quits or reaching a conclusion.

Then the term was coined by Scott Fletcher of Podcheck Review: *podfading.*

As easily as it can happen to you, it can also be prevented.

Factors That Contribute to Podfading

Podfading is the community's scarlet letter to podcasts that launched out of the box strong only to scale back production values around the tenth show, then change posting frequency, and then finally stop. In much the same manner as a Roman candle, a podcast makes a sudden, bright impression only to disappear. Podfading is easily preventable, but before coming up with the solutions, it's a good idea to diagnose the problem. What causes podfading?

Time

Perhaps the leading cause of podfading is the time people invest in their podcasts. It gets to be too much; a lot of us can empathize with the podfaders. Friends ask Tee, "You're writing, you've got a family, you've got a day job, you travel for both, and you have four podcasts you produce. How do you do it?!" His usual answer is, "I don't know, but when you figure it out, tell me how!"

If you've got a lot of energy, or your muse refuses to let you sleep, or you're a master at time management (hmm . . . a lot of us had better strike that last one!), then you have a lot of what you need to podcast. Equally important is getting a handle on the value of time and a realistic estimate of the demands when you're creating a podcast. Earlier in this book, we discuss the value of producing five (or more) episodes for a podcast. That experience will quickly give you an idea of exactly *how much time* your podcast will demand of you.

Effort

Some podcasts are simply a host or a group of hosts kicking back and enjoying a good chat over the state of the world . . . or the contents of their fridge. With the *Weekly Anime Review* podcast, Aaron sits back and provides commentary on the world of anime. With *Two Girls and a Podcast,* Chris and Eliza link up via Skype and talk about whatever is striking their fancy that particular week. Production is kept to the bare-bones minimum.

When it comes to podcasts like *Variant Frequencies, Shadow Falls, Stranger Things,* or *Silent Universe,* the production demands increase exponentially. Organizing the vocal talent. Efficient post-production work. Wrestling with bandwidth issues. Keeping up with these demands — and keeping the content free to the public — can be extremely taxing.

The earlier-mentioned podcasts are still podcasting, but only because their creators are willing to clock in the extra time and keep the production quality and posting frequency consistent. The effort you put

into a podcast should be in sync with the podcast's production demands. When the podcast's demands extend beyond your own limits, it can lead to podfading.

Personal matters

A top-rated iTunes show, *The Transmission* (http://hawaiiup.com/lost), a *Lost* podcast based out of Hawaii, closed up shop unexpectedly in 2006. Show hosts Ryan and Jen Ozawa found that the demands of producing a weekly show (sporting a listenership of over 15,000) — along with the financial demands of providing sufficient bandwidth — took up too much time and energy when coupled with their daily lives.

Whether the problem is the blurring of the lines between reality and podcasting, an unexpected change at home, the sudden disruption of sickness, death, *or* the double-edged sword of success, podfading can occur if your heart just isn't in it anymore.

The *Honeymooners* Syndrome

Podfading tends to make many in the podosphere sneer, "Those podfaders just couldn't cut it!" (No lie — such aspersions have come from both podcasters and listeners!) Here at *Expert Podcasting Practices For Dummies*, we're of the mindset to accept that life happens. It is sadder still the loss of content (no matter what the show is) on account of someone's honest life decision.

That empathy, however, doesn't extend to those podcasters who get caught up in the *Honeymooners* Syndrome.

What is that, you ask? Hearken back to the days of early TV, when *Honeymooners* stars Jackie Gleason and Art Carney would come across a scheme that offered to set them up in the lap of luxury. "Norton," Ralph would say, a smile beaming brightly on his face, "I'm telling you, this plan can't miss." Inevitably, it did.

The same thing happens to podcasters who get into this medium with one objective: *big money.* Oh, the occasional wild success story is there, sure, but podcasting is hardly a get-rich-quick vehicle. What it really amounts to is a long-term *investment* of time and resources that may (or may not) pay off down the road. When you podcast, your first priority should be the content — and you have to back up that content with a desire and passion to produce it on a regular basis. If your first priority is landing the big sponsors, quitting your day job, and making a mint in podcasting, then you're not podcasting for the right reasons, and you're likelier to podfade.

Taking a Break

Now that you have a good idea of what can cause a podfade to occur, how do you keep this fate from befalling a project that has come to mean so much to listeners?

There is something to be said about stepping away from a podcast for a moment or two, now and then, just to catch your breath.

In many cases, a break is needed because demands of real life are getting too intense. Tee's immediate schedule (while writing this practice) was a case in point. In addition to writing, he had several seminar and teaching commitments to attend to — and all this while, still doing a weekly podcast.

But practicality prevailed: Tee's podcast announced that all his present time commitments left no realistic room to record. He stepped back to take care of the other business, and his podcast went dark for two weeks. Upon returning, he found the listeners were there, glad to hear the story return with a new drive and determination.

The break (while maybe not a relaxing one) was necessary to the life of the show. Tee had to wait until his schedule lightened up before he could produce episodes at his personal quality level.

Regardless of whether the break you take is due to your day job, family commitments, a change in your life's routine, or just a need to get control of the podcast (instead of the podcast controlling you),

what's important here is to *let your listeners know*. If there's a break coming up in the show posting's frequency, your listeners will stay with you so long as you keep the lines of communications open.

Produce a five-minute quickcast that lets people know what's going on; it may surprise you just how understanding your audience will be. Let the listeners know how long a break you're taking; if you feel comfortable about letting them know why, do that. From there, you can step away from your podcast's schedule with a clear conscience. It beats a burnout followed by a podfade.

Reconnecting with Your Passion

Sometimes, Jack Bauer needs a break between his bad days of saving the world. Cylons probably need to recharge their batteries from time to time. It's no surprise that actors, writers, and production crews need to take a break during the summer (or, in the case of *The Sopranos* cast, for a majority of the year!) so they can remain fresh with the characters and situations they face. Podcasters need breaks, too. One of the reasons a podcast may podfade is the podcaster's loss of passion for what he or she is podcasting about. After six months of podcasting on a weekly or a bi-monthly schedule, your message could sound tired.

Why you may need to go on hiatus

There are a variety of natural reasons to take a break simply to give yourself some downtime, and here are a few to consider:

- ✔ **The holidays.** Whichever holidays take priority in your life definitely should provide you a respite from your podcasting schedule. Between Thanksgiving and Christmas, the time just isn't there to podcast. Usually, after the confetti is cleared from the New Year's celebrations, the time is right, and podcasters are ready (pretty anxious, in fact) to get back to it.

✔ **The end of a season.** Tee happily hosted the *Podcasting For Dummies Companion Podcast* until Episode #20 when he announced it was time for a break. As Tee signed off, he assured everyone that there would be a new season of the podcast as soon as the new book was completed. What could be a more natural (and true) explanation?

 The number of episodes that make up a season varies from podcast to podcast. It all depends on how often you're podcasting and what feels right for you. Many podcasts follow a network-television model: A *season* lasts for about 20 to 25 episodes.

✔ **Health issues.** *Skepticality* (www.skepticality.com) was one of the original trailblazers of podcasting, bringing an unabashed, critical look at politics, religion, consumerism, and the world. Its hosts Derek Colanduno and Swoopy inspired others to voice their viewpoints (such as *Truth Seekers* at http://audioaddict.libsyn.com and George Hrab's *GeoLogic Podcast* at http://geologicpodcast.net), caught the attention of *Business Week* and even Apple's Steve Jobs, and the show was named "the Official Podcast of *Skeptic* Magazine."

These accomplishments are nothing less than inspiring, especially considering the long break the hosts took unexpectedly in September 2005 when Derek suffered a kind of aneurism that sent him into a coma. Swoopy made an announcement on *Skepticality* about Derek's condition, and then the show went dark for close to a year.

The podcast launched again once Derek deemed himself ready and able. Not only were the show's hosts ready to bring their views to the world, but the listenership was ready to listen.

✔ **A death in the family.** On April 1, 2007, the podosphere lost one of its own. Joe Murphy of FarPoint Media (http://farpointmendia.net) lost a battle with leiomyosarcoma, an extremely aggressive form of cancer. When his death happened, the FarPoint crew with whom Joe worked closest took several of their shows and repeated past episodes — while *Wingin' It* aired a tribute show before going dark for a month.

The listeners understood.

Because the subscribers were part of the experience, hearing regular discussion on how Joe was doing, they understood that this was coming. It was a time of mourning; and for the FarPoint Media crew, it was a necessity to pay respect to "their fallen ninja."

Regardless of health issues, the important thing here is that both *Skepticality* and FarPoint Media communicated to their audience that there would be a break. The break was unexpected and unplanned in both situations, but audiences knew what was up and stayed subscribed.

Communication, in both these situations, kept the audience in the loop and kept them subscribed. Provided you take a moment to let people know what is happening, your subscribers will understand and won't desert you.

 Along with your podcast, take advantage of your blog. Sure, the blog is a convenient place for your show notes, but you can also use it for updates in personal or health matters that affect your podcast's production schedule. How personal the info gets — and whatever details you choose to reveal on the blog — is completely up to you, but remember: Your blog is a means of keeping your listenership informed and in the loop on the status of your podcast and its crew.

What to do during your break

The break taken here should be a moment for you and your crew (or just you, if you're working solo) to step away from the recording, the editing, and the podcast as a whole. This is the downtime that lets you focus on nothing else but the passion behind your podcast. If your podcast is about gardening, clock in some time in the herb garden. If your podcast is about writing, write. If your podcast is about underwater basket-weaving, go for a swim. Whatever you do, invest some time into the passion you podcast about.

Another option for this downtime is stepping away from this passion. Make a clean break and step away from it completely. Stopping a passion cold-turkey can actually shock you back into a renewed love for what you talk about.

When you do something for nothing, it should be something you look forward to doing. This applies to the experts just as much as it applies to the rookies or the casual podcaster who is merely exploring the media as an audio hobby. If you don't love what you do, the podcast becomes a chore — and there's very little you can do to mask that ennui in your delivery when the mic goes live.

Step away from the mic and take a sabbatical. When you're ready, make the return with a new-found fire and heavy fanfare. Not only will your loyal fans return, but you might even catch a few new listeners, too.

It's a Great Idea for a Podcast, but . . .

"I feel thin . . . sort of stretched, like butter scraped over too much bread."

—Bilbo Baggins, in *The Lord of the Rings: The Fellowship of the Ring*

When you read that, did you groan a bit because you feel that way every day? (A forest of authorial hands goes up.) If you tend to have a tough time saying no to people, podcasting will only intensify the need to say no now and then.

Perhaps the idea you get for yet *another* podcast is for a good cause, or perhaps you think of a show that would be a roller-coaster ride for yourself and your audience. However, instead of rushing into the idea headfirst with blinders on, the best thing you can do in developing this idea is to evaluate your time commitments first:

✔ Is there room in your schedule for this Next Big Thing in podcasting?

✔ Do you enough time available to host and produce *and* promote *and* maintain this podcast?

✔ If you do start this podcast, how will it affect the other podcasts you're currently running?

Yes, consider your other podcasts, ranging from the five-minute quickcasts to the full hour-long productions. You may think one more podcast may not have a profound effect on your other shows, but it will — because any time you spend on those shows is time away from that particular new show. In essence, it's another commitment you will want to meet.

Consider your time before you agree to assist other podcasters, as well. Nothing is as aggravating as committing to helping out a podcast with some audio, only to end up forced to later admit, "I can't do it." Before agreeing to help out other podcasters with audio, ask the following:

✔ How much audio is needed?

✔ When do you need it by?

✔ Will you want it edited or just recorded, with all editing and post-production handled elsewhere?

✔ Will you need me in later episodes? Will you need more audio later?

Supplying audio for other podcasts is a commitment that should be honored, and there is no love lost if you just say no. Timing is everything in both comedy and podcasting. If the time is right, throw your hat into the ring and have fun. If you are swamped and overcommitted, then concentrate on clearing your desk. Otherwise, you will just continue to clear your desk with no end in sight.

A final note on why saying no is a good thing: Get away from the computer and enjoy life. Part of the charm and appeal of podcasting is hearing about the life experiences of your show hosts. There is only so much living you can do from your computer. Whether you are a writer, a musician, or a podcaster, life experience is what makes shows fun and entertaining. Make time to enjoy the world, and the world will assuredly enjoy listening to you talk about it.

New Hosts, New Podcast?

Podcasts can be a personality-driven enterprise. Good hosts forge a connection with listeners — and have the personality, knowledge, and charisma to keep the masses coming back for more. Hopefully, you have just such a host at the helm of your program, whether it's you or somebody else. And yet, people move on and times change. Hosts go elsewhere, whether it's David Letterman moving from NBC to CBS or your friend deciding to leave his more general videogame podcast to focus solely on his love of small-leaping-Italian-plumber games (but only the original work — those new games corrupted this message).

There are a lot of factors to consider at this point, including how a new host affects both the podcast itself and the program's listeners. You have to decide what (if any) changes need to be made in the program itself, and you need to decide who's going to come on board to replace the familiar voice at the mic. That person may, in turn, require more changes in the program. With all these priorities flying around, you'll need to get a pen and paper to write all this down and make sure you keep everything straight.

Heading Toward the Door

If you have a little lead time before you know a podcast host is going to be moving on, it might be best to lay the groundwork for a graceful exit. Audiences don't like to be surprised, and losing a regular part of their regular podcast schedule can leave them a little cold. Take advantage of the personalized nature of podcasts. You're not broadcasting to society as a whole — you're narrowcasting to (hopefully a sizeable) segment of the population, folks who are interested in what you're talking about. Let them know what's going on, and they'll appreciate it — it's kinder to them than just letting 'em download an entirely new program with new hosts one day (they tend to wonder where their show went). Fans don't always take kindly to change, so if you're transitioning from a program that already has some popularity to something new, it's good to give them a heads-up.

Good, that is, if it can be done gracefully. If you're moving on due to "irreconcilable differences" with folks who are still involved with the show, it's best to cut the cord immediately and move on with the program before things get too bad. Continuing with a podcast after it's clear that things are going wrong will only serve to annoy or turn off the listeners. If there's a quick and definite solution that can be taken to solve the problem, take it. It's hard to win back listeners after they've been turned off.

We'd Like to Introduce to You . . .

So now that you need to find a replacement, where do you start? It was probably hard enough to find your first podcast host — and now you have to go out and get somebody else. So what do you do? The first step is to re-evaluate the nature of your podcast and decide what needs to remain the focus of your program:

- ✔ Is this an informational podcast, or are you focused more on entertainment?

- ✔ Should the host be from a certain region of the country (or the world)?

- ✔ Does the show thrive on the host's personality traits, or are you worried about how a new personality will carry the show?

For example, you wouldn't necessarily try to put on a podcast about your city's happenings without having your host reside in that city. How believable is someone going to sound talking about this weekend's art festival from hundreds of miles away over a Skype line? Alternatively, if you're producing a podcast that represents your corporation's activities around the country ("Look at how our paper products improve San Diego! Now we'll take a look at notebook activities in the greater Chicagoland area . . ."), that locality isn't going to be as important.

It also means keeping the focus of the podcast in mind. In this example, that paper corporation is going to remain the focus, no matter who the host is. You're going to keep the subject consistent from story to story, from storyteller to storyteller. Therefore you want to find somebody who can deliver the podcast well, interact with whoever appears on the podcast, and still stay out of the way of the podcast's focus.

If the podcast, however, is more personality-driven (a television feature with a host who has a lot of contacts in the field, for instance), you're going to have some trouble. That host is an integral part of the show, and you'll have to find somebody else with that same sort of credibility to take over. Nobody will buy your new videogaming podcast (for example) if the host doesn't know the difference between a Commodore 64 and a Wii.

So you need somebody who's at ease doing the speaking and hosting duties that make a podcast work. If interviews are going to be part of the show, you need somebody who can interact naturally with others. And that person (or those persons) will have to make a regular commitment to hosting this podcast. Infrequent episodes turn off the listeners; be sure to find somebody who can do the job.

Taking a Step Back to Re-evaluate the Show

So now that you've located your new host (or decided to soldier on with him or her), it's time to decide how the personality of the show has been changed — and how the program must adapt to that personality change. You may have to drop the ten-minute monologue at the beginning of a podcast if your new host can't carry that off, or you might want to play to the host's strengths if he or she is a naturally charismatic and friendly person. If the podcast has a tight structure with well-defined seg-ments, it can be an easier transition. If the podcast is organized more loosely, you'll find that you'll have to adapt more to the host's personality.

Incorporating Changes to Your Show

After you've identified the changes necessary to keep your podcast up and running, you have a cou-ple of choices to make: Do you work the changes in quickly, or do you allow them to evolve over time?

You have to take into account both your audience and your show at this point. Would your listeners tol-erate a quick change? Would the show sound better if you made the changes quickly or more slowly? Again, if the podcast is well structured and doesn't depend on the host as much, you could probably make changes relatively quickly. A personality-driven podcast takes some creative thought and time to make the switchover so the change doesn't turn off audiences. Give 'em some time to come around.

 Above all, make sure that you hold your pod-cast to the same high standards you've been using up to this point. A change for the worse is the road to an untimely podfade.

Change of Passion, Change of Podcast?

Practice 50

L ike most things that make their way to the Internet (remember the dancing gerbils and all those e-mail forwards you still get, even though they've been circulating since the beginning of time?), the vast majority of podcasts are driven by passion. Whether it's a love of cooking or the need to rant for hours about their neighbors, podcasters have a strong internal motivation to create their shows. They podcast not only because they want to, but almost because they *need* to. That makes these podcasts personal — almost intimate — and it's a factor that draws listeners in and keeps them coming back.

However, time moves on, things change, and podcasters may become interested in something else. Given the fast pace and the intense information saturation on the Internet, you can quickly get burnt out on doing a podcast, even if it's a topic you love talking about. It takes a lot of effort to research, write, record, and produce a podcast on a regular basis, and the schedule can be a little grueling. When you start wishing you could spend your podcasting time doing . . . well, just about anything else, it might be time to take a step back and see exactly why you're producing this program.

Performing an Annual Evaluation

So you've been creating your podcast for a while now, and it just doesn't have the same lure as it did before. Or you still want to create a podcast, but you're not sure about the subject matter anymore. It's possible that something else is influencing your decision, so you might want to start looking at the reasons why. Once you know why you're feeling the way you do, you can look at how to change it.

Time

Taking the time to create a podcast can eat into other parts of your life, and you may be having problems keeping everything balanced. Your day job (unless podcasting *is* your day job, of course), your family, other leisure activities (I NEED MY NEEDLEPOINT TIME!), and more can make you feel a little stressed out or overcommitted. If the podcast is taking too much time out of your life, it's time to make a change.

It may not be time to chuck the whole thing, though. Consider ways to reduce your time commitment to the show, and you may find yourself feeling a little better about it. Try getting some help with creating the show, or shorten the actual time of the show. Once you get a little more time to yourself, you could find you have a little more energy for the show.

Effort

Depending on what you include in your podcast, you may end up doing a lot more than just turning on the mic and letting your mind run free. If you have to keep up to date on all the current happenings in a subject (from technology to cars to movies to the latest in postage-stamp innovations), it can mean doing a lot of show preparation, and that can be a little exhausting. Fatigue doesn't just have to be physical — you could be experiencing a classic case of burnout.

Maybe a little vacation is in order. You don't see *new* episodes of your favorite television shows every week, do you? Taking some time to rest, rejuvenate, and re-evaluate could be just what you need. It could also mean that you're ready to leave the podcast behind and move on to something else. Before you do that, though, it couldn't hurt to take a little break. After you've put it aside for a bit, you'll have more perspective on what you want to do.

New subject matter

Sure, your half-hour treatises on funny-car racing pleased both you and your listeners. Yet, one day, you realize that Formula One is starting to catch your attention. Sure, it's a little different from what you're used to, and it's not something you've focused on before. Still, more and more, you realize you have vital thoughts and opinions on the state of F1, and you must share these with the world. Funny cars are great and all, but you're moving onto a global stage now.

As mentioned in the introduction to this practice, passions can change, evolve, or move on. Because you're most likely the boss of your own podcast, you have license to explore different subjects and matters. It may mean starting a new program in addition to your current podcast, expanding your current show to include your new interest — or even discontinuing your current program and starting a new one, with new theme music, scripts, and the like. This can be a big step, so it might be worth spending some time considering your new direction. As with burnout, you may find that taking a little time out could bring you back to where you want to be. It may also lead you to an entirely new show.

Keep in mind, however, that you've already established an agreement or relationship of sorts with your audience. They've come to expect a certain type of program from you, and drastic changes may have a major impact on your listenership. Be ready to absorb some major changes from them as they absorb some major changes from you.

 Don't be afraid to explore a new show — it's not like you have to start canceling other programs or make room on the evening lineup. Remember, only time and bandwidth can limit what programs you want to produce.

Who's Counting on You?

The vast majority of podcasts are individual efforts, but that doesn't necessarily mean that your show is made in a vacuum. You should take into account some folks when making your decision to switch things around and change from (say) a music podcast to a serious economic roundtable program (time to put that degree to work, we suppose).

Podcasting co-workers

If you do work with other people on your podcast, you should definitely consult with them before making any major programming changes. After all, they share your passion for the current show, and they may not be as ready as you are to make a transition.

Talk with them seriously about why you want to make this change. It might be time to start your own different podcast and let them take over the current project.

Advertisers

While this probably isn't a concern for most podcasts out there, you do have to consider the wishes of anybody who provides support to your podcast, whether it's a financial or barter (trade) arrangement. They bought into your podcast in some fashion because they wanted to reach your audience. If a major programming shift takes place, your program might not be reaching that same audience. A local auto shop probably won't want to spend any money on your new podcast *Bicycling Away*. It's not that you're producing a bad podcast — you're no longer speaking to its target audience. If you're comfortable moving on without the benefit of that support, then you're ready to go.

 Don't forget to take into account any legal agreements or contracts you may have entered into with those advertisers. If you have any of those things lying around, it's definitely in your best interest to fully complete the terms of those contracts before moving on. Nobody needs too many lawyers in their lives.

Your boss and company

If you're podcasting for your boss or your company, you're not the only one responsible for the show. This program represents the interests and image of your business, and therefore it definitely has a say in what happens with the podcast. Your new program could either attract or repel potential customers, so you need to run any changes by your company to make sure the higher-ups are good with it. It may be your show, but ultimately the company is paying the bills.

Listeners

They're mentioned last in this section, but the needs and attitudes of your listeners should also be considered. If you're producing your show mainly for a small group of fans you know personally, they'll probably understand if you choose to move on. However, you may have already developed a large and loyal following with your podcast (who knew Amish quilts would be so popular on the Internet?), and a change in focus for your podcast could turn off some of your listeners. If it's just a slight switch in subject matter, you can probably ride out the change with no problem.

Don't expect an audience to follow you through a major transition, though. If you want to keep your audience, look at what they want, and take that into consideration when you make your switch. If you're the only one out there doing a podcast on your subject, you could be leaving a big hole to fill. That's not to say that you should feel obligated to pursue your podcast far past the point of caring about doing it. It's your life, after all. But if you're going to be leaving said large hole, consider turning over the show to somebody else who can keep it going. Your audience may miss you, but the show will still be there.

Time for an Overhaul

So suppose, after taking all the factors mentioned here into consideration, you've decided to cast your former podcast aside and jump headlong into a new project. The good news is that you're already an experienced podcaster, so you won't have as much trouble starting your show over again. The bad news is that you're basically starting your show over again. Even with your experience, making a major change like this means that you're essentially creating a new show from scratch, and you have to go through all the work of plotting, planning, recording, and promoting one more time. Have fun!

Changing the podcast itself

If you produced your old podcast for a long time, you probably became pretty set in your ways. You had a regular schedule of preparation and recording, and you knew what program segments went where. With a new podcast, all that changes. It doesn't mean you have to completely overhaul your style, but you're dealing with new subject matter now — and your programming habits might need to change in a way that better serves the subject matter. For example, if your podcast is focused more on current events, you might have to make a short program more often than you did before. If your new podcast is longer, you could possibly cut back on your production schedule.

Back to square one

You're also not married to the same theme music, format, or anything having to deal with the last show you produced. It can be hard to do, but you can take this opportunity to totally reimagine the show you put together and try new and different things. You first started podcasting because it was a wide-open field for you to express what you wanted to, right? It may be difficult to snap out of your old habits, but now is the perfect opportunity to make your new podcast different from your last one. The change of topic (and maybe pace) could keep you from getting burned out as easily, as well.

Take a look at this checklist and make sure you know what you're getting into when you're starting over:

- ✔ New show title
- ✔ New theme music and sound effects
- ✔ New show length
- ✔ New production schedule
- ✔ New entries in podcast directories and networks

Drawing a New Crowd

Now that you have got your program ready to go, it's probably a good idea to re-read this entire book. Just bend the corner of this page and get back to it when you're finished.

All right, maybe you don't need to subject yourself to that again. But a refresher might help. Remember

that starting from scratch means that you have to repeat a lot of the steps you'd already gone through with your last podcast. And there's really nothing that you should skip simply because you've done it before with your other show. You're tackling a new project now, and it's likely that the listeners will be a different crowd. You have to lure them in with your new show just the way you did with your old one. Even if you're using the same Web site and feed, you need to entice the audience to stick around.

Targeting a new audience

You probably have an idea of the people who would listen to your new podcast, if only because they share your passion for the subject. So you already have an idea of where they go for information and entertainment — probably the same places you do. Still, get out there and put your search engine through the paces. Find all the possible locations online (and offline, if possible) that can give you a look at what your potential audience is doing and what they want to listen to. This is basic market research, but it certainly gives you some places to spread the word about your show and help you know what people want to listen to. Refer to the practices in Part V for a refresher course on building your new audience.

Mixing the old and the new

If you didn't make a drastic transition in podcasting focus (we suppose it's possible your punk-rock compatriots might share your newfound interest in locally produced polka music), you could conceivably take members of your old audience with you. Don't be afraid to tell your old listeners about your new endeavors. They may follow you for your new subject matter, and they may follow you just because they enjoy the programs you've put together in the past and they want to see what you're up to now. Don't count on a mass exodus to your new program, but do encourage your audience to at least give you a shot. It's not like they have to pay an extra cable bill to check out your new creation.

The Hard Podfade

Practice 51

Podfading, whether you like it or not, is something to consider when you launch a podcast. It may seem a bit sad to think about the end when you're caught up in the excitement of launching a podcast — and even reaching milestones like Episode #100 — but it is a reality. So far, you have been keeping the fires burning in your podcast studio. You have focused on ways of keeping the interests and the passions of your podcast running, ranging from reconnecting with your podcast's subject matter to stepping away from the production for a little perspective.

There are situations, however, where the only option is to sweep the floors, put the chairs on the top of the tables, turn off the lights, and lock up the studio. How to say goodbye is up to you.

No Announcement, No More Show

Perhaps the most common kind of podfade is anything but a fade; it's more like a vanishing. The feed begins promisingly enough with a few shows, be it three episodes or even five, and then the show suddenly stops in its posting.

Shows like this are easy to find on iTunes, provided the podcasts are still on their host's server. A good indication of the sudden podfade is to look at the time stamps displayed in the podcast's listing. The existing episodes usually have a consistent timing in their schedule early on, suddenly coming to an abrupt stop. The next step in confirming a podcast's demise is to check the podcast's host site or blog. Find out whether anyone is still posting there; and if they are, search for any relevant posts from the show's host or hosts. If all appears quiet, it would not be out of line to drop a *friendly* e-mail asking whether the show has, in fact, ceased production. Provided the tone of your e-mail is not confrontational and more out of concern than demanding, "Where is my next episode?!", you may receive a pleasant, cordial reply explaining either that the show has gone on hiatus — or that the podcast has, in fact, closed its doors. Such was the case for Kiki Anika, a voice that charmed writers everywhere with her sassy Australian accent and perspectives on writing romance. Her podcast, *The Kissy Bits,* steadily climbed in its listenership until episodes came to an abrupt halt in December 2006. At first, it was assumed the holidays had claimed all her free time; but as 2007 continued on without her, e-mails asking when *The Kissy Bits* would return began arriving in her mailbox. Sadly, encouragement from all parts of the world failed to ignite the interest for an Aussie comeback. Still, her Web site (www.kikianika.com, shown in Figure 51-1) reassured her loyal listeners that while her podcasting was tabled for the time-being, her writing was gaining momentum.

• **Figure 51-1: Romance author Kiki Anika came on to the podosphere strong, but a budding writing career detoured her podcasting interests, bringing an end to *The Kissy Bits.***

Heartbreaking as it was to hear that Kiki would not return with her romance writing podcast, the good news was that the plucky Australian hostess was heading in the right direction with her writing and still only an e-mail away. Remember, when writing to podcast hosts, keep queries brief and (most important) positive. If you receive no reply at all or get the bad news of "no more podcast," shut down the feed and remember the good times while they lasted.

Good Night, and Good Luck

Some shows reluctantly look at the time and effort invested in the podcast, and after a lot of re-evaluation, the producers (who, in most cases, are also the hosts, editors, writers, and directors) try to streamline the production. Following the pruning of the show's demands, the ugly truth continues to raise its ugly head: It's time to call it quits.

If you end up at this point, the decision to fold the tents does not make you a bad podcaster — but what you do at this stage of your podcast says a lot about you to your listeners, as well as about the way you regard them as a community. The *hard* podfade, as mentioned in the previous section, sends out a message of "Well, I really don't care . . ." to a listenership. Regardless if your podcast-generated listenership is an audience of 2 or 200, your audience deserves more than just the cold shoulder of silence.

Because our stock in trade here is *expert* podcasting practices, it's worth noting that one of those is the professional approach to podfading — again, something many podcasters never really consider at the beginning of their projects: To communicate with your listeners and let them know that your podcast is heading off into the sunset, much in the same way that Indy, his dad, Sallah, and Dr. Marcus did at the end of *Indiana Jones and The Last Crusade.* Something clear, final, and upbeat, also known as . . .

The farewell episode

Many podcasters believe the first episode to be the toughest. They figure it sounds awkward and comes across as a touch tense and a bit jittery. New ventures often do. But if you think the premiere episode is difficult, just wait until you tackle the last one.

When recording the last episode, consider how you sound. Do you sound elated or exhausted? Distracted or depressed? Whimsical or whiny? This is the lasting, final impression — at least to this audience — that you are leaving in the place of your show. How do you want to be remembered by your listeners? It may come as a shock to you when your final podcast is the topic of much debate, and people talk that episode up as they did the final episode of *Quantum Leap*. Was it a good way to wrap things up? Did listeners get a real reason as to why the podcast has come to a close? What do they listen to now?

So here are some points to hit in your farewell episode that your listeners will appreciate:

✔ **The reason why this is the last episode.** Ultimately, it's no one's business other than yours, true — but depending on the nature of the podcast and the rapport you've built over a season (or two) with your listenership, it's good manners to explain to your listenership exactly why your microphone is going dark. How personal you make those reasons is strictly up to you and your own boundaries. Even if it's "I simply don't have the time," you may be surprised to find that even such a humble reason is enough for your listener base. Offering that kind of simple honesty and candor may inspire one of your listeners to pick up the proverbial podcasting torch and keep the show rolling along without you, provided you're comfortable with that notion and see your podcast more as a service than as a property.

 By giving your reasons behind the end of your production, you also give audience members a clear idea of what's behind the decision, reassure them that their attention matters to you, and maybe alleviate any possible conspiracy theories about your podcast's close. ("It was the space aliens, man. They're trying to take over the podosphere.")

✔ **Other shows of similar interest.** When people interested in podcasting tell us "I have an idea for a podcast — but it's been done before . . . " we usually reply with, "So? This is your podcast and your perspective." If *Face the Nation* were to shut down its podcast, other podcasters (and listeners) would find political commentary to fill the void left behind. But give 'em a break: When you believe that the podcast you are recording is your last one, listeners will probably begin to wonder, "Great, so what do I listen to now?!" Why not offer a few recommendations?

Podcasters are also pod*catchers* as well; we listen to podcasts that either go with or against our grain. As George Hrab of *The GeoLogic Podcast* stated in one of his episodes, "It's always a good idea to know what the other side is saying." Giving your audience some tips for recommended listening not only fills the void, but is also a gesture of respect; they'll appreciate that touch. It says, in effect, *"Okay, so maybe I'm not doing this anymore, but I like what these other folks are saying, or at least find it important or useful, so why not give them a try?"*

 Okay, this may seem obvious, but before you recommend other shows, it behooves you to *listen* to a few of their episodes beforehand. Simply searching through a category and saying *"Yeah, give this show a listen . . ."* is a bit reckless; some podcasts are not always listed in the appropriate category or may change their focus without making a note of the change in the show description. While you don't have to become a regular listener to anybody's podcast, it wouldn't be a bad idea to listen to two or three episodes of whichever unknown podcast you're thinking of recommending, just to make certain that the description matches the actual podcast — and that it's actually something you feel comfortable recommending. If you know what the podcast is all about, then your sincere recommendation leaves a good impression on your community.

✔ **Thank your audience for listening.** Three words that, even though you hear them again and again, carry so much weight: "Thank you for listening." (Okay, three words and a preposition!) No one is compelled or forced to listen to your podcast, and acknowledging that with a simple "Thanks . . ." — especially at the end — lets your listeners know how much you appreciate the time they invested in you and how much fun they've made this ride of yours through the podosphere.

And don't make the thank-you a throwaway. Mean it. When you think about it, the folks subscribing to your podcast got there in various ways — from the recommendation of other podcasters, listener word-of-mouth, or a search for podcasting topics and keywords. Your community is always there, hanging on your every post. They don't have to stick it out with you, but they do. If you're shutting things down, your listenership deserves a binary High Five (as created by the hosts of *Technorama*) and a sincere thank you for being there.

The farewell episode is also a popular finale for podcasters who know their productions have a planned end in sight. J.C. Hutchins (of the widely popular potboiler thriller *7th Son*) creates, at the end of each complete book, a Fan Appreciation or a Listener Feedback show — which includes everything from voice mail to listener-inspired fiction, as well as a heartfelt thank you and stay tuned from Hutchins himself.

The blog-post farewell

A number of podcasters, after laboring over the decision to continue a podcast, draft a letter of resignation to their audience, go back and polish it up, and then finally log on to their podcast's host blog and make the post.

For that matter, why not record something? For some podcasts, that's too emotional a task. You've invested time, energy, and personal resources into your show, and now you're coming on pod to say, "It's time for me to say goodbye." This may sound a bit sappy, but it's also true: Goodbye is not always easy. What makes a blog announcement "easier" (and if we could make the quotes bigger around that without wrecking the typography of this book, we would) is being able to get your thoughts, decisions, and opinions out to your listenership without actually hearing yourself saying, "This is it." The silent word on-screen has its advantages. It may not seem like a big deal, but trust us — it is.

The farewell on the blog also gives you the option of keeping in touch with your core group of listeners. In this farewell post, you can announce that while the podcast is closing shop, the blog will remain open for business. Even after some podcasts have concluded their runs, their accompanying blogs still have recent posts, updates, and links of interest — continuing the community that the show built.

The Yard Sale: Selling Your Podcast Rigs

Now that you've closed shop, your audio equipment simply sits there in the shadows of your reclaimed office or guest room. There is a slim chance — depending on how *loved* (a better alternative to the word *used*) your equipment is — that you can recoup some of your investment, especially if you have your upgrades still in shrink-wrap. Yes, there will be monetary losses (depreciation, old gear giving up the ghost, and the like). Instead of approaching this as a way of breaking even, look at this as a Going Out of Business sale: *Everything must go!!!*

Your papers, please . . .

Before you start pricing out your used microphones or mixer boards, try to find all the original documentation that goes with the items you're offering for sale. Instruction manuals are a given, but other original documentation to consider including would be warranty policies, serial numbers, CDs and DVDs (which would include the basic drivers), and — if at all possible — the original box the device came in. The original packaging also makes shipping or exchange of the equipment a lot easier and more convenient for the buyer.

If manuals have gone missing, consider looking online at the manufacturer's Web site. User manuals may be available online for download and easy printing at home.

Selling your sound supply

So where is a good place to offer up equipment for sale, and what are the pros and cons in selling your rigs? It's not so easy to slap a red tag on your stuff (and you might devalue the mic if a big ol' sticker is slapped across it!) and then hold a sale. Consider your possibilities, what makes the sale as convenient and stress-free as possible?

- ✔ **eBay:** Yes, the absolute answer to getting rid of stuff you don't want in your house anymore, the eBay online auction site is a good place to unload your podcasting rigs. Granted, this approach may involve a little more work on your part. (To find out how you can economize this investment of time, maximize the potential of reselling your audio equipment, and make the most from your sale, pick up *eBay For Dummies*, or *eBay Timesaving Techniques For Dummies*, both by Marsha Collier [Wiley]). Remember: You can reach a global audience of would-be podcasters and audio enthusiasts, all in the market for something. True, what you're selling may not be "new" to you, but it is to the person stopping by your eBay Merchant Page.

 eBay has plenty of good security measures, but unsavory, unscrupulous characters are still lurking about. Before giving the okay on a purchase or even setting up a store for yourself, check all the policies of eBay (and scrutinize those aforementioned *For Dummies* books) to find out what you may need to do if some shady transaction crops up (be it a delay in payment, a bounced check, and the like) and what you can do to defend yourself against these problems.

- ✔ **PodCamps and podcast conventions:** *PodCamps* (http://podcamp.org) are held across the United States and around the world. At these events, podcasters — and people interested in podcasting — gather together and participate in panel discussions and hands-on workshops. There is also a great deal of networking — and part of that networking includes a bit of bartering and bargaining for used equipment, whether it's face-to-face selling or an exchange of leads to the Web sites with the best deals.

Note, however, that some podcamps discourage the selling and marketing of merchandise. If that is the case, look into podcast conventions like the Podcast and New Media Expo (http://newmediaexpo.com, shown in Figure 51-2) and podcasting tracks at science fiction conventions (such as Dragon*Con and Balticon). At these events, bartering and bargaining abound; and there are plenty of good deals to take advantage of. You can also pre-arrange transactions if you have a rapport with another podcaster (or listener-wanting-to-podcast) over Skype: You can set up times, places, and prices before you meet to do the deal. A terrific advantage of conducting business in this manner is face-to-face transaction. Instead of a nondescript e-mail and profile on eBay, you have a contact (albeit someone you probably just met!) and that person-to-person relationship makes commerce a lot easier. (And why not? It used to be the *only* way to buy and sell.)

- ✔ **Online discussion groups and forums:** Swap meets take place 24-7 online, outside of eBay. Perhaps these transactions are missing the instant gratification and quick purchases with Visa or MasterCard, but these communities are the equivalent of small towns: Everyone knows everyone and shares everything from gossip to the latest news in the podosphere.

Online discussion groups like Yahoo! Podcasters (http://tech.groups.yahoo.com/group/podcasters/) are well-established communities, welcoming new members into the fold and offering all sorts of (ahem) sound advice. After getting to know the community, ask either on or off the list if anyone is interested in relieving you of used equipment. This kind of transaction combines the best of the eBay and face-to-face worlds: You "know" the person you are directly dealing with.

• Figure 51-2: The Podcast and New Media Expo is a great place for podcasters to network, but can also be a great place to buy and sell used podcasting equipment.

Handling with care and confirmation

If you're selling your equipment and you're fortunate enough to receive your payment upfront, don't keep the customer waiting. Make sure you invest in packing materials that make the item's ride from your house to its destination as ding- and damage-free as possible.

You can use Styrofoam popcorn or newspaper as your padding, but consider the mess and hassle involved with both. Take that extra step and find bubble wrap or Rapid Fill bags. They can be an inexpensive and easy-to-dispense packing material. You can find bubble wrap, Rapid Fill bags, and even newspaper and popcorn through online vendors of packing materials such as ULine (www.uline.com) and PackingPrice.com (www.packing price.com).

If you go with the United States Post Office as your courier service, say Yes to the Delivery Confirmation service. It is an excellent way to confirm that the package you're sending has reached its destination. If you make the investment in UPS (www.ups.com) or Federal Express (www.fedex.com), make sure you keep track of the paperwork from shipping your merchandise. The receipt gives you a tracking number that you can enter into a tracking page on the shipper's Web site and zero in on the progress of your merchandise from shipping center to destination.

Bonus Content on the DVD

Appendix A

I n this appendix, we play show-and-tell with the DVD that comes with this book. You'll find extra lessons on the disc, along with various types of sample podcasts and music to check out. Like the book, feel free to browse the DVD contents at your leisure, checking out what's interesting and coming back to the rest later. Pop it in and check it out!

System Requirements

Make sure your computer meets the minimum system requirements shown in the following list. If your computer doesn't match up to most of these requirements, you may have problems using the software and files on the DVD. For the latest and greatest information, please refer to the ReadMe file located at the root of the DVD-ROM. Here's what you need (the no-frills list):

✔ A PC running Microsoft Windows 98, Windows 2000, Windows NT4 (with SP4 or later), Windows Me, Windows XP, or Windows Vista

✔ A Macintosh running Apple OS X or later

✔ A PC running a version of Linux with kernel 2.4 or greater

✔ An Internet connection

✔ A DVD-ROM drive

If you need more information on the basics, check out these books published by Wiley Publishing, Inc.: *PCs For Dummies,* by Dan Gookin; *Macs For Dummies,* by David Pogue; *iMacs For Dummies* by David Pogue; *Windows XP For Dummies* and *Windows Vista For Dummies,* both by Andy Rathbone.

Using the DVD

To install the items from the DVD to your hard drive, follow these steps.

1. **Insert the DVD into your computer's DVD-ROM drive.**

   The license agreement appears.

   Note to Windows users: The interface won't launch if you have Autorun disabled. In that case, choose Start⇨Run. (For Windows Vista, choose Start⇨All Programs⇨Accessories⇨Run.) In the dialog box that appears, type **D:\Start.exe**. (Replace *D* with the proper letter if your DVD drive uses a different letter. If you don't know the letter, see how your DVD drive is listed under My Computer.) Click OK.

   Note for Mac Users: When the DVD icon appears on your desktop, double-click the icon to open the DVD, and then double-click the ClickMe icon.

2. **Read through the license agreement, and then click the Accept button if you want to use the DVD.**

   The DVD interface appears. The interface allows you to access the contents with just a click of a button (or two).

What You'll Find on the DVD

The following sections are arranged by category; they provide a summary of the goodies you'll find on the DVD. If you need help with installing the items provided on the DVD, refer to the installation instructions in the preceding section.

Podcast audio

For Windows and Mac.

There's no better way to find out how to make a good podcast than listening to those who do just that. We wanted to make sure you had some great examples to listen and learn from, so this DVD includes several episodes from different types of podcasts. You'll hear what goes into making a professional podcast, learn how to organize and structure a good show, and probably enjoy the actual episode as well. Here's what we put on the disc:

- The entire first season of *Podcasting For Dummies* and two episodes from the second season.

- Sample promos you can use in your own podcast from the authors of this book.

- Samples of podsafe music you can include on your podcasts. Podsafe music can be used on any podcast. You will need to contact the artists for use outside of podcasts. Be sure to credit the artist and the name of the track when you use it in a podcast. The artist's and track's names are both included in the filename. Authors include Diane Arkenstone, George Hrab, Lisa Furukawa, Jonathan Coulton, Beatnik Turtle, and Background Trash.

- Excerpts from podcasts and podiobooks created by top podcasters. These excerpts demonstrate the various styles and approaches that go into creating a podcast.

Podcast video

For Windows and Mac.

This section gives you some video examples of practices we've discussed in the book, as well as a sample video podcast from *Stranger Things* for you to study and learn from. Topics covered in these examples include these:

- Setting Sound Levels
- Adding Special Effects
- Editing Audio
- Creating an mp3 File
- Creating an Enhanced Podcast

Sample media kits

When it comes time to publicize your podcast, you'll find these media kits extremely helpful. These examples show you great ways to tell others about your show and give you an idea of what you might want to include in your own media kit.

Podcast XML template

If you want to put together your own RSS feed for your podcast, this XML file is a great place to start. It's been set up for you — all you have to do is insert your own information and you're ready to go.

Sample files

If you want to follow along with some of the step lists in this book, look for the sample files (organized by practice number) on the DVD.

Links galore!

It might seem a little cruel to send you off searching for some of the things we talked about in this book on the Internet without a road map. The disc links to an online page where you'll find a plethora of links to all sorts of useful information. You'll find out about software, vendors, equipment, and more with just the click of a mouse!

Troubleshooting

We tried our best to compile content that works on most computers with the minimum system requirements. Alas, your computer may differ, and some programs may not work properly for some reason.

The two likeliest problems are that you don't have enough memory (RAM) for the programs you want to use, or you have other programs running that are affecting installation or the running of a program. If you get an error message such as Not enough memory or Setup cannot continue, try one or more of the following suggestions and then try using the software again:

- **Turn off any antivirus software running on your computer.** Installation programs sometimes mimic virus activity — and may make your computer incorrectly believe that it's being infected by a virus.

- **Close all running programs.** The more programs you have running, the less memory is available to other programs. Installation programs typically update files and programs; so if you keep other programs running, installation may not work properly.

- **Have your local computer store add more RAM to your computer.** This is, admittedly, a drastic and somewhat expensive step. However, adding more memory can really help the speed of your computer and allow more programs to run at the same time.

Customer Care

If you have trouble with the DVD-ROM, please call the Wiley Product Technical Support phone number at (800) 762-2974. Outside the United States, call 1 (317) 572-3994. You can also contact Wiley Product Technical Support at http://support.wiley.com. John Wiley & Sons will provide technical support only for installation and other general quality control items. For technical support on the applications themselves, consult the program's vendor or author.

To place additional orders or to request information about other Wiley products, please call (877) 762-2974.

Index

Wiley Publishing, Inc. End-User License Agreement

READ THIS. You should carefully read these terms and conditions before opening the software packet(s) included with this book "Book". This is a license agreement "Agreement" between you and Wiley Publishing, Inc. "WPI". By opening the accompanying software packet(s), you acknowledge that you have read and accept the following terms and conditions. If you do not agree and do not want to be bound by such terms and conditions, promptly return the Book and the unopened software packet(s) to the place you obtained them for a full refund.

1. **License Grant.** WPI grants to you (either an individual or entity) a nonexclusive license to use one copy of the enclosed software program(s) (collectively, the "Software") solely for your own personal or business purposes on a single computer (whether a standard computer or a workstation component of a multi-user network). The Software is in use on a computer when it is loaded into temporary memory (RAM) or installed into permanent memory (hard disk, DVD-ROM, or other storage device). WPI reserves all rights not expressly granted herein.

2. **Ownership.** WPI is the owner of all right, title, and interest, including copyright, in and to the compilation of the Software recorded on the physical packet included with this Book "Software Media". Copyright to the individual programs recorded on the Software Media is owned by the author or other authorized copyright owner of each program. Ownership of the Software and all proprietary rights relating thereto remain with WPI and its licensers.

3. **Restrictions on Use and Transfer.**

(a) You may only (i) make one copy of the Software for backup or archival purposes, or (ii) transfer the Software to a single hard disk, provided that you keep the original for backup or archival purposes. You may not (i) rent or lease the Software, (ii) copy or reproduce the Software through a LAN or other network system or through any computer subscriber system or bulletin-board system, or (iii) modify, adapt, or create derivative works based on the Software.

(b) You may not reverse engineer, decompile, or disassemble the Software. You may transfer the Software and user documentation on a permanent basis, provided that the transferee agrees to accept the terms and conditions of this Agreement and you retain no copies. If the Software is an update or has been updated, any transfer must include the most recent update and all prior versions.

4. **Restrictions on Use of Individual Programs.** You must follow the individual requirements and restrictions detailed for each individual program in the "Bonus Content on the DVD" appendix of this Book or on the Software Media. These limitations are also contained in the individual license agreements recorded on the Software Media. These limitations may include a requirement that after using the program for a specified period of time, the user must pay a registration fee or discontinue use. By opening the Software packet(s), you agree to abide by the licenses and restrictions for these individual programs that are detailed in the "Bonus Content on the DVD" appendix and/or on the Software Media. None of the material on this Software Media or listed in this Book may ever be redistributed, in original or modified form, for commercial purposes.

5. **Limited Warranty.**

(a) WPI warrants that the Software and Software Media are free from defects in materials and workmanship under normal use for a period of sixty (60) days from the date of purchase of this Book. If WPI receives notification within the warranty period of defects in materials or workmanship, WPI will replace the defective Software Media.

(b) WPI AND THE AUTHOR(S) OF THE BOOK DISCLAIM ALL OTHER WARRANTIES, EXPRESS OR IMPLIED, INCLUDING WITHOUT LIMITATION IMPLIED WARRANTIES OF MERCHANTABILITY AND FITNESS FOR A PARTICULAR PURPOSE, WITH RESPECT TO THE SOFTWARE, THE PROGRAMS, THE SOURCE CODE CONTAINED THEREIN, AND/OR THE TECHNIQUES DESCRIBED IN THIS BOOK. WPI DOES NOT WARRANT THAT THE FUNCTIONS CONTAINED IN THE SOFTWARE WILL MEET YOUR REQUIREMENTS OR THAT THE OPERATION OF THE SOFTWARE WILL BE ERROR FREE.

(c) This limited warranty gives you specific legal rights, and you may have other rights that vary from jurisdiction to jurisdiction.

6. Remedies.

(a) WPI's entire liability and your exclusive remedy for defects in materials and workmanship shall be limited to replacement of the Software Media, which may be returned to WPI with a copy of your receipt at the following address: Software Media Fulfillment Department, Attn.: *Expert Podcasting Practices For Dummies*, Wiley Publishing, Inc., 10475 Crosspoint Blvd., Indianapolis, IN 46256, or call 1-800-762-2974. Please allow four to six weeks for delivery. This Limited Warranty is void if failure of the Software Media has resulted from accident, abuse, or misapplication. Any replacement Software Media will be warranted for the remainder of the original warranty period or thirty (30) days, whichever is longer.

(b) In no event shall WPI or the author be liable for any damages whatsoever (including without limitation damages for loss of business profits, business interruption, loss of business information, or any other pecuniary loss) arising from the use of or inability to use the Book or the Software, even if WPI has been advised of the possibility of such damages.

(c) Because some jurisdictions do not allow the exclusion or limitation of liability for consequential or incidental damages, the above limitation or exclusion may not apply to you.

7. U.S. Government Restricted Rights. Use, duplication, or disclosure of the Software for or on behalf of the United States of America, its agencies and/or instrumentalities "U.S. Government" is subject to restrictions as stated in paragraph (c)(1)(ii) of the Rights in Technical Data and Computer Software clause of DFARS 252.227-7013, or subparagraphs (c) (1) and (2) of the Commercial Computer Software - Restricted Rights clause at FAR 52.227-19, and in similar clauses in the NASA FAR supplement, as applicable.

8. General. This Agreement constitutes the entire understanding of the parties and revokes and supersedes all prior agreements, oral or written, between them and may not be modified or amended except in a writing signed by both parties hereto that specifically refers to this Agreement. This Agreement shall take precedence over any other documents that may be in conflict herewith. If any one or more provisions contained in this Agreement are held by any court or tribunal to be invalid, illegal, or otherwise unenforceable, each and every other provision shall remain in full force and effect.

BUSINESS, CAREERS & PERSONAL FINANCE

0-7645-9847-3

0-7645-2431-3

Also available:
- Business Plans Kit For Dummies
  0-7645-9794-9
- Economics For Dummies
  0-7645-5726-2
- Grant Writing For Dummies
  0-7645-8416-2
- Home Buying For Dummies
  0-7645-5331-3
- Managing For Dummies
  0-7645-1771-6
- Marketing For Dummies
  0-7645-5600-2

- Personal Finance For Dummies
  0-7645-2590-5*
- Resumes For Dummies
  0-7645-5471-9
- Selling For Dummies
  0-7645-5363-1
- Six Sigma For Dummies
  0-7645-6798-5
- Small Business Kit For Dummies
  0-7645-5984-2
- Starting an eBay Business For Dummies
  0-7645-6924-4
- Your Dream Career For Dummies
  0-7645-9795-7

HOME & BUSINESS COMPUTER BASICS

0-470-05432-8

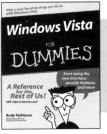

0-471-75421-8

Also available:
- Cleaning Windows Vista For Dummies
  0-471-78293-9
- Excel 2007 For Dummies
  0-470-03737-7
- Mac OS X Tiger For Dummies
  0-7645-7675-5
- MacBook For Dummies
  0-470-04859-X
- Macs For Dummies
  0-470-04849-2
- Office 2007 For Dummies
  0-470-00923-3

- Outlook 2007 For Dummies
  0-470-03830-6
- PCs For Dummies
  0-7645-8958-X
- Salesforce.com For Dummies
  0-470-04893-X
- Upgrading & Fixing Laptops For Dummies
  0-7645-8959-8
- Word 2007 For Dummies
  0-470-03658-3
- Quicken 2007 For Dummies
  0-470-04600-7

FOOD, HOME, GARDEN, HOBBIES, MUSIC & PETS

0-7645-8404-9

0-7645-9904-6

Also available:
- Candy Making For Dummies
  0-7645-9734-5
- Card Games For Dummies
  0-7645-9910-0
- Crocheting For Dummies
  0-7645-4151-X
- Dog Training For Dummies
  0-7645-8418-9
- Healthy Carb Cookbook For Dummies
  0-7645-8476-6
- Home Maintenance For Dummies
  0-7645-5215-5

- Horses For Dummies
  0-7645-9797-3
- Jewelry Making & Beading For Dummies
  0-7645-2571-9
- Orchids For Dummies
  0-7645-6759-4
- Puppies For Dummies
  0-7645-5255-4
- Rock Guitar For Dummies
  0-7645-5356-9
- Sewing For Dummies
  0-7645-6847-7
- Singing For Dummies
  0-7645-2475-5

INTERNET & DIGITAL MEDIA

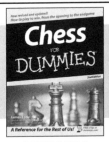

0-470-04529-9

0-470-04894-8

Also available:
- Blogging For Dummies
  0-471-77084-1
- Digital Photography For Dummies
  0-7645-9802-3
- Digital Photography All-in-One Desk Reference For Dummies
  0-470-03743-1
- Digital SLR Cameras and Photography For Dummies
  0-7645-9803-1
- eBay Business All-in-One Desk Reference For Dummies
  0-7645-8438-3
- HDTV For Dummies
  0-470-09673-X

- Home Entertainment PCs For Dummies
  0-470-05523-5
- MySpace For Dummies
  0-470-09529-6
- Search Engine Optimization For Dummies
  0-471-97998-8
- Skype For Dummies
  0-470-04891-3
- The Internet For Dummies
  0-7645-8996-2
- Wiring Your Digital Home For Dummies
  0-471-91830-X

* Separate Canadian edition also available
† Separate U.K. edition also available

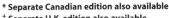

Available wherever books are sold. For more information or to order direct: U.S. customers visit www.dummies.com or call 1-877-762-2974.
U.K. customers visit www.wileyeurope.com or call 0800 243407. Canadian customers visit www.wiley.ca or call 1-800-567-4797.

SPORTS, FITNESS, PARENTING, RELIGION & SPIRITUALITY

0-471-76871-5

0-7645-7841-3

Also available:

- Catholicism For Dummies
  0-7645-5391-7
- Exercise Balls For Dummies
  0-7645-5623-1
- Fitness For Dummies
  0-7645-7851-0
- Football For Dummies
  0-7645-3936-1
- Judaism For Dummies
  0-7645-5299-6
- Potty Training For Dummies
  0-7645-5417-4
- Buddhism For Dummies
  0-7645-5359-3

- Pregnancy For Dummies
  0-7645-4483-7 †
- Ten Minute Tone-Ups For Dummies
  0-7645-7207-5
- NASCAR For Dummies
  0-7645-7681-X
- Religion For Dummies
  0-7645-5264-3
- Soccer For Dummies
  0-7645-5229-5
- Women in the Bible For Dummies
  0-7645-8475-8

TRAVEL

0-7645-7749-2

0-7645-6945-7

Also available:

- Alaska For Dummies
  0-7645-7746-8
- Cruise Vacations For Dummies
  0-7645-6941-4
- England For Dummies
  0-7645-4276-1
- Europe For Dummies
  0-7645-7529-5
- Germany For Dummies
  0-7645-7823-5
- Hawaii For Dummies
  0-7645-7402-7

- Italy For Dummies
  0-7645-7386-1
- Las Vegas For Dummies
  0-7645-7382-9
- London For Dummies
  0-7645-4277-X
- Paris For Dummies
  0-7645-7630-5
- RV Vacations For Dummies
  0-7645-4442-X
- Walt Disney World & Orlando
  For Dummies
  0-7645-9660-8

GRAPHICS, DESIGN & WEB DEVELOPMENT

0-7645-8815-X

0-7645-9571-7

Also available:

- 3D Game Animation For Dummies
  0-7645-8789-7
- AutoCAD 2006 For Dummies
  0-7645-8925-3
- Building a Web Site For Dummies
  0-7645-7144-3
- Creating Web Pages For Dummies
  0-470-08030-2
- Creating Web Pages All-in-One Desk
  Reference For Dummies
  0-7645-4345-8
- Dreamweaver 8 For Dummies
  0-7645-9649-7

- InDesign CS2 For Dummies
  0-7645-9572-5
- Macromedia Flash 8 For Dummies
  0-7645-9691-8
- Photoshop CS2 and Digital
  Photography For Dummies
  0-7645-9580-6
- Photoshop Elements 4 For Dummies
  0-471-77483-9
- Syndicating Web Sites with RSS Feeds
  For Dummies
  0-7645-8848-6
- Yahoo! SiteBuilder For Dummies
  0-7645-9800-7

NETWORKING, SECURITY, PROGRAMMING & DATABASES

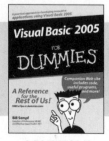

0-7645-7728-X

0-471-74940-0

Also available:

- Access 2007 For Dummies
  0-470-04612-0
- ASP.NET 2 For Dummies
  0-7645-7907-X
- C# 2005 For Dummies
  0-7645-9704-3
- Hacking For Dummies
  0-470-05235-X
- Hacking Wireless Networks
  For Dummies
  0-7645-9730-2
- Java For Dummies
  0-470-08716-1

- Microsoft SQL Server 2005 For Dummies
  0-7645-7755-7
- Networking All-in-One Desk Reference
  For Dummies
  0-7645-9939-9
- Preventing Identity Theft For Dummies
  0-7645-7336-5
- Telecom For Dummies
  0-471-77085-X
- Visual Studio 2005 All-in-One Desk
  Reference For Dummies
  0-7645-9775-2
- XML For Dummies
  0-7645-8845-1